Biographical Dictionary of
Congressional Women

Biographical Dictionary of Congressional Women

Karen Foerstel

Greenwood Press
Westport, Connecticut • London

Library of Congress Cataloging-in-Publication Data

Foerstel, Karen.
    Biographical dictionary of congressional women / Karen Foerstel.
      p. cm.
    Includes bibliographical references and index.
    ISBN 0–313–30290–1 (alk. paper)
    1. United States. Congress—Biography—Dictionaries. 2. Women
legislators—United States—Biography—Dictionaries. I. Title.
JK1012.F57   1999
328.73'0082—dc21
  [B]   99–17950

British Library Cataloguing in Publication Data is available.

Library of Congress Catalog Card Number: 99–17950
ISBN: 0–313–30290–1

First published in 1999

Greenwood Press, 88 Post Road West, Westport, CT 06881
An imprint of Greenwood Publishing Group, Inc.
www.greenwood.com

Printed in the United States of America

The paper used in this book complies with the
Permanent Paper Standard issued by the National
Information Standards Organization (Z39.48–1984).

10 9 8 7 6 5 4 3 2 1

Copyright Acknowledgments

The editor and publisher gratefully acknowledge permission to use excerpts from *A Minority of Members: Women in the U.S. Congress* by Hope Chamberlin, © 1973 by Hope Chamberlin. Reprinted by permission of Henry Holt and Company, LLC.

CONTENTS

Introduction   1

Biographies   17

Notes   285

Selected Bibliography   293

Index   295

A photographic essay follows page 148.

Biographical Dictionary of
Congressional Women

INTRODUCTION

Throughout the history of the United States, a total of 200 women have served in Congress. That's about half the number of men currently sitting in the House and Senate today. It has not been an easy ride for women in federal office. Jeannette Rankin—the very first woman to serve in Congress—was elected before women across the country were even granted the right to vote. Since then, women have been forced to overcome prejudice and stereotyping from the voters as well as their male colleagues in order to represent their country in the halls of Congress.

Currently, women make up only 9 percent of the Senate and 13 percent of the House—an all-time record. One would think their small numbers would make it nearly impossible for them to have any major impact on legislation. Indeed, it was only recently that women were even afforded the same congressional perks granted their male colleagues. It was not until the mid-1980s that the House leadership allowed women lawmakers to use the House gym, which had been a longtime male bastion. The Senate did not build a bathroom for women members until 1993. Previously, women had to walk down a level to reach the nearest facility, while men were within several feet of a bathroom.

Even the artwork in the Capitol building shows the male dominance of Congress. Only seven of the 190 statues and busts in the Capitol are of women. And it was not until 1996 that the Senate added the likeness of one of its female alum to its extensive portrait gallery. It was a painting of Sen. Hattie Caraway (D-Ark.), the second woman to serve in Congress and the first to chair a Senate committee.

Women hold very few of the top leadership or committee assignments in Congress. In fact, only 10 women have ever chaired full committees in the House, and only two have led full committees in the Senate (see Chart 1). A woman has never chaired the House's most powerful committees on Appropriations, Commerce, or Ways and Means. The highest leadership position ever held by women in the House is vice chair of the Democratic and Republican caucuses—the fourth-ranking spots in the party leaderships. Following the 1998 elections, two women made bids to break that glass ceiling. Rep. Rosa DeLauro (D-Conn.) ran for chair of the Democratic Caucus—the third-ranking spot in the party—and Rep. Jennifer Dunn (R-Wash.) ran for the second-ranking post of Republican Leader. Both women, however, lost their bids to male colleagues.

"We're mad as hell," said Rep. Diana DeGette (D-Colo.) of DeLauro's loss and the lack of any women in top leadership posts. "We're almost 60 women [in the House] and we deserve a voice in the leadership."[1]

In the Senate, Sen. Barbara Mikulski (D-Md.) is the highest-ranking woman ever in that body, holding the post of secretary of the Democratic Conference—the fourth-ranking spot in the Democratic leadership.

But many of today's legislators concede that women's historically late entrance into the congressional arena—Rankin was elected in 1917—and the trend among women to run for public office later in life after they have finished raising their children have prevented them from attaining the seniority and clout needed to wield the same power as their male counterparts. Until recent years, the vast majority of congressional women did not enter office until they were in their late 40s or 50s. Most men enter Congress at a younger age, serving longer and gaining the seniority needed to chair committees or serve in the leadership. Since Rankin first came to Congress in 1917, just 46 women have served 10 years or more in office and only 14 women have served two decades or longer. That's compared to the more than three dozen men currently sitting in the House and Senate who have held their seats for 20 years or more. Women have also had a tendency to leave Congress after relatively few years to run for higher office—further limiting their congressional seniority.

"The Congress was here a hundred and some years before women [even] had the right to vote so our limited seniority is understandable," said Rep. Louise Slaughter (D-N.Y.). She added, "Every time an incumbent woman approached a safe election, the people who supported her would try to convince her to try for something else when it came up. . . . That's something that you really have to factor in as to why there aren't more women in the leadership. The men have just stayed around longer."[2]

In the first half of the century, most of the women in Congress came to fill out the terms of husbands who had died while in office. Up until 1970, more than half the women ever to have served in Congress came by way of the "widow's path." But many of those women—after sampling the pleasant taste of power—went on to later win election in their own right and surpass the success that had been attained by their husbands.

Despite their small numbers, women have helped craft some of the country's most important legislation. Rep. Mary Teresa Norton (D-N.J.) introduced the first constitutional amendment to repeal the Volstead Act (Prohibition) and, as chair of the Labor Committee, helped pass the Fair Labor Standards Act of 1938, which established a minimum wage and maximum work hours.

Rep. Edith Nourse Rogers (R-Mass.), who first came to the House to fill the seat of her deceased husband and ended up staying for 36 years, rose to chair the Veterans' Affairs Committee and helped pass the GI Bill of Rights and legislation creating the Women's Auxiliary Army Corps (WAACs).

Rep. Leonor Sullivan (D-Mo.) also succeeded her husband, but held on to her seat for another 24 years. Her lengthy congressional service led to passage of numerous consumer protections, including a ban on carcinogens in food, compulsory federal inspection of poultry, and pretesting of all chemical additives used in food.

WOMEN'S LEGISLATION

Along with their work on legislation benefiting all American citizens, female lawmakers have also been forced to take the lead on measures that specifically protect women's rights. Such legislation, obviously, could not pass without the support of their male colleagues, and, indeed, men have often been in the forefront of equal rights legislation. The first member of Congress ever to introduce the Equal Rights Amendment was, in fact, a man, Rep. Charles Curtis (R-Kan.) in 1923.

But women lawmakers have traditionally led the fight for equality among the sexes. Their mere presence on Capitol Hill has forced male politicians to give women's issues a greater priority. As more and more women have joined the House and Senate over the years, national attention given to women's issues has jumped significantly. In 1969, when there were just 10 women in the House and one in the Senate, the *Congressional Record* index listed 43 House bills introduced on women's issues—39 of them referring to the Equal Rights Amendment. In the Senate that same year, no bills on women's issues were introduced.

In 1993, after the historic "Year of the Woman" elections that nearly doubled the number of women in Congress, 357 bills were introduced on women's and family issues in the House and Senate. Some 230 of those bills were introduced by men.

The legislation that perhaps had the greatest impact on women's rights ever—the woman's suffrage constitutional amendment—was taken up by Congress when there was just one woman in office. But Jeannette Rankin (R-Mont.)—Congress's first woman member—was pivotal in the amendment's passage. She co-sponsored the legislation, and, when the measure was stalled in committee, introduced a bill creating a Woman Suffrage Committee of which she became ranking minority member.

She was given the honor of opening House debate on the amendment in 1918.

"We are facing today a question of political evolution," Rankin told her male colleagues. "Our country is in a state of war. . . . But something is still lacking in the completeness of our national effort. With all our abundance of coal, with our great stretches of idle, fertile land, babies are dying from cold and hunger; soldiers have died for lack of a woolen shirt. Might it not be that the men who have spent their lives thinking in terms of commercial profit find it hard to adjust themselves to thinking in terms of human needs? Might it not be that a great force that has always been thinking in terms of human needs, and that always will think in terms of human needs has not been mobilized? Is it not possible that the women of the country have something of value to give the nation at this time?

"It would be strange indeed if the women of this country through all these years had not developed an intelligence, a feeling, a spiritual force peculiar to themselves, which they hold in readiness to give to the world," she continued. "It would be strange if the influence of women through direct participation in the political struggles, through which all social and industrial development proceeds, would not lend a certain virility, a certain influx of new strength and understanding and sympathy and ability to the exhausting effort we are now making to meet the problem before us."[3]

Obviously, passage of the Suffrage Amendment hinged on Rankin's male colleagues. During the debate, Rep. John Raker (D-Calif.)—who supported the women's vote—pointed out that many of the men serving in the House had in fact won election with the help of women. Although women were not allowed to vote nationally in 1918, several states, including California, did permit women to go to the polls. In speaking of the 20 million American women who were of voting age at that time, Raker argued that the entire Democratic leadership of the House owed their position to women.

"To my Democratic friends I want to say this: The Speaker of this House, the chairmen of the committees of this House, and the officers who constitute the organization of this House hold their positions today as the result of the votes of women. Without the votes of the Democratic members from California, the Speaker would not be in the chair. These Democratic Members from California would not have been elected without the votes of the women of California. Every man who holds a chair-manship of a committee owes it to the women vote of the West."[4]

But not all men agreed. Rep. Frank Clarke (D-Fla.) argued that female voting would, at best, be irrelevant and, at worst, lead to the eventual destruction of the American family and the country as a whole.

"If this resolution should pass and the proposed amendment should be ratified by three-fourths of the states of the Union, then we would find a condition where the wife would either follow the husband in the casting of her vote or she would disagree with his views and have her vote counted in opposition to his. If the former is to be the case, then it occurs to me that all will agree that this would be an entirely superfluous and useless piece of legislation, as the only result would be to practically double the number of votes cast without changing in the slightest the political complexion of the state or the nation, but adding largely to the expense of holding our elections. If the latter should be the case, then we would find the husband and wife constantly engaged in political disputation, which would grow warmer, more heated, and more acri-monious as the campaign advanced, until finally a veritable conflagra-tion of domestic infelicity would be kindled, consuming the marital tie, destroying the home, and sending the children, to all intents and pur-poses, orphaned out on the cold charity of the world to become charges on the state."

And what about unmarried women and their right to vote? Clark had an answer to that as well.

"The unmarried woman who has passed marriageable age is the ex-ception to her class, and no general law should ever be passed to fit the exceptions to the class upon which it is intended to operate," he said.[5]

Several hours after Rankin's opening statement, the Suffrage Amend-ment passed the House on Jan. 10, 1918, by a vote of 274 to 136, barely the two-thirds required for passing a constitutional amendment. The Senate, 10 months later, failed to garner the two-thirds vote and it was defeated 53 to 31. But the House once more passed it in 1919, by a vote of 304 to 90 and a month later the Senate passed it 56 to 25. It was ratified by the states in 1920.

Women members of Congress again faced strong opposition 50 years later when the House took up the Civil Rights Act of 1968, a bill aimed at prohibiting racial discrimination. During debate, conservative south-ern male lawmakers tried to use the issue of gender equality to kill the overall legislation. Rep. Howard Smith (D-Va.), the chair of the powerful Rules Committee, introduced an amendment to the Civil Rights Act call-ing for the prohibition of discrimination based on gender. He had as-sumed the amendment would draw so much opposition from his fellow lawmakers that the entire bill would be defeated. Indeed, after Smith offered his amendment, it was met with laughter from his fellow male legislators.

But women members, led by Rep. Martha Griffiths (D-Mich.), seized the opportunity to use Smith's amendment to their advantage. In her floor speech in favor of the amendment, Griffiths told the male legislators, "A vote against this amendment today by a white man is a vote against his wife, or his widow, or his daughter or his sister."[6]

Years later, Griffiths recalled the obstacles women faced in pushing for gender equality. "I can remember that just before I went up there once [Smith's] amendment had been offered, there was uproarious laughter. Now we had been debating this bill since Tuesday, and this was now Thursday and [Rep.] Lee Sullivan looked back at me—there had never been any laughter on the rest of the bill, but when the amendment was offered there was tremendous laughter, uproarious laughter— and Lee looked back and she said, 'Martha, if you can't stop that laughter, you're lost.' . . . There was not laughter after I stood up."[7]

In the end, an odd coalition of southern segregationists and women lawmakers prevailed, and the amendment passed 168 to 133. When the entire Civil Rights Act came up for a vote, Smith and every one of the southerners who had voted for the gender amendment opposed the broader legislation. The act, however, passed 290 to 130.

Griffiths again proved pivotal in the women's rights movement in 1970 when she successfully pushed through a House discharge petition to pry the Equal Rights Amendment out of the Judiciary Committee where it had languished without a single hearing since it was first introduced in 1923.

Debate on the amendment paralleled many of the arguments made against women's suffrage 50 years earlier.

"Feminists clamor for equal rights," Emanuel Celler (D-N.Y.), chair of the House Judiciary Committee, said during his speech against bringing the ERA to the floor for a vote. "Nobody can deny that women should have equality under the law. But ever since Adam gave up his rib to make a woman, throughout the ages we have learned that physical, emotional, psychological, and social differences exist and dare not be disregarded. Neither the National Women's Party, nor the delightful, delectable, and dedicated gentlelady from Michigan [Griffiths] can change nature. They cannot do it. Beyond that, let me say that there is as much difference between a male and a female as between a horse chestnut and a chestnut horse, and as the French say, *Vive le difference*. Any attempt to pass an amendment that promises to wipe out the effects of these differences is about as abortive as trying to fish in a desert, and you cannot do that. There is no really genuine equality and I defy anyone to tell me what 'equality' in this amendment means. Even your five fingers, one is not equal to the other, they are different."[8]

Despite such arguments, Griffith's resolution to discharge the ERA from the Judiciary Committee passed 333 to 22. An hour's debate was then granted for floor consideration of the amendment, which read simply: "Equality of rights under the law shall not be denied or abridged by the United States or by any state on account of sex." It was eventually passed by the House 352 to 15. Two months later, when the Senate took up the amendment, it muddied the water by inserting language to exempt women from the draft. With only a few weeks left in the session, there was no time for the two chambers to resolve the difference in language and the ERA was effectively dead for the year.

A year later, in 1971, the ERA was again introduced and this time the Judiciary Committee held hearings on it. But chairman Celler inserted two amendments into it exempting women from the draft and allowing Congress and the states to enact special protective labor standards for women.

"Women represent motherhood and creation," Celler said on the floor in defense of his amendment. "Wars are for destruction. Women, integrated with men in the carnage and slaughter of battle, on land, at sea, or in the air, is unthinkable. Can you imagine women trained by a drill sergeant to charge the enemy with fixed bayonets and bombs?"

Rep. Thomas Abernathy (D-Miss.), a supporter of the Celler amendments, argued: "With all deference to the courage, the beauty, the charm, and the sacrifice that have been made by American women, how many of you believe that this country can be made safe with women standing in times or war at the triggers of cannons?"[9]

But when the ERA hit the House floor in October 1971, both of Celler's amendments were defeated. The House then passed the full measure 354 to 24, and the Senate went on to approve it 84 to 8. But the states never ratified the ERA, which had a seven-year ratification deadline.

Women have not only confronted the prejudices of their male colleagues during floor debate, but they have often been the victims of sexism in their day-to-day workings on Capitol Hill. Women have historically faced obstacles in gaining prominent committee assignments in Congress. In 1949, Rep. Reva Bosone (D-Utah) was told she could not have a seat on the Interior Committee because, as the only woman on the panel, she would be too "embarrassed" when her male colleagues discussed "the sex of animals."[10] But Bosone did not give up and eventually pushed her way onto the panel. In 1973, Rep. Pat Schroeder (D-Colo.) had to fight her way onto the Armed Services Committee because its chairman did not think women could understand war issues since they had never been in battle. Even today, women requesting assignments to the committee of their choice are often told the "women's slot" on that committee has been filled.

Former Rep. Leslie Byrne (D-Va.) said male lawmakers often do not realize their sexist comments are offensive to women. She said such comments—which she called "grandpa talk"—were frequent on Capitol Hill. Byrne related a story of one of the first times she went before the Rules Committee asking for permission to introduce an amendment on the floor.

"It was an amendment to the budget bill on intangible property, pretty esoteric stuff," Byrne said. "And so I was pitching this amendment, how important it was, and one of the gentlemen who had been sitting there quietly for a long time kind of looked up at me when it came time for the committee to ask questions and he said, 'I don't think I like your amendment, but you sure brighten the place up.' And my response was, 'I can't tell you how much that means to me.' "[11]

But not all such comments are so easily brushed off. During the 1991 Senate confirmation hearings on Supreme Court nominee Clarence Thomas and his alleged sexual harassment against Anita Hill, Rep. Jill Long (D-Ind.) shocked the nation when she spoke on the House floor about her experience with sexism on Capitol Hill.

"It was not too long ago that a colleague of mine complimented me on my appearance and then said that he was going to chase me around the House floor. . . . I was offended and I was embarrassed," Long said. "Sexual harassment is serious. It is not funny and it is not cute, and it is certainly not complimentary."[12]

Even on the campaign trail, women must overcome sexism before ever getting elected to office. In 1972, when Schroeder first ran for the House, she was constantly asked how she could serve in Congress and raise her children while her husband also worked. Eventually, the exasperated Schroeder told one reporter: "Jim and I get up very early—about 6 a.m. We bathe and dress the children and give them a wonderful breakfast. Then we put them in the freezer, leave for work and when we come home we defrost them. And we all have a wonderful dinner together."[13]

As more and more women have entered the political arena, gender has become less of an issue. Younger women—with young children still at home—are running for Congress without having to face criticism about being bad mothers. In 1974, Rep. Yvonne Brathwaite Burke (D-Calif.) became the first woman to have a child while serving in Congress. In 1995 and 1996, Reps. Enid Greene (R-Utah) and Susan Molinari (R-N.Y.) became the second and third women, respectively, to have children while in office.

The male-dominated congressional leadership has been forced to accept the changing culture of Capitol Hill. Recent years have brought efforts to schedule more "family-friendly" work weeks to allow both congressional mothers and fathers to spend more time at home. During the pregnancies of Waldholtz and Molinari, GOP leaders pledged to create nursery rooms near the House floor so the women could care for their infants between votes.

RUNNING AS A WOMAN

Women's growing representation in Congress has generally come in slow but steady increments. From 1976 to 1990, women increased their numbers in the House an average of less than two seats every election. Those small gains prepared nobody for the historic 1992 elections when 24 new women were elected to the House, nearly doubling their numbers from 29 to 48. In the Senate, women tripled their numbers from two to six. The huge increase prompted analysts to dub it the "Year of the Woman."

Several political factors led to those amazing gains. First, there was an unusually high number of "open seats"—seats vacated by incumbents due to redistricting, retirements, or resignations. Open seats offer political newcomers—men or women—their best chance of winning office. Women in 1992 ran for 35 of the 91 open House seats. Of the 24 new women elected to the House that year, 22 were open-seat victors.

Another factor that led to women's success that year was the growing anti-incumbent mood of voters and the nationwide debate on sexual harassment prompted by the Clarence Thomas hearings. Polls showed that voters wanted change, new faces, and new political ideas. The Thomas hearings and the Navy Tailhook sexual harassment scandal brought women's issues to the forefront. Ross Perot's third-party presidential bid highlighted the appeal of "independent" candidates, and women fit the bill precisely.

But two years later, in 1994, the elections crushed any hopes that women would continue to make huge electoral gains on a regular basis. The elections that year brought no net increase in the number of House women. In fact, six of the women first elected in 1992—one-quarter of the historic class—were defeated in 1994. And unlike the 1992 elections, gender was not a major issue on the campaign trail.

Political analysts, ironically, point to the historic gains for women in the 1992 elections as a contributing factor in their poor showing two years later. In 1992, women ran as political outsiders, crusaders against big government, and catalysts for change. Many of the Democratic women who won that year took over districts that leaned Republican in registration or were at best marginally Democratic. Those women immediately became Republican targets. The unprecedented numbers of women joining the House and Senate in 1992 also pushed the women's image closer to the mainstream, diminishing their "outsider" status.

But while the 1994 elections proved unimpressive for women overall, they handed Republican women a huge success. The number of Democratic women in Congress fell following those elections, but the number of GOP women increased. Seven of the 11 new women elected to the House were Republicans. The lone female addition in the Senate was also a Republican. Overall, however, Democratic women still outnumber Republican women in Congress more than two-to-one.

The 1996 elections proved more successful for women lawmakers overall, giving them a net gain of four in the House, and the 1998 elections increased the number of female House members by two for an all-time high of 58 (including two nonvoting delegates). The number of women elected to the Senate in 1998 remained unchanged at nine. Although those numbers seem minimal compared to 1992, women political analysts still heralded the 1998 elections as a triumph. And open seats again proved the greatest opportunity for women running for office.

"We think it was a great night," said Ellen Malcolm, president of EMILY's List, which provides campaign funds to Democratic women who support abortion rights. "The open-seat victories show that we need to take advantage of such opportunities so we can maximize our efforts to help women win. The biggest barrier to getting women elected is not gender-related, it is the power of incumbency."[14]

The 1998 elections also set a record for the number of women who won major party nominations for Congress. A total of 121 women were nominated for House offices and 10 women were nominated for the Senate. That's more than twice the number of major party nominees just 10 years earlier when 59 women were nominated for House offices and just two women were nominated for the Senate.

"We know that women can win tough races, and we know that women office holders make a difference," said Mary Hawkesworth, director of the Center for the American Women and Politics at Rutgers University. "Now we need to make sure that more women are well placed to take advantage of opportunities to win."

Among the most important changes in recent years for women running for office is the growing ease of fund-raising. Incumbents generally have an easier time raising money than challengers, and because most incumbents are male, they have a distinct advantage over women challengers. But as more women win office, their fund-raising abilities have greatly increased. Their growing numbers in office have also opened the minds—and wallets—of political contributors.

"Women aren't facing the daunting fund-raising problems that I faced in 1982," said Rep. Nancy Johnson (R-Conn.), referring to the year she was first elected to Congress. "Many of the men you were asking for money had never even made a serious decision with a woman. There has been a tremendous culture change, and I think it's for a much better society."[15]

Barbara Burrell, a University of Wisconsin political researcher, said that, until 1988, female congressional candidates raised only about three-fourths of what men did. Since then, female candidates have on average raised about the same or more than male candidates. Much of that fundraising success is due to the growing number of political action committees created specifically to raise money for women candidates. Groups like EMILY's List and the Women's Campaign Fund have pumped millions of dollars into targeted campaigns. In 1983, there were just 16 women's PACs. By 1992, that number more than doubled with 42 PACs giving money predominantly to women or receiving donations primarily from women. The total financial support for female congressional candidates from these PACs in 1992 was $11.5 million, a 400 percent increase over the $2.7 million raised by women's PACs just two years earlier.

But despite women's growing fund-raising success, polls show they are still more reluctant to run for office than men. A survey conducted in the summer of 1994 by Democratic pollster Celinda Lake for the National Women's Politics Caucus (NWPC) showed that 18 percent of men have considered or would consider running for political office, while only 8 percent of women ever thought of launching a campaign. A second survey of male and female executives and lawyers—a likely pool for recruiting candidates—found that 38 percent of the men, but only 25 percent of the women lawyers and executives had considered running for office.

NWPC President Harriett Woods commented, "Women win as often as men, [yet] this survey shows that women still aren't convinced."

Rep. Sue Myrick (R-N.C.) said that the fears women have in running for office are deeply ingrained from childhood. "Women are afraid to take risks," she said. "Men are raised to play football, to bash their heads and come back for more. Women are raised to stand back. We aren't raised to be risk takers."[16]

But the NWCP survey did show that younger women felt more confident and qualified to run for political office. Slightly less than half of the younger women polled expressed fears of political inadequacy, while 61 percent of older women did.

Despite the growing number of opportunities for women to run for office, there are still six states that have never elected a woman to Congress—Alaska, Delaware, Iowa, Mississippi, New Hampshire, and Vermont. If women continue to win election to Congress at the slow rate of just a few seats every election, it will take centuries to reach parity with men. But not all women believe gender parity is a realistic or even necessary goal in Congress.

"You belong to your party. You don't just vote by sex," said former Rep. Lynn Martin (R-Ill.). "The ballot says Lynn Martin (Representative), not Lynn Martin (Feminist)."[17]

Republican women in general have tended to downplay the importance of gender in politics. In 1925, Rep. Florence Kahn (R-Calif.) advised

Republican women planning to run for office to "obliterate sex in politics." The most prominent Republican woman ever to serve in Congress, Sen. Margaret Chase Smith (Maine), spent almost 33 years in the House and Senate, during which she frequently expressed resentment at being singled out as a woman. In 1994, the still feisty 96-year-old Smith reiterated her feelings about gender and politics. "I was elected as a person. I served as a member. I was never considered a woman in Congress. I was a member."[18]

In the years since the historic 1992 elections, gender as a campaign issue has greatly declined in importance. It appears that without major media events or sexual scandals—such as the Clarence Thomas hearings or the Navy Tailhook convention—gender will be secondary to other political issues.

Ironically, the biggest sex scandal of the century—President Bill Clinton's affair with 22-year-old White House intern Monica Lewinsky—was at first considered a detriment to women running for Congress in 1998. The scandal was used against three of the women first elected to the Senate in the 1992 "Year of the Woman"—Barbara Boxer (D-Calif.), Patty Murray (D-Wash.), and Carol Moseley-Braun (D-Ill.)—in their bids for re-election. All three had been critics of Clarence Thomas during his Supreme Court confirmation hearings, and all had condemned Sen. Bob Packwood (R-Ore.) following their '92 elections after it was revealed he sexually harassed women on his staff.

Republican challengers to the three women turned the tables in 1998 and attacked them for not criticizing their Democratic president aggressively enough for his sexual peccadilloes.

"When it comes time [to criticize] Democrats, you have a different standard than for Republicans," said Matt Fong, the GOP challenger to Boxer, during the 1998 campaign. "Barbara, your silence on this issue is deafening."[19]

The Republican candidate against Murray, Rep. Linda Smith, also charged that Murray was being inappropriately quiet on Clinton's sex scandal. Murray first ran for office in 1992 under the slogan "a Mom in tennis shoes." But during the 1998 campaign, Smith slammed Murray for turning "her tennis shoes in for a pair of Hush Puppies."[20]

The scandal put Democratic women running for office in a tough bind. Clinton had long been perceived as "pro-women" in his policy agenda and it was difficult for them to now attack him as a sexual predator. Most of the women criticized Clinton for his personal behavior, but continued to praise him as an effective policy-maker.

Many pundits believed Clinton's scandal would further hurt women candidates by supressing the women's vote. Female voters who in 1992 thought their activism would make a difference in how elected leaders treated women said that the Clinton scandal left them feeling discouraged and disillusioned.

"In 1992, seeing the image of Anita Hill, millions of women voted who never voted before," observed Rep. Jane Harman (D-Calif.), who was first elected in 1992. "There were clearly positive feelings toward Hill and against an all-male Senate Judiciary Committee, so the goal was clear: to change the face of Congress. In 1998, the feelings toward this president are so ambivalent. So many deplore his conduct, including me, but they applaud the positions he has taken on issues. Now the situation is more ambiguous."

Some women predicted the scandal might help women candidates because they are generally seen as more ethical and less likely to have affairs than men.

"Women could get a boost. On the values part of it, women probably have a slight edge," said Rep. Tillie Fowler (R-Fla.), first elected in 1992. "Women are looked to as being above all this, more honest, less likely to engage in this kind of conduct."[21]

In the end, to the suprise of most pundits, the investigation into Clinton's affair backfired on Republicans and handed Democrats—and women—gains in Congress. Voters were more disturbed by the strong-arm investigative tactics of special prosecutor Ken Starr than they were with Clinton's lies about the affair. Of the seven new women elected to Congress in 1998, only one was a Republican.

Boxer and Murray were re-elected. Moseley-Braun, the first black woman to serve in the Senate, was defeated, but her loss was attributed to a variety of factors, with the Clinton scandal at the bottom of the list. And women overall increased their numbers in Congress. Much of that success was attributed to get-out-the-vote programs launched by women's groups who worked hard to bring women to the election polls and counteract any negative fallout from the scandal. But gender as a political issue did not play a major role in the 1998 elections. Unlike 1992, when women used the Thomas–Hill scandal as a platform to elect more women to office, not a single female candidate used the Clinton scandal in 1998 to make a similar call for more women legislators. And the small two-seat gain for women in Congress indicated that we will not soon see another huge influx of female legislators as we did in 1992.

"I think 1992 may have been the last election where gender was a significant issue, an issue you could rally around," said Rep. Karen McCarthy (D-Mo.), elected in 1994. "I think we're beyond that now. The idea of having more women in Congress has not gone away, because women do bring a unique perspective to Congress that would be left out if we were not present, but I didn't see it in 1994 as the sort of rallying cry that it was in '92. Whether we'll return to the issues of women and minorities, I don't know."[22]

Chart 1
Women Who Have Chaired Full Committees

Senate

Sen. Hattie Caraway (D-Ark.)
Committee on Enrolled Bills, 1933 to 1945

Sen. Nancy Kassebaum (R-Kan.)
Committee on Labor and Human Resources, 1995 to 1997

House

Rep. May Ella Nolan (R-Calif.)
Committee on Expenditures in the Post Office, 1921 to 1925

Rep. Mary Norton (D-N.J.)
Committee on the District of Columbia, 1931 to 1937
Committee on Labor, 1937 to 1947
Committee on House Administration, 1947 to 1949

Rep. Caroline O'Day (D-N.Y.)
Committee on Election of the President and Vice President, 1937 to 1943

Rep. Edith Nourse Rogers (R-Mass.)
Committee on Veterans' Affairs, 1947 to 1949 and 1953 to 1955

Rep. Martha Griffiths (D-Mich.)
Select Committee on the House Beauty Shop, 1967 to 1975

Rep. Leonor Sullivan (D-Mo.)
Committee on Merchant Marine and Fisheries, 1973 to 1977

Rep. Yvonne Brathwaite Burke (D-Calif.)
Select Committee on the House Beauty Shop, 1975 to 1979

Rep. Patricia Schroeder (D-Colo.)
Select Committee on Children, Youth, and Families, 1991 to 1993

Rep. Jan Meyers (R-Kan.)
Committee on Small Business, 1995 to 1997

Rep. Nancy Johnson (R-Conn.)
Select Committee on Standards of Official Conduct, 1995 to 1997

Chart 2
Number of Women by Congress*

65th Congress (1917)
House: 1R
Senate: 0

66th Congress (1919)
House: 0
Senate: 0

67th Congress (1921)
House: 2R
Senate: 1R

68th Congress (1923)
House: 1R
Senate: 0

69th Congress (1925)
House: 1D, 2R
Senate: 0

70th Congress (1927)
House: 2D, 3R
Senate: 0

71st Congress (1929)
House: 4D, 5R
Senate: 0

72nd Congress (1931)
House: 4D, 3R
Senate: 1D

73rd Congress (1933)
House: 4D, 3R
Senate: 1D

74th Congress (1935)
House: 4D, 2R
Senate: 2D

75th Congress (1937)
House: 4D, 1R
Senate: 2D

76th Congress (1939)
House: 4D, 4R
Senate: 1D

77th Congress (1941)
House: 4D, 5R
Senate: 1D

78th Congress (1943)
House: 2D, 6R
Senate: 1D

79th Congress (1945)
House: 6D, 5R
Senate: 0

80th Congress (1947)
House: 3D, 4R
Senate: 1R

81st Congress (1949)
House: 5D, 4R
Senate: 1R

82nd Congress (1951)
House: 4D, 6R
Senate: 1R

83rd Congress (1953)
House: 5D, 7R
Senate: 1R

84th Congress (1955)
House: 10D, 7R
Senate: 1R

85th Congress (1957)
House: 9D, 6R
Senate: 1R

86th Congress (1959)
House: 9D, 8R
Senate: 1R

87th Congress (1961)
House: 11D, 7R
Senate: 1D, 1R

88th Congress (1963)
House: 6D, 6R
Senate: 1D, 1R

89th Congress (1965)
House: 7D, 4R
Senate: 1D, 1R

90th Congress (1967)
House: 5D, 5R
Senate: 1R

91st Congress (1969)
House: 6D, 4R
Senate: 1R

92nd Congress (1971)
House: 10D, 3R
Senate: 1R

93rd Congress (1973)
House: 14D, 2R
Senate: 1D

94th Congress (1975)
House: 14D, 5R
Senate: 0

95th Congress (1977)
House: 13D, 5R
Senate: 0

96th Congress (1979)
House: 11D, 5R
Senate: 1D, 1R

97th Congress (1981)
House: 10D, 9R
Senate: 2R

98th Congress (1983)
House: 13D, 9R
Senate: 2R

99th Congress (1985)
House: 13D, 9R
Senate: 2R

100th Congress (1987)
House: 12D, 11R
Senate: 1D, 1R

101st Congress (1989)
House: 14D, 11R
Senate: 1D, 1R

102nd Congress (1991)
House: 19D, 9R
Senate: 1D, 1R

103rd Congress (1993)
House: 36D, 12R
Senate: 5D, 1R

104th Congress (1995)
House: 31D, 17R
Senate: 5D, 3R

105th Congress (1997)
House: 35D, 16R
Senate: 6D, 3R

106th Congress (1999)
House: 39D, 17R
Senate: 6D, 3R

*Numbers do not include nonvoting delegates.
Source: Vital Statistics on Congress.

NOTES

1. Author's interview with Rep. Diana DeGette (D-Colo.), Nov. 16, 1998.

2. Karen Foerstel and Herbert Foerstel, *Climbing the Hill: Gender Conflict in Congress* (Westport, Conn.: Praeger, 1996), p. 103.

3. *Congressional Record*—House, Jan. 10, 1918, p. 771.

4. Ibid., p. 772.

5. Ibid., pp. 785–786.

6. Emily George, *Martha Griffiths* (Washington, D.C.: University Press of America, 1982), p. 151.

7. *New York Times* Oral History Program, Former Members of Congress Oral History Collection, No. 32, Martha Griffiths (Sanford, N.C.: Microfilming Corporation of America, 1981), p. 84.

8. *Congressional Record*—House, Aug. 10, 1970, pp. 28000–28001.

9. *Congressional Record*—House, Oct. 12, 1971, pp. 35785–35787.

10. Foerstel, *Climbing the Hill: Gender Conflict in Congress*, p. 95.

11. Ibid., p. 99.

12. Linda Witt, Karen M. Paget, and Glenna Matthews, *Running as a Woman: Gender and Power in American Politics* (New York: The Free Press, 1994), p. 51.

13. Barbara Boxer, *Strangers in the Senate: Politics and the New Revolution of Women in America* (Bethesda, Md.: National Press Books, 1993), p. 62.

14. Norah M. O'Donnell, "Gender Gap? Lincoln, Six New House Members Set Record for Women," *Roll Call*, Nov. 5, 1998, p. 3.

15. Terry Neal, "As More Women Run, Gains in Congress Predicted," *Washington Post*, Oct. 1, 1998, p. A16.

16. Foerstel, *Climbing the Hill: Gender Conflict in Congress*, p. 71.

17. Ibid., p. 185.

18. Author's interview with Margaret Chase Smith, Nov. 14, 1994.

19. Karen Foerstel, "Three Endangered Senators," *Congressional Quarterly*, Oct. 3, 1998, p. 2640.

20. Ibid.

21. Ibid.

22. Author's interview with Rep. Karen McCarthy (D-Mo.), Feb. 15, 1995.

BIOGRAPHIES

HAZEL ABEL (R-Neb.)
(July 10, 1888–July 30, 1966)
Senate: Nov. 8, 1954, to Dec. 31, 1954

Most Nebraskans thought it odd that anyone would want to run for a two-month unexpired Senate term—especially since the Senate wasn't even supposed to meet during that period. But in the winter of 1954, 14 men and one woman made a full-scale race for it, and the woman won. Hazel Abel became the first woman in history to succeed another woman in the Senate. The short term was a result of a technicality in Nebraska's election law that prevented Abel's predecessor Eva Bowring from serving the final two months of the session. Abel campaigned across the state in an air-conditioned Cadillac, earning her the nickname "Hurricane Hazel." She went on to beat her closest primary challenger by 20,000 votes and her Democratic general election opponent by 60,000. "To me it was more than a short term in the Senate. I wanted Nebraska voters to express their approval of a woman in government. I was a sort of guinea pig," Abel said.[1]

Abel had been active in state politics before running in the special election and was serving as the vice chair of the Nebraska Republican Central Committee when she won the Senate seat. A former high school teacher, Abel later worked for 20 years for her husband's construction company and took over as company president following his death.

Her brief time in the Senate began on a dramatic note. Two days after being sworn into office, the Senate began censure hearings against Sen. Joseph McCarthy. After listening to "every single minute" of testimony for and against the motion, Abel was the first Senator to answer the roll call and cast her ballot with the majority to condemn McCarthy's conduct.[2]

Abel—who was assigned to the Finance Committee and the Committee on Interstate and Foreign Commerce—maintained a hectic schedule during her short service. She mailed 3,000 government documents—maps, cookbooks, and farm yearbooks—to Nebraska schools, libraries, and farm organizations. She appointed four students to the Air Force Academy. She lunched twice with First Lady Mamie Eisenhower, once with Vice President Richard Nixon, and conferred with President Dwight D. Eisenhower at the White House. She also visited Europe at her own expense to inspect military bases and foreign aid programs.

Abel voluntarily made her short term even shorter, resigning from the Senate two days early in order to give Carl Curtis, who was elected to succeed her, an edge in seniority. She remained active in Republican state politics after leaving office, serving as the chair of the state delegation at the national convention in 1956. In 1960, at the age of 72, she ran for governor, taking second place in the GOP primary.

BELLA ABZUG (D-N.Y.)
(July 24, 1920–March 31, 1998)
House: Jan. 3, 1971, to Jan. 3, 1977

Bella Abzug is one of the best-known women ever to serve in Congress, famous for her flamboyant hats and sharp tongue. She was the first woman since Jeannette Rankin in 1916 to run for Congress on a women's rights platform. "The other women in Congress were running not because they were women, but because they happened to be women. I was running because I was a woman," Abzug said.[3] During her time in Congress Abzug fought tirelessly against the Vietnam War and for women's rights, but her outspokenness and abrasive personality often alienated her from many of her congressional colleagues.

Abzug first became involved in politics while attending Hunter College where she served as president of the student council and worked for Zionism. After graduating in 1942, she wanted to go to Harvard Law

School, but was denied because it didn't accept women. She instead enrolled in Columbia Law School on a scholarship, but soon dropped out
to help the war effort by working in a shipbuilding factory. She returned
to law school at the end of World War II and specialized in labor issues.
She worked for the Civil Rights Congress and the American Civil Liberties Union and gained worldwide fame in the late 1940s as chief counsel for the two-year appeal of Willie McGee, a black man sentenced to
death in Mississippi for raping a white woman. During the case, Abzug
argued that the death penalty for rape was applied almost exclusively
to blacks. She lost the case and McGee was executed in 1951.

Abzug continued to work for liberal causes and in 1961 helped to
found Women Strike for Peace, which lobbied for an international nuclear test ban. During the 1960s, Abzug also fought against the war in
Vietnam and it was during this time that she decided to run for Congress. Campaigning on the slogan "A woman belongs in the House,"
Abzug challenged Democratic Rep. Leonard Farbstein. She won the primary and went on to defeat her Republican challenger to become the
first Jewish woman elected to Congress.

On her very first day in office, Abzug upset the old bulls when she
introduced a bill requiring the withdrawal of American troops from Vietnam within six months. She then made more waves at the end of her
inaugural day when she walked outside to the Capitol steps to take a
second oath of office—a "people's oath" administered to her by her colleague and friend from Brooklyn, Rep. Shirley Chisholm.

Abzug had requested a seat on the Armed Services Committee, where
no woman had been a member since Margaret Chase Smith in 1948. She
was refused and was instead assigned to the Public Works Committee.
In that position she offered an equal rights amendment to every bill that
emerged from the panel. Abzug was also placed on the Government
Operations Committee. At that panel's very first meeting, Abzug angered the chairman when she opposed his motion to close the doors to
the press. When she was outvoted, she defied the motion by giving re-
porters a detailed account of the proceedings.

During her first term in office, Abzug fought President Nixon's Vietnam policies, calling compulsory military service "slavery" and saying
Nixon was "motivated by insane priorities."[4] She was the first member
of Congress to openly call for Nixon's impeachment. In her first term,
Abzug also co-authored with Chisholm the Comprehensive Child Development Act to establish federally funded day-care centers in most
major cities. Nixon eventually vetoed the bill.

Throughout her three terms in office, Abzug pushed for an Equal
Rights Amendment to the Constitution, helped found the National
Women's Political Caucus, called for a congressional probe into the com-

petence of FBI director J. Edgar Hoover, and concentrated on local New York issues. She forced a rollback of New York rent increases, prevented the destruction of housing, and helped assure greater police protection. She also launched a drive to get statehood for New York City.

Abzug faced a political setback in 1972 when redistricting eliminated her seat. Forced to retire or fight, Abzug made the difficult decision to challenge fellow Democratic Rep. Bill Fitts Ryan who represented a neighboring district. Abzug told voters that they had the opportunity to choose the "greater of two goods," but, in a bitter race, Ryan won the primary by almost 2 to 1. Eight weeks before the general election, Ryan died and the Democratic County Committee nominated Abzug to replace him. Ryan's widow entered the race against Abzug, but Abzug won what turned out to be another bitter and personal race.

In 1976, Abzug decided to run for New York's open Senate seat, but lost the primary to Daniel Patrick Moynihan. A year later, Abzug ran an unsuccessful bid for New York mayor. When the winner of that race—Ed Koch—resigned from Congress to take his new post, Abzug ran for but lost a race for his House seat. She later launched another bid for the House against Rep. Joseph DioGuardi, but again lost.

She was appointed by President Jimmy Carter to head his National Advisory Committee on Women—and was later fired by him when she had the committee pass a resolution criticizing him for ignoring women's issues while increasing military spending. In 1990, she founded the Women's Environment and Development Organization (WEDO) to make women more visible in government and society. She remained a political activist on women's issues up until her death, caused by a heart ailment in 1998.

BOOKS BY ABZUG

Bella! Ms. Abzug Goes to Washington (1972)
Gender Gap: Bella Abzug's Guide to Political Power for American Women (1984)

MARYON ALLEN (D-Ala.)
(Nov. 30, 1925–   )
Senate: June 8, 1978, to Nov. 7, 1978

Maryon Allen's brief Senate career was filled with controversy arising from her outspoken statements to the press and her attempt to win election to the remainder of her husband's term. Allen was appointed to the Senate in 1978 by Gov. George Wallace after her husband, James Allen, died in office. Maryon Allen had been expected to hold the seat only until a special election was held several months later. She decided, however, that she wanted to run in the election for the remaining two years of her husband's term.

Shortly after her appointment to the Senate, Allen alienated Wallace when she gave an interview to the *Washington Post* in which she was quoted as being highly critical of the governor and his wife. Although Allen later insisted the interview had distorted her comments, the controversy caused quite a stir back home and damaged her chances in the special election. She led the September primary with 44 percent of the vote, but was forced into a runoff with state Senator Donald Stewart who defeated her by more than 120,000 votes.

After leaving the Senate, Allen worked as a columnist for the *Washington Post* and for *McCall's Needlework* magazine. Allen was a trained journalist and had earlier worked as a reporter, editor, and lecturer before entering politics. A graduate of the University of Alabama, Allen first met her husband while working as a reporter for the *Birmingham News*. She interviewed him for an article in 1964 while he was Alabama's lieutenant governor and they were married four months later. After her husband was elected to the Senate in 1968, Allen followed him to Washington and wrote a syndicated newspaper column entitled "The Reflections of a News Hen." She was preparing a series of televised news commentaries at the time of her husband's death in 1978.

ELIZABETH ANDREWS (D-Ala.)
(Feb. 12, 1911–)
House: April 4, 1971, to Jan. 3, 1973

Elizabeth Andrews faced no Republican opposition in the special election to fill the seat of her husband, 15-term Rep. George Andrews, who died while in office. She spent so little money on her campaign that, after her victory, she returned all political contributions that had been given to her. Before the Alabama Democratic Executive Committee overwhelmingly selected Andrews as their nominee in the race, conservative Gov. George Wallace—famous for standing in a schoolhouse door to block black students from entering—vowed to support her as an independent candidate if she did not get the Democratic nod. Wallace's endorsement led the committee to select Andrews as the Democratic candidate by a 72 to 17 vote. Opposition came largely from the black committee members.

Andrews had learned much about politics during her husband's extensive congressional career. She had, in fact, helped run his first bid for office, campaigning for him in Alabama while he served with the Navy at Pearl Harbor.

Once in office, Andrews was assigned to the Post Office and Civil Service Committee. During her brief nine months of congressional service Andrews introduced a number of bills, including one to increase the limit on earned income for Social Security recipients and another prohibiting cuts in welfare due to increases in Social Security benefits. Andrews favored withdrawing troops from Vietnam, saying a "military victory has been abandoned as a goal."[5] She also offered a constitutional amendment banning busing as a means to end school segregation.

Andrews declined to run for re-election when her term ended in 1973.

JEAN ASHBROOK (R-Ohio)
(Sept. 21, 1934–   )
House: July 12, 1982, to Jan. 3, 1983

Jean Ashbrook was elected to the House after the death of her husband, 11-term Rep. John Ashbrook. During her brief six months in office, she sat on the Merchant Marine and Fisheries Committee and established herself as a solid conservative. Shortly after being sworn in, Ashbrook introduced a bill to deny federal law enforcement funds or criminal justice assistance to any jurisdiction that implemented certain gun control ordinances. She also drafted legislation to require mandatory minimum sentences for anyone convicted of federal felonies against senior citizens. She supported the Enterprise Zone Tax Act of 1982 that encouraged businesses to relocate to poor areas by giving them tax cuts. She also backed a bill that would have created a U.S. Academy of Freedom to promote democracy in other countries and educate citizens about the dangers of Communism.

Ashbrook left Congress after just six months when her seat was eliminated through redistricting.

IRENE BAKER (R-Tenn.)
(Nov. 17, 1901–April 2, 1994)
House: March 10, 1964, to Jan. 3, 1965

Irene Baker was elected to Congress to fill out the unexpired term of her husband, Rep. Howard Baker, who died during his sixth term in office. The local GOP endorsed her campaign for the open seat, and Baker ran on a platform that promised she would follow her husband's pursuit of a balanced budget and job protection for workers in the local coal mines and nuclear laboratories. Baker had extensive political experience before coming to Congress. She had worked on all of her husband's campaigns and served for four years as a Republican National Committeewoman from Tennessee. Baker had also previously chaired the Grass Roots Organization of Republican Women—a statewide committee aimed at recruiting more women Republican voters. From 1918 to 1924, Baker worked as a county court clerk.

Once in the House, Baker pushed for cost-of-living increases for Social Security recipients and for less government spending. At the end of her brief term, Baker decided not to run for re-election. She instead returned to Knoxville, Tenn., where she served as director of public welfare from 1965 to 1971. Two years after she left Congress, Baker's stepson, Howard Baker, Jr., was elected to represent Tennessee in the U.S. Senate. He served until 1985.

TAMMY BALDWIN (D-Wisc.)
(Feb. 11, 1962–   )
House: Jan. 6, 1999, to present

Tammy Baldwin was the first openly gay woman to win election to Congress. Although she acknowledged the "historic nature of my campaign and my candidacy," she said her sexuality would not have a major influence on her agenda in the House.[6] She noted that her legislative priorities would include universal medical insurance coverage and improved educational programs. She was assigned to the Judiciary Committee and the Budget Committee.

Baldwin entered public office in 1986, at the age of 24, when she won a seat on the Dane County Board of Supervisors. During her four terms as a supervisor, she established and chaired the Dane County Task Force on AIDS.

In 1992, she was elected to the Wisconsin state assembly. During her six years in the state legislature, she worked to advance the civil rights of women, the disabled, gays, minorities, and the poor.

HELEN DELICH BENTLEY (R-Md.)
(Nov. 28, 1923–)
House: Jan. 3, 1985, to Jan. 3, 1996

Throughout her lengthy career as a journalist and member of Congress, Helen Delich Bentley established a reputation for being salty, gruff, and tough as nails. Once, while reporting a story by radio aboard a tanker, she used a four-letter expletive that led to the barring of her and her fellow journalists from the ship's radio room. Years later, when she ran for Congress, she dubbed herself the "fighting lady," and, once in office, she smashed a Toshiba radio with a sledgehammer to demonstrate her anger over the Japanese firm's sale of sensitive technology to the Soviet Union.[7] She also gained notoriety in 1990 when a process server accused the 5-foot, 2-inch 66-year-old Bentley of assaulting him as he was handing her a subpoena to be a potential witness in a murder trial. The server—a 230-pound ex-cop—later dropped the assault charges.

Bentley began her interest in politics while a high school student, serving as her senior class president. While attending the University of Nevada, Bentley worked as a campaign aide for James Scrugham in his successful bid for the U.S. Senate and, following the election, moved to Washington to work as his secretary. She later returned to college at the University of Missouri and after graduation went to work for the *Baltimore Sun*. She worked with the paper for 24 years, specializing in maritime issues. She also produced a weekly TV show focusing on the Baltimore shipping industry.

Bentley entered public service in 1969 when President Nixon appointed her chairman of the Federal Maritime Commission—making her the highest-ranking woman in federal government at that time. She held that post until 1975 and then returned to work as a columnist for the *World Port Magazine* and as an executive with a shipping company.

In 1980 and 1982, Bentley ran for Congress but failed to defeat the Democratic incumbent. She finally won with her third attempt in 1984. Once in office, she was assigned to the Merchant Marine and Fisheries Committee and the Committee on Public Works and Transportation. She later served on the Budget Committee and the Select Committee on Aging.

Throughout her House career, Bentley was a fierce protectionist of American businesses, supporting "Buy America" programs and opposing the free-trade NAFTA deal. "I'm tired of employing foreigners all the time in foreign countries and helping them out. I want to help out Americans," she said.[8]

She also was one of the few pro-union Republicans. During heated negotiations between waterfront management and dock workers at the Baltimore port in 1989, Bentley volunteered to serve as mediator.

In 1995, Bentley left Congress after losing the primary bid for governor of Maryland.

SHELLEY BERKLEY (D-Nev.)
(Jan. 20, 1951–   )
House: Jan. 6, 1999, to present

Shelley Berkley first became involved in politics in high school when she served as student body secretary. She continued her activism in college when she was elected student body president at the University of Nevada. She went on to earn her law degree from the University of San Diego in 1976, and from 1982 to 1983 served in the Nevada state assembly. She also served in a variety of non-elected positions with the Democratic party, including delegate to local and national Democratic conventions and national committeewoman.

Outside of politics, Berkley worked with Las Vegas gambling interests as the director of government and legal affairs at the Sands Hotel Casino and chair of the Board of the Nevada Hotel and Motel Association. From 1990 to 1992, she served on Nevada's University and Community College System Board of Regents. Immediately before winning election to Congress, Berkley worked as a consultant for PCS World, a telecommunications company.

Berkley said she will look out for the interests of her Las Vegas-area constituents during her time in Congress. She emphasized that she will be a strong opponent of any attempts to regulate or tax the gambling

industry and will fight efforts to establish a temporary nuclear waste
storage facility near Yucca Mountain. She was assigned to the Transportation Committee and the Veterans Affairs Committee.

JUDY BIGGERT (R-Ill.)
(Aug. 15, 1937–   )
House: Jan. 6, 1999, to present

Before entering politics, Judy Biggert was a lawyer and suburban "soccer
mom" who coached a neighborhood school team in her spare time. She
launched her political career in 1983 when she became president of the
local school board. Ten years later, she found herself serving in the Illinois House and after just one term was elected to be part of the Republican leadership team. During her time at the state level she sponsored
the Illinois law limiting pain and suffering awards in lawsuits.

    After winning election to the House, she was assigned to the Banking
Committee, the Government Reform Committee, and the Science Committee. Biggert supports abortion rights but is opposed to gun control.
She is considered a good negotiator and a hard worker who understands
the lingering prejudices against women. She relates a story of how one
of her college law professors once complained that Biggert was taking
the space of a man. "Women had to work harder than men," she said.
"They still do."[9]

IRIS BLITCH (D-Ga.)
(April 25, 1912–Aug. 19, 1993)
House: Jan. 3, 1955, to Jan. 3, 1963

Iris Blitch first decided to run for public office in 1940 when she couldn't
find a candidate to support for the state legislature. Her husband suggested she run for the seat, and she did. She lost the race, but at the age
of 28 set off to build a base of support for her future political career. She
worked in local Democratic politics and in 1946 ran for and won a seat
in the state Senate. That same year she became assistant secretary of the
state Democratic executive committee. Two years later, in 1948, she won

a seat in the state House. Because there were so few women in state politics at the time, she was crowned "Queen of the Legislature."[10] One of her proudest accomplishments was passage of a bill giving women the right to serve on juries in Georgia.

Her defeat for re-election to the state House in 1949 did not deter her. Blitch went back to college to study political science, accounting, and English. In 1952, she ran again for the state Senate and won.

In 1954, Blitch launched a primary challenge against four-term U.S. Rep. William Wheeler, charging him with absenteeism and party disloyalty. She narrowly defeated the incumbent and became the first woman in Georgia history to win the Democratic nomination to the U.S. Congress. She ran unopposed in the general election.

After coming to Capitol Hill, Blitch was assigned to the Public Works Committee where she fought to preserve the Okefenokee Swamp in her district from drought and fire. She also passed an amendment that gave small property owners federal aid for water-conservation projects and introduced legislation to protect the jute-yarn industry in her district by making it more difficult for foreign-made jute to enter the country.

In her second term in the House, Blitch joined 100 other southern lawmakers in signing a "manifesto" against civil rights. They opposed a bill that established a committee on civil rights and protected the voting rights of every citizen. They blasted the legislation as "an iniquitous and flagrant violation of states rights."[11] They also presented a petition against the 1954 Supreme Court ruling that called for the desegregation of schools.

Blitch, suffering from arthritis, declined to run for re-election in 1962. Two years later, she announced that she would leave the Democratic party and support the presidential bid of GOP Sen. Barry Goldwater.

CORRINE "LINDY" BOGGS (D-La.)
(March 13, 1916–   )
House: March 20, 1973, to Jan. 3, 1991

When Lindy Boggs left Congress in 1991, she ended 50 years of work on Capitol Hill—in and out of office. Boggs was first elected to the House in 1973 after her husband Hale Boggs—the powerful House majority leader—disappeared in a plane crash over Alaska during a campaign trip for a colleague. Weeks were spent searching for the plane, and Mrs. Boggs initially refused to launch a campaign for her husband's seat. "Oh, no, we already have a Congressman," she would tell supporters who urged her to run.[12] Two months after the plane disappeared, Congress finally declared the seat vacant and Mrs. Boggs emerged as the top contender.

Mrs. Boggs was no newcomer to politics. She was raised in a political family—her grandfather was a Louisiana state legislator and district attorney, her cousin was mayor of New Orleans, and her family tree included Louisiana's first governor after it became a state. After marrying in 1938, Boggs and her husband became involved with local politics. The couple came to Washington in 1940 when Hale Boggs won a House seat. He was defeated for re-election two years later, but returned to the House in 1947. During the next 25 years, Lindy Boggs worked closely with her husband, managing his campaigns and his Capitol Hill office. Lindy Boggs also established a name for herself. She worked on Adlai Stevenson's presidential campaign in 1956, worked with Lyndon Johnson's vice presidential whistle-stop tour through the South, chaired John Kennedy's and Johnson's inaugural ball committees in 1961 and 1965, and served as president of the Women's National Democratic Club.

When it came time for Lindy Boggs to run for office, voters accepted her overwhelmingly. She won the special election to fill her husband's seat with 81 percent of the vote and became the first woman from Louisiana to be elected to the House. Boggs asked for and was given a seat on the Banking Committee, on which her husband had served. On that panel, Boggs worked to end credit discrimination against women. When the committee took up the Equal Credit Opportunity Act of 1974, which prohibited discrimination based on race, age, and veteran status, Boggs introduced an amendment to also ban discrimination based on sex and marital status. Boggs wrote the new language on her copy of the bill and without saying a word, made copies for each committee member. Calling up her southern charm, she told her colleagues, "I'm sure it was just an oversight that we didn't have sex or marital status included."[13] Her amendment passed unanimously. Boggs later served on the powerful Appropriations Committee—one of only a handful of women ever to serve on that panel—and looked out for the interests of her state, directing millions of dollars to local projects.

Throughout her congressional career, Boggs worked for women's rights. In 1977, she introduced the first domestic violence bill, which called for the creation of a research program at the National Institute of Mental Health aimed at ending spousal abuse. In 1983, she led efforts to shift the emphasis in the $4-billion appropriations job bill away from construction work and toward jobs women perform. "The longer you stay here," she once remarked, "the more aware of inequities you become."[14] Boggs helped establish the Congressional Women's Caucus and the Select Committee on Children, Youth, and Families, but she was often criticized by outside women's groups because she opposed abortion. Boggs, however, did back family planning legislation. In honor of her commitment to women's issues, the House voted to rename a room off the Capitol Rotunda the "Lindy Clairborne Boggs Congressional Women's Reading Room."

Boggs was also a strong supporter of civil rights. While her husband was alive, the two opened their house up to young civil rights marchers and even dubbed their basement the "underground railroad." While in office, Boggs worked to create the National Museum of African Art in Washington. When she left Congress, she was the only white member of Congress representing a majority black district.

Along with her congressional duties, Boggs was greatly interested in history (she was a high school history teacher before coming to Washington). She was a board member of the American Revolution Bicentennial Administration and chaired the joint Senate–House arrangements committee for the 1976 congressional celebrations. She helped establish the Office of Historian in the House, and in 1987 was chosen by her colleagues to preside over the special congressional ceremony in Philadelphia honoring the 200th anniversary of the Constitution. Boggs herself made history in 1976 when she chaired the Democratic National Convention, the first woman to preside over a national political convention.

In 1990, Boggs decided to leave Congress to spend more time with her daughter Barbara Sigmund—the mayor of Princeton, N.J.—who was dying of cancer. Boggs's other children have also made names for themselves. Daughter Cokie Roberts is a nationally known journalist and son Thomas Hale Boggs is a prominent Washington lobbyist.

After leaving office, Boggs wrote her biography, *Washington Through a Purple Veil*. The title stems from an incident Boggs encountered when she first came to Washington with her husband in 1941. Her husband was attending Lend Lease hearings for weapons and food aid to Britain and China. Hale Boggs called his wife—just 24 years old—at home and told her to hurry down to hear the arguments.

"I threw a jacket over my sweater and skirt, and made up my face, brushed my hair and put on high heels," she said. When she arrived at the hearings, there was a huge crowd of people waiting to get in. Boggs approached the guard and said she was Hale Boggs's wife. " 'Oh, sure, honey,' he said, looking away. He totally disbelieved me . . . I suddenly thought of Mrs. Dugas, a beautiful New Orleans socialite who had told me . . . that the most sophisticated and becoming thing a woman could wear was a purple veil." Boggs went home, put on her best black suit, pearl pin, hat, and gloves, and went to the Palais Royal and asked to have a purple veil draped over her hat. She returned to the Capitol and again approached the guard. "I took off one glove and then the other with as much authority as I could muster. In my sweetest Southern accent I said, 'I'm Mrs. Boggs. I'd like to be seated, please.' The guard said, 'Oh, yes, ma'am. Come right in.' "[15]

Her daughter Barbara once said, "Whenever I want to do something directly, I think of what Daddy would have done. And whenever I want to accomplish something indirectly, I try to emulate what Mama would do."[16]

In November 1997, Boggs—at the age of 81—launched another political career. She was sworn in as the U.S. ambassador to the Vatican.

BOOK BY BOGGS

Washington Through a Purple Veil: Memoirs of a Southern Woman (1994)

VERONICA BOLAND (D-Pa.)
(March 18, 1899–June 19, 1982)
House: Nov. 19, 1942, to Jan. 3, 1943

During her brief 45 days in office, Veronica Boland received no committee assignments and made no speeches on the floor. She came to the House after running unopposed in a special election to fill out the unexpired term of her late husband, Rep. Patrick Boland, the House majority whip. She, however, was not a candidate in the election held simultaneously for the following full term. After leaving Congress, Boland returned to her home town of Scranton, Pa., and worked as an executive secretary for the Dutch Manufacturing Company.

FRANCES BOLTON (R-Ohio)
(March 29, 1885–March 9, 1977)
House: Feb. 27, 1940, to Jan. 3, 1969

When Frances Bolton decided to run for the unexpired term of her late husband, Rep. Chester Bolton, state party leaders supported her bid only because "they were sure I would get tired of politics in a few months and flit on to something else." But she soon surprised and annoyed them when she declared she would run for the next full term. "The men so much wanted to get me out, that I determined they would have to put up with me," she said.[17] She made just one short campaign speech during her first run for office and managed to win with a bigger majority than her husband ever had. In 1960, after 20 years in office, she became the longest serving woman in the House up to that time. Earlier in her career, in 1952, Bolton's son Oliver won election to the House and the two became the only mother–son team ever to serve in Congress simultaneously.

The daughter of a wealthy Ohio family, Bolton, at the age of 32, was bequeathed a huge trust fund from her uncle, a founder of the Standard Oil Company. That fund, along with the wealth of her deceased husband, would give her the label of the "richest man in Congress." Before coming to office, Bolton used her wealth to give generously to various causes, including education, nursing, literacy, and radio communication. In 1929, she donated $1.25 million for a school of nursing at Western Reserve University. She also sponsored a five-year survey of the social value of motion pictures and funded a study on the use of radio in education. After being elected to Congress, Bolton gave back to the U.S. Treasury the $10,000 she was entitled to as the widow of a representative.

Bolton was assigned to serve on the Indian Affairs Committee, the Expenditures in the Executive Departments Committee, and the Committee on the Election of the President, Vice President and Representatives. In her second term, she resigned from those assignments to serve on the Foreign Affairs Committee, where she sat for the next 28 years and eventually became the ranking Republican on the panel. She traveled extensively at her own expense—never charging the taxpayer for her committee excursions—and in 1947 became the first woman to head an overseas congressional delegation and the first member of the Foreign Affairs committee to travel to the Soviet Union. Bolton was responsible for reorganizing the panel into geographical subcommittees; she served on the Eastern Europe, the Balkans, and the Middle East subcommittee. Late in her career, at the age of 70, she journeyed to East Africa where she climbed mountains, fled from a charging elephant, and studied the educational and health development of the native peoples.

Bolton came to Congress an isolationist, opposing the creation of the selective service and President Roosevelt's Lend-Lease program to aid Britain and the Soviet Union before the war. But once World War II began, Bolton slowly began to support the effort with a focus on the military's nurses. (Bolton's interest in nursing started as a young girl when she volunteered with nurses who worked with the poor.) She authored and pushed through Congress the $5 million Bolton Act, which created a U.S. Cadet Nurse Corps that trained 124,000 nurses who would serve in the war effort. She also crafted legislation that required uniformed nurses to receive the same pay as male officers. Bolton did not just speak about nurses' rights, but also donned a nurse's uniform and traveled through Europe to inspect the working conditions of the military nurses during World War II.

She believed that women and men should be treated equally and spoke out in favor of drafting women into the military. "I am afraid that gallantry is sorely out of date, and as a woman I find it rather stupid," she said. "Woman's place includes defending the home."[18] In the 1960s, she sponsored an equal-rights-for-men bill authorizing the Army and Navy to commission male nurses. She also spoke out against racial segregation in the military. In 1953, President Eisenhower appointed Bolton as the first female congressional delegate to the United Nations, and one year later she gave a historic speech before the UN against South Africa's apartheid policies. "Prejudice [must be put down] wherever it raises its head, whether we are the victims or not. . . . [A]n attack on any group endangers everyone's freedom."[19]

Although Bolton concentrated on international issues, she also worked hard for her constituents and even paid the salaries of additional staff in her district office out of her own pocket. Her popularity kept her in office for 29 years, but her career ended when she was forced to run against Rep. Charles Vanik (D) when their two districts were merged. Her age of 83 was an issue in the race against the younger Vanik. She moved back to Ohio and continued her philanthropic work until her death in 1977, just a few weeks short of her 92nd birthday.

Throughout her life, Bolton believed women had to work twice as hard as men—especially in Congress. She once told the Women's National Press Club, "The Lord, after creating the world, put a man in charge of it. He messed everything up, so the Lord turned everything over to a woman, and He gave her everything He had given man, plus two more things: pain, so she would understand what creation is, and laughter, so that she could stand that and the man."[20]

MARY BONO (R-Calif.)
(Oct. 24, 1961–   )
House: April 21, 1998, to present

Mary Bono was elected to Congress to fill the seat of her husband, two-term Rep. Sonny Bono (R), who was killed in a skiing accident. Like many congressional widows, Bono campaigned on a promise to continue the legislative work of her husband. She ran as a fiscal conservative and social moderate. Like her husband, she supports abortion rights in the first trimester but favors some restrictions, including parental notification for minors. She also supports lower taxes, debt reduction, and privatization of Social Security.

The special election to fill the late Bono's open seat received heavy media attention for its Hollywood connections. Sonny Bono, although he served in the House for three years and previously as the mayor of Palm Springs, was best known for his early entertainment career as the singing partner of Cher. During the special election, Bono's widow was pitted against Democrat and actor Ralph Waite, who portrayed "Pa" on the television show *The Waltons*. The race also made headlines when Sonny Bono's mother publicly opposed her daughter-in-law's run for Congress, saying a woman could not serve in Congress and raise children at the same time.

In the end, Mary Bono easily won the April 7 special election and Waite later decided not to challenge her again during the November election for a full two-year term. A former gymnast and personal trainer, Bono had never before held public office.

Once on Capitol Hill, Bono was assigned to the National Security Committee and the Judiciary Committee where she participated in the impeachment hearings against President Bill Clinton. She voted for all four impeachment articles against Clinton.

Among her first moves in Congress was to push for passage of a bill her husband had introduced to clean up the Salton Sea, a polluted desert lake in her district. She also introduced legislation to end recreational fees at national parks.

REVA BOSONE (D-Utah)
(April 2, 1895–July 21, 1983)
House: Jan. 3, 1949, to Jan. 3, 1953

When Reva Bosone was first elected to the House, she requested a seat on the Committee on Public Lands (later called the Interior Committee), but was turned down because she was a woman. No woman had ever served on that panel. Although she was brand new in Congress, Bosone wasn't going down without a fight. She sent her top aide to approach Rep. Jere Cooper (D-Tenn.), the chair of the Ways and Means Committee and the man in charge of committee assignments. Bosone later recalled,

"So she went to him and he said 'Oh, my. Oh, no. She'd be embarrassed
. . . to be on the committee and discuss the sex of animals.' And she called
me back and said he didn't think it advisable. He wouldn't appoint me.
And I said you go right back and tell him it would be refreshing to hear
about animals' sex relationships compared with the perversions among
human beings. She did and she came back and said to me he laughed,
and said 'She can go on the committee.' "[21]

Bosone's unwillingness to accept defeat was a trait that helped her
establish a distinguished career both in and out of Congress. Bosone
started out as a teacher, but after seven years of teaching high school
English and speech, she decided to follow her real dream and earn a law
degree. After working in private practice for a year, Bosone in 1932 ran
and won a seat in the Utah House of Representatives—becoming the
first woman in Utah's history to be elected to the state legislature. For
the next four years, Bosone rose through the ranks to become the first
woman to chair a major committee and the first to serve as floor leader.
She secured passage of a women's and children's wage and hour law
and a child labor amendment to the state constitution.

In 1936, Bosone scored another first—the first woman to be elected a
municipal judge. During her 12 years on the bench, Bosone established
herself as tough yet compassionate. She often took a personal interest in
rehabilitating offenders, sending wayward girls to psychiatrists and
drunks to Alcoholics Anonymous. In recognition of her efforts to help
the troubled, Bosone was named to the Utah Hall of Fame in 1943. In
1947, Bosone served as the first director of the Utah State Board for Education on Alcoholism. During World War II, she was chair of the
Women's Army Corps Civilian Advisory Committee of the Ninth Service
Command and was an official observer at the United Nations' founding
conference in San Francisco in 1945.

In 1948, Bosone defeated a freshman Republican to win a seat in the
U.S. House. During her first term in office, she pushed for Native-
American self-government and introduced a bill to gradually reduce federal administration of Indian affairs. She favored extension of Social
Security, funding for public housing for military personnel, and statehood for Hawaii and Alaska. Bosone voted against the Subversive Activities Control and Communist Registration Act and the 1949 Central
Intelligence Act. She also called for federal statutes outlawing the poll
tax and lynching. Bosone won a second term for Congress against GOP
challenger Ivy Baker Priest—who would later become U.S. Treasurer—
but failed in her bid for a third term after she experienced legal problems
and charges that she was soft on Communism. In 1952, the Justice Department ordered an investigation into accusations that she had violated
the federal Corrupt Practices Act by accepting a $630 campaign contri-

bution from two staff members. Bosone insisted she was not aware of the contribution and the Justice Department decided not to pursue charges. But the damage had been done.

Bosone tried to make a comeback to the House in 1954, but was again defeated. She returned to Capitol Hill in 1957, this time as a legal counsel to the safety and compensation subcommittee of the House Education and Labor Committee. In 1961, she was named a judicial officer with the Post Office Department, a seat she held until her retirement in 1968.

EVA BOWRING (R-Neb.)
(Jan. 9, 1892–Jan. 8, 1985)
Senate: April 26, 1954, to Nov. 7, 1954

When Gov. Robert Crosby appointed Eva Bowring to fill the vacancy created by the death of Sen. Dwight Griswold, Bowring was splitting her time between serving as the vice chair of the Nebraska Central Republican Commitee and herding cattle on her 10,000-acre ranch. Bowring almost turned down the governor's appointment. "He kept talking about the honor. But I told him it would be just a burden. I think that what really convinced me was myself. I've been saying for years that women should get into politics, and so when I got the chance, I just didn't feel I could turn it down," she said shortly after accepting the seat.[22]

Bowring was assigned to the Interstate and Foreign Commerce Committee, the Labor and Public Welfare Committee, and the Post Office and Civil Service Committee. In her maiden speech on the Senate floor, she spoke out against the Senate Agriculture Committee's vote to continue rigid price supports of farm crops. She instead supported the program of flexible agricultural price supports proposed by the Eisenhower administration. Bowring also paid special attention to her constituents, introducing bills for flood control and reservoir projects back in her district.

Bowring's interest in politics came from her second husband, a county commissioner and state legislator. She worked as a Republican precinct worker for 20 years and became the first woman county GOP chairman in the state. She was also the first female chair of the Nebraska Stockgrowers Association.

Because of a technicality in Nebraska election law, Bowring was forced to end her Senate service two months before the end of the congressional session. Another woman—Hazel Abel—was elected to fill out those last two months. It was the first time a woman succeeded another woman in the Senate.

After leaving Capitol Hill, Bowring was named to serve on the Mental Health Advisory Council of the National Institutes of Health. She was later appointed to the Federal Bureau of Prisons Parole Board.

BARBARA BOXER (D-Calif.)
(Nov. 11, 1940–   )
House: Jan. 3, 1983, to Jan. 5, 1993
Senate: Jan. 5, 1993, to present

Barbara Boxer—one of only four women to serve in both the House and Senate—has proven herself one of the most independent and liberal-minded members of Congress. She was elected to the Senate in 1992 and, along with former San Francisco Mayor Dianne Feinstein (D), became part of the first female duo to hold a state's two Senate seats. Throughout her campaign for the Senate, Boxer used her "feisty" image to her advantage and even handed out bright yellow "BOXER" shorts along with her campaign literature.

Before entering politics, Boxer worked as a stockbroker and newspaper reporter. In 1974, she joined the staff of Rep. John Burton (D-Calif.) as a district worker. Two years later, she won election to the Marin County Board of Supervisors and in 1981 became the first woman president of the board. When Burton announced in 1982 that he was leaving Congress, Boxer jumped into the race. With Burton's endorsement, Boxer won the primary against five other opponents and sailed to victory in the general election.

In the House, Boxer was a leading critic of wasteful Defense Department spending—she pointed out the absurdity of the Pentagon's purchase of the now infamous $7,622 coffee pot. She sat on the powerful Budget Committee and the Armed Services Committee, and served as co-chair of the Military Reform Caucus, but she rarely won passage of her many amendments aimed at cutting defense spending and increasing funds for domestic social programs. Boxer also sat on the Government Operations Committee, the Committee on Merchant Marines and Fisheries, and the Select Committee on Children, Youth and Families.

Boxer, an avid supporter of women's rights, was thrown into the battle of the sexes among her own congressional colleagues during her first term in office. When she found out that there was an all-male gym in the House, she complained but to no avail. In her second term, she recruited several of her male colleagues to lobby for the gym's integration. When they were turned down, Boxer gathered together several women members and wrote a song—set to the tune "Has Anybody Seen My Gal?"—to dramatize the "gym problem." After the women sang the ditty to several members of the House leadership, the gym was opened to women.

On more serious women's issues, Boxer fought tirelessly throughout her House service for abortion rights and drafted the Violence Against Women's Act aimed at curbing domestic violence and helping abused wives. In 1991, when the Senate was poised to confirm Clarence Thomas to the Supreme Court, Boxer was one of seven House women who marched across the Capitol to the Senate to protest his confirmation without first hearing from Anita Hill and her charges of sexual harassment against Thomas.

One year later, Boxer was elected to the Senate in the 1992 "Year of the Woman" elections that brought an unprecedented number of female lawmakers to Congress. In the Senate, Boxer continued to make waves and headlines on women's issues. In 1994, Boxer spoke out against the Tailhook Navy scandal and voted against allowing two Navy admirals to retire at full rank—holding them responsible for the sexual abuse that took place during the Tailhook convention. In 1995, she called for public hearings against Sen. Bob Packwood (R-Ore.), who was charged with sexual harassment by his former aides.

Boxer serves on the Appropriations Committee; the Banking, Housing, and Urban Affairs Committee; the Budget Committee; and the Committee on Environment and Public Works. She has worked on a variety of children's issues, calling for child safety devices on all guns sold in America, and she introduced the After School Education and Safety Act. She also pushed for new environmental safety standards to take into account the health of children and the elderly. Most standards are set to protect the health of average adults.

Although a staunch liberal and opponent of military spending, Boxer in 1995 attacked the base-closing commission that shut down military installations in her state and cost California thousands of defense jobs. Boxer also joined with Republicans in toughening immigration standards and sought to force the federal government to reimburse states for costs associated with illegal immigration.

BOOK BY BOXER

Strangers in the Senate: Politics and the New Revolution of Women in America (1993)

CORRINE BROWN (D-Fla.)
(Nov. 11, 1946–   )
House: Jan. 5, 1993, to present

Before coming to Congress, Corrine Brown served in the Florida House where she helped draw three new majority black congressional districts following the 1990 census. She would go on to win one of those districts in 1992, but four years later, in 1996, the courts ruled that her district lines were unconstitutional. The state legislature was forced to redraw Brown's district, reducing the number of black voters. Nonetheless, Brown easily overcame the obstacle and won re-election that year with 60 percent of the vote—her biggest victory.

Brown had served in the state legislature for 10 years. Before that, she worked as a professor and counselor at Florida Community College. She also opened a travel agency, but later sold it when it became the center of controversy during her first run for the U.S. House. The loser of the Democratic primary charged Brown with using her state employees to work in the agency. He filed a complaint with the Florida Commission on Ethics, and, while Brown maintained her innocence, she eventually agreed to pay a $5,000 fine.

In Congress, Brown has generally supported liberal causes, but she places the concerns of her constituents above ideological leanings. She voted against the wishes of President Clinton on two high-profile issues: lifting the ban on homosexuals in the military and the North American Free Trade Agreement. Brown's district is home to several military installations as well as many retired military personnel and her vote against gays in the military likely reflected the opinion of her constituents. And she argued that NAFTA would drain jobs from her district. She worked behind the scenes with the Clinton administration to help formulate a policy that would provide assistance to the huge flow of Haitian refugees to her district without draining local resources.

She has also worked to bring federal funds back to her district, securing a $100-million federal courthouse for Jacksonville and working to keep a defense contractor in the city to provide jobs. She supports capital punishment and is a strong law-and-order proponent, but she fought local police departments when, after a series of violent car-jacking incidents plagued her district, police officers began rounding up young black men and holding them in jail without due process.

Brown sits on the Transportation and Infrastructure Committee and the Committee on Veterans' Affairs. In 1997, she was elected secretary of the Congressional Black Caucus. She also headed a Black Caucus task force on campaign finance reform, working to protect contributions from political action committees.

VERA BUCHANAN (D-Pa.)
(July 20, 1902– Nov. 26, 1955)
House: Aug. 1, 1951, to Nov. 26, 1955

When Vera Buchanan was elected to the House to fill out the term of her late husband, the local *Pittsburgh Post-Gazette* wrote that her "foremost attribute was that she was the widow of Frank Buchanan."[23] But she soon proved that she could hold office in her own right, going on to win re-election twice with large majorities.

Throughout her career, Buchanan fought for organized labor and was a strong backer of the Truman administration. In 1952, she voted against using the Taft-Hartley Act to end a steelworkers strike and force the men back to work on the company's terms. She introduced bills to combat inflation, increase railroad retirement benefits, and provide housing for poor senior citizens. She served on the Merchant Marine and Fisheries Committee, the Banking and Currency Committee, and the Committee on Public Works.

Buchanan would have likely won election to a fourth term in the House, but midway through her third term she died of cancer.

Before serving in Congress, Buchanan gained political experience by working as a secretary in her husband's Capitol Hill office. She also previously served on the Democratic Women's Guild.

JOCELYN BURDICK (D-N.D.)
(Feb. 6, 1922–   )
Senate: Sept. 16, 1992, to Dec. 14, 1992

Jocelyn Burdick was appointed to the Senate after her husband, five-term Sen. Quentin Burdick, died in office. Although her term was brief, it was significant in two ways: she became the first woman to represent North Dakota in Congress and, second, her appointment brought to three the number of women serving in the Senate—a record high at that time.

Jocelyn Burdick, the great-granddaughter of Matilda Joslyn Gage, a suffragist and colleague of Susan B. Anthony, maintained a low public profile during her husband's three decades in office, but she was active in Fargo civic affairs for many years. She was a founding member of the Fargo Democratic Women Plus, a political group organized in the 1980s. She was the local chair of the United Fund (now the United Way) and served on the boards for Fargo's Florence Crittenden Home for unwed mothers and Frazier Hall for the Developmentally Disabled. A graduate of Northwestern University, Burdick spent her early career as a radio reporter and announcer in Minnesota.

Before meeting her husband, Burdick was a Republican. She met the future senator in 1952 at a local debate on adding fluoride to the Fargo water supply. She supported allowing individuals to choose on this issue, while he was against choice. They were married in 1960, one week after he was elected to the Senate.

After her appointment to the Senate, Jocelyn Burdick was assigned to the Special Committee on Aging, the Select Committee on Indian Affairs, and the Environment and Public Works Committee. During her brief three-month term (the Senate was in session and voting for just one of those months), Burdick said she wanted to carry on the agenda of her husband. She, however, cast one of her votes exactly opposite to her husband's vote months earlier. Although he had voted to sustain a veto by President Bush of a bill to restrict trade with China, she voted to override the veto several months later when the issue came up a second time.

Following her appointment to the Senate, Burdick announced she would not run in the special election to fill out the remaining two years of her husband's term. She instead endorsed Rep. Kent Conrad (D-N.D.), who went on to win the seat.

YVONNE BRATHWAITE BURKE (D-Calif.)
(Oct. 5, 1932–   )
House: Jan. 3, 1973, to Jan. 3, 1979

In her very first year in office, Yvonne Brathwaite Burke set a milestone for women in politics. It had nothing to do with legislation or elections—

she was the first woman to give birth while serving in Congress. It would be 20 years before another congresswoman would have a child in office (Rep. Enid Greene Waldholz in 1995). Although Burke is best remembered for her maternal achievement, she was also an effective legislator and leader. She was the first black woman to be elected to the California General Assembly, the first woman to serve as vice chair of the Democratic National Convention, and the first woman to chair the Congressional Black Caucus.

Even as a child, Burke showed outstanding leadership skills. A talented student, Burke was transferred out of public elementary schools and placed in a special "model school" associated with the University of Southern California. Burke later served as vice president of her high school student body and worked her way through college as a model, appearing in such magazines as *Ebony*. After graduating from the University of California at Los Angeles with honors, Burke entered the University of Southern California law school where she was forced to confront racism from her fellow students. The school's women's law society refused to admit blacks and Jews, so Burke and two Jewish students formed their own professional sorority, which remained in existence long after they graduated.

After passing the California bar, Burke found that no law firms would hire a black woman, so she opened her own practice specializing in civil, probate, and real estate law. Burke later served as the state's deputy corporation commissioner and as a hearing officer for the Los Angeles Police Commission. In 1965, following the riots in Watts, Burke organized a legal defense team for the rioters and later served as an attorney for the McCone Commission, created to investigate the cause of the violence. She also worked with the NAACP defense team and produced an analysis of the housing conditions of Los Angeles that helped shed light on some of the causes of the riots.

Burke first became interested in politics in 1964 when she worked as a volunteer with the re-election campaign of President Lyndon Johnson. In 1966, she entered her first race for the state legislature. She defeated six men for the Democratic nomination, and after a bitter general election race in which she was labeled a black militant and a Communist, Burke became the first black woman elected to the California General Assembly. During her six years on the state level, she worked for equal job opportunities for women, free child-care centers on college campuses, affordable child care for the poor, and federal aid for education.

After the creation of a new, majority black congressional district, Burke decided to run for the U.S. House. She defeated four challengers for the Democratic nomination and ended up marrying the campaign aide for one of her toughest opponents. Following her primary victory, Burke was selected to serve as vice chair of the 1972 Democratic National Convention. She won national attention for her cool-handed oversight of the raucous proceedings. A few months later, Burke won a landslide victory over her Republican opponent with 73 percent of the vote.

"There is no longer any need for anyone to speak for all black women. I expect Shirley Chisholm is feeling relieved," Burke said after her election, referring to the first black woman elected to Congress four years earlier.[24]

Burke was assigned to the Interior and Insular Affairs Committee, but a year later transferred to the powerful Appropriations Committee. Burke worked to increase the minimum wage, issue food stamps to striking workers, and extend unemployment compensation to farm workers, domestics, and state and local employees. A liberal, Burke consistently supported federal programs to help the poor and needy. During consideration of the Trans-Alaska Pipeline Authorization Act, Burke introduced an amendment requiring affirmative action programs to ensure that construction contracts be awarded to minority businesses. A version of the amendment would later require that *any* project receiving federal funding implement an affirmative action plan. In 1977, Burke backed a human rights amendment to the foreign aid bill and supported other efforts to pressure foreign governments to improve their human rights records. That same year she introduced the Displaced Homemakers Act that authorized job training centers for women entering the labor market.

In 1978, Burke declined to run for re-election. She instead launched an unsuccessful bid for California state attorney general. In 1979, she was appointed by the governor to the Los Angeles County Board of Supervisors. In 1997, Burke became chair of the Board.

SALA BURTON (D-Calif.)
(April 1, 1925–Feb. 1, 1987)
House: June 21, 1983, to Feb. 1, 1987

Sala Burton was elected to the House to fill out the term of her husband, Rep. Phillip Burton, who died while in office. Phillip Burton was one of the most powerful men in the House—having lost his bid for House majority leader by just one vote in 1976—and his widow was quickly accepted into the fold of top Democrats following her election. But Sala Burton did not simply ride the coattails of her husband. She had a solid political background and was a longtime liberal activist before coming to Congress.

Burton founded the California Democratic Council and served as its vice president from 1951 to 1954. She later served as president of the San Francisco Democratic Women's Forum and was a member of both the San Francisco County and California State Democratic Central Committees. She also worked with the NAACP to fight job and housing discrimination. During her husband's tenure in Congress, she served as president of the Democratic Wives of the House and Senate.

Burton announced that she would run for Congress just eight days after the death of her husband. She went on to easily defeat 10 other candidates in the special election. Once in office, she was appointed to her husband's old seats on the Education and Labor Committee and the Committee on the Interior. In her second term, she sought a seat on the powerful Appropriations Committee, but was turned down. Instead, Speaker Tip O'Neill gave her an equally exclusive assignment to the Rules Committee, which oversees all legislation headed to the House floor. She also served on the Select Committee on Hunger.

Burton maintained a solidly liberal voting record, supporting the Equal Rights Amendment and opposing military spending. She backed social welfare programs, child nutrition assistance, and bilingual education. (Burton was a native speaker of Polish, having fled the country at the age of 14 with her parents just before the Nazi invasion.)

After her re-election in 1986, Burton was too ill to take the oath of office on the House floor and was instead sworn in at her home. She died shortly thereafter on Feb. 1, 1987.

VERA BUSHFIELD (R-S.D.)
(Aug. 9, 1889–April 16, 1976)
Senate: Oct. 6, 1948, to Dec. 26, 1948
(never sworn into office)

When South Dakota Gov. George Mickelson appointed Vera Bushfield to fill out the last three months of her late husband Sen. Harlan Bushfield's term, he made it clear that her service was to be minimal. "The appointment is being made with the understanding that shortly before the 80th Congress reconvenes she will resign and thus enable me to give seniority right to the new senator-elect," Mickelson told the public.[25] Her husband's death was not unexpected, for he had announced earlier in the year that he would not seek re-election due to failing health. Mrs. Bushfield had worked closely with her husband while he was in the Senate and during his earlier two terms as governor. She traveled to all parts of the state and "doubled as a capable sounding board and effective supporter of issues important to women and children."[26] But after being appointed to the Senate, Bushfield's biggest decision was whether to bother coming to Washington or stay at home during her three-month term. Knowing she would not be sworn into office because Congress had already recessed for the year, she opted to stay in South Dakota and make herself "as accessible as possible" to her constituents.

Keeping her promise to the governor, Bushfield resigned her seat six days before the end of the Congress so that Karl Mundt—the winner of the November election—would gain seniority over the other newly elected senators. Her brief tenure in the Senate was Bushfield's first and only official public service.

LESLIE BYRNE (D-Va.)
(Oct. 27, 1946–   )
House: Jan. 5, 1993, to Jan. 3, 1995

During her brief one term in office, Leslie Byrne established herself as a tough, hard-nosed legislator who wasn't afraid to challenge her own leadership. In her first year in office, she led an unsuccessful effort to remove from their posts all Democratic committee chairs who did not support President Clinton's 1993 deficit-reduction plan. Ironically, it was her vote for the budget plan that helped lead to her defeat for re-election in 1994. Her Republican opponent attacked Byrne's support for the plan, saying it was a vote for higher taxes, and she was soundly defeated for a second term.

Byrne was the first woman elected to Congress from Virginia. She was well known in Virginia politics from her years as a leader in local community affairs. She headed a business consulting firm and was president of the local League of Women Voters. In 1985, Byrne was elected to the Virginia House of Delegates where she served for seven years. During her time in the state House, Byrne became the first nonlawyer appointed to the prestigious Courts of Justice Committee. She also held the top

Democratic position on the Finance Committee and pushed through a bill to require trucks traveling in Virginia to cover their loads so debris wouldn't be blown across highways.

After her election to Congress, Byrne was named to the Post Office and Civil Service Committee and the Public Works and Transportation Committee. She also won appointment as "at-large" whip, the first rung on the House leadership ladder. She generally supported Democratic initiatives to expand social programs such as child immunization and Head Start. She faced opposition from her leadership however, when she pushed for an amendment to a health care bill that would have forced Congress to subject itself to any health plan it passed for the rest of the country. With few exceptions, she sided with environmentalists and labor unions, voting against the North American Free Trade Agreement and for bills to add land to the national park system. She strongly supported abortion rights as well as waiting periods for handgun purchases.

After her defeat for a second term in the House, Byrne launched a Senate bid in 1996, but dropped out after it became clear she could not win the Democratic primary. She later worked for the Clinton administration as the head of the U.S. Office of Consumer Affairs and in 1998 was named a special assistant to the U.S. Information Agency.

BEVERLY BYRON (D-Md.)
(July 27, 1932–   )
House: Jan. 3, 1979, to Jan. 3, 1993

Family history repeated itself when Beverly Byron succeeded her husband, four-term Rep. Goodloe Byron, who died of a heart attack while jogging in 1978. Nearly 40 years earlier, Goodloe Byron's father, U.S. Rep. William Byron, had been killed in a plane crash and his widow, Katharine Byron, was elected to fill out his term.

When the younger Byron died in 1978—just one month before the general election—local Democratic leaders immediately looked to Beverly as his replacement. She had worked closely with her late husband during his bids for the Maryland state legislature and later assisted with his House campaigns. She first met her husband while she was a high school teacher and decided to work with him in his political endeavors because, she said, "It meant I either stayed at home by myself or joined him."[27]

She had no problem easily winning his House seat and was given his place on the Armed Services Committee. Like her husband, Byron was a pro-defense conservative. In 1988, she supported GOP President Reagan on almost half of the House votes on which he took a position, and had the fourth-highest pro-Reagan percentage of House Democrats. She supported most of the Defense Department's priority projects, including the MX missile, and fought to weaken proposed nuclear test bans. Byron eventually rose to chair the Armed Services subcommittee on military personnel and compensation—the first woman to chair an Armed Services subcommittee. She also served as chair of the House Special Panel on Arms Control and Disarmament from 1983 to 1986 and sat on the Select Aging Committee.

Although Byron spent most of her career focusing on defense and military issues, she was also a physical fitness buff who worked to improve the country's recreational areas. She used her seat on the Interior and Insular Affairs Committee to lobby for more money to improve hiking trails in Maryland and to make a federal inventory of hiking trails across the nation. In 1988, she wrote a bill encouraging the Interior Department to convert abandoned railroad tracks into recreational trails. She also fought to require physical fitness programs on a daily basis for all school children.

In 1992, Byron lost her bid for the Democratic nomination against Thomas Hattery, who attacked her for supporting a congressional pay raise. Hattery went on to lose the general election to Republican Roscoe Bartlett. In 1994, Byron was elected to the board of directors of McDonnell Douglas Corp. In 1995, she was appointed by President Clinton to the Naval Academy Board of Visitors.

KATHARINE BYRON (D-Md.)
(Oct. 25, 1903– Dec. 28, 1976)
House: June 11, 1941, to Jan. 3, 1943

Katharine Byron served less than one term in the House, but her brief time in office coincided with some of the most tumultuous years in American history—just before and after America's entry into World War II. Byron came to the House after winning a special election to fill out the unexpired term of her late husband Rep. William Byron, who died in a plane crash. During her campaign for office, she faced an anti-war

Republican who warned voters that Byron would simply be one more vote for the Roosevelt administration "whose present inclination is to spill the blood of our boys in the squabbles of Europe."[28] Byron, in contrast, voiced support for countries fighting against the Nazis and called for increased American military preparedness. She was joined on the campaign trail by such Democratic bigwigs as First Lady Eleanor Roosevelt and Rep. Estes Kefauver (D-Tenn.). In the end she narrowly won the seat by 1,115 votes.

She was assigned to the Committee on the Civil Service and the Committee on War Claims. She supported amending the Neutrality Act to permit the arming of U.S. merchant vessels and urged her colleagues to speed up the delivery of war supplies to Great Britain and the Soviet Union. On Dec. 8, 1941, the day following Japan's attack on Pearl Harbor, House Speaker Sam Rayburn designated Byron as one of five lawmakers to declare on the floor their support for U.S. entry into the war.

Byron's support for the war indirectly led her to cut short her political career. She had actually filed for re-election in 1942 and delivered her first speech on the campaign trail for a second term. But the call had gone out for women to pitch in on behalf of the war effort, and when the governess of Byron's five sons wanted to volunteer as a military nurse, Byron did not feel she could stand in her way. Byron withdrew her name as a candidate so she could take care of her children. After leaving office, Byron spent much of her time as a Red Cross volunteer. She returned to the campaign trail 30 years later, this time to help her third eldest son, Goodloe Byron, win election to the House. Goodloe Byron served until 1978 when he, like his father, died in office and was succeeded by his widow, Beverly Byron.

MARIA CANTWELL (D-Wash.)
(Oct. 13, 1958–)
House: Jan. 5, 1993, to Jan. 3, 1995

Maria Cantwell came to the House during the historic 1992 "Year of the Woman" that brought a record number of female legislators to Congress. She was the first Democrat to win her Washington state seat in 40 years. A self-described "pro-business Democrat," Cantwell campaigned against traditional politicians who "had lost touch with reality." She said: "We didn't campaign to 'throw the bums out.' We campaigned on the idea of getting things done."[29]

Cantwell first arrived in Washington state from Indiana in 1983 to work for Sen. Alan Cranston's (D-Calif.) presidential campaign. After the campaign fizzled, Cantwell stayed in Washington and started a public relations business. In 1986, when she was just 28, Cantwell was elected to the state legislature where she chaired the Committee on Trade and Economic Development.

During her campaign for the U.S. House, Cantwell won the backing of women's groups, business leaders, environmentalists, and labor organizations. She supported the line-item veto as well as large defense cuts and said she was philosophically closer to presidential candidates Paul Tsongas and Ross Perot than Bill Clinton. After coming to the House, Cantwell won the support of Speaker Tom Foley (D-Wash.), who helped her win a prestigious seat on the Public Works Committee. She also served on the Merchant Marine and Fisheries Committee and the Committee on Foreign Affairs. Cantwell was one of only three freshmen to be named to the Democratic Steering and Policy Committee, which made committee assignments.

During her one term in office, Cantwell led a freshman class task force that pushed for internal reforms in the House, including term limits for committee chairmen. Cantwell also helped break the longtime taboo against female legislators playing in the annual congressional baseball game. She donned a Seattle Mariners jersey in the 1993 game and, after being walked, became the first woman to reach base in a congressional game.

On legislative issues, Cantwell worked on behalf of the computer software industry located in her district and challenged President Clinton's export restrictions on cryptographic software. When Vice President Al Gore agreed to review the export controls, a spokesman for the Microsoft corporation exulted: "Maria Cantwell has gone head-to-head with the powers-that-be and they blinked."[30]

Cantwell continually pushed for smaller government spending during her time in office. She voted against the superconductor-supercollider and the space station. Her reform task force also lobbied the White House to increase the budget cuts in its economic stimulus package. But all of Cantwell's fiscal conservatism was politically erased when she voted in favor of Clinton's budget plan, which was attacked by Republicans as a huge tax-increase package. The vote was used against her during her re-election bid in 1994, which she narrowly lost to the Republican challenger 48 to 52 percent. After leaving Congress, Cantwell returned to Washington state to work for a computer software company where she now serves as senior vice president.

LOIS CAPPS (D-Calif.)
(Jan. 10, 1938–)
House: March 17, 1998, to present

Lois Capps was elected to Congress to fill the seat of her husband, Rep. Walter Capps (D), who died of a heart attack just 10 months into his first term. The special election to fill the seat was an ugly one between Capps and her Republican challenger. Special interest groups supporting term limits, opposing abortion, and pushing for tax cuts spent millions of dollars in outside advertising—pouring more money into the election than the two candidates combined. During the campaign, Capps focused on education, health, and the environment, and went on to win the race by an eight-point margin.

A former school nurse, Capps had never before held public office, but she had gained plenty of campaign experience during her husband's political career. She campaigned by his side during his first unsuccessful run for the House in 1994 against Republican Andrea Seastrand and again in 1996 when he ousted Seastrand from office. The latter campaign forced Capps to act as the surrogate candidate while her husband spent months recuperating from a car accident.

In the House, Capps serves on the Science Committee and the International Relations Committee. She says she will focus on educational issues, advocating smaller class sizes and greater access to the Internet. She also wants to require health maintenance organizations (HMOs) to allow their doctors to inform patients about all available treatments. She supports abortion rights, but says she will support a ban on a certain technique—called partial birth abortion by its opponents—as long as it includes an exemption to protect the woman's health.

Capps ran for a full two-year House term in November and won against the same Republican she beat in the special election.

HATTIE CARAWAY (D-Ark.)
(Feb. 1, 1878–Dec. 21, 1950)
Senate: Nov. 13, 1931, to Jan. 2, 1945

Hattie Caraway—the first woman elected to the Senate, the first woman to chair a Senate committee, and the first woman to preside over the Senate—made history again in 1996, 46 years after her death, when she became the first woman senator to have her portrait hung in the Upper Chamber. The unveiling of the painting doubled the number of women's portraits in the Senate's collection: a painting of Pocahontas is the only other one.

Caraway came to the Senate in 1931, when Gov. Harvey Parnell appointed her to the seat left vacant by the death of her husband, Sen. Thaddeus Caraway. A few months later, Caraway, with Parnell's backing, also won a special election to fill out the remaining year of her late husband's term. Most of Arkansas's male politicians—including Parnell—assumed Caraway would not run for the next six-year term, but would simply keep the seat warm for a male successor. They were wrong.

On May 10, 1932—the last day before the filing deadline for the Democratic primary—Caraway sent in her filing fee and forms for re-election. The local headlines declared, "Bombshell Explodes in Arkansas Politics." Caraway wrote in her journal that she filed for re-election "because I really want to try out my own theory of a woman running for office."[31] The six prominent men who had already lined up for the seat—including ex-Gov. Charles Brough and former Sen. William Kirby—did not consider Caraway a serious threat. She had no campaign funds, no campaign manager, and not a single political leader endorsed her. Local politicos predicted she would receive no more than 3,000 out of the estimated 30,000 votes to be cast.

But Caraway's chances of winning quickly turned around when the outspoken Sen. Huey Long (D-La.)—who had his eye on the White House—agreed to come to Arkansas and campaign for her. One week before primary day Long and his "Louisiana Medicine Show" rolled into the state. His entourage included a long black limousine, two trucks equipped with loudspeakers and rooftop platforms for speeches, four vans covered with campaign posters, and a slew of campaign workers on "temporary leave" from the Louisiana Highway Department.[32] Long told voters, "We're out here to pull a lot of pot-bellied politicians off a little woman's neck."[33] Caraway spoke less often but appealed to the poverty-stricken farmers of her state. In just one week, the unlikely duo covered 2,103 miles and made 39 speeches to 200,000 voters. In the end, Caraway garnered 128,000 votes—almost the same amount earned by all six of her primary challengers combined. She went on to easily win the general election a few months later.

In office, Caraway was a dedicated worker. She got to the Senate at eight each morning to read every bill and every line of the *Congressional Record*. In 1933, she was named chairman of the Enrolled Bills Committee, on which Harry Truman was a member. She also served on the Agriculture and Forestry Committee, where she became an advocate of farm and labor groups. Throughout her years in the Senate, she concentrated on constituent services and fought to bring federal funds back to her state. She won the construction of a $15-million aluminum plant back home—paid for with federal grants—and secured the first federal education loan for a college in her state. She was a strong supporter of President Roosevelt's New Deal legislation, but considered her greatest achievement the passage of a bill that kept Arkansas from losing a seat in the U.S. House of Representatives. She was never able, however, to pass her bill that would have required all airline passengers to wear parachutes.

She became the first congresswoman to co-sponsor the proposed Equal Rights Amendment, but was opposed to granting the same rights to blacks. Like most of her southern colleagues, she voted against the anti-lynching law of 1938 and opposed legislation that would have ended the poll tax. Caraway also showed her independence when she turned down a request by her former champion Huey Long to vote with him against the United States's entry into the World Court. She said she had "no great hopes for the Court," but felt that "at least it was a move in the direction of world peace."[34]

Throughout her career in the Senate, Caraway spoke on the floor just 15 times and won the nickname Silent Hattie. She once explained, "I haven't the heart to take a minute away from the men. The poor dears love it so."[35] Caraway also made note in her journal of the marginal role women were given in the Senate. "I have the same desk as the one used by Mrs. Felton [the first woman to serve in the Senate]. I guess they wanted as few of them contaminated as possible."[36]

In 1938, without the help of Long who was assasinated three years earlier, Caraway won a second full term in office against Rep. John McClellan, who had run on the slogan, "Arkansas needs another man in the Senate." But six years later, Caraway lost her bid for a third term when former University of Arkansas President William Fulbright defeated her in the Democratic primary. After her loss, President Roosevelt named Caraway to the Employees' Compensation Commission, on which she served from 1946 until her death in 1950.

BOOK BY CARAWAY

Silent Hattie Speaks: The Personal Journal of Senator Hattie Caraway (1979)

JULIA CARSON (D-Ind.)
(July 8, 1938–)
House: Jan. 7, 1997, to present

Julia Carson's rise to political power is a true rags-to-riches story. Born into poverty to a teenage mother who worked as a housekeeper, Carson worked her way up through such jobs as waitressing, delivering newspapers, and working as a farm hand. Carson's political life began to take shape in 1965 when she was hired away from her job as a secretary for the local United Auto Workers union by Rep. Andy Jacobs (D-Ind.). She worked for Jacobs as his secretary and later as his office manager for eight years. In 1972, Carson decided to make her own bid for public office and ran successfully for the Indiana House of Representatives. After two terms in the House she was elected to the Indiana Senate in 1976. In 1990, Carson was elected to serve as head of the Marion County Center Township, which administers relief to the poor. When Jacobs announced his retirement from office, Carson ran for and won her boss's old House seat and became the first African American to represent the Indianapolis area in Congress.

In the House Carson serves on the Banking and Financial Services Committee and the Veterans' Affairs Committee. She is much more liberal than her former boss and predecessor. Carson is an unapologetic advocate of government intervention to help people and improve the standard of living. She favors universal access to health care and contends that spending money on education is cheaper and more productive than building prisons.

During her first term in office, Carson co-sponsored bills to curb smoking among minorities and keep guns out of the hands of children. The latter bill called for manufacturers to make child-resistant guns and for criminal penalties to be imposed against adults who fail to keep loaded guns out of the reach of children. Carson also fought against a bankruptcy bill that gave credit card debt the same legal weight as child support payments. The bill allowed creditors to collect money that might otherwise go toward child payments.

HELEN CHENOWETH (R-Idaho)
(Jan. 27, 1938–   )
House: Jan. 4, 1995, to present

Helen Chenoweth, who prefers to be called a "congressman" rather than a "congresswoman," is among the most conservative members ever to serve in the House. She has been criticized by her opponents as "extremist," "right wing," and "crazy," but she has continued to win the support of her western constituents.

Chenoweth first ran for office vowing to fight the "War on the West"—the name many Westerners used for President Clinton's proposals to raise fees and impose new restrictions on mining, grazing, and logging on federal lands. Before coming to Congress, Chenoweth served as the executive director of the Idaho Republican party from 1975 to 1977 and was co-founder of the conservative religious group Focus on the Family. She also worked as a staffer with former Sen. Steve Symms (R-Idaho).

In the House, Chenoweth sits on the Agriculture Committee, the Veterans' Affairs Committee, and the Resources Committee where she chairs the subcommittee on Forests and Forest Health.

Chenoweth is an outspoken supporter of private property rights and has fought hard against new environmental regulations. One of her top targets is the Endangered Species Act that she charges denies private property owners the right to use their own land. She made headlines when she held "endangered salmon bakes" to make fun of protection of Idaho's endangered fish, and she once said the only truly endangered species is "the white Anglo-Saxon male."[37]

Chenoweth again triggered an uproar when she said the U.S. Forest Service should stop trying to recruit blacks and Hispanics to work in her state.

"The warm climate community just hasn't found the colder climate that attractive. It's an area of America that has simply never attracted the Afro-American or the Hispanic," she said.[38]

A strong opponent of abortion rights and affirmative action, Chenoweth supported a state ballot initiative that would have restricted civil rights protections for homosexuals. She also pushed in 1995 for an end to federal financing of abortions in cases of rape and incest.

But Chenoweth may be best known for her outspoken support for gun owners' rights and the reining in of federal law enforcement. With the backing of citizen militia groups, Chenoweth has called for the dismantling of the Bureau of Alcohol, Tobacco, and Firearms. One of her first acts in Congress was to introduce legislation that would require federal officials to receive written permission from local or state officials before carrying out law enforcement or bringing a weapon into their areas of jurisdiction.

Following the tragic bombing of the federal building in Oklahoma City in 1995, Chenoweth told local papers: "I'm not willing to condemn militias. While we can never condone this, we still must begin to look at the public policies that may be pushing people too far."[39]

But for all her conservative stances, she is not always a reliable Republican vote. She, in fact, has charged her GOP leadership with being too moderate. In 1996, she was one of just 15 House Republicans to oppose a GOP plan to reopen the government after an extended shutdown caused by an impasse between Congress and the White House over the budget. She again bumped heads with her leadership in 1996 when she refused to support a budget resolution.

SHIRLEY CHISHOLM (D-N.Y.)
(Nov. 30, 1924–   )
House: Jan. 3, 1969, to Jan. 3, 1983

The 1968 elections brought just one woman to Capitol Hill, and she happened to be the first black woman ever elected to Congress. Shirley Chisholm was one of the most liberal, outspoken, and independent women ever to grace the halls of Congress. Never weighing more than 100 pounds, Chisholm often found herself fighting against the leaders of her own Democratic party as well as her black male colleagues.

"When I decided to run for Congress, I knew I would encounter both antiblack and antifeminist sentiments. What surprised me was the much greater virulence of the sex discrimination.... I was constantly bombarded by both men and women exclaiming that I should return to teaching, a woman's vocation, and leave politics to men," she once said.[40]

Chisholm was the daughter of immigrants from the Caribbean and spent much of her formative years living with her grandmother in Barbados. She graduated cum laude from Brooklyn College in 1946 and went on to earn a master's degree in elementary education from Columbia University. Chisholm later served as director of two child-care centers in New York and from 1959 to 1964 was an educational consultant in the day-care division of New York City's Bureau of Child Welfare.

During this time Chisholm became involved with the local Democratic party. In 1964, she ran for the New York State Assembly and became the second black woman to win a seat there. Chisholm quickly established herself as a maverick. She pushed for state legislation to provide public funding of day-care centers and unemployment insurance for domestic workers. She also passed a bill creating the SEEK program (Search for Elevation, Education and Knowledge), which allowed undereducated black and Puerto Rican students to enter state universities and receive remedial training.

Chisholm decided to run for the U.S. Congress in 1968 when a black welfare mother came to her house and offered a campaign donation of $9.62 in change collected from a bingo game. The woman said if Chisholm ran for Congress, she would raise funds for the campaign every Friday night. Using the slogan "Unbought and Unbossed," Chisholm narrowly won the primary election against the preferred candidate of the local Democratic party. She then went on to face a general election race against James Farmer, the nationally known civil rights leader and founder of CORE (Congress of Racial Equality).

Farmer focused on the gender issue in the race, calling Chisholm a "mere" black woman.[41] Farmer warned that women had controlled the black community for too long and that a "stong male image" was needed in Washington to break this matriarchal dominance. Chisholm suffered a major setback in the race when she was forced to undergo major surgery and was bedridden for weeks. But Chisholm went on to win the race by a more than two-to-one margin. Her victory is credited in large part to the mobilization of women as well as the fact that Chisholm—who earned a minor in Spanish in college—was able to directly communicate with many of the Puerto Rican voters in her district.

Once in office, Chisholm ran head-on into the male-dominated culture of Capitol Hill. She asked party leaders to assign her to the Committee on Education and Labor—because of her extensive background in educational policy—or to the Foreign Affairs Committee, because of her interest in African nations. Instead, she was placed on the Agriculture Committee and its subcommittee on forestry and rural villages—an assignment that had no relevence to her Brooklyn ghetto district. Chisholm was outraged and refused to accept the assignment. "Apparently all they know here in Washington about Brooklyn is that a tree grew there," she said. "Only nine black people have been elected to Congress, and those nine should be used as effectively as possible."[42]

Chisholm went straight to House Speaker John McCormack to complain, but he responded that she should be a "good soldier" and accept the assignment quietly. She again refused and McCormack agreed to talk to Ways and Means Committee chairman Wilbur Mills who controlled committee assignments. When no action was taken, Chisholm took her complaint directly to the House floor. She insisted she be given a chance to speak and made a plea to her colleagues that she be reassigned. She was eventually placed on the Veterans' Affairs Committee—not the perfect assignment but one that prompted her to say "There are a lot more veterans in my district than trees."[43] Later in her congressional career, Chisholm served on the powerful Rules Committee.

In her maiden speech on the House floor, Chisholm attacked the Nixon administration and said taxpayer dollars should go to fight poverty and racism within the country and not wars overseas. She vowed to vote against any defense appropriation "until the time comes when our values and priorities have been turned right-side up again."[44] Chisholm later introduced legislation to end the draft and create an all-volunteer military, and she called for an end to British arms sales to South Africa. She also held a series of hearings with Rep. Ron Dellums (D-Calif.) to investigate racism in the Army.

Chisholm backed an increase in the minimum wage, called for increased spending for Medicare and Medicaid, and supported the Office of Economic Opportunity—which funded anti-poverty programs in urban areas. She supported abortion rights and served as honorary president of the National Association for the Repeal of Abortion Laws (NARAL). A dedicated feminist, she helped form the National Women's Political Caucus.

Chisholm, however, had limited legislative success. She authored a bill with Rep. Bella Abzug (D-N.Y.) to establish federally funded day-care facilites in most major cities, but Nixon eventually vetoed that bill.

In 1971, Chisholm—at the age of 47—announced her candidacy for President of the United States. Surprisingly, Chisholm did not have the initial support of many women's groups or her black colleagues in Congress. They felt Chisholm had no chance of winning and attacked her candidacy as nothing more than self-promotional. Although most women's groups eventually backed her candidacy, black male lawmakers continued to oppose it, attacking Chisholm as a young upstart who refused to seek their permission before launching her bid. "Black male politicians were no different from white male politicians," Chisholm said. "This 'woman thing' is so deep. I've found it out in this campaign if I never knew it before."[45]

Running on an educational and anti-Vietnam War platform, Chisholm carried her presidential campaign across the country and was on the ballot in 12 state primaries. At the 1972 Democratic convention, she received 152 delegate votes.

In 1982, Chisholm announced she would not seek re-election to the House. She went on to co-found the National Political Congress of Black Women and campaigned for Jesse Jackson's presidential bids in 1984 and 1988. She taught briefly at Wellesley College and in 1994 was nominated by President Clinton for ambassador to Jamaica. She was forced to decline the nomination because of poor health. She now lives in Palm Coast, Fla., and is still active with writing, ballroom dancing, and giving speeches.

BOOKS BY CHISHOLM

Unbought and Unbossed (1970)
The Good Fight (1973)

DONNA CHRISTIAN-GREEN
(D-Virgin Islands)
(Sept. 19, 1945–   )
House: Jan. 7, 1997, to present

Donna Christian-Green is the first woman physician to serve in Congress. A former family practitioner, Christian-Green sat on numerous medical boards in the Virgin Islands before entering politics and served as the territory's acting Commissioner of Health from 1993 to 1994.

Christian-Green first entered politics in 1980 when she became a member of the Virgin Islands Democratic Territorial Committee, acting as its chair from 1980 to 1982. She also served on the Virgin Islands Board of Education from 1984 to 1986.

In Congress, Christian-Green sits on the Small Business Committee and the House Resources Committee. She is also an active member of the Women's Congressional Caucus and the Congressional Black Caucus, where she was named chair of the group's task force on health issues.

Although Christian-Green, as a territorial delegate, does not have voting privileges on the House floor, she has worked with her fellow lawmakers to introduce legislation that benefits her Caribbean constituents. She has fought to increase federal child-care funding for the Virgin Islands and pushed through legislation that allows the Virgin Islands— not the federal government—to determine the size of its territorial legislature.

MARGUERITE CHURCH (R-Ill.)
(Sept. 13, 1892–May 26, 1990)
House: Jan. 3, 1951, to Jan. 3, 1963

Marguerite Church was first elected to Congress to replace her husband Rep. Ralph Church, who had died in office. She, however, went on to win re-election five times in her own right. Church had gained much of her early political experience while working as a close adviser to her husband during his 14 years in the House, often accompanying him on investigative trips or traveling alone at his request to observe conditions in Europe. Church was active in Republican politics, embarking on her own speaking tours for the Republican National Committee during the 1940 and 1944 presidential campaigns. She also served as president of the Congressional Club, a group composed of the wives and daughters of members of Congress, the Cabinet, and the Supreme Court.

When Ralph Church died in the midst of a House committee hearing, local GOP leaders convinced Marguerite to vie for the open seat. She defeated her Democratic opponent with a more than three-to-one margin, the highest number of votes recorded for a House candidate in that district. In her freshman term, she was assigned to the House Committee on Expenditures in the Executive Departments, the same panel before which her husband had died. She was later named to the Government Operations Committee and the Committee on Foreign Affairs.

As a member of Foreign Affairs, Church traveled extensively, visiting nearly half of the world's nations. In 1958, she was one of two House members selected to serve as delegates to the inauguration of Mexico's president, and in 1959 she traveled over 40,000 miles to 17 countries in the Middle East, Asia, Europe, and Africa. After seeing swastikas scrawled on synagogues in Europe, she called on Congress to make religious desecration in the United States a federal offense. In 1962, President Kennedy named her a delegate to the 16th General Assembly of the United Nations.

Church focused much of her legislative efforts on calling for better oversight of foreign aid. She chastised Congress for not taking more control over the foreign aid program and complained that overseas financial help had become an indiscriminate tool of U.S. foreign policy.

As a member of the Government Operations Committee, Church

fought for effective government and lower taxes. She introduced a bill to enact recommendations by the Second Hoover Commission to reorganize the government and make it more efficient. She was also instrumental in passing a bill to place the federal budget on an annual appropriations schedule.

Church worked hard for the education and protection of children. She introduced bills to increase pension benefits for women and exempt students' tuitions from taxes. She also won passage of her bill banning the transportation of fireworks into states where they were illegal.

In her twelfth year in office, Church turned 70 and decided it was time for her to retire. Church believed that people who refused to retire from office would "reach the stage when it is difficult, if not impossible, for them to face life any place else."[46] Indeed, Church remained active after leaving the House. She served on the national board of directors for the Girl Scouts of America and on the board of the U.S. Capitol Historical Society. She later worked for the presidential campaigns of Barry Goldwater in 1964 and Richard Nixon in 1968.

MARIAN CLARKE (R-N.Y.)
(July 29, 1880–April 8, 1953)
House: Dec. 28, 1933, to Jan. 3, 1935

Marian Clarke came to Congress after winning a special election to fill the seat of her husband, six-term Rep. John Clarke, who had been killed in a car accident. Clarke was the only female Republican elected to Congress during the first seven years of the New Deal and was unable to make much of a legislative impact in the overwhelmingly Democratic House. During her one year in office she introduced a bill to restore cuts in the equipment allowance for rural mail carriers and fought for an amendment to the Tariff Act of 1930 to protect shoe manufacturers in her district from cheap labor and unfair competition abroad. She was assigned to the Committee on Civil Service, the Committee on Claims, and the Committee on Invalid Pensions.

Clarke first met her husband on the campus of Colorado College, where he was doing postgraduate work while she earned her bachelor's degree. Before coming to Congress, she worked on a newspaper in Colorado Springs and later assisted her husband in his congressional office.

After serving out the one year remaining in her late husband's term,

Clarke declined to run for re-election in 1934. She remained active in GOP politics and in 1936 served as an alternate delegate to the Republican National Convention in Cleveland. In 1939, Clarke's only son died like his father in an automobile crash. Clarke returned to the family farm near Delhi, N.Y., where she lived in relative seclusion until her death in 1953.

EVA CLAYTON (D-N.C.)
(Sept. 16, 1934–   )
House: Nov. 4, 1993, to present

Eva Clayton made history in 1992 when she became the first black woman elected to Congress from North Carolina. The 58-year-old mother of four was quickly named president of her Democratic freshman class, the first woman to hold that office. As class president, she was responsible for organizing and leading the 63 new House Democrats, the largest freshman class in two decades. During the consideration of President Clinton's controversial budget package in 1993, Clayton served as a liaison between her class and the White House, organizing meetings between the administration and her fellow freshmen.

During her years in Congress, Clayton generally supported the party agenda, although she opposed Clinton on the North American Free Trade Agreement, arguing that it would hurt the small farmers in her agricultural district. She has consistently fought for government assistance for small peanut and tobacco farmers, often going head-to-head with liberal and urban members of her own party who want to cut back on agriculture subsidies. She has also been an outspoken opponent of Republican efforts to scale back welfare benefits and other federal programs for the poor.

Clayton has steadily risen through the Democratic ranks. In 1995, following the Republican takeover of Congress, Democratic Leader Richard Gephardt picked Clayton to sit on the Policy Committee to help formulate strategies to counter the new GOP agenda. In 1997, the Democratic leadership tapped Clayton for the powerful Budget Committee. She accepted the assignment and gave up her seat on the Small Business Committee. She also serves on the Agriculture Committee.

Clayton came to Congress by winning the special election to fill out the remainder of the term of Rep. Walter B. Jones (D), who died in office.

At the same time, Clayton also won election to the following full two-year term. Clayton used the support of organized labor, women's groups, and minority leaders to defeat Jones's son for the Democratic nomination going into the election.

Before coming to Congress, Clayton served as chair of the Warren County Commission from 1982 to 1990. On the commission she oversaw economic development, delivery of health care, and maintenance of infrastructure projects for the county. Clayton first became involved in politics shortly after earning her master's degree in biology from North Carolina Central University in 1965. She worked with voter registration and education projects in North Carolina and in 1968 decided to make a bid for Congress. She lost, but earned an impressive 30 percent of the vote for a political neophyte. She continued to work as a community leader and from 1974 to 1976 served as executive director of the Soul City Foundation, a black civil rights group. In 1977, she was appointed by Gov. James Hunt to serve as assistant secretary for natural resources. Along with her political work, Clayton also ran her own economic development consulting company from 1981 until her 1992 election to Congress.

BARBARA-ROSE COLLINS (D-Mich.)
(April 13, 1939–)
House: Jan. 3, 1991, to Jan. 3, 1997

Barbara-Rose Collins came to Congress with a far-reaching agenda to renew America's inner cities and "save the black male."[47] But Collins's ambitious work in Congress was cut short by charges of ethical and financial misconduct.

Collins had worked for two decades in the Detroit political system before running for Congress. A former purchasing agent for Wayne State University, Collins was urged to enter the political arena in the early 1970s by her pastor. She ran for and won a seat on the Detroit School Board in 1971 and for the next two years worked to improve the local school system. In 1973, she set her sights on the Detroit City Council, but lost. She later won a seat in the Michigan House where she was the founder and chair of the Michigan Legislative Black Caucus. During her time in the state House she successfully pushed through a fair housing bill, sexual harassment legislation, and a bill to equalize treatment of women and men who received pension benefits. Collins served for seven years in the state legislature before she tried again for a seat on the Detroit City Council and this time she won. She served on the Council from 1982 to 1990. In 1988, she launched a primary challenge against U.S. Rep. George Crockett (D-Mich.), but narrowly lost by just eight points. Two years later, Crockett retired and Collins overwhelmingly won the Democratic nomination and the general election.

Once in Congress, Collins was assigned to the Public Works and Transportation Committee, the Government Operations Committee, and the Post Office and Civil Service Committee, where she chaired the postal operations subcommittee. As head of that panel, she took U.S. Postmaster General Marvin Runyon to task for a series of violent incidents in post offices across the country, including Michigan. She charged Runyon with having a "benign and cavalier" attitude toward the violence.[48]

From her seat on the Public Works Committee, Collins worked to bring jobs and money to Detroit. She won funding for the city when it was designated a federal empowerment zone and brought money back to the district for infrastructure projects. On national issues, Collins generally voted with her Democratic leadership, but she opposed President Clinton on NAFTA and GATT, voting against both trade agreements. She also initially opposed Clinton's crime bill because it expanded the use of the death penalty, but she later voted for a modified version of the bill. She was pro-abortion rights and introduced a bill that would have calculated the worth of housework—primarily performed by women—into the gross national product. The bill received widespread press attention but never went anywhere.

Collins's ethical and financial problems arose shortly after she came to office. In her first term, Collins confessed to campaign finance irregularities and paid a fine. More charges arose throughout Collins's next few terms in office, and the Justice Department and House Ethics Committee launched investigations into her campaign practices and use of official staff. Collins was known to have an extraordinarily high rate of staff turnover. In her third term, a gay aide claimed he was fired after Collins found out that his roommate had died from AIDS. Collins was found guilty of unfair employment practices and reached a $50,000 settlement. The scandals prompted six Democrats to challenge Collins in the 1996 primary. She managed to win just 31 percent of the vote, losing the nomination to Carolyn Cheeks Kilpatrick. Following her primary defeat, the House ethics committee found Collins guilty of 11 violations of laws and House rules, ranging from forcing employees to do personal chores for her to taking campaign contributions for personal use.

CARDISS COLLINS (D-Ill.)
(Sept. 24, 1931–   )
House: June 7, 1973, to Jan. 7, 1997

Although Cardiss Collins served almost 25 years in the House—the longest serving African-American woman in the history of Congress—her quiet, low-key style made her one of the lesser known women in the House. She preferred to work diligently behind the scenes rather than in the spotlight. Collins had never thought about running for political office until her husband, two-term Rep. George Collins, died in a plane crash in 1972. Collins agreed to run for the vacant seat only after Chicago Mayor and Democratic powerhouse Richard Daley, Sr., convinced her it was for the good of the party.

Collins had never planned a career in politics. Her very first job was as a seamstress in a mattress factory, but she later studied accounting during night school at Northwestern University and eventually became an auditor with the Illinois Department of Revenue. Her only political experience was the help she lent her husband during his campaigns for city alderman, committeeman, and congressman. Despite her lack of political experience, she easily won the special election for her husband's seat with 82 percent of the vote.

Two days after her election, Collins began to work on a bill to eliminate credit discrimination against women and she continued to fight for women's rights throughout her lengthy career in Congress. "One thing that I'm very proud of having done was to have introduced the first mammogram bill ever in the House of Representatives, and when that finally became a reality and became payable under Medicare, it was a very proud moment for me," Collins said.[49]

In 1993 and 1994, Collins led an investigation into college sports and proposed legislation to force schools to report how their funds were divided between men and women's teams. She helped gain passage of language aimed at creating gender equity among college sports, and for her work she was inducted into the Women's Sports Hall of Fame in 1994.

Collins served on the powerful Energy and Commerce Committee and eventually rose to chair its subcommittee on commerce, consumer protection, and competitiveness. She was the first woman and the first black to chair a subcommittee on the prestigious committee. She also sat on the Government Operations Committee where she eventually served as the second-ranking Democrat.

On the Commerce Committee, Collins worked to expand minority opportunities within the telecommunications field. She introduced numerous bills to preserve preferences for minority and female applicants seeking broadcasting licenses from the Federal Communications Commission. She also wrote legislation to create the Office of Minority Health at the National Institutes of Health.

On Government Operations, Collins chaired the government activities and transportation subcommittee where she held oversight hearings on the Federal Aviation Administration and criticized it for not doing enough to recruit minority and women air traffic controllers. When the full House debated the airport authorization bill of 1987, Collins offered an amendment requiring at least 10 percent of airport concession revenues go to minority or women-owned businesses. It passed unanimously.

In 1979, Collins became chair of the Congressional Black Caucus and used the post to criticize President Carter for his flagging civil rights record. When the House failed to make Martin Luther King Jr.'s birthday a federal holiday, Collins charged racism and blamed the Carter administration—which had endorsed the idea—for not working hard enough to round up the votes.

During her career, Collins was a leader in the call for sanctions against South Africa. She was also one of the first lawmakers to introduce gun-control legislation, and she was a driving force behind the passage of the Child Safety Protection Act of 1993, which required warning labels on dangerous toys and established federal safety standards for bicycle helmets.

Despite Collins's long list of legislative accomplishments, her quiet personality typically kept her out of the spotlight. "I'm not as vocal as a lot of members of Congress," she once admitted.[50] But in the final years of her congressional career, Collins did gain national attention for two controversial events. In 1993, Collins was involved in a bitter and highly publicized exchange on the House floor with Rep. Henry Hyde (R-Ill.) over his amendment that banned Medicaid funding for abortions.

"We tell poor women, 'You can't have a job, you can't have a good education, you can't have a decent place to live,'" Hyde sarcastically argued on the floor. "[But] we'll give you a free abortion because there are too many of you people, and we want to kind of refine the breed."

At that, Collins leapt to her feet saying she was offended by his comments. Hyde responded by telling Collins to consult with "some of the black clergymen in her district" about their views on abortion, at which point Collins insisted that Hyde's remarks were a violation of House rules and that they should be stricken from the *Congressional Record*.

Hyde eventually apologized to Collins and his words were removed from the record.[51]

Collins again gained national attention in 1994 when she called widely publicized hearings to look into the influence of "gangsta rap" on teen violence. Collins said she did not want to legislate morality, but called on the recording industry to do more than simply put parental warning labels on records.

In 1996, Collins declined to run for election to a 13th term.

SUSAN COLLINS (R-Maine)
(Dec. 7, 1952–   )
Senate: Jan. 7, 1997, to present

Susan Collins came to the Senate by succeeding the man she once worked for. Collins started her political career as an intern in the office of Sen. Bill Cohen (R-Maine) in 1975. She stayed with Cohen's office in Washington for 12 years, rising to become one of his top staffers on the Governmental Affairs Committee's subcommittee on oversight of government management. After leaving Cohen's office in 1987, Collins returned to her home state of Maine, where she joined the cabinet of Gov. John McKernan (R) as commissioner of the Department of Professional and Financial Regulation. She stayed for five years until her appointment in 1992 as the New England regional director of the U.S. Small Business Administration. Collins later directed the Center for Family Business at Husson College in Bangor, Maine.

For all her public service experience, Collins had never held elected office before winning her Senate seat in 1996. In 1994, Collins ran for governor of Maine, but came in last in a three-way race. During her bid for the Senate two years later to fill the seat of Cohen, who was retiring, Collins emphasized her previous work with the departing senator. Her victory made her—along with Maine's other Senator, Olympia Snowe (R)—part of the only Republican female team to represent a state in the Senate.

In office, Collins is generally a moderate on social issues and a conservative on money matters. She supports abortion rights and voted against a ban on a certain type of procedure called partial birth abortion by its opponents. She also opposes the death penalty and favors protections of gay rights. She, however, is a backer of gun owners' rights, supporting a repeal of the five-day waiting period for handgun purchases mandated by the Brady Law. She also wants to repeal the ban on certain assault weapons.

On fiscal matters, Collins supports a balanced budget constitutional amendment and wants to require a two-thirds vote of Congress to raise taxes. She is pro-small business, and has pushed to repeal estate taxes to make it easier for families to pass their businesses on to their children. She has also criticized burdensome government regulations on business.

Collins serves on the Labor and Human Resources Committee, the Special Committee on Aging, and the Governmental Affairs Committee—the same panel on which she once served as a staffer. The Senate Republican leadership also named Collins as a member of its task force on managed care in 1998. The task force was charged with drafting legislation to overhaul the managed health care system. Collins also serves on the Senate GOP task force on education.

In 1998, Collins asked the Navy to pay special tribute to the late Sen. Margaret Chase Smith (R-Maine) by naming a missile destroyer after her. Smith once held the Senate seat Collins now holds.

BARBARA CUBIN (R-Wyo.)
(Nov. 30, 1946–)
House: Jan. 4, 1995, to present

Barbara Cubin, the first woman elected to the U.S. Congress from Wyoming, gained notoriety during her 1994 campaign when it was reported that she had distributed penis-shaped cookies to her colleagues in the Wyoming state legislature. She denied making the cookies, but admitted to distributing them. Despite the controversy, she easily won election, besting a wide field of candidates that included a state House speaker and a former congressional aide.

A chemist by training, Cubin first became involved in politics through community grass-roots organizations. She won a seat in the state House in 1996 and six years later was elected to the Wyoming state Senate.

Once arriving on Capitol Hill, she was elected by her 72 fellow Republican freshmen to serve as class secretary. She was also given a low-level leadership position of deputy whip. A solid conservative, Cubin shortly after her election presented conservative talk show host Rush Limbaugh with a plaque declaring him an honorary class member and promising him, ''There's not a femiNazi among us.''[52]

Cubin was first assigned to the Resources Committee and the Science Committee, but later gave up the Science post for a prestigious spot on the Commerce Committee. On Resources she became chair of the subcommittee on energy and mineral resources in 1997.

Legislatively, Cubin has focused on protecting western landowners from federal land regulations. She supported a measure rewriting federal rules for grazing livestock on public lands and giving ranchers additional influence in managing 260 million acres of federal rangeland. She is also strongly pro-business and is an ardent supporter of Wyoming's mining industry. She has fought increases of federal royalties on mined minerals.

Cubin is a reliable Republican vote in the House, voting against increases in the minimum wage, backing a repeal of a ban on certain assault weapons, supporting a balanced budget constitutional amendment, and voting to deny public education to illegal immigrants. She is an opponent of abortion rights, but joined with several other Republican women in 1995 in asking the GOP leadership to curb the growing number of anti-abortion votes brought to the House floor.

"I am very pro-life," Cubin said. "And I think debate is good, but I don't know how many times you have to debate abortion, or any issue, in one week."[53]

Cubin has called for a "big tent" Republican platform—stating that all points of view are welcome on abortion. She said she fears the abortion issue will split the Republican party.

PAT DANNER (D-Mo.)
(Jan. 13, 1934–   )
House: Jan. 5, 1993, to present

Pat Danner came to Congress by defeating eight-term GOP Rep. Tom Coleman. Well aware of the conservative leanings of her district, Danner has since consistently bucked her party agenda and is perhaps the most conservative woman in the Democratic Caucus. Danner, in fact, is the only Democratic woman not to belong to the Congressional Caucus for Women's Issues. When she dropped out of the caucus in 1994, she insisted that her departure had nothing to do with the group's pro-choice stance on abortion rights. Instead, she said, she simply didn't think membership was worth the $1,800 fee.

But Danner regularly votes against pro-abortion rights bills. She opposed legislation requiring states to fund Medicaid abortions for poor women, permitting abortions at overseas military hospitals, and allowing federal employees' health plans to cover abortions.

Danner also sides with Republicans on gun control issues. As a freshman she opposed a five-day waiting period for handgun purchases. She voted against a ban on certain assault weapons and against the Clinton-backed crime bill that included a gun ban. In 1996, she supported the repeal of the assault weapons ban. She also joined Republicans in backing a constitutional amendment requiring a balanced budget and was one of just 28 Democrats in 1995 to vote for a GOP-backed measure that tried to block President Clinton from deploying U.S. forces to Bosnia unless Congress approved funds for the operation.

But Danner usually sides with Democrats on labor issues. She supported an increase in the minimum wage and backed the Family and Medical Leave Act requiring businesses to give workers unpaid leave for medical emergencies. Danner is also a deficit hawk and has backed cuts in defense spending. She serves on the International Relations Committee and the Committee on Transportation and Infrastructure.

Before coming to Congress, Danner served from 1982 to 1992 in the Missouri state Senate where she worked to overhaul the state's criminal probation system and improve victims' rights. She also worked to create after-school programs across the state and increase funds for programs for the disabled.

Danner's very first governmental experience was as a district assistant in the early 1970s to Rep. Jerry Litton (D-Mo.), who held the same congressional seat Danner would later be elected to. During the administration of President Carter, Danner was appointed to the Ozark Regional Commission, the first woman to chair a regional commission.

DIANA DEGETTE (D-Colo.)
(July 29, 1957–   )
House: Jan. 7, 1997, to present

Diana DeGette was elected to replace feminist icon Rep. Pat Schroeder (D) when she retired after 24 years in the House. DeGette, a former civil rights lawyer and state representative, follows much of the same ideology as Schroeder, vowing to fight for abortion rights, the environment, and the poor.

During her four years in the Colorado state House, DeGette led several high-profile fights as assistant minority leader. She successfully sponsored the "Bubble Bill," which ensured women unobstructed access to abortion clinics. She also helped rewrite the state's domestic violence law and led the floor opposition to a Republican bill banning same-sex marriages.

In the U.S. House, DeGette has continued her work for liberal causes. From her seat on the House Commerce Committee, DeGette pushed to retain funding for "brownfields" legislation, which provides grants and loans to businesses who buy and clean up environmentally contaminated abandoned property.

DeGette has also focused on gun control issues. Following a schoolyard shooting in Arkansas in 1998, DeGette introduced legislation to ban all ammunition clips that hold more than 10 bullets. Her bill would amend the 1994 Crime Bill, which banned the manufacturing of such clips but allowed gun dealers to import and sell clips made before the ban. She also introduced a bill that would force gun shows to comply with the same laws that federally licensed gun-shop owners must follow, such as enforcing age requirements and background checks before selling guns.

During her first term in office, DeGette sponsored bills to allow patients to sue their health management organizations, prohibit insurance companies from denying coverage to abused spouses, and raise the smoking age from 18 to 21.

ROSA DELAURO (D-Conn.)
(March 2, 1943–   )
House: Jan. 3, 1991, to present

Rosa DeLauro has spent most of her life surrounded by politics. Both her parents sat on the New Haven, Conn., Board of Aldermen, and her mother—in her 80s—is today its longest serving member. After receiving her master's degree in international politics from Columbia University and studying at the London School of Economics, DeLauro returned to Connecticut, where she was a community organizer for the War on Poverty program. She went on to manage the successful campaign of New Haven's mayor Frank Logue—the first woman to run a statewide campaign in Connecticut—and later worked as his executive assistant. In 1979, DeLauro managed Sen. Chris Dodd's (D-Conn.) campaign and worked as his administrative assistant for the next seven years. In 1987, DeLauro became the executive director of Countdown '87, the national campaign that successfully stopped U.S. military aid to Nicaraguan Contras. Just before winning election to the House, DeLauro was the executive director of EMILY's List, a political action committee that helps elect women candidates who support abortion rights.

Ironically, DeLauro's extensive political background almost caused her to lose her first bid for the House in 1989. Her opponent attacked DeLauro as a Washington insider. DeLauro's marriage to well-known Democratic pollster Stanley Greenberg was also used against her. But in the end, DeLauro raised more than $1 million for her campaign and managed to win by just four percentage points. "There was never any question that I wanted a political career," she said after winning her first election.[54]

After coming to Congress, DeLauro was appointed to the Public Works and Transportation Committee, the Government Operations Committee, and the Select Committee on Aging. Her outspokenness and liberal stance on issues quickly caught the eye of the Democratic leadership and in 1993 she won a spot on the exclusive Appropriations Committee. But a year later, following the 1994 GOP takeover of Congress and the subsequent cuts in Democratic committee slots, DeLauro lost her Appropriations seat, and was instead placed on the National Security Committee. On that panel she fought unsuccessfully to lift the ban on female military personnel and their dependents from getting abortions on bases overseas—even if they pay for the procedure themselves. In 1997, after several senior Democrats retired from the House, DeLauro was able to return to Appropriations to fill a vacancy. She also served as a deputy whip for the Democratic leadership and in 1998 made an unsuccessful bid for chair of the Democratic Caucus. If she had won, she would have been the highest-ranking woman to serve in the House.

DeLauro is one of the more outspoken members of the House, frequently taking the floor to blast Republican policies. She was one of five Democrats who filed an ethics complaint against Speaker Newt Gingrich (R-Ga.) that eventually led to a formal reprimand against him for misusing tax-exempt groups for political purposes. DeLauro has opposed most of the Republican agenda, including their welfare reform bill, efforts to deny public education to illegal immigrants, attempts to repeal the assault weapons ban, and broad tax cuts. When President Clinton in 1997 hammered out a budget deal with congressional Republicans that included capital gains and estate tax cuts, DeLauro organized a petition signed by 110 Democrats opposing the plan. When the House debated a bill that would have required public housing residents to conduct community service, DeLauro attacked the measure as forced labor.

A survivor of ovarian cancer, DeLauro has fought for increased funding for breast and cervical cancer research. She introduced legislation to guarantee appropriate hospital stays for women undergoing breast cancer surgery and to prevent "drive-through mastectomies." She has also drafted bills to improve education for children under the age of three and organized an anti-tobacco "Kick Butts Connecticut" campaign aimed at preventing teen smoking.

EMILY TAFT DOUGLAS (D-Ill.)
(April 10, 1899–Jan. 28, 1994)
House: Jan. 3, 1945, to Jan. 3. 1947

The original plan of the Douglas family was for husband Paul Douglas to win a seat in Congress with his wife quietly standing by his side. But 10 days after losing a bid for the Senate in 1942, the 50-year-old Mr. Douglas joined the Marine Corps as a private. It never occurred to Emily Taft Douglas that she might go to Congress in his stead, but after she was approached by Chicago Democratic leaders, she reluctantly agreed to run for the House in 1944. In a major upset, she defeated the sitting Republican by 200,000 votes and became the first woman to precede her husband in Congress. (Paul Douglas would eventually win a Senate seat in 1948 after his wife was defeated for re-election to the House.)

Emily Taft Douglas campaigned almost exclusively on a platform in support of President Franklin Roosevelt's foreign policy, and she continued her drive for world peace once she was sworn into office and granted a seat on the House Foreign Affairs Committee. Douglas's interest in international policy was sparked at an early age. Her father was the famous sculptor Lorada Taft, who often traveled to Europe's art centers. As a teen, Douglas was profoundly impressed with Woodrow Wilson and his efforts on behalf of the League of Nations. "My first political enthusiasm came after World War I with Woodrow Wilson and his League of Nations. I really went all out for that concept of no more war and the League of Nations as a civilized way of settling disputes between mankind," Douglas said. "I made a vow to myself as a teenager that if ever I could do anything to help his cause, I would do it. Later when I worked on international affairs in Congress, I hoped that he would have approved."[55]

In 1935, Douglas and her husband took a life-altering vacation through prewar Europe. "Paul and I stood under the palace balcony in Rome on the day Mussolini announced he had sent his troops into Ethiopia. . . . It came crystal clear to us then and there that if Hitler and Mussolini and the forces they represented were not stopped, the whole world would be engulfed."[56] On their return to Chicago, the couple dedicated themselves to spreading word of the danger of Naziism and Fascism. Mr. Douglas won election as alderman to the Chicago City Council and Mrs. Douglas became an organizer for the League of Women Voters. She soon took over as state chair of the League's department of government and foreign policy and worked for a variety of liberal candidates. In 1942, she became executive secretary of the International Relations Center in Chicago. Throughout her life, Douglas emphasized the importance of women in peacemaking. "If they understood and exercised their power they could remake the world," she said on several occasions.[57]

Once in Congress, Douglas offered legislation to empower the United Nations to control armaments and outlaw the atomic bomb. She also came out in favor of drafting nurses into the armed forces. On the Foreign Affairs Committee, she was the only woman on the seven-member subcommittee selected to tour postwar Europe in 1945 to study the progress being made by the United Nations Relief and Rehabilitation Administration. Among Douglas's major concerns during the tour was the growing number of refugees; on her return she proposed a program "to regenerate the youngsters reared under the tyranny of Naziism and Fascism."[58] At the same time, Douglas drafted legislation to bring books and libraries to impoverished areas of the United States. The Hill–Douglas bill called for the creation of bookmobiles and federal grants of $25,000 to $50,000 to states for library demonstration projects. The bill was not enacted during Douglas's one term in office, but her husband reintroduced it after he was elected to the Senate and the Library Services Act was signed by the president in 1956.

During her time in office, Douglas also offered a bill to outlaw oppressive labor practices such as the use of labor spies and strikebreakers, and she voted for a school lunch bill. Douglas's very first vote in the House was against the continuation of the Dies Committee on Un-American Activities.

Douglas lost her bid for a second term in office during the 1946 elections that ousted 54 Democrats from the House. Following her husband's election to the Senate two years later, Douglas served on the legislative committee of the Unitarian Fellowship for Social Justice and as vice president of the American Unitarian Association. She was a representative to UNESCO and other United Nations conferences, and remained active in many civil rights and political causes. In 1964, she took part in the historic march on Selma, Ala. She also set off on a writing career that produced *Remember the Ladies: The Story of Great Women Who Helped Shape America*, *Margaret Sanger: Pioneer of the Future*, and the children's book *Appleseed Farm*.

Before entering politics, Douglas had a brief career as a stage actress. She studied at the American Academy of Dramatic Art in New York and toured in a series of plays. Her greatest acting success came in the lead role in the 1926 Broadway hit *The Cat and the Canary*.

BOOKS BY DOUGLAS

Appleseed Farm (1948)
Margaret Sanger: Pioneer of the Future (1969)
Remember the Ladies: The Story of Great Women Who Helped Shape America (1966)

HELEN GAHAGAN DOUGLAS (D-Calif.)
(Nov. 25, 1900–June 28, 1980)
House: Jan. 3, 1945, to Jan. 3, 1951

Helen Gahagan Douglas's political career may be best known for the race she didn't win—her 1950 bid for the Senate against Rep. Richard Nixon (R-Calif.). The race epitimized the Cold War era and was the first time Nixon gained his reputation as "Tricky Dick." Throughout the campaign, Nixon tried to label Douglas as a Communist. Years earlier, Douglas had opposed funding for the House Un-American Activities Committee on which Nixon served, and he repeatedly reminded voters that Gahagan had said, "Communism is no real threat to the democratic institutions of our country." Douglas had indeed uttered those words during a speech against the scare tactics of Sen. Joseph McCarthy (R-Wis.), but Nixon failed to mention the rest of her speech in which she blasted Communism as having "no place in our society."[59]

Nixon circulated half a million campaign flyers—printed on pink paper to emphasize the "pink lady's" politics—that showed similarities between Douglas's voting record and that of leftist New York Rep. Vito Marcantonio, a member of the American Labor Party. Nixon, of course, never mentioned the numerous times he voted with Marcantonio against aid to Korea, for the reduction of Marshall Plan funds, against the Reciprocal Trade Agreement, and other foreign policy issues.

Nixon's campaign staff even implied that Douglas's support of civil rights proved that she was disloyal. Nixon volunteers mailed thousands of postcards from the fictitious "Communist League of Negro Women" that read, "Vote for our Helen for Senator. We are with her 100 percent."[60] There were also anonymous phone calls made to thousands of voters charging that Douglas was a Communist and reminding them that her husband was Jewish. After Douglas lost the race, her good friend Eleanor Roosevelt—who had campaigned for her—encouraged her to file charges of voter fraud against Nixon. Roosevelt also launched her own attack against Nixon in her newspaper column, on radio, and on television. Douglas had come to know Eleanor Roosevelt years earlier when she was just beginning to work in Democratic politics. In 1940, she made over 150 speeches in California for Franklin Roosevelt and was often a guest at the White House.

Douglas was a world famous stage actress and opera singer before entering the political arena. She married actor Melvyn Douglas in 1931, after the two met on Broadway, and the couple eventually became leading Democrats in the film industry. During their move from New York to California, Douglas grew particularly aware of the nation's social inequities. During the cross-country trip she saw up close the poverty of migrant farm families. "Thousands of them, living in box cars and in caves dug out of the sides of the hills. I saw this. I was shocked, and I really came of age at that time. I watched the New Deal cope with these problems and I became convinced it was the most enlightened administration that we'd had. At the same time I realized that the Republicans had allowed this situation to come to pass," Douglas said.[61] She later joined the Farm Security Administration and was active in the John Steinbeck Committee that assisted migrant workers. In 1939, Roosevelt appointed Douglas to the National Advisory Committee of the Works Progress Administration and she served with the National Youth Administration and the California Housing and Planning Association.

In 1937, Douglas made another trip that changed her life—a European concert tour that exposed her to the horrors of Naziism. All music by non-Aryan composers was censored, and her Jewish accompanist was shunned. On her return to the United States, she joined every anti-Nazi organization she could find. In 1940, Douglas was elected a Democratic committeewoman from California and attended her first Democratic National Convention. Four years later, at the urging of the Roosevelts, Douglas decided to run for the House to fill the seat of retiring Democratic Rep. Thomas Ford. With the campaign help of such Hollywood luminaries as Eddie Cantor and Virginia Bruce—as well as migrant workers and organized labor—Douglas won the election by almost 4,000 votes.

Once in office, Douglas won a rare freshman appointment to the Foreign Affairs Committee. She was a staunch supporter of the United Nations and the Marshall Plan. When the May-Johnson bill, which gave control of atomic energy to the military, was quietly making its way through the Military Affairs Committee without title or number, Douglas brought its dangers to the attention of lawmakers and voters. She then introduced her own legislation placing atomic patents under civilian control. "If we permit the military to determine our policy on atomic energy, we serve notice in unmistakable terms that we believe this new power is a better sword than plow, and that we intend to live by the sword," she said. The Federation of Atomic Scientists called her measure the most important bill ever passed by Congress.[62]

Douglas also made headlines when she brought a basket of food on the House floor to dramatize what the high cost of living meant to the average housewife. She said she had purchased the basket of food for $15, but showed that just one year earlier—before Congress removed price controls—the food would have cost only $10.

As the representative for the largest black neighborhood in the West, Douglas was active in civil rights. She was the first white representative to hire black staff, and she appointed black constituents to West Point and helped desegregate the dining facilities in the Capitol. After Rep. John Rankin (D-Miss.) claimed on the House floor that black soldiers were responsible for massive fatalities in World War II, Douglas studied military records and gave a speech on the achievements and heroism of black troops. The *New Republic* called her "the most courageous fighter for Liberalism in Congress," while the Daughters of the America Revolutions branded her a "nigger lover."[63]

Douglas's loss to Nixon in 1950 effectively ended her political career, although she came out of retirement in 1972 to campaign for Geroge McGovern in his bid against Nixon for the White House. "Nixon will cut anything. He'll cut schools, he'll cut drug progams, he'll play with the nation's health. He doesn't care what he cuts as long as it isn't defense. His whole record shows that he has no compassion for people," she said during the McGovern campaign.[64]

JENNIFER DUNN (R-Wash.)
(July 29, 1941–)
House: Jan. 5, 1993, to present

Jennifer Dunn became the highest-ranking woman in the House in 1997 when she was elected by her fellow Republicans to serve as vice chair of the Republican Conference. GOP leaders hoped her high-profile post will attract more women to the Republican party, and Dunn said she wanted to deliver "the conservative message with a softer edge."

"I have always been a proponent of softening our rhetoric. I believe we can pursue the same positions we have been, but we don't need to be as harsh and scary about it," Dunn said.[65]

In that vein, Dunn has spearheaded efforts to explain how Republican tax-cut proposals benefit women and led numerous political summits for Republican women. During congressional debate on overhauling the welfare system, Dunn joined with other Republican women in moving to provide additional money for child care, and she has sought to direct NASA to devote some of its weightless microgravity research to ovarian and breast cancer research. She also sponsored legislation that was signed into law allowing homemakers to save money in individual re-tirement accounts (IRAs).

Dunn is a moderate on abortion issues, supporting a ban on so-called partial birth abortions and opposing federal employee health care plans from covering abortions. But she opposed banning abortions at overseas military hospitals and voted to require states to pay for Medicaid abor-tions in the case of rape or incest or to protect the life of the mother. On other social issues, however, Dunn is a strict conservative. She voted against the Family and Medical Leave Act in 1993 and opposed the Brady Bill, which required a waiting period for handgun purchases. Dunn is also conservative on economic issues. She is an outspoken critic of the Internal Revenue Service and supports cuts in the capital gains tax.

A favorite of her GOP leadership, Dunn quickly rose through the Re-publican ranks. As a freshman, Dunn was picked to serve on the GOP Committee on Committees that makes Republican assignments—the first woman appointed to that panel. Dunn was also the only freshman member named to the high-profile Joint Committee on the Organization of Congress, which studied internal reforms for Congress. During her first term, she also served on the House Oversight Committee, the Com-mittee on Public Works and Transportation, and the Science, Space, and Technology Committee. In her second term, Dunn was appointed to the prestigious tax-writing Ways and Means Committee and has since given up her other committee assignments. She is only the fifth woman in his-tory to serve on Ways and Means. Before being elected vice chair of the House Republican Conference in 1997, she served as conference secre-tary.

Dunn has reciprocated the GOP leadership for all its support. When Speaker Newt Gingrich (R-Ga.) was under attack in 1996 for violating House ethics rules, Dunn was one of his strongest defenders. She also retaliated against Democrats and filed her own ethics complaint against Democratic Leader Richard Gephardt, accusing him of improperly re-porting income on land he owned.

But Dunn's rising star hit a ceiling following the 1998 elections. Re-

publicans lost five seats in the elections, which sparked a flurry of chal-
lenges to GOP leaders. Dunn entered the race for Majority Leader,
challenging the incumbent leader Rep. Dick Armey of Texas. She was
the first woman to make a run for the top seat.

"I'm someone who has broken a lot of glass ceilings," she said after
she entered the leadership race. "I was the first woman president of our
student body in the sixth grade and was the first woman Republican
state party chairman."[66]

Dunn lost her bid, coming in third place.

Before joining Congress, Dunn served for 10 years as the chair of the
Washington State Republican Party. Her accomplishments with the state
party led to her active involvement with the Republican National Committee, where she was elected vice chair from the Western Region and
served as chair of all the state party chairmen nationwide from 1988 to
1991. During the administration of President Reagan, she was a presidential appointee to several advisory councils on volunteer service and
historic preservation. Prior to her work with the Republican Party, Dunn
served in the King County Department of Assessments from 1978 to 1980
directing legislation and public relations.

FLORENCE DWYER (R-N.J.)
(July 4, 1902–Feb. 29, 1976)
House: Jan. 3, 1957, to Jan. 3, 1973

Florence Dwyer began her lengthy congressional career with a narrow
upset victory over the Democratic incumbent, but she went on to win
re-election seven more times by large margins and often with the help
of Democratic voters. Dwyer was considered a "progressive" Republican, sometimes crossing party lines to oppose her own GOP leadership
on such issues as housing and internal House procedures.

Dwyer first became interested in politics when she was raising her
young son and became active in the PTA. She learned the legislative
process when she began working as a state lobbyist for the New Jersey
Business and Professional Women's Clubs and later as a secretary and
parliamentarian in the state assembly. In 1949, Dwyer decided she was
finally ready to run for office and won a seat in the state assembly. She
served for six years, during which she chaired the Education Committee
and introduced the first mandatory minimum salary schedule for public

school teachers. She also introduced legislation regulating the sale of flammable fabrics and controlling air pollution, and she pushed through a bill guaranteeing equal pay for women in the state. While serving in the state assembly, Dwyer also attended Rutgers University Law School to further her knowledge of taxation and law and improve herself as a legislator.

After coming to the U.S. House in 1957, Dwyer served on the Government Operations Committee and the Banking and Currency Committee. On the Government Affairs Committee, Dwyer sought to eliminate "pork barrel" projects slipped into spending bills by her colleagues. "It's a common failing, I suppose, to take all you can get, but it's a failing people in public office should try to resist," she once said.[67]

Dwyer eventually rose to the ranking Republican position on Government Affairs and focused much of her efforts on consumer rights. She introduced bills to establish a permanent office of Consumer Affairs and outlaw discrimination in lending. She was one of the early proponents of federal support for mass transit and helped bring into being the Department of Transportation. She also pushed for the creation of the National Commission on Population Growth and the Environmental Protection Agency.

In 1962, Dwyer was one of only 13 Republicans to join Democrats in voting for President Kennedy's request to create an Urban Affairs and Housing Department. Several years later, Dwyer again opposed her party leadership when she backed a Democratic plan to enlarge the powerful Rules Committee. She led a small group of Republicans who believed the larger committee would water down the influence of southern Democrats and conservative Republicans who had blocked social and civil rights legislation.

Dwyer maintained a strong interest in parliamentary procedure and in 1965 introduced a bill calling for sweeping congressional reforms. Among her proposals were lengthening lawmakers' terms to four years, better scheduling of committee hearings, and creating a code of ethics for members and their staffs. Dwyer also authored an amendment to the Legislative Reorganization Act of 1970 requiring public disclosure of how members cast their ballots on teller votes. Before, members were simply counted but not listed by name.

Dwyer also worked hard for women's rights. She helped lead the fight for passage of the Equal Rights Amendment in the early 1970s, and when her Republican colleague Richard Nixon was elected president, she urged him to appoint more women to federal office. Although she fought against sexual discrimination, Dwyer did not make gender an issue in her own campaigns. "I have never campaigned as a woman," she said. "If I can't take on any man running against me, I don't deserve to represent the women and men of this country." Dwyer, however, admitted that women lawmakers often have to work harder than their male counterparts. "A Congresswoman must look like a girl, act like a lady, think like a man, speak on any given subject with authority and most of all work like a dog."[68]

ELAINE EDWARDS (D-La.)
(March 8, 1929–   )
Senate: Aug. 1, 1972, to Nov. 13, 1972

When Sen. Allen Ellender died in office in 1972, Louisiana Gov. Edwin Edwards was placed in an awkward situation. A long list of Senate hopefuls—including several of Edwards's financial backers—lined up for the seat. Edwards knew he would be in hot water if he were forced to endorse one of them, so he instead made the politically safe move and appointed his wife to fill the vacancy. (Ironically, Ellender himself had been elected 36 years earlier to succeed Louisiana's first woman senator, Rose McConnell Long.) Elaine Edwards accepted the appointment by her husband, but promised to serve out only the remaining few months of the term and not run for re-election. Mrs. Edwards, in fact, would have preferred not to have held office at all.

"I never wanted to be liberated from sewing, cooking, or even gardening," she said.[69]

Assigned to the Agriculture and Forestry Committee and the Public Works Committee, Edwards was criticized during her brief tenure for being little more than the mouthpiece for her husband. Her staff was ordered to call the governor's office before every Senate vote.

In her first speech on the Senate floor, Edwards spoke out in favor of the proposed Equal Education Opportunities Act, which would have restricted the use of busing to end school segregation. One of her first legislative acts was to join Sen. Hubert Humphrey in sponsoring a bill to create an educational fellowship in the name of her predecessor Ellender. She supported an increase in the earned income limits for Social Security recipients and worked for new highway construction in Louisiana.

Edwards resigned from her seat on Nov. 13, two months before the end of her term, to allow her successor, J. Bennett Johnston, to be sworn in early to gain an edge in seniority over other newly elected senators.

JO ANN EMERSON (R-Mo.)
(Sept. 16, 1950–   )
House: Nov. 5, 1997, to present

Jo Ann Emerson was elected to Congress to fill the seat of her husband, eight-term Rep. Bill Emerson (R), who died of lung cancer. Jo Ann Emerson originally said she would not run for the seat, but eventually conceded to pressure from local and national Republican leaders. She was required to run as an Independent because her husband's death occurred after the state's filing deadline for the primary had closed. She campaigned on a platform vowing to follow her husband's legislative agenda and nicknamed her organization "Team Emerson." On election day in November, she actually won two races—the special election to fill out the remaining two months of her husband's term and the general election for a full term in the following Congress.

After being sworn into office, Emerson quickly switched from Independent to Republican. House leaders placed her on the two committees her husband had served on—the Transportation and Infrastructure Committee and the Agriculture Committee. She also received an assignment to the Small Business Committee.

Emerson is a reliable conservative vote. She opposes abortion and is a strong supporter of gun owners' rights. She backs a balanced budget constitutional amendment as well as an amendment to ban flag burning. She supports voluntary prayer in public schools and thinks taxes should only be raised if two-thirds of the Congress votes to do so. She is also concerned with issues of importance to her district. She has worked to win money for local infrastructure projects and wants to expand markets for crops grown in the district, including soybeans, rice, and cotton.

Emerson had never held public office before coming to Congress, but she was no political novice. She grew up in a political family. Her father had worked with the Republican National Committee and her mother was a lobbyist and political activist. As a child growing up in Maryland, her family lived next door to House Majority Leader Rep. Hale Boggs (D-La.).

As an adult, Emerson worked for years as a lobbyist on Capitol Hill. She also served as the deputy communications director for the National Republican Congressional Committee. Immediately before winning election to Congress, Emerson served as the vice president for public affairs of the American Insurance Association in Washington.

KARAN ENGLISH (D-Aríz.)
(March 23, 1949–   )
House: Jan. 5, 1993, to Jan. 3, 1995

Karan English first became involved in politics when, as a member of her neighborhood association fighting to resolve local water and sewer problems, she was urged to seek a post on the Coconino County Board of Supervisors. She won election to the board in 1980 and became its chair four years later.

English was elected to the state House in 1986 and to the state Senate in 1990. She chaired the state Senate Environment Committee as a freshman and pushed through measures cracking down on hazardous waste and requiring environmental education in the state's elementary and high schools.

During her race for Congress, English not surprisingly won the backing of environmental groups as well as feminist organizations. It was a surprise, however, when she also won the support of Arizona's most famous Republican, former senator and presidential contender Barry Goldwater. His endorsement, along with English's conservative economic views, brought her to victory in the swing political district and made her a member of the historic 1992 "Year of the Woman" class.

Once in Congress, English served on the Education and Labor Committee and the Committee on Natural Resources, where she continued to focus on environmental issues. English also worked on reforming congressional operations. She lost a highly publicized battle to change House rules and prohibit lawmakers from converting to personal use frequent-flyer miles accumulated through taxpayer-financed trips.

English established a solidly liberal voting record on social issues. She voted for abortion rights, a ban on certain assault weapons, the Brady gun control bill, and Clinton's tax-raising budget package. Her votes made her the target of religious conservatives and prompted Goldwater to remove his support for her during her bid for a second term. She spent $700,000 in the campaign and still lost by 20,000 votes.

During a special meeting of House Democrats following the elections, many of English's colleagues suggested that she and other defeated freshmen should have cast politically safer votes in order to win re-election. English shot back: "I am angry, not that I lost the election, but that some of you are taking away the very things that made my service valuable to me. I am proud that I voted for the Brady bill and the assault-weapons ban. I am proud of my vote for the budget bill. Many of us in the Women's Caucus have a slogan: We didn't come here to be somebody, we came here to do something."[70] English received a standing ovation from the assembled Democrats.

ANNA ESHOO (D-Calif.)
(Dec. 13, 1942–   )
House: Jan. 5, 1993, to present

Anna Eshoo has spent much of her congressional career working to help the large technology industry in her district. Although she is liberal on social issues, she is more conservative on fiscal matters, supporting cuts in the capital gains tax that benefit small businesses. She is a firm believer in free trade and backed the North American Free Trade Agreement, despite opposition from labor organizations in her district.

Keeping in step with the high-tech industry that dominates her Silicon Valley district, Eshoo helped launch the Internet Caucus in Congress and pushed for enhanced tax incentives for computer donations to public schools. Eshoo fought hard to overhaul security litigation laws and tighten restrictions on investor lawsuits. Clinton vetoed a bill that made it harder to file such lawsuits, but Eshoo joined with other pro-tech lawmakers and helped override Clinton's veto. She also encouraged parents to use technology to control their children's access to online materials and pushed to prevent government laboratories from competing with private industry. Eshoo's assignment on the Commerce Committee helps her look out for the technology industry. She took the seat on Commerce in her second term, giving up her original assignments on the Science, Space and Technology Committee and the Committee on Merchant Marine and Fisheries.

Along with her strong pro-business stance, Eshoo is a reliable liberal vote on social issues such as abortion and the environment. She is a vocal advocate for coastal protection, fighting to make coastal management programs a bigger federal priority and introducing the California Ocean Protection Act to permanently protect the state's outer continental shelf from new offshore drilling. She has worked for stricter enforcement of the Clean Water Act and the Endangered Species Act.

The former head of a local hospital board, Eshoo has pushed for expanded funding for women's health issues. She is a sponsor of the

Women's Health Equity Act, which calls for expanded testing for gender differences in new drugs, improved medical school education for women's health issues, and expanded women's health care and research in the military and the Veterans' Administration. She also introduced legislation to guarantee insurance coverage for reconstructive breast surgery following mastectomies.

Before coming to Congress, Eshoo served for 10 years on the San Mateo County Board of Supervisors. Eshoo began her public service career in 1980 when she became the first woman chair of the San Mateo County Democratic Party. She became chief of staff for California Assembly Speaker Leo McCarthy in 1981 before winning election to the county board a year later. While on the board, Eshoo was responsible for securing funds for California's first freestanding nursing facility for AIDS patients and was instrumental in increasing fifteen-fold the AIDS funding in San Mateo County.

WILLA ESLICK (D-Tenn.)
(Sept. 8, 1878–Feb. 18, 1961)
House: Dec. 5, 1932, to March 3, 1933

On June 14, 1932, Willa Eslick watched from the House galleries as her husband, Rep. Edward Eslick, died on the chamber floor. During an impassioned speech for passage of a bonus bill for World War I veterans, Rep. Eslick collapsed mid-sentence and died of a heart attack. Two months later, Mrs. Eslick defeated three male challengers to fill out the remainder of her husband's unexpired term.

Mrs. Eslick's service in the House was just a brief three months. The House was in recess when she won election in August 1932, so she was not sworn into office until a lame duck session was called on Dec. 5. Because her husband had died after the election filing deadline, Eslick was not allowed to run for election to the following two-year term. During her brief service, Eslick focused on the plight of farmers in her largely rural district that had been devastated by the Depression. She joined an ad hoc group of 75 House members who met at night to discuss possible legislative remedies to the agricultural crisis. She supported a bill that offered relief to cotton farmers who reduced production, and backed the proposal by President-elect Franklin Roosevelt to develop the Tennessee

River Valley. She also endorsed Roosevelt's plan to construct an electricity-generating plant at Muscle Shoals, Ala.

Before coming to Congress, Eslick served on the state Democratic committee. Born and raised in Tennessee, Eslick left her home state only to study music during her younger years at New York's Metropolitan College of Music and to accompany her husband to Washington. She died in Tennessee at the age of 82.

MARY FARRINGTON (R-Hawaii)
(May 30, 1898–July 21, 1984)
House: Aug. 4, 1954, to Jan. 3, 1957

Throughout her time in office, Mary Farrington dedicated herself to winning statehood for the territory of Hawaii. As a delegate to the House of Representatives, she could not cast her vote on the House floor, but she introduced statehood legislation, met with President Eisenhower, and lobbied powerful lawmakers to gain support for her cause. She defended statehood against those who claimed that Hawaii was a hotbed of Communism, attacking the charges as "extravagant, undocumented, and unsupported."[71]

Farrington came to the House after winning a special election to succeed her husband Joseph Farrington, who died in his sixth term in office. During her husband's congressional service, Farrington became active in Republican politics. She served as president of the League of Republican Women in Washington from 1946 to 1948. From 1949 to 1953, she was president of the National Federation of Women's Republican Clubs. Earlier, Farrington founded a Washington-based newspaper syndicate that distributed news clips from the capital to publications in the Midwest.

After coming to the House, Farrington was assigned to the Agriculture Committee, the Armed Services Committee, and the Interior and Insular Affairs Committee. Three months after winning the special election, she ran for a full term and defeated Democrat John Burns by just 818 votes. Two years later, Burns launched a rematch and this time won.

Farrington returned to her earlier career in journalism and served as president of the *Honolulu Star Bulletin* from 1957 to 1961. She was also director and chair of the Honolulu Lithograph Company, Ltd., and president of the Hawaiian Broadcasting System, Ltd.

In 1969, President Nixon appointed Farrington director of the Office of the Territories in the Interior Department. When the department abolished that post in 1971, she worked in the congressional liaison office until 1973.

DIANNE FEINSTEIN (D-Calif.)
(June 22, 1933–   )
Senate: Nov. 4, 1992, to present

Dianne Feinstein's career is a history of political firsts. She was the first woman to serve as president of the San Francisco Board of Supervisors, the first woman to be elected mayor of San Francisco, the first woman to be nominated by a major party for governor of California, and the first woman to represent California in the U.S. Senate.

Feinstein began her public service career with an interest in criminal justice. In 1960, she was appointed by Gov. Pat Brown to serve on the California Women's Parole Board. During the next six years, Feinstein helped oversee the sentences and paroles of 5,000 women convicted of felonies. In 1968, she also served as a member of the San Francisco Committee on Crime.

In 1969, Feinstein was elected to the San Francisco Board of Supervisors and served for three terms as its president. She ran for mayor in 1971 and again in 1975, losing both times. In 1978, after mayor George Moscone and a city supervisor were assassinated by a disgruntled former supervisor, Feinstein was elected by her colleagues on the board to fill out the rest of Moscone's term. She stayed on as mayor until 1988. In 1984, she was a leading contender for the Democratic party's vice presidential nomination, and in 1990 she ran for governor of California, but lost to GOP Sen. Pete Wilson.

When Wilson left the Senate, he appointed John Seymour to "hold" his seat until a special election could be held in 1992 to fill out the remainder of Wilson's term. Feinstein ran in the special election against Seymour and won. Two years later, Feinstein ran again for a full six-year term. The race between her and conservative GOP Rep. Michael Huffington turned into the most expensive Senate race in history. Huffington spent $29 million on his campaign—$28 million coming from his own pockets—compared to the $14 million Feinstein spent. The race was ugly, with each candidate accusing the other of hiring illegal immigrants as domestic workers. In the end, Feinstein won a narrow victory over Huffington.

Throughout her political career, Feinstein has maintained an odd mix of liberal and conservative stances. She has supported environmental protection and abortion rights, but also supports the death penalty and a tougher border patrol to stem illegal immigration from Mexico. She has voted to ban employment discrimination against homosexuals, but also backed a proposed constitutional amendment against flag burning. She is known for effectively working with her Republican colleagues and has authored numerous bills with GOP lawmakers covering breast cancer treatment, victims rights, and tobacco regulation.

When she first won election to the Senate in 1992, Feinstein was assigned to the powerful Appropriations Committee, but her support of a line-item veto so angered the committee's Democratic chair that she was removed from the panel two years later. Feinstein also serves on the Foreign Relations Committee, the Judiciary Committee, and the Committee on Rules and Administration.

In the first two years of her Senate service, Feinstein pushed through two major pieces of legislation: the California Desert Protection Act, which put in place the largest federal land protection measure in nearly two decades, and a ban on 19 different kinds of assault weapons. The historic gun ban, which Feinstein tirelessly championed despite strong opposition from gun rights groups, was signed into law in 1994 as part of President Clinton's comprehensive crime bill.

"It really comes down to a question of blood or guts—the blood of innocent people or the Senate of the United States having the guts to do what we should do when we take that oath to protect the welfare of our citizens," she said of the ban.[72]

Feinstein has focused much of her legislative attention on criminal justice. She co-authored with her Republican colleagues a bill to fight the rise of gang violence as well as a victims' rights constitutional amendment that would require that victims of crimes be heard during the legal proceedings of their assailants, including sentencing and release of the perpetrators. She also pushed to passage her bill setting tougher sentences for the use and distribution of the highly addictive drug methamphetamine.

Feinstein has also focused on women's health issues. She introduced legislation creating a special postage stamp in which a portion of the 40-cent price would go toward breast cancer research. The bill was signed into law in 1997 and the Postal Service issued the stamp in 1998. She also authored legislation to prevent "drive-through mastectomies." The bill would require doctors—and not insurance companies—to determine the length of time a breast cancer patient must stay in the hospital.

REBECCA FELTON (D-Ga.)
(June 10, 1835–Jan. 24, 1930)
Senate: Nov. 21 to Nov. 22, 1922

Rebecca Felton has the distinction of serving the shortest term of any senator in history—just two days—but her career in politics and civic affairs spanned decades. Before becoming the first woman to serve in the Upper Chamber, Felton entered the world of politics as the campaign manager and close adviser to her husband, Dr. William Felton, who served in the House of Representatives for three terms in the 1870s. On the campaign trail and through her editorials in the newspaper she and her husband ran, Felton gained a reputation as a sharp-tongued and unyielding politician. She was seen as the driving force behind her husband's career, prompting one newspaper to ask, "Which Felton is the Congressman and which the wife?"[73]

Mrs. Felton got her chance to emerge from behind the scenes and hold office herself in 1922 when Georgia Sen. Thomas Watson suddenly died. Gov. Thomas Hardwick decided he would appoint a woman to hold the seat until a successor could be elected. Hardwick, who had opposed the suffrage amendment when he served in Congress four years earlier, quickly saw the opportunity to cozy up to the newly enfranchised women voters. He hoped the appointment would clear the path for his own ambitions to win the vacant seat, never thinking the "interim" woman would actually get a chance to step foot on Capitol Hill. He appointed Felton, 87 years old and widowed, calling her a "noble Georgia woman now in the sunset of a splendid, useful life."[74]

During her appointment ceremonies, Felton said, "The biggest part of this appointment lies in the recognition of women in the government of our country. It means, as far as I can see, there are now no limitations upon the ambitions of women. They can be elected or appointed to any office in the land."[75]

Women across the country quickly mobilized a lobbying campaign to have Felton officially sworn in and seated among her senatorial colleagues. This could only happen if the president called a special session of Congress, or if the Senate agreed to swear her in before the elected successor was seated. President Harding was overwhelmed with letters and telegrams urging him to allow Felton to be sworn in, but he decided it would be too expensive to call a special session of Congress just to seat a single senator.

In the meantime, Walter Franklin George won the primary for the vacant Senate seat—ending Hardwick's political aspirations. The nation's women quickly turned their focus onto George and flooded him with requests to defer the presentation of his credentials and allow Felton to be sworn in. Felton sent a personal note to President Harding asking again that he call a special session of Congress. He ignored her request, but, by apparent coincidence, decided to convene a special session to allow the passage of an administration-sponsored ship-subsidy bill. This was the opportunity Felton was waiting for. Senator-elect George agreed to hold off on the presentation of his credentials until after she presented hers. He warned, however, that the objection of a single senator could deny her the right to be sworn in.

On Nov. 20, 1922, Felton took her seat in the Senate chamber amid cheers from a gallery crowded with women. The next day she was sworn in as the body's first woman member and the oldest senator at the time. The following day, Felton answered the roll call and stood to give the first and last speech of her senatorial career.

"When the women of the country come in and sit with you, though there may be but a very few in the next few years, I pledge you that you will get ability, you will get integrity of purpose, you will get exalted patriotism and you will get unstinted usefulness," Felton told her male colleagues.[76]

After her brief service in the Senate, Felton returned to Cartersville, Ga., where she continued to write and lecture on public issues. She became an advocate for World War I veterans and campaigned against future involvement in foreign wars. After Felton died in 1930 at the age of 94, researchers discovered the speech she prepared in case the Senate refused to swear her into office. In it she argued that the temporary presence of a woman should be granted in the Senate "not as a favor or a compliment, not as a bequest to a charity patient, not as a tribute to personal vanity, but as a tribute to the integrity, the patriotism and the womanhood of blessed wives and mothers of our common country."[77]

Felton's commitment to women's rights had developed long before she ever came to the Senate. In the 1880s, she became known as one of the leading figures in the Georgia Woman's Christian Temperance Union, speaking tirelessly across the state in support of women's rights. She focused much of her energy on calls for higher education for women and often drew parallels between the treatment of women and slavery.

Felton was also an outspoken advocate of reforms in southern farming policies, and tied her feminist beliefs to calls for changes in agricultural politics. She charged that the wives of farmers often found themselves in a state of "actual and peremptory bondage" and declared, "The Bible saying that 'a man and his wife are one' reads correctly, for man is the only one."[78] In 1891, Felton proposed a program to the Georgia Agriculture Society aimed at improving women's rights as well as the plight of farmers dependent on a sagging market. Her "Wife's Farm" program proposed that farmers set aside a portion of the farm for their wives, and while the women were in the house cooking his breakfast, the men would be working her fields. The crops produced would belong solely to the wife and would be used for home consumption rather than for market production.

But Felton's calls for equality of the sexes did not extend to other sections of the population. She attacked Jews, Catholics, and blacks, at one time endorsing mass lynchings of blacks as a warning against suspected rapists.

Born into a farming family outside of Decatur, Ga., in 1835, Felton married her husband when she was 18 and became the head of a slave plantation. Felton was opposed to Georgia's secession from the Union in 1861, but she stood by her husband, who supported it. When he volunteered as a surgeon during the war, she worked by his side nursing wounded soldiers. By the end of the war, she had lost both her sons to poor living conditions, her plantation had been razed by passing troops, and she and her husband had lost most of their wealth. They later opened a school in the Catersville Methodist Church before her husband made his first run for Congress in 1874.

MILLICENT FENWICK (R-N.J.)
(Feb. 25, 1910–Sept. 16, 1992)
House: Jan. 3, 1975, to Jan. 3, 1983

When Millicent Fenwick won election to the House in 1974, it was hailed in the papers as a "geriatric triumph." The 64-year-old Republican had beat the odds in the post-Watergate tide that swept Democrats—mostly young and male—into office. One month after being sworn in, Fenwick celebrated her 65th birthday aboard a military plane flying to Indochina as part of an eight-member delegation asked by President Ford to evaluate his request for additional military and economic aid to South Vietnam and Cambodia. During the trip, Fenwick was stunned by the horrors of war and ultimately opposed Ford's request for military funds. "I think we must face the fact that military aid sent from America will not succeed. It will only delay the development of the kind of stable situation—whatever form that takes—that will at least stop the horrible suffering of war," she said.[79] That was just the first of many times Fenwick would oppose her GOP president. A fiscal conservative, Fenwick was a social liberal who supported the Equal Rights Amendment, federal funding for abortions, the creation of a consumer protection agency, and the food stamp program.

Fenwick had always been an independent and strong-minded thinker. The daughter of the U.S. ambassador to Spain (her mother died aboard the British passenger ship *Lusitania* when it was torpedoed by a German submarine in 1915), Fenwick had little formal education as an adolescent but instead learned during her travels through Europe with her father. After returning to the United States at the age of 19, Fenwick took courses at Columbia University and later studied philosophy at the New School of Social Research in New York. During the 1930s, Fenwick worked as a model for *Harper's Bazaar* and later joined the feature staff of *Vogue* magazine where she remained for 14 years and wrote *Vogue's Book of Etiquette*. In 1952, Fenwick belatedly received her mother's $5-million inheritance. She quit her job at *Vogue* and began doing volunteer and political work.

Fenwick first became interested in politics during World War II when she observed Hitler's atrocities against the German people. "Since then, I have never really trusted government and it is because I don't trust government that I am a Republican," she said.[80] In 1954, she volunteered as an aide in a successful Senate campaign and later served as chair of the Somerset County Legal Aid Society. From 1958 to 1964, Fenwick served on the Bernardsville Borough Council and was vice chair of the New Jersey advisory committee to the U.S. Commission on Civil Rights for 14 years. During that time, she visited building sites to investigate charges of discrimination and attended rallies of black and Hispanic demonstrators.

In 1969, at the age of 59, Fenwick won a seat in the New Jersey General Assembly and for the next three years in office she pushed for civil rights, consumer interests, prison reform, and conservation. She showed her independence during a debate on her proposed equal rights amendment for women. "One colleague rose and with real anguish in his voice . . . said, 'I just don't like this amendment. I've always thought of women as kissable, cuddly and smelling good,'" Fenwick recalled. "The only answer, of course, was, 'That's the way I felt about men, too. I only hope for your sake that you haven't been disappointed as often as I have.'"[81] In 1973, Fenwick left the General Assembly to become director of New Jersey Consumer Affairs, a post she held for one year until her election to the U.S. Congress.

During her four terms in the U.S. House, Fenwick served on a variety of committees and worked on a wide range of issues. In her first term she sat on the Small Business Committee and the Committee on Banking, Currency and Housing. She also later served on the District of Columbia

Committee, the Foreign Affairs Committee, the Committee on Education and Labor, the Select Committee on Aging, and the Ethics Committee.

Fenwick was not afraid of taking on her senior colleagues. In her first term she rose on the House floor to chastise Rep. Wayne Hays, who was eventually forced out of office in the wake of a sex scandal. In her second term, as a member of the Ethics Committee, she demanded a thorough investigation of the "Koreagate" scandal involving members who took gifts in exchange for policy decisions. She later pushed for changes in campaign finance laws to prevent lawmakers from getting donations from special-interest groups.

Fenwick also worked to establish the Helsinki Commission on human rights and introduced bills to eliminate the "marriage penalty" tax and make it easier for seniors to get credit. In 1982, Fenwick ran and lost a bid for the Senate. A year later she was named the U.S. ambassador to the United Nations Agencies for Food and Agriculture, a post she held until 1987.

Fenwick's outspoken style—and her unabashed habit of smoking a pipe—made her the model for the fictional character Rep. Lacey Davenport in the "Doonesbury" cartoon series.

BOOK BY FENWICK

Speaking Up (1982)

GERALDINE FERRARO (D-N.Y.)
(Aug. 26, 1935–   )
House: Jan. 3, 1979, to Jan. 3, 1985

Geraldine Ferraro had a relatively brief congressional career, but her accomplishments laid down a new foundation for women's participation in American politics. Ferraro began her political life in 1974 as an assistant district attorney for Queens County in New York, prosecuting cases involving rape, child abuse, and domestic violence. She had previously taught public school while putting herself through Fordham University School of Law. She received her law degree in 1960 and was admitted to the bar a year later. After joining the district attorney's office, she became head of a new unit, the Special Victim's Bureau, where she became a forceful advocate for abused children. In 1978, Ferraro ran for and won a seat in the U.S. House where she focused much of her work on wage and pension issues and women's rights.

Ferraro was assigned to the Post Office and Civil Service Committee where she defended the interests of displaced federal employees and worked to enforce flex-time employment laws. On the Public Works and Transportation Committee, she fought for increased federal funds for urban mass transit systems. In 1981, Ferraro introduced a bill to make private pensions fairer and to recognize marriage as an economic partnership. The bill permitted all workers to begin participating in pension plans at age 20—rather than 25—and allowed them to remain eligible for pensions during job absences, including maternity leave. She introduced a bill to allow homemakers to open individual retirement accounts (IRAs) and was a co-sponsor of the 1983 Women's Equity Act.

Along with her legislative work, Ferraro established close ties to House Speaker Tip O'Neil (D-Mass.) and other members of the House leadership. She was elected secretary of the House Democratic Caucus during her second term in office, entitling her to a seat on the influential House Steering and Policy Committee. She later gave up her seat on the Post Office panel to take a spot on the powerful Budget Committee.

In 1984, Ferraro decided to leave Congress and accept Walter Mondale's invitation to join his presidential ticket as vice president. She became the first woman in American history to receive a major party's nomination for vice president. Although Ferraro helped energize many female and young voters, she and Mondale lost to the Reagan–Bush ticket in a landslide.

In 1992, Ferraro returned to the political arena and entered the Senate race against Sen. Alfonse D'Amato. Three other Democrats entered the race—ex-Rep. Elizabeth Holtzman, state attorney general Robert Abrams, and civil rights activist Al Sharpton. The primary race quickly turned ugly and bitter as Holtzman accused Ferraro of having ties to the Mafia. In the end, Abrams narrowly defeated Ferraro for the nomination, but lost the general election to D'Amato.

For the next six years, Ferraro worked as a lawyer and television commentator on CNN's *Crossfire* show, until she decided to launch yet another bid against D'Amato in 1998. "I believe this high office requires more than being Senator Pothole," Ferraro said in her announcement of a second Senate bid, referring to D'Amato's self-proclaimed obsession with constituent service. "It demands a genuine, continuing commitment to repair the holes in our social fabric and to chart a road into the future."[82] Ferraro was defeated in the Democratic primary by Rep. Charles Schumer. After the loss, Ferraro announced she would never again run for public office.

BOOKS BY FERRARO

Changing History: Women, Power and Politics (1993)
Framing a Life: A Family Memoir (1998)

BOBBI FIEDLER (R-Calif.)
(April 22, 1937–   )
House: Jan. 3, 1981, to Jan. 3, 1987

Bobbi Fiedler's election to the House was one of the biggest upsets in the 1980 congressional races. It was her first run for national office, but she managed to defeat 20-year representative and head of the Democratic Congressional Campaign Committee James Corman by just 752 votes. Her victory was credited in part to the landslide election of Ronald Reagan and also to the anger of California parents who had been forced to send their children to school under a new state busing law aimed at ending segregation. The law forced many students to travel up to 50 miles from their homes every day. Although Corman defended busing as a last resort to desegregate schools, Fiedler was an active opponent of it. She was an organizer of the anti-busing group BUSTOP and served on the Los Angeles School Board where she also fought to overturn the busing law.

After winning election to the House, Fiedler sat on the Budget Committee and was a strong advocate of fiscal conservatism. Although she generally supported the policies of the Reagan administration, she broke with some of her Republican colleagues by supporting the Equal Rights Amendment and other feminist issues. Fiedler's congressional career ended after three terms, when she ran for the Senate but lost the primary for the GOP nomination.

TILLIE FOWLER (R-Fla.)
(Dec. 23, 1942–   )
House: Jan. 5, 1993, to present

Tillie Fowler had spent more than two decades in public and community service before winning election to the House in the historic 1992 "Year of the Woman." She served as a legislative assistant to former Rep. Robert Stephens, Jr. (D-Ga.) and as general counsel in the White House Office of Consumer Affairs during the Nixon administration. In 1989, she became the first woman ever elected as Jacksonville, Fla., City Council president. She later chaired the council's finance committee. She served as chair of the Florida Endowment for the Humanities and was a member of Jacksonville's Commission on the Status of Women.

When Fowler ran for Congress in 1992, she used her experience as a former Capitol Hill staffer to help her in the campaign. She traveled to Washington and asked then-Republican House Leader Bob Michel (Ill.) to promise her a seat on the National Security Committee if she won the election. The promise of the prestigious committee assignment helped her win the race.

Michel kept his word following the election, and Fowler also won a seat on the Transportation and Infrastructure Committee. Fowler is a strong proponent of increased defense spending. She has continually fought against cuts in Pentagon funding, saying the U.S. armed forces are being stretched to the limit. She said the United States cannot be the world's peacekeeper if it continues to slash military spending. In her second term, Fowler backed a measure that would have prohibited the deployment of ground troops to Bosnia unless Congress specifically approved the funding.

The only Republican woman on the National Security Committee, Fowler has also fought efforts to separate the sexes in military training. During congressional investigations into sexual harassment in the armed services and consideration of gender separation, Fowler introduced an amendment that would have allowed the individual services to decide if men and women should be trained together. It was defeated in committee.

During her freshmen year, Fowler co-chaired her class's task force on congressional reform. The group endorsed a constitutional balanced budget amendment, the line-item veto, a super-majority to approve tax increases, and term limits for lawmakers. Fowler introduced legislation to limit House members to eight years and senators to 12 years. It was defeated.

Fowler, a Republican deputy whip, generally votes along party lines. She is conservative on crime and immigration issues. She voted in 1996 to repeal the ban on certain assault weapons and has called for tough crackdowns on legal and illegal immigration. On other issues, however, she is more moderate. She backed an increase in the minimum wage and supports some abortion rights. She voted to require states to pay for Medicaid abortions in cases of rape or incest and to allow women at overseas military bases to have an abortion if they paid for the procedure themselves. But Fowler opposed efforts to allow federal employee health care plans to cover abortions, and she voted to ban a certain procedure called partial birth abortions by its opponents.

In 1998, Fowler was elected to serve as vice chair of the GOP Conference for the 106th Congress, the highest-ranking woman in the Republican hierarchy.

SHEILA FRAHM (R-Kan.)
(March 22, 1945–   )
Senate: June 11, 1996, to Nov. 6, 1996

When Senate Republican Leader Bob Dole (R-Kan.) resigned from office in 1996 to launch a full-time bid for the White House, Kansas Gov. Bill Graves appointed Sheila Frahm to fill the vacancy. But Frahm's service in the Senate was short-lived. She ran for the special election to fill out the remainder of Dole's full term and although she won the endorsement of Kansas's other Senator Nancy Kassebaum (R), she was defeated in the August primary for the GOP nomination by Rep. Sam Brownback. Frahm, who was pro-abortion rights and against congressional term limits, was targeted by conservative political groups during the race and was soundly defeated 55 to 42 percent by the more conservative Brownback. During her brief five months in office, Frahm served on the Banking Committee and the Armed Services Committee.

Frahm had worked in state politics for more than a decade before coming to the Senate. In 1985, Frahm—who had previously worked with her family's agriculture business—was appointed to the Kansas Board of Education. Three years later, she ran for and won a seat in the state Senate. While in the state Senate, she sponsored legislation to cut income taxes and supported bills to crack down on sexual predators. In 1993, Frahm was elected by her colleagues to become the first woman majority leader of the state Senate. A year later, she ran for lieutenant governor with Graves and became the first woman in state history to win that post.

After Frahm was defeated for the U.S. Senate nomination by Brownback, she returned to Kansas and became the executive director of the Kansas Association of Community Colleges.

WILLA FULMER (D-S.C.)
(Feb. 3, 1884–May 13, 1968)
House: Nov. 16, 1944, to Jan. 3, 1945

Willa Fulmer served less than two months in office, never receiving a committee assignment or speaking on the House floor. She came to Congress after winning a special election to fill out the unexpired term of her late husband, Rep. Hampton Fulmer. Mr. Fulmer—who with 23 years of service under his belt was one of the most senior House members at the time of his death—was the chair of the Agriculture Committee.

Unlike many congressional spouses of her time, Mrs. Fulmer was not active in her husband's political career. She knew little about public service and had no desire to run for the following full term in office. She won the special election unopposed, but attracted less than 8,000 votes out of the district's total population of 361,933.

After leaving Congress, Mrs. Fulmer devoted most of her time to traveling around the world. She suffered a heart attack and died in 1968 while on board a luxury liner bound for Europe.

ELIZABETH FURSE (D-Ore.)
(Oct. 13, 1936–)
House: Jan. 5, 1993, to Jan. 6, 1999

Elizabeth Furse, born in Nairobi, Kenya, to British parents and raised in South Africa, began working for peace and human rights at an early age. In her teens, she marched against apartheid with her mother, the founder of the Black Sash, a South African women's anti-apartheid group.

Furse became a U.S. citizen in 1972, and worked as a community organizer in the Watts neighborhood in Los Angeles. She moved to Oregon in 1978 and became a peace activist working on behalf of Northwestern Indian tribes. During the 1980s, she successfully lobbied Congress to pass legislation restoring legal status to three Oregon tribes. In 1985, she cofounded the Oregon Peace Institute, dedicated to teaching peace and nonviolent conflict resolution, and in 1988 she organized the "Citizens Train" that took 300 citizens from the Northwest to Washington, D.C., in a high-profile effort to educate Congress on the need for a "citizens budget."

After winning election to Congress in 1992—in her first bid for public office—Furse continued to work on behalf of peace and other liberal issues. She focused much of her legislative attention on cutting military spending. For four years in a row she successfully offered budget amendments that slashed millions of dollars from the Pentagon's budget. In

1993, she won a $150-million cut in the "Star Wars" ballistic missile defense program and later passed amendments cutting an additional $87 million from various military programs.

Furse charged that "every exotic weapon you could possibly think of" will not overcome the nation's real enemies, which, she said, are "decaying schools, neglected children, violent streets, too few jobs, disgraceful housing."[83]

During her first term in the House, Furse was assigned to the Banking, Finance, and Urban Affairs Committee, the Merchant Marine and Fisheries Committee, and the Armed Services Committee. She gave up all those assignments in her second term for a seat on the exclusive Commerce Committee.

Furse generally backed the agenda of President Clinton, supporting gun control and gays in the military, but she split with the administration when she voted against the North American Free Trade Agreement. She said the trade deal would be damaging to the environment.

Furse also worked on behalf of women's issues and was a strong supporter of abortion rights. In 1997, on the 24th anniversary of the *Roe v. Wade* Supreme Court ruling that legalized abortion in the United States, Furse publicly admitted she once terminated a pregnancy. In a newspaper column, Furse described how, when she was 25 and abortion was illegal, she underwent a hysterectomy rather than give birth to a child who would likely have been blind, deaf, and severely brain damaged.

"What a terrible set of choices: I could risk a back-alley abortion, carry a severely brain-damaged fetus to term or lose my fertility forever," she wrote. "In my generation, many lives were lost or permanently changed because abortion was not an available medical option. The young women in this country need to learn a lesson from our pain."[84]

In 1995, when allegations of sexual harassment were launched against fellow Democratic Oregonian Sen. Bob Packwood, Furse repeatedly called for him to agree to public hearings or resign. After Packwood announced his resignation, Furse jumped into the race to fill his open seat. She, however, dropped the bid three weeks later, citing fund-raising difficulties.

In 1997, Furse announced she would not run for a fourth term in office. She said she planned to start a new political action committee emphasizing environmental and children's issues.

ELIZABETH GASQUE (D-S.C.)
(Feb. 26, 1896–Nov. 2, 1989)
House: Sept. 13, 1938, to Jan. 3, 1939 (never sworn into office)

Elizabeth Gasque won the special election to fill the seat of her late husband—eight-term Rep. Allard Gasque—but because Congress had already adjourned for the year, she was never actually sworn into office. The only candidate to run in the September special election, Gasque became the first woman elected to represent South Carolina. During her brief four months in office, Gasque did not get a chance to do any legislating, but made the most of her position in the Washington social circuit, hosting one of the gala balls given in honor of President Roosevelt's birthday.

Gasque did not run for re-election, but maintained her social ties in Washington after leaving Congress. She died in 1989 at the age of 93.

FLORENCE GIBBS (D-Ga.)
(April 4, 1890–Aug. 19, 1964)
House: Oct. 3, 1940, to Jan. 3, 1941

Florence Gibbs's brief time in office was uneventful—she never even received a committee assignment. She was elected to fill out the last three months of the unexpired term of her husband Rep. Willis Gibbs, who died in his first term in office. In the special election to fill the seat, a mere 2,469 voters went to the polls in the 20-county district. She was uncontested in the race.

Gibbs, the mother of two, had never before participated in politics and she never returned to public life after leaving Congress. "She was good for political patronage—mainly post office appointments," said one associate. "The job wasn't really to her liking."[85]

A graduate of Brenau College in Gainesville, Ga., after leaving Congress Gibbs returned to Georgia where she died at the age of 74.

KATHRYN GRANAHAN (D-Pa.)
(Dec. 7, 1894–July 10, 1979)
House: Nov. 6, 1956, to Jan. 3, 1963

Kathryn Granahan was a decisively liberal Democrat when it came to civil rights, labor, and urban renewal. But Granahan gained support from many conservatives when she launched a highly publicized and controversial crusade against the sale of pornography through the mail. As chair of the Post Office and Civil Service subcommittee on postal operations, Granahan held two months of hearings in 1959 on the growing business of pornography and its effects on children. She introduced legislation requiring mandatory jail sentences for anyone found guilty of selling indecent material through the mail and co-sponsored a bill passed by the House giving more power to the Post Office to seize the mail of suspected pornography distributers. "The peddling of smut to children is a heinous crime that must be stopped," Granahan declared.[86]

Granahan was first elected to Congress in 1956 to fill the seat of her husband, Rep. William Granahan, who died during his fifth term in office. At the same time she was also named to succeed her husband as the leader of the 52nd Ward of Pennsylvania—a post she, like her husband, kept throughout her congressional career. In hopes of changing the stereotypical image of the tough, cigar-chomping ward bosses, she refused to supply the traditional barrels of beer during ward meetings. Instead, she served tea and cookies.

Granahan first met her husband in 1941 while she worked as the supervisor of public assistance in Pennsylvania's auditor general's office and he served as the chief disbursing officer for the state treasury. William Granahan was elected to the House in 1944, and Kathryn worked closely with him throughout his congressional career.

After she was elected to Congress, Granahan asked to succeed her husband on the Interstate and Foreign Commerce Committee, but was turned down because no woman had ever served on that panel. Instead, she was assigned to the District of Columbia Committee, the Committee on Government Operations, and the Post Office and Civil Service Committee.

In 1960, at the start of her third term in office, the census showed that Philadelphia would lose one of its six House seats. State Democratic leaders selected Granahan's district as the one to be eliminated, but they also persuaded President Kennedy to appoint Granahan as the U.S. treasurer. She took over that position in 1963, and her signature can be seen on every piece of paper currency issued during her service. In 1965, Granahan underwent brain surgery after suffering a serious fall. In 1966, a court set aside a petition asking her to be declared incompetent, but later that year Granahan resigned from the treasurer's position due to her ill health.

KAY GRANGER (R-Texas)
(Jan. 18, 1943–   )
House: Jan. 7, 1997, to present

Both Democrats and Republicans courted Kay Granger to run for Congress when conservative Democratic Rep. Peter Geren (Texas) decided to retire in 1996. Granger had served for four years as the mayor of Fort Worth, but was a registered Independent. Eventually, Granger decided to side with the GOP and went on to become the first Republican woman ever elected to the House from Texas. She also became the first Republican in almost 100 years to hold the Fort Worth area House district— which had once been held by House Speaker Jim Wright (D).

A former school teacher and insurance agent, Granger made a name for herself as mayor by balancing the city's budget and cutting the crime rate in half during her tenure from 1991 to 1995. She had also previously served for three years on the Fort Worth City Council.

After winning election to the House, Granger became a favorite of the party leadership. She was immediately made a deputy whip and was selected to serve on an advisory committee to Speaker Newt Gingrich (R-Ga.). She was also appointed to two freshman class committees to draft tax-cutting legislation and study the overhaul of the managed health care system. She was assigned to the prestigious Budget Committee, as well as the House Oversight Committee and the Transportation and Infrastructure Committee, where she helped secure $25 million for construction of a local highway project. In 1997, following the death of Rep. Sonny Bono (R-Calif.), Granger was appointed to fill his spot on the powerful National Security Committee.

Granger is a strong fiscal conservative. On her very first day in the House, she introduced a balanced budget proposal. She supports streamlining government agencies to reduce spending, although she lobbied against cuts in defense funding. She also backed a Republican "comp time" bill that would allow businesses to offer employees a choice between receiving money or time off in exchange for working extra hours. Drawing from her experience as a mayor, she strongly supports increasing local control over such issues as crime and education.

Granger is more moderate on social issues. She supports abortion rights, although she opposes late-term abortions and taxpayer-funded abortions except in the cases of rape, incest, or to save the life of the woman. She has opposed racial quotas, but backed affirmative action admissions to public colleges and universities. Overall, Granger votes along party lines more than 90 percent of the time.

In 1998, Granger pushed a proposal to deny leadership roles to Republicans who abandon the party in key House votes by creating a formal system to enforce party unity. She said she wanted to reduce party infighting. The plan was never adopted.

ELLA GRASSO (D-Conn.)
(May 10, 1919–Feb. 5, 1981)
House: Jan. 3, 1971, to Jan. 3, 1975

Ella Grasso was already a veteran politician by the time she was elected to Congress. Throughout her extensive political career, Grasso racked up an impressive list of firsts, including becoming the first woman ever elected as governor in her own right.

Grasso got her start in politics when she joined the League of Women Voters when she was in her 20s. She had graduated Phi Beta Kappa from Mount Holyoke College with a master's degree in economics and sociology. She later worked on various local Democratic organizations and in 1952 decided she was ready to launch her own campaign for elective office. She won a seat in the state House and was re-elected two years later. In her second term she became the first female floor leader in the state. During her tenure in the legislature, Grasso pushed through a law forbidding housing discrimination on the basis of race, religion, or national origin. After leaving the state House in 1956, Grasso served as a Democratic National Committeewoman and chaired the Democratic State Platform Committee—the first woman in Connecticut ever to hold that post.

In 1958, Grasso was elected as Secretary of State for Connecticut and quickly became one of the best-known and most popular political figures in the state. During her 12 years as state secretary, Grasso also remained active in national Democratic politics. She twice co-chaired the Resolutions Committee at the Democratic National Conventions and in 1968 proposed a platform plank condemning U.S. involvement in the Vietnam War.

In 1970, Grasso entered the race for an open seat in the U.S. House. Running on an anti-war platform, she also focused on the economic needs of her district. She won the seat despite being outspent nearly two-to-one by her GOP opponent. Once in office, Grasso was named to the Education and Labor Committee and the Committee on Veterans' Affairs.

During her two terms in office, Grasso worked for a higher minimum wage and a hike in Social Security payments. She helped draft the Comprehensive Employment and Training Act and the Emergency School Aid Act. To keep in touch with the voters back home, Grasso set up a toll-free "Ellaphone" in her office that allowed constituents to call her at no cost. She also offered a bill that would allow voters free postage on all correspondence to members of Congress, the President, and other federal officials.

Early in her second term, Grasso began to miss her home state and ran for governor of Connecticut. She defeated a fellow Congressman to become the country's first female governor elected in her own right. As part of her efforts to cut state spending, she refused a pay raise for herself. She won re-election to the governor's mansion in 1978 and a year later became the chair of the Democratic Governors' Conference. Ill health forced Grasso to resign in December 1980 and she died one month later.

DIXIE GRAVES (D-Ala.)
(July 26, 1882–Jan. 21, 1965)
Senate: Aug. 20, 1937, to Jan. 10, 1938

Alabama Gov. Bibb Graves sparked a flurry of controversy in 1937 when he named his wife Dixie to the Senate seat vacated by Hugo Black, who had resigned to become an associate justice of the U.S. Supreme Court. By choosing his wife, Gov. Graves avoided a messy intraparty struggle that could have cost him political allies, but he instead brought on charges of nepotism. In his own defense, Gov. Graves declared, "She has as good a heart and head as anybody."[87]

Dixie Graves, in fact, came well prepared for the office, having spent years actively working with local civic groups. She was a pioneer of the "Votes for Women" movement in Alabama, campaigning under the slogan "All citizens should be permitted to take part in government."[88] She taught Bible classes at the Central Christian Church, worked with groups to wipe out illiteracy in the state, and was a member of the Women's Christian Temperance Union and the Alabama Federation of Women's Clubs. From 1915 to 1917, she served as president of the United Daughters of the Confederacy. When her husband ran for governor in 1934, she helped write his campaign speeches and even filled in for him occasionally at campaign rallies. The *New York Times* declared that she was "at home with deep-sea fishing tackle, a shotgun, a garden spade, or a silver ladle at the banquet table."[89]

Once Graves was sworn into the Senate, she quickly proved her ability to the voters back home. Graves gave her maiden speech in opposition to the Wagner-Van Nuys anti-lynching bill—a popular stance among Alabama voters. Although Graves spoke out against the horrors of lynching, she charged that the bill was a dangerous infringement on states' rights and an insult to Southern law enforcement officers. She predicted that without the federal law, lynching would be eliminated in five years. Northern newspapers attacked her for opposing the bill, but her husband the governor ordered 10,000 copies of her speech and declared he was the "chestiest man in Alabama—prouder than ever of my appointment and appointee."[90] The speech also prompted a write-in campaign by Alabama voters who wanted her to run in the special election to fill out the remainder of Black's term. She declined.

During her brief five months in the Senate, Graves was assigned a seat at the rear of the chamber known as the "Cherokee Strip." The nickname came from the fact that there were 76 Democratic senators in 1937 and some had to be seated on the Republican side, where they were said to be "off their reservation." Her remote seating assignment prompted her to say, "I'm supposed to be seen, perhaps, but certainly not heard."[91]

While in office, Graves served on the Committee on Claims, the Committee on Education and Labor, and the Committee on Mines and Mining. She racked up a nearly perfect attendance record during her five months. On her final day in office, Graves made a moving speech praising her Senate colleagues— particularly the only other woman senator at the time, Sen. Hattie Carraway (D-Ark.). "I am grateful indeed, to my fellow woman Senator, a woman who, though she first came to the Senate by appointment, yet has made such a name for herself and for womanhood that her own people have honored her with election to this great office. I do devoutly hope that in time to come their example will be followed in other states."[92] Sen. Alben Barkley, the Democratic leader who would later serve as vice president under Truman, said of Graves,

"No Senator who has come into this body by appointment in recent years has made quite so good an impression."[93]

After leaving the Senate, Graves remained active in civic affairs. She worked for the USO, the American Red Cross, and spearheaded a statewide recruitment drive for the Women's Army Auxiliary Corps (WAAC). She also served as state adviser to the National Foundation for Infantile Paralysis, for which she frequently traveled to Washington, sometimes as the guest of President and Mrs. Harry Truman.

EDITH GREEN (D-Ore.)
(Jan. 17, 1910–April 21, 1987)
House: Jan. 3, 1955, to Jan. 3, 1975

Edith Green, nicknamed Mrs. Education, left her mark on nearly every schooling bill enacted during her 20 years on Capitol Hill. A member of the Education and Labor Committee—she eventually rose to the second-ranking Democratic position on that panel—she pushed for passage of the historic 1963 Higher Education Facilities Act. Described by President Johnson as the "greatest step forward" in education in 100 years, the act paid for the construction of classrooms, libraries, and laboratories at colleges and universities.[94] The very first bill Green ever introduced in the House became law in 1956 and provided $7.5 million in federal funds to help states improve their library services in rural areas. Two years later, she fought for passage of the National Defense Education Act, aimed at improving American learning of science and math. And in 1965, Green wrote and helped pass the Higher Education Act, which for the first time established a federal financial aid program for undergraduate students.

Along with her tireless work in the field of education, Green also fought for equal rights for the sexes. In 1970, as chair of the Special Subcommittee on Education, Green launched the first hearings ever on discrimination against women in education. Although Green tried to convince her male colleagues for months, she could not win enough votes on her subcommittee to pass a bill banning sexual discrimination in education. "If this passes, you are going to have male stewards on airplanes," one of her fellow congressmen argued. But Green's relentless efforts eventually brought her proposal—known as Title IX—to the

House floor where it was passed into law in 1972. "I was really in seventh heaven. I went back to my office; I don't know when I have ever been so pleased, because I had worked so long and it had been such a tough battle," Green said.[95]

Ten years earlier, Green tried to get her Education and Labor Committee to take up equal pay legislation. Green targeted committee member Phil Landrum (D-Ga.), pretending to seek his support for a bill that would raise the salaries of male lawmakers over their female counterparts. "Of course I won't do it," Landrum told her. "You know that you women have to work harder than men do." Green replied, "Phil, I'm so glad to hear you say that because I've got a bill that's been before your ad hoc committee now for several years that requires equal pay for equal work. Would you have hearings on it?" He accepted her ploy with good nature, but ignored her request.[96] Eventually, hearings were held on the bill, which was signed into law in 1963 as the Equal Pay Act.

Green, however, was the only woman in the House to vote against an amendment adding "sex" to the Civil Rights Act of 1964. The amendment was aimed at preventing discrimination against women as well as racial minorities, but Green, a strong advocate of civil rights, feared it would kill the entire bill. The amendment passed without her support and the Civil Rights Act went on to victory.

Although Green was viewed as a liberal when she first came to office, she grew more conservative through the years and eventually alienated herself from many of her Democratic colleagues. In 1971, Green sided with President Nixon and opposed forced busing to racially integrate school children. "I don't think the evidence supports the conclusions that if we just mix youngsters so that there are so many blacks and so many whites in a schoolroom that they will get a better education," she said.[97] She also joined a coalition of southern Democrats and Republicans in passing an amendment that barred the Department of Health, Education and Welfare from denying funds to southern schools that refused to integrate their students. Green again bucked her leadership in 1965 when she joined just five other House members to vote against President Johnson's request to increase military funding for the Vietnam War.

Earlier in her career, Green was a favorite among Democratic presidential hopefuls. At the 1956 Democratic National Convention, Green seconded the presidential nomination of Adlai Stevenson and four years later gave the seconding speech for John Kennedy. She had managed Kennedy's surprise victory in the Oregon primary that year. After his inauguration, Kennedy offered to make Green the ambassador to Canada, but she declined. Instead he named her to his Presidential Committee on the Status of Women. Oddly, Green's drift from the Democratic party reached its peak in 1976, after she had left the House, when she became co-chair of National Democrats for Gerald Ford during his presidential campaign.

Before entering politics, Green worked for 10 years as a school teacher and later served for three years as legislative chair of the board of the Oregon Congress of Parents and Teachers. After retiring from Congress in 1974, Green returned to her educational roots and taught at Warner Pacific College. In 1979, she was appointed to the Oregon Board of Higher Education.

ENID GREENE (R-Utah)
(Oct. 5, 1958–   )
House: Jan. 4, 1995, to Jan. 7, 1997

Enid Greene came to Congress a rising star, but her political career quickly plummeted after her husband was caught in a $4-million check-kiting scheme.

Greene—the former national chair of the Young Republicans and deputy chief of staff to Utah's governor—first ran for the House in 1992 but lost to Democrat Karen Shepherd. Two years later, after getting married and taking her husband's name, Waldholtz, she launched a rematch against Shepherd and won. She campaigned extensively on the GOP's "Contract with America," advocating a balanced budget and pledging to serve no more than 12 years in the House. She also drafted her own congressional reform package, including calls to abolish franked mail, end congressional pensions, cut staff, and roll back lawmakers' salaries.

Once arriving on Capitol Hill, Greene was singled out by the House Republican leadership and given a presitigious seat on the Rules Committee, which oversees all legislation that comes to the House floor. She was the first freshman named to that powerful committee in 80 years.

Greene also gained prominence when she had a child during her first year in office, only the second woman in history to give birth while serving in Congress.

But Greene soon ran into major personal and political problems when her campaign committee and husband, Joe Waldholtz, came under investigation for financial improprieties. During the fall of 1995, it was discovered that Waldholtz, who also served as his wife's campaign manager, had embezzled $4 million from his wealthy father-in-law and illegally funneled much of it into his wife's congressional campaign while spending the rest. He was also charged with filing fradulent income tax returns, financial disclosure forms, and federal election reports. He was later indicted on 27 counts of bank fraud and pled guilty to other lesser charges. He was sentenced to three years in jail in 1996.

The congresswoman distanced herself from her husband as the scandal began to emerge and divorced him on the day he entered his guilty plea. She announced she would not seek a second term and changed back to her maiden name Greene. She also held a daylong tearful press conference during which she denied knowing about any of the wrongdoing by her husband.

In November 1996, just days before the elections, the Justice Department cleared Greene of any wrongdoing. After the Justice Department's announcement, Greene said she may again run for office in the future.

ISABELLA GREENWAY (D-Ariz.)
(March 22, 1886–Dec. 18, 1953)
House: Oct. 3, 1933, to Jan. 3, 1937

The voters of Arizona were suffering from massive unemployment and poverty when they sent Isabella Greenway to Congress in 1933. She didn't let them down. Within 10 days of her election, Greenway was in the office of Harold Ickes, Secretary of the Interior and the head of the Public Works Administration, asking for financial help to create jobs back home. The meeting typified Greenway's charm and determination "in the tradition of those women who once moved kingdoms," as one of her contemporaries wrote. Greenway is said to have entered Ickes's office only to find him tired and work weary. "I hate to talk to a man just before he has lunch," she said as she pulled an apple out of her bag. She then sent his assistant out to buy a bottle of milk. "Now we can talk," she said as she poured him a glass. Ickes asked her to compress her demands into one page. "Arizona would never forgive me if I could get all it wanted onto one page," she smiled.[98] By the time she left Ickes, she had secured $14 million for an irrigation project that would put 3,000 men to work for three years. She also arranged for flood control construction at Nogales and a post office building in Pheonix that would employ another 6,000 people.

Greenway had long worked on behalf of Arizona residents. Before coming to Congress, Greenway opened a center in Tucson where 80,000 World War I veterans were taught the woodcrafting trade. When they made more things than tourists could buy, she built the Arizona Inn resort, furnishing it with the veterans' crafts, which she also sold to the hotel's guests.

Greenway first became involved in politics in 1928 when she was elected to the Democratic National Committee, largely as a tribute to her late husband, a former Rough Rider and a local copper magnate. But Greenway turned the position into a full-time job and traveled across the state campaigning for Democratic candidates. She worked tirelessly for her friend Franklin Roosevelt and seconded his nomination for president before the Democratic National Convention. Greenway had become close friends with the future First Lady Eleanor Roosevelt when the two attended Miss Chapin's school in New York. She later served as a bridesmaid at the Roosevelts' wedding.

Observers credited Greenway's success in Congress to her friendship with the First Family, but she did not always walk lockstep with the administration. Greenway split with the President over the Economy Act of 1933, which cut veterans' pensions. After leaving Congress, Greenway also worked against President Roosevelt's bid for a third term and chaired the Arizona chapter of Democrats for Wendell Willkie, the Republican nominee, in 1940.

While in Congress, Greenway dedicated herself to helping the voters back home. When the Depression hit Arizona's main industry of copper mining, Greenway won a $1-million federal loan to raise chrysanthemums that would then be processed into an insecticide. This variety of flowers had until then been imported from Japan. With the loan, miners grew the chrysanthemums intead of digging for copper. Greenway also offered measures to transfer Veterans' Administration land to the Interior Department for the benefit of Yavapai Indians, protect land resources against soil erosion, improve public grazing lands, and use relief funds to build homes for the elderly. She continued to work on behalf of veterans by introducing bills to build additions to VA facilities in Tucson and Whipple, Ariz., and to help veterans who settled on homesteads.

Greenway declined to run for a third term in 1936, saying she wanted to spend more time with her family. She later served as national chair of the American Women's Volunteer Service during World War II and was active in international cultural exchange programs before she died in Tucson in 1953.

MARTHA GRIFFITHS (D-Mich.)
(Jan. 29, 1912–)
House: Jan. 3, 1955, to Jan. 3, 1975

Although Martha Griffiths is best known for her work for women's rights (she is known as the "Mother of the ERA"), she also fought hard for tax and welfare reform during her two decades in office. Early in her congressional career, Griffiths backed food stamp and urban renewal programs and introduced a bill to promote public library services in rural areas. In 1962, Griffiths became the first woman to serve on the presitigious Ways and Means Committee and proposed legislation to repeal the excise tax on cars, provide tax relief for single parents, and reduce Social Security taxes paid by low-income families. In conjunction with her efforts on tax reform, Griffiths introduced the first recycling bill in Congress in 1972, which she proposed should be financed by taxes that would come with the repeal of the oil depletion allowance. The bill was never acted on.

Griffiths also served on the Joint Economic Committee and chaired its subcommittee on fiscal policy. As chair, she launched a three-year sudy of the nation's welfare system. The study's findings led Griffith to introduce the 1974 Tax Credits and Allowances Act, designed to reorganize and improve national public assistance programs by providing per capita tax credits for moderate and low-income families. In 1970, Griffiths joined Sen. Edward Kennedy (D-Mass.) in pushing for a national health insurance program financed through payroll, self-employment, and unearned income taxes, as well as federal revenue.

Griffiths also worked hard to reform Social Security, which she called the "most unfair law that was ever drafted." Griffiths spoke out against the program's differing standards for men and women. "The drafters of the law really believed, in my opinion, that a woman's work was worth nothing, that a woman's work in the home was worth nothing." In 1967, she persuaded her colleagues to amend Social Security so that minor children could receive benefits from their working mothers who retired, died, or became disabled.[99]

Griffiths's biggest accomplishments on behalf of women's rights came with the Civil Rights Act and later the passage of the Equal Rights Amendment. In 1964, as the House Judiciary Committee began deliberating civil rights legislation to prevent racial discrimination, Griffiths decided that sex must be added to the bill. She did not testify at the committee hearings because she feared the publicity would spark enough opposition to kill her plans. She instead resolved to offer an amendment on the floor protecting women from discrimination. Ironically, Rep. Howard Smith (D-Va.)—a conservative southerner—also decided to offer a sexual protection amendment on the floor in hopes of actually killing the overall Civil Rights Act.

"Judge Smith was chairman of the Rules Committee and leader of the conservative bloc, who would, if they could, have killed the bill. I realized that Mr. Smith would get more than a hundred votes just because he offered the amendment. . . . Without saying anything to anyone, I decided to let him offer it, and use my powers of persuasion to get the rest of the votes," Griffiths said later. "I used Smith."[100]

When Smith offered the amendment on the floor there was uproarious laughter. Griffiths would later recount, "When I arose, I began by saying: 'I presume that if there had been any necessity to point out that women were a second-class sex, the laughter would have proved it.' There was no further laughter."[101] A strange coalition of women lawmakers and southern segregationists formed to push the amendment to victory. While those same southerners later voted against the broader civil rights bill, it was passed by the House and Senate and signed into law by President Johnson in 1964.

But Griffiths didn't let her fight end there. She kept a close eye on the Equal Employment Opportunity Commission created by the act to make sure it enforced the ban on sexual discrimination. Griffiths spoke angrily on the House floor when she discovered the commission was failing at its job, and she received letters from women across the country seeking advice on equal employment. One of the worst complaints sent to Griffiths came from a United Airlines stewardess who was fired after she announced she was getting married. When Griffiths wrote the personnel officer, he responded that this was a bona fide occupational requirement—that all stewardesses must be young, single, and attractive. Griffiths shot back, "What are you running, an airline or a whorehouse?"[102]

In 1970, Griffiths again proved pivotal in passing the Equal Rights Amendment. Griffiths first introduced the constitutional amendment in her second term and reintroduced it each succeeding Congress. After years of seeing the amendment linger without any action in the House Judiciary Committee, Griffiths decided to bypass the committee system and seek a discharge petition to bring the language directly to the House floor for a vote. A discharge petition requires the signatures of half the House—218 lawmakers. Griffiths went after those signatures with a vengeance. "I chased fellow congressmen ruthlessly. I'd even listen to roll call for the names of any who hadn't signed. Having spotted the face, I'd promptly corner him for his autograph."[103] She managed to gain the required number of signatures in 40 days. The House eventually went on to pass the ERA 350 to 15. The victory was short-lived, however. When the Senate voted to amend the ERA to exempt women from the draft, the House and Senate were unable to resolve their differences before the Congress adjourned for the year. Griffiths launched her second push for the ERA in 1971. The House passed it again, and in 1972 the Senate gave its approval without changing the original language. The ERA, however, has yet to receive ratification by the states.

Griffiths grew up in a family of strong women. Griffiths's grandmother dared to enter the traditionally male field of tailoring following her husband's death and used the income to raise three children on her own. Griffiths's mother is believed to have been the first female rural mail carrier in America, and Griffiths herself was the only woman in her law school class at the University of Michigan.

Griffiths was admited to the bar in 1941 and joined the legal department of the American Automobile Insurance Company. She later became a contract negotiator for the Army where she worked until 1946 when she opened her own law practice. Later that year, she ran for the state House of Representatives but lost. She ran again in 1948, and this time won the seat, which she held until 1952. In 1953, she became the first woman judge of the Detroit Recorder's Court.

Griffiths ran for the U.S. House in 1952. She won the primary over three rivals, but lost the general election. In 1954, after campaigning out of a house trailer and traveling extensively across the district, she ousted the same Republican who defeated her two years earlier.

In 1982, eight years after retiring from Congress and at the age of 70, Griffiths became the first woman elected lieutenant governor of Michigan. She was re-elected to that post in 1986, but four years later Gov. James Blanchard tried to drop Griffiths as his running mate because of her age. Griffiths refused to go quietly and after launching a public campaign she stayed on the ticket. The two, however, ended up losing their bid for a third term.

KATIE HALL (D-Ind.)
(April 3, 1938–   )
House: Nov. 29, 1982, to Jan. 3, 1985

Katie Hall's brief congressional career was distinguished by her successful efforts to establish a federal holiday honoring the birthday of civil rights leader Dr. Martin Luther King, Jr. The holiday had been hotly debated for 15 years before Hall came to Congress, but the timing was finally right in 1983 when Hall introduced her own bill creating the holiday. Congressional leaders named Hall floor manager of the bill and she won praise for her cool handling of the often acrimonious debate.

Hall—the first black elected to Congress from Indiana—had fine-tuned her political acumen during her eight years in the Indiana state House and Senate. She had also served as the chair of the Lake County Democratic Committee. While in the state legislature, the former social studies teacher concentrated on education as well as labor and women's issues. She pushed through a bill clarifying Indiana's divorce laws by defining marital property and devoted much of her time calling for ratification of the Equal Rights Amendment—which the state finally did in 1977.

When U.S. Rep. Adam Benjamin (D) died of a heart attack in 1982, the local Democratic leader—Gary, Ind., Mayor Richard Hatcher—selected Hall to run for the open seat. Hall had previously worked with Hatcher as a campaign aide. But many local white Democrats opposed the selection of Hall and instead wanted Benjamin's widow to run. They even filed a lawsuit to try to block Hall's designation as the Democratic nominee. Hall, however, went on to win the special election to fill out the remainder of Benjamin's term as well as the next full term.

Once in Congress, Hall was assigned to the Committee on Post Office and Civil Service and the Committee on Public Works and Transportation. She supported a variety of bills aimed at creating jobs back home and fixing many of the social problems caused by the high unemployment in her district. She backed the Fair Trade in Steel Act—which was intended to revitalize the steel industry—and the Humphrey-Hawkins bill for full employment. She also focused on bills to prevent child abuse and family violence.

When Hall ran for re-election in 1984, she found herself caught in a bitter Democratic primary. She faced two challengers, including a former aide to the late Benjamin. Both challengers attacked Hall for her close ties to Hatcher, but Hall felt she was really being attacked because of her race. "If I wasn't black and female, there wouldn't be a contest," Hall said. "I have an excellent record, and under other circumstances I wouldn't have an opponent."[104]

Hall lost the Democratic nomination, but tried again in 1986 and 1990 to come back to Congress. She failed both times. After leaving Congress, she served as vice chair of the Gary Housing Board of Commissioners and was elected as the city clerk of Gary.

JULIA BUTLER HANSEN (D-Wash.)
(June 14, 1907–May 3, 1988)
House: Nov. 8, 1960, to Dec. 31, 1974

When Julia Butler Hansen retired from Congress in 1974, she complained that she was tired of being "pursued by an endless string of people who want everything from post offices to gasoline." She also declared that she "had never considered that politics was really a career."[105] But, in fact, Hansen had made a lifelong career of politics. She served for 21 years in the state legislature before she was elected to the U.S. House of Representatives in 1960 to fill the seat left open by the death of Rep. Russell Mack (R-Wash.). Even after leaving Congress 14 years later, Hansen remained active in civic life. She served from 1975 to 1981 on the Washington State Toll Bridge Authority and State Highway Commission and chaired the Washington State Transportation Commission.

Hansen began her career in politics in 1938 when she was elected to the Cathlamet, Wash., city council. In 1939, Hansen won a seat in the state legislature and over the next 21 years would go on to chair several panels including the Education Committee, the Roads and Bridges Committee, and the Highways Committee. She sponsored bills calling for higher wages for teachers, school lunch programs, nursery schools, improved state highways, and for the creation of the state highway commission. During her last five years in the state House, Hansen served as the speaker pro tempore.

When Hansen was elected to the U.S. Congress in 1960, she was appointed to the Veterans' Affairs Committee, the Education and Labor Committee, and the Interior and Insular Affairs Committee. In 1963, however, she gave up all those posts to take a seat on the exclusive Appropriations Committee—only the second woman in history to serve on that panel. Four years later, Hansen became chair of the Appropriations subcommittee on the Interior and Related Agencies—the first woman in history to chair an Appropriations subcommittee. [It would take almost 30 more years until another woman would reach that milestone. In 1995, Rep. Barbara Vucanovich (R-Nev.) became chair of the Appropriations subcommittee on Military Construction.]

Hansen recalled the trouble she had getting the subcommittee chairmanship. "I had a little struggle to get it. The [full committee] chairman was running around and asking the members if I would be a good chairman. . . . And finally, one day I pounced on him and I said, 'Mr. Chairman, have you ever run around and asked the members of the committee if a man would make a good chairman?' He looked kind of sheepish," Hansen said. "No, no, you don't get on the Approriations Committee if you are a woman very easily."[106]

During her 14 years in Congress, Hansen introduced bills creating a national traffic safety agency and an independent Federal Maritime Administration. She was generally considered liberal in her voting record, supporting the Civil Rights Act of 1964, the Voting Rights Act of 1965, and the Equal Rights Amendment in 1972.

In her final term in Congress, Hansen was named chair of the Democratic Committee on Organization, Study and Review, which was responsible for recommending changes to House procedures and the committee system. Hansen's committee drafted a package of reforms that the House approved by a vote of 203 to 165 in October 1974. Although Hansen's reform package was considered much milder than several other proposals that were voted down, it did impose a number of major changes, including a ban on proxy voting in committee, an increase in the power of the Speaker to refer bills to committee, and a requirement that the House organize itself in December before the start of a new session in January. It was the first overhaul of House procedures since 1946.

BOOK BY HANSEN

Singing Paddles (n.d.)

CECIL HARDEN (R-Ind.)
(Nov. 21, 1894– Dec. 5, 1984)
House: Jan. 3, 1949, to Jan. 3, 1959

Cecil Harden's ten years in the House were relatively uneventful. She introduced few bills of national importance, but instead focused on helping the voters back home in Indiana. She promoted flood control for the Wabash Valley and secured funding for a local dam and recreational center. In 1956, she attacked the Defense Department's plans to close the Atomic Energy Commission's heavy water plant in her district, saying that it would put 900 people out of work. She generally stuck to the Republican party line, speaking out against big government and "left-wing extremists." She was also friendly to business interests. As chair of the subcommittee on intergovernment relations she conducted a study of government-run businesses and concluded they were a "real threat to private enterprise."[107] Her investigation showed that the federal government had dozens of commercial and industrial ventures ranging from the manufacturing of sleeping bags to coffee roasting.

As a member of the Committee on Expenditures in Executive Departments, she toured military supply installations in the United States and Asia to study ways of improving the armed forces' procurement procedures. She also sat on the Government Operations Committee and the Committee on Post Office and Civil Service.

Harden first became involved in Republican politics when her husband lost his presidential appointment as a local postmaster following the Democratic victory of 1932. That year she became a GOP precinct vice chair and in 1938 moved up to become chair of the Fountain County Republican party. She was later elected a Republican National Committeewoman and was a delegate to four Republican national conventions. In her first run for the U.S. House in 1948, she defeated the Democratic nominee by just 483 votes. She went on to win her next four elections, but was finally defeated in 1958 when a Democratic sweep ousted a total of 47 Republicans from the House. Two months after leaving Congress, Harden was appointed special assistant for women's affairs to the Postmaster General's office. In 1970, when Harden was 76, President Nixon appointed her to the National Advisory Committee for the White House Conference on Aging.

JANE HARMAN (D-Calif.)
(June 28, 1945–   )
House: Jan. 5, 1993, to Jan. 6, 1999

Despite her extensive political experience before coming to Capitol Hill, Jane Harman continually faced tough battles during her three successful bids for congressional office. In her 1994 race for a second term, Harman was originally declared the loser. But weeks later, after absentee ballots were counted, Harman squeaked through to victory by just 812 votes.

Harman entered the world of politics at a young age, attending her first Democratic convention in 1960 at the tender age of 16. A few years later she worked on the staff of former Sen. John Tunney (D-Calif.) and eventually became chief counsel and staff director of the Senate Judiciary subcommittee on constitutional rights. During the Carter administration, she served as a deputy secretary to the Cabinet.

In 1984, Harman served as counsel to the Democratic Convention's platform committee; in 1987 she co-chaired a $2.2 million Democratic Party fund-raiser; and from 1986 to 1990 she chaired the National Lawyers' Council, a legal network for the Democratic party.

But with all her political experience, Harman had never run for elective office until 1992. The California district she ran in was split evenly between Democratic and Republican voters and Harman was considered the underdog against a Republican female candidate. Harman eventually won the race, campaigning as a social liberal and fiscal conservative.

Harman maintained that political reputation throughout her three terms in the House. A strong supporter of abortion rights and gun control, Harman also worked against plans to segregate the sexes in the military and opposed moves to automatically discharge all HIV-infected personnel from the military.

Although Harman voted for Clinton's deficit reduction budget plan in 1993, she opposed him on the North American Free Trade Agreement a year later. Harman also stood with conservatives in backing a constitutional balanced budget amendment and pushing for cuts in the budget. She was resolutely pro-defense, largely because of the large defense industry in her district. Harman repeatedly pushed for increased spending on such big-ticket defense items as B-2 bombers. The radars for the bombers were built in Harman's district.

Harman used her seat on the National Security Committee—one of only three women on the panel—to look out for the defense interests in her district. But while Harman worked on behalf of these companies, she also pushed for tax incentives to encourage defense companies to convert their operations to peacetime uses. During her time in the House, Harman also served on the Science Committee and the Select Committee on Intelligence.

In 1998, Harman announced her retirement from Congress to run for the Democratic nomination for governor of California. After spending $20 million in the campaign—much of it from her own pocket—she came in third in the Democratic primary.

PAULA HAWKINS (R-Fla.)
(Jan. 24, 1927–   )
Senate: Jan. 1, 1981, to Jan. 3, 1987

During her one term in the Senate, Paula Hawkins gained national attention when she bravely revealed that she had been a victim of sexual abuse as a child. Hawkins made child abuse the focus of her legislative agenda and her revelation gained congressional support for her initiatives to combat the problem. In the Senate, Hawkins initiated a yearlong investigation of the problem of missing children, which eventually led to passage of the Missing Children's Act of 1982 and the creation of a central information center for missing children. She sponsored other legislation to help in the search for missing children and provide federal guidelines for the prevention of abuse in child-care centers.

Hawkins first became involved in politics in the 1960s as a community activist to improve public utilities. She also worked with the local Republican party. In 1966, she organized the successful House bid of Edward Gurney and served as the Florida co-chair of Richard Nixon's presidential campaigns in 1968 and 1972. Hawkins won her first elective office in 1972 on the state Public Services Commission. During her two terms on the commission, she earned a reputation as a consumer-rights advocate and opponent of rate increases by utility companies. She resigned from the commission in 1979 to become vice president for consumer affairs for Air Florida.

While serving on the Public Services Commission, Hawkins ran two unsuccessful bids for higher office—the U.S. Senate in 1974 and lieutenant governor in 1976. She again ran for Senate in 1980 and this time was helped by the landslide presidential victory of Ronald Reagan and the GOP sweep that wrested control of the Senate from the Democrats.

"It's a tremendous advantage being a woman in government," Hawkins said. "Most of us still stay in touch with reality. I go [to] buy groceries at midnight. Most people in Washington are so isolated by their staffs [that] they are isolated from the world. You need to rub shoulders with the people."[108]

Hawkins was assigned to the Committee on Agriculture, Nutrition, and Forestry and the Committee on Labor and Human Resources, where she chaired the subcommittee on investigation and oversight. She also served on the Banking, Housing, and Urban Affairs Committee, the Committee on Foreign Relations, the Joint Economic Committee, and the Special Committee on Aging.

Hawkins was generally supportive of the Reagan administration in foreign policy and economic matters. She backed cuts in social spending, but supported funds for programs for the elderly.

Long concerned about drug abuse and its link to social problems, Hawkins was instrumental in the passage of legislation creating federal programs for the prevention and treatment of substance abuse in women and she sponsored bills making drug-related murder a federal offense.

Hawkins called herself "feminine" rather than a "feminist," and opposed federal funding for abortions and the Equal Rights Amendment. "As women, we're all for equality—or superiority," she said. "But there are better ways to attack problems which have come to be known as women's issues. Elect more women to the United States Senate. It's women's fault for not running for office."[109]

Hawkins lost her bid for a second term in 1986, when the Democrats regained control of the Senate. After leaving the Senate, Hawkins served for seven years representing the United States on the Organization of American States Inter-American Drug Abuse Commission. In 1997, Hawkins joined the board of directors for Nu Skin Asia-Pacific, Inc., a marketer of personal care products.

MARGARET HECKLER (R-Mass.)
(June 21, 1931–   )
House: Jan. 3, 1967, to Jan. 3, 1983

Margaret Heckler started off her congressional career without the backing of her own Republican party. She ignored the pleas of party leaders in 1966 and decided to challenge 21-term representative and former House Speaker Joseph Martin for the GOP nomination. She narrowly won the primary against the 84-year-old incumbent and then faced an equally difficult race in the general election. Top Democratic names—including Vice President Hubert Humphrey and Robert and Edward Kennedy—came out to campaign for Heckler's opponent. In the end, Heckler won the House seat, largely with the help of women voters who had supported her during her earlier elections to the Massachusetts Governor's Council.

Heckler first became involved in politics while she was still in college. In her sophomore year she won her first election as a member of the student government at Albertus Magnus College in Connecticut. She later became the first woman to be elected Speaker of the Connecticut Intercollegiate Student Legislature. In 1953, Heckler enrolled in the Boston College Law School as the only woman in her class. She became editor of the law review and founded the school's Young Republican Club. From 1958 until her election to Congress, she was a member of the Republican town committee of Wellesley, Mass. In 1962, she won a seat on the Massachusetts Governor's Council, an advisory group to the state's top executive.

Because Heckler won her House seat without the support of her own party, she was free to buck GOP leaders, and often did throughout her congressional career. She was considered a "liberal" Republican and often crossed party lines. She was an early opponent of the Vietnam War and voted against two of President Nixon's pet projects—the anti-ballistic missile system and the supersonic transport plane. Heckler also bumped heads with Nixon in 1971 when he vetoed her comprehensive child-care bill. But a year later, Heckler created a firestorm during the Republican National Convention when she demanded that federally funded day care be included in the party platform.

In her first year in office, Heckler was assigned to the Committee on Government Operations and the Veterans Affairs Committee, where she eventually rose to become the second-ranking Republican. On that panel, Heckler pushed for counseling for Vietnam War veterans and supported the creation of aging centers in Veterans Administration hospitals. Heckler also helped uncover the widespread problem of defective body armor being shipped to U.S. troops in Vietnam. Although the Defense Department balked at her complaints and said "defective armor is bettern than no armor at all," Heckler eventually forced the Pentagon to improve its specifications and testing of body armor.[110] An opponent of the Vietnam War, Heckler also supported the publication of the *Pentagon Papers*, saying the public had the right to know what the government does.

Throughout her career, Heckler served on a variety of committees—Banking and Currency, Agriculture, Science and Technology, Ethics, and the Joint Economic Committee. She was a strong supporter of women's rights, backing the Equal Rights Amendment and the subsequent extension for its ratification deadline. She drafted the Equal Credit Opportunity Act of 1974 with Rep. Ed Koch (D-N.Y.), which granted equal credit access regardless of race, sex, or marital status. She sponsored bills that would secure the pensions of working women on maternity leave, set up a national center for the prevention of rape, and provide shelters for victims of domestic violence. In 1977, she joined Rep. Elizabeth Holtzman (D-N.Y.) to create the Congressional Caucus for Women's Issues. "Women are the one minority group it is still considered fashionable to discriminate against," she once said.[111]

Heckler's congressional career ended in 1982 when her district was redrawn and she was forced to run against Rep. Barney Frank (D). Although Heckler often opposed her Republican leadership—she backed just 40 percent of the proposals President Reagan put before Congress—Frank successfully attacked her for her support of Reagan's budget and economic plan of 1981.

After her defeat, Reagan nominated Heckler as Secretary of the Department of Health and Human Services. During her two years at the department, she established new guidelines for the Social Security disability program and increased research and care for patients with Alzheimer's and AIDS. But Heckler's time at HHS was tumultuous as she often battled with other, more conservative Reagan appointees.

In 1985, Reagan appointed Heckler ambassador to Ireland, where she served until 1989. She now practices law in Arlington, Va.

LOUISE HICKS (D-Mass.)
(Oct. 16, 1923–   )
House: Jan. 3, 1971, to Jan. 3, 1973

Louise Hicks' brief stay in Congress belies the intense controversy she sparked in Massachusetts and across the nation with her strong opposition to busing to integrate schools. Before coming to Congress, Hicks served for nearly a decade on the Boston School Committee and the Boston City Council, where she continually battled with the NAACP and other civil rights groups that favored busing.

"I know I've been called . . . a bigot and anti-Negro," Hicks said. "But I haven't said 'no' to the Negroes. I have said 'no' to civil rights leaders using children as pawns in the national struggle. Civil rights infiltrators are not interested in good education for the children of Boston."[112]

Hicks believed that integration should come "naturally" and not be forced. During her three terms on the school committee from 1961 to 1967, Hicks repeatedly assaulted the Supreme Court's school desegregation order. In 1965, as chair of the committee, she vetoed a locally sponsored busing proposal—defying a state law that required schools to establish anti-segregation plans or lose state funds. Her move cost Boston schools $6.3 million, but her stance won her widespread support from conservative white voters. She lost a bid for state treasurer in 1964 but easily won a third term on the committee in 1965.

In 1967, Hicks ran for mayor using the slogan "You know where I stand." She lost the race to liberal Secretary of State Kevin White who had the backing of Democratic Sen. Ted Kennedy and Republican Gov. John Volpe. After losing the race, Hicks returned to elective office in 1969 when she won a seat on the Boston City Council. A year later, when U.S. House Speaker John McCormack announced his retirement Hicks ran for and won the open seat on a law-and-order platform.

Once in Congress. Hicks was generally liberal on domestic issues and conservative on racial and military policies. Her stance on the Vietnam

War was mixed. Although she supported the invasion of Cambodia, she called for the "orderly withdrawal" from Vietnam, saying the money could be better spent on the inner cities. She was assigned to the Education and Labor Committee and the Committee on Veterans' Affairs. Hicks focused on educational issues and proposed a system of tax credits for parents of children in private schools. She continued to oppose school busing and tried to ban it on a federal level. She also pushed to allow voluntary prayer in public schools. On other issues she supported increased benefits for disabled veterans, a 50-percent hike in Social Security benefits, and a cut in mass transit fares for seniors.

Less than six months after being sworn into office, Hicks challenged White to a rematch for mayor. Hick's congressional district was set to be redrawn, and many critics charged that she was more interested in holding onto political office than with returning to Boston. Hicks launched a grass-roots campaign for mayor, vowing to overhaul the state's tough desegregation laws. In the end, White beat her by more than 40,000 votes. She also lost her bid for re-election to the House in her redrawn district. But less than a year later, Hicks was overwhelmingly elected back to the Boston City Council.

Before entering politics, Hicks was a first grade teacher. Later, after marrying and having children, Hicks enrolled in Boston University and earned a bachelor's degree in education. She went on to earn a law degree in 1958 and opened a law office with her brother.

MARJORIE HOLT (R-Md.)
(Sept. 17, 1920–   )
House: Jan. 3, 1973, to Jan. 3, 1987

Marjorie Holt was a strong conservative who spent much of her seven terms in Congress pushing for increased defense spending and improved benefits for military personnel. She also opposed many women's rights bills and fought against school busing.

Much of Holt's conservative ideology came from her southern roots. Born in Alabama, she graduated from the University of Florida College of Law. After practicing in Florida, she moved to Maryland in the 1960s and continued to work as a lawyer. She served for two years as a supervisor of elections and from 1966 to 1972 she worked as clerk of the Anne Arundel County Circuit Court. At the same time, she became active in GOP politics as a precinct leader and local campaign organizer. She served as counsel for the Maryland State Federation of Republican Women and in 1968 was the state co-chair of the Nixon-Agnew presidential ticket. Vice President Spiro Agnew—a former governor of Maryland—repaid Holt for her support by campaigning for her four years later when she ran for Congress. Her victory in the race was much helped by Nixon's landslide victory in the district.

Once in office, Holt followed up on her campaign theme of reducing nonmilitary spending. In 1978, she offered a Republican substitute budget proposal and, although the effort failed, it became a standard party strategy in the future. Holt served on the Budget Committee and the Armed Services Committee, where she supported development of the MX missile and the B-1 bomber. "The most important responsibility of federal government is national defense," Holt said. "The peace of the world depends absolutely on American military strength."[113]

In her very first term in office, Holt gained national attention when she tried to amend a supplemental spending bill to stop a Health, Education and Welfare Department probe into discrimination charges against a school in her district. If passed, the amendment would have prevented the department from enforcing integration requirements in all schools. Although the amendment passed the House, it failed in the Senate.

Holt, overall, was opposed to government intervention into state affairs—including busing, abortion, and sex integration in physical education classes. "Things usually get fouled up when the Feds get in," she said.[114] Holt was strongly anti-abortion and supported constitutional amendments that would have given human rights to fetuses and returned state control over abortion laws. She also voted to ban the use of federal funds for abortions.

Holt was strongly opposed by most women's groups, and once called a woman lobbyist an "unnatural mother" because she wasn't at home with her preschool child.[115] Holt did, however, support the Equal Credit Opportunity Act—which prohibited banks from discriminating against women when it came to loans—and voted to increase the availability and scope of insurance coverage for women. Holt also said that she helped pave the way for other local female candidates. "I think that just by being in the House of Representatives, I fight for women. Instead of getting in there and fighting for abortions for everyone, I work hard to represent my district. This gives other women the courage to run and shows that women can do the job."[116]

Holt declined to run for re-election in 1986 and returned to her law practice in Baltimore.

ELIZABETH HOLTZMAN (D-N.Y.)
(Aug. 11, 1941–   )
House: Jan. 3, 1973, to Jan. 3, 1981

Elizabeth Holtzman was a virtual unknown when she shocked politicos and defeated 84-year-old Emanuel Celler in the Democratic primary. She was dubbed "Liz the Lion" by *Time* magazine for toppling the 25-term Celler who had chaired the Judiciary Committee for 22 years. At the age of 31, Holtzman also became the youngest woman ever elected to Congress. Unlike Celler—who had a well-entrenched political machine and financial backing—Holtzman had little money and was forced to run a grass-roots campaign. She used an army of unpaid volunteers to hand out leaflets and spoke to small community groups. "Thank God for the *Godfather*," said Holtzman, who spoke and handed out campaign literature to moviegoers as they waited outside in huge lines to see the blockbuster film.[117] During the campaign, Holtzman criticized Celler for not spending enough time back in the Brooklyn district and for his support of the Vietnam War. Holtzman also attacked his opposition to the Equal Rights Amendment, which he had kept bottled up in his Judiciary Committee for 20 years. In the end, Holtzman won the Democratic nomination by just 600 votes. She then sailed to a lopsided victory in the general election.

Holtzman did not have extensive political experience before coming to Congress. A 1965 graduate of Harvard Law School, she worked with the civil rights movement in Georgia before returning to New York City, where she practiced law and worked as an assistant to Mayor John Lindsay for two years. She then became involved in party politics as a Democratic state committee member and a district leader for several years.

Once in Congress, Holtzman filled the vacancy left on the Judiciary Committee by Cellar's departure. On that committee she participated in the Watergate impeachment hearings against President Richard Nixon. She also later served on the Budget Committee. Holtzman made her mark early as a freshman when she led a move to block implementation of new federal rules of evidence promulgated by the Supreme Court. She also made headlines when she sued in a federal court to stop the bombing of Cambodia on the grounds that it had not been authorized by

Congress. She won her case in a district court that ruled the Cambodian invasion was unconstitutional, but her victory was later overturned by an appeals court. She pressed an appeal to the Supreme Court, but it refused to hear her case.

In 1977, Holtzman co-founded the Congressional Caucus for Women's Issues with Rep. Margaret Heckler (R-Mass.). The two persuaded 13 female colleagues from both parties to join the group. "[There was] a lot of hesitancy," Holtzman recalled. "Some women felt their constituents wouldn't understand working on women's issues. Some were very worried they would be embarrassed politically."[118] One of the group's first acts was to get an extension of the ratification deadline for the Equal Rights Amendment. Holtzman led the fight to pass a seven-year extension beyond the original 1979 deadline. In the end, however, Congress extended the deadline by just three-and-a-half years.

In 1980, Holtzman decided to run for the Senate but lost to Republican Alfonse D'Amato. She returned to New York and was elected district attorney of Brooklyn and served until 1989 when she was elected as the city's comptroller. In 1992, Holtzman decided to make a second bid for the Senate seat. This time she faced a bitter four-way primary election that included former congressional colleague Geraldine Ferraro. The race turned ugly as Holtzman launched attacks against Ferraro, accusing her of Mafia ties and ethics violations in the House. In the end, both women lost the primary and many felt Holtzman had effectively ended her political career. She now practices law in New York.

BOOK BY HOLTZMAN

Who Said It Would Be Easy? One Woman's Life in the Political Arena (1996)

NAN HONEYMAN (D-Ore.)
(July 15, 1881–Dec. 10, 1970)
House: Jan. 3, 1937, to Jan. 3, 1939

Nan Honeyman was a 55-year-old grandmother when she was elected to Congress. She ran on Roosevelt's New Deal platform and continued to fight for the president's initiatives after winning office. Her opponents, in fact, attacked her for blindly following Roosevelt's policies and ignoring her constituents' interests. When legislation crucial to the operation of the Bonneville Dam in her district was taken up by Congress, she stated that she had no opinion of her own and wanted only what Roosevelt wanted. Honeyman also snubbed the voters back home when they rose in opposition to Roosevelt's liberal Supreme Court nominees. She answered her constituents' protest mail with a form letter declaring her support for the president. The form letter sparked criticism—even from Democrats—that she was a "stencil for the White House duplicating machine."[119]

During her one term in office, Honeyman also spoke out in favor of a stronger national defense, proposed a federally sponsored national poetry award, and sought to have a street in the District of Columbia named Oregon Avenue. But Honeyman's unbending support for President Roosevelt cost her re-election in 1938, when only one Democrat in the state was elected to a major office. Even with the campaign help of Interior Secretary Harold Ickes, Honeyman lost the race to Republican Homer Angell. Honeyman tried to make a comeback in 1940 but again lost to Angell despite the active support of Eleanor Roosevelt. One year later, Honeyman was appointed to fill a vacancy in the state Senate, where she served for three months until she resigned to become senior representative of the Pacific Coast Office of Price Administration. In 1942, President Roosevelt appointed Honeyman collector of customs in Oregon, a post she held for 11 years.

Honeyman had extensive political experience before she won election to Congress. In 1933, she served as president of the state constitutional convention that ratified the 21st Amendment repealing Prohibition. Although Honeyman was a teetotaler herself, she opposed Prohibition because she "didn't believe that any law governing people's personal conduct should be a part of the Constitution."[120] From 1935 to 1937, she was a member of the Oregon House of Representatives and was a delegate to the Democratic National Conventions in 1936 and 1940.

DARLENE HOOLEY (D-Ore.)
(April 4, 1939–   )
House: Jan. 7, 1997, to present

Darlene Hooley first got involved in politics when her son fell off a playground swing and cut his head on the asphalt below. Hooley, a teacher, complained to the city council, but was told it was too expensive to remove the asphalt. That's when she decided to run for office.

In 1977, Hooley was elected to the West Linn City Council, where she served until 1981. She then won a seat in the Oregon House of Representatives, where she was instrumental in establishing Oregon's recycling laws and played a key role in reforming the state's welfare system. Six years later, Hooley was appointed to the Clackamas County Commission and oversaw a program that sought to counsel welfare recipients and reduce the number of people on public assistance.

Hooley won election to Congress in 1996 by defeating a freshman Republican incumbent. She became the third person in six years to be elected to the swing district.

As a member of Congress, Hooley has pledged to work to protect funding for early childhood education programs, such as Head Start. She supports abortion rights and environmental protection. In 1998, Hooley joined with environmentalists and demanded that the U.S. Forest Service do a more extensive environmental review before allowing a massive cutting and sale of timber in her district. She said the logging could clog streams and cause landslides.

But Hooley, well aware of the district's large timber and fishing industry, generally believes the federal government should set environmental standards but give local governments and industry the power to choose how to meet those standards.

On another local issue, Hooley joined with Oregon lawmakers in 1998 to oppose federal legislation that would overturn a state-passed "Death with Dignity" law that allows physicians to prescribe lethal doses of medication to terminally ill patients.

On fiscal issues, Hooley supports balancing the budget but opposes cutting taxes before doing so. She did, however, introduce legislation to simplify the process of tax filing.

Hooley serves on the Banking and Financial Services Committee and the Committee on Science.

JOAN KELLY HORN (D-Mo.)
(Oct. 18, 1936–   )
House: Jan. 3, 1991, to Jan. 3, 1993

Joan Kelly Horn came to Congress after defeating three-term Rep. Jack Buechner (R) by just 54 votes. During her campaign, she charged Buechner with using public office for personal gain and ran television ads showing images of pigs snorting in the mud. Horn, in contrast, pledged not to accept a congressional pay raise and never to travel at taxpayer expense—two pledges she kept during her one term in office. Her congressional bid was initially given no chance of winning, but her tough campaigning style led her to win her first bid for federal office.

Horn had learned her political expertise by heading a research and polling firm with her husband before running for Congress. Among her clients were House Democratic leader Richard Gephardt (Mo.). She began working with the Democratic party in the 1970s and went on to become a committeewoman of the Clayton Township (Mo.) in 1987.

After coming to Congress, Horn was appointed to the Public Works and Transportation Committee, the Science, Space and Technology Committee, and the Select Committee on Children, Youth, and Families. On the Public Works panel, Horn worked to bring home money for local projects such as the Metro-Link light-rail system, and she used the Science Committee to promote projects important to St. Louis businesses such as McDonnell Douglas.

Horn was generally liberal on social issues and more conservative on fiscal matters. She worked to kill the $40-billion Space Station and the superconductor-supercollider. She supported abortion rights and voted against the "gag rule" that prohibited doctors in government-funded clinics from giving advice about abortions. She backed the Brady gun control bill and supported requiring employers to give their workers unpaid leave for family emergencies. One of her first votes in the House was against granting President Bush permission to use force in the Persian Gulf to remove Iraqi President Saddam Hussein from Kuwait. She voted against the balanced budget constitutional amendment, even though she had promised during her campaign to support it. She defended her vote, charging that the final amendment language was changed from the original bill. "They made it loud and clear that they weren't going to balance the budget through defense and military cuts but through domestic programs," Horn said. "I didn't change. The amendment changed."[121]

But the vote was used against her by her GOP opponent during her bid for a second term. Her district had also been redrawn following the 1990 census making it more Republican. She was defeated for re-election by more than 8,000 votes. After leaving Congress, Horn headed a Defense Department task force on converting military industries into civilian projects. She later went to the Commerce Department to work as an undersecretary for technology. In 1996, she ran again for Congress but lost.

WINNIFRED MASON HUCK (R-Ill.)
(Sept. 14, 1882–Aug. 24, 1936)
House: Nov. 7, 1922, to March 3, 1923

Huck may have served just four months in Congress, but during her short tenure she spoke out on more issues and introduced more major pieces of legislation than many of her colleagues who served for years. She backed a constitutional amendment requiring a direct popular vote before the United States could enter any war overseas. In her very first speech on the House floor she declared, "In a country where the people control their government, there is no opportunity for a war to originate."[122]

Huck, the daughter of William E. Mason, who served for 16 years in the House and Senate, grew up in Washington, D.C., in the shadow of the Capitol. Just two weeks after the death of her father in 1921, Huck announced she would be a candidate for the remainder of his term as well as for the following two years. Despite being denied the endorsement of the Illinois Republican Women's Club, Huck narrowly won the unexpired term but lost the nomination for the next full term.

Huck—the first wife and mother to serve in Congress—inherited her distaste for war from her father, who during his congressional career attacked World War I as a "dollar war." After Huck came to Congress, she pledged to devote her legislative efforts "chiefly toward a constructive educational plan which will show the folly of war."[123] She offered legislation barring any U.S. trade with or financial concessions to nations that did not permit their citizens to participate in referendums on declarations of war. She also introduced a resolution declaring the Philippine Islands to be free and independent and fought for self-government for Cuba and Ireland.

Before the end of Huck's congressional career in 1923, she made an unsuccessful bid to fill the seat left open by the death of Rep. James Mann. She said her opponent defeated her only after he illegally spent well over the $5,000 limit on congressional campaigns, but she failed to get a House investigation into the matter. A year later, Huck lost another bid for the House, but continued to be active in politics and civil affairs after leaving office. She became the national chair of the Political Council of the Woman's Party, pushing for congressional passage of the Equal Rights Amendment. She vowed that if the amendment did not pass in 1924, "We shall endeavor to elect a large number of women to the next

Congress so that we shall have sufficient strength to pass the measure without further delay."[124] She also worked as an investigative reporter for the *Chicago Evening Post*, delving into the conditions of the criminal justice system and prison life. With the help of Ohio Gov. Vic Donahey, Huck took an assumed name, committed a theft, and was sentenced to six months in the state prison. After serving 30 days in jail, she was officially pardoned and began seeking various odd jobs throughout the Northeast and Midwest only to be fired after her employers found out about her "criminal past." Her series of articles and lectures relating her experiences created a sensation across the country.

MURIEL HUMPHREY (D-Minn.)
(Feb. 20, 1912–Sept. 20, 1998)
Senate: Feb. 6, 1978, to Nov. 7, 1978

Muriel Humphrey made the most of her brief 11 months in office, speaking out frequently on the Senate floor and introducing several pieces of legislation that were passed and signed into law. Humphrey was appointed by Gov. Rudy Perpich to the Senate after her husband Sen. (and former U.S. vice president under Lyndon Johnson) Hubert Humphrey died in office. She declined to run in the special election held several months later to fill out the remainder of her husband's term.

In her first speech as a senator, she urged ratification of the treaties turning over control of the Panama Canal to Panama and guaranteeing the canal's neutrality. She served on the Foreign Relations Committee and the Committee on Governmental Operations. On the Foreign Relations panel, she voted in favor of President Carter's proposal to sell jet fighter planes to Egypt, Israel, and Saudi Arabia. She was the sponsor of a successful amendment to the Civil Service Reform Act of 1978 to give better job security to federal employees who exposed fraud and waste. And she was co-sponsor of the joint resolution extending the ratification deadline of the Equal Rights Amendment. In September 1978, the Senate approved her amendment to the Department of Education Organization Act that changed the name of the Department of Health, Education, and Welfare to the Department of Health and Human Services.

Humphrey resigned from the Senate following the election of David Durenberger to serve out the remainder of her husband's term. Humphrey later remarried a man named Max Brown, who had been friends with Humphrey since high school. Humphrey stayed out of the public light after leaving the Senate, but in 1988, when President George Bush disparaged liberalism, Humphrey responded. "There's something I've been wanting to say for a long time. I'm a liberal and I'm proud of it. In fact, I was probably a little more liberal than Hubert was. I just wanted to say that."[125]

KAY BAILEY HUTCHISON (R-Texas)
(July 22, 1943–   )
Senate: June 14, 1993, to present

Kay Bailey Hutchison made history in 1993 when she won a special election to become the first woman ever elected to the U.S. Senate from Texas. Her election came after the resignation of Sen. Lloyd Bentsen (D), who was appointed as treasury secretary under President Clinton. The Texas governor named Democrat Bob Krueger to replace Bentsen in the Senate, but Hutchison soundly trounced Krueger in the special election a few months later, 67 to 33 percent. Her victory gave Republicans control of both Texas Senate seats for the first time since Reconstruction.

Hutchison had made Texas history years earlier when in 1972, at the age of 29, she became the first female Republican elected to the state legislature. In 1982, she made a run for Congress but lost. For the next few years, she worked as a successful businesswoman heading several banks and a candy manufacturing company. In 1990, Hutchison returned to politics and won the seat of Texas state treasurer.

During her Senate bid in 1993, Hutchison campaigned as a fiscal conservative and social moderate. She successfully linked her Democratic opponent to Clinton and his tax-raising budget package. She said her vote was needed in the Senate to defeat the plan. She also touted her moderate stance on abortion, supporting *Roe v. Wade* but favoring some restrictions and opposing federal funding for most abortions.

Just months after her election to the Senate, Hutchison made history once more, becoming the first Senator from Texas ever to be indicted while in office. She was charged with four felony counts of misusing state workers and computers for personal and political reasons while she was Texas treasurer. She was later acquitted of all wrongdoing and was easily re-elected in 1994 when she ran for a full six-year term.

During her first three years in office, Hutchison served on the Commerce Committee, the Select Committee on Intelligence, the Small Business Committee, and the Armed Services Committee—where she was the only woman on the panel. In 1994, Hutchison was one of only two members of the Armed Services Committee to vote against allowing Navy Adm. Frank Kelso to retire at the top level of four stars. Kelso had been in charge of naval operations during the Tailhook sex scandal in which female sailors had been physically harassed. When the issue of Kelso's retirement came to the floor of the full Senate, Hutchison joined with the other five women senators to fight the four-star honor. "The issue is his captaincy of the ship, what happened on his watch, and the signal his performance sends to the Navy and the world," Hutchison said on the floor. "When I voted in committee last week, I did not know if I would be the lone vote. I did not know if I would be the lone vote in the U.S. Senate. But I did what I thought was right."[126]

Hutchison in 1997 left her seat on the Armed Services Committee and took a spot on the powerful Appropriations Committee. On that committee she continued to work to protect the numerous military bases in her state and improve conditions for personnel.

Hutchison is a reliable Republican vote, working with conservatives in her party to rein in government regulations, cut taxes, and pass a balanced budget constitutional amendment. But Hutchison ran into trouble with conservative anti-abortion groups in 1996 when they tried to prevent her from speaking at the Republican presidential convention. Hutchison, who has voted in favor of criminal penalties for people who block entrances to abortion clinics, was ultimately allowed to speak at the convention when other prominent Republicans rushed to her defense. She was later mentioned as a possible vice presidential candidate with presidential nominee Bob Dole.

Hutchison bumped heads with the majority of her Senate colleagues— as well as the Clinton administration—in 1995 when she was an outspoken opponent of sending U.S. troops to Bosnia. The Senate narrowly rejected her resolution expressing Congress's disapproval of Clinton's decision to deploy troops. In 1998, Hutchison called for troops to pull out within three years and said military funds should be diverted to other, more immediate national security needs.

Hutchison, one of only seven women in her University of Texas Law School graduating class in 1967, has worked to promote women's economic empowerment and criminal protection. She won Senate passage of a provision allowing homemakers to contribute up to $2,000 to tax-deductible individual retirement accounts. She also sponsored an anti-stalking law that makes it a crime to cross state lines to harass or harm a victim. In 1998, Hutchison won passage of her amendment that gives pubic schools the option to use federal funds for voluntary single-sex schools and classrooms. She said single-sex classes have been proven to help girls earn higher grades and graduation rates.

SHEILA JACKSON-LEE (D-Texas)
(Jan. 12, 1950–)
House: Jan. 4, 1995, to present

Sheila Jackson-Lee made headlines when she first came to Congress by being the only black woman elected during the 1994 elections as well as one of only four challengers that year to defeat incumbents during the primary elections. The man Jackson-Lee brought down in the primary was a giant in Texas politics. Rep. Craig Washington (D) had served for 22 years in state politics before coming to Capitol Hill in 1989. During the campaign, Jackson-Lee hit Washington for opposing the North American Free Trade Agreement, the superconducting supercollider, and the space station—three issues that were extremely important to local Houston businesses. The business community poured money into Jackson-Lee's campaign and she soundly defeated Washington 63 to 37 percent. She then sailed to victory in the general election. She was assigned to the Science Committee and the Judiciary Committee. She was also elected president of her freshman class.

Before coming to Congress, Jackson-Lee served as an associate judge in Houston's municipal court for three years. She had also previously worked from 1977 to 1978 as a staff counsel on Capitol Hill with the Select Committee on Assassinations, charged with investigating the murders of Martin Luther King and President John F. Kennedy. In 1990, Jackson-Lee was elected to the Houston City Council and gained a reputation as a tireless worker. She served on 11 council committees and was known for attending every community or political event to which she was invited. As a city council member, Jackson-Lee gained recognition for pushing through tough gun safety laws creating penalties for parents who failed to safely lock up their guns to keep them out of reach of their children. She also pushed for expanded hours at city parks and recreation centers during the summer as a way to reduce gang activity.

Jackson-Lee has maintained her reputation as a hard worker on Capitol Hill. She is one of the more outspoken members of the House, taking the House floor on an almost daily basis to criticize the Republican agenda. She has attacked the GOP for its efforts to make it more difficult to get welfare assistance and has fought Republican legislation to ban a certain abortion technique labeled partial birth abortion by its opponents. During the welfare debate, Democratic leaders made Jackson-Lee the leader of a party task force aimed at drafting an alternative welfare reform package.

Jackson-Lee chairs the 57-member Children's Congressional Caucus. She has sponsored bills to create affordable child care for working families, protect child support payments from creditors, and enact comprehensive tobacco legislation to reduce the number of teenage smokers.

VIRGINIA JENCKES (D-Ind.)
(Nov. 6, 1877–Jan. 9, 1975)
House: March 4, 1933, to Jan. 3, 1939

Virginia Jenckes was one of the few women pioneers in Congress who did not succeed a husband into office but was elected in her own right. She was also one of the few congresswomen who never went to college. Although she had little political experience before coming to Congress, she won her first campaign by defeating incumbents in both the primary and general elections (the district had been redrawn, forcing several sitting members to compete against each other for the new seat).

Jenckes was well known in her district as the founder and secretary of the Wabash and Maume Valley Improvement Association. During her ten years at the helm of that organization, she continually badgered the federal government to construct floodwalls and drainage canals to halt the $2-million annual loss suffered by area farmers. She once also rallied local farmers together to work throughout the night as she directed the laying of 3,000 sandbags to dam a flood that would have destroyed expensive crops. Her efforts sparked one local reporter to write, "It's easy to see her getting in the hay before a storm. [She's the] type of individual who inevitably takes charge of drives."[127]

Her first election victory was bolstered by her opposition to the Volstead Act. Both her incumbent challengers supported Prohibition, but Jenckes argued successfully that its repeal would boost the price of locally grown corn and grains as well as provide new jobs. Jenckes was an outspoken campaigner and traveled across the district in a car chauffered by her daughter. In office, Jenckes requested but was denied seats on the Argriculture and the Rivers and Harbors committees. Instead she was assigned to the Civil Service Committee, the District of Columbia Committee, and the Mines and Mining Committee. Although she gained few points back home for her work on the DC Committee, Jenckes became the self-appointed guardian of overworked and underpaid District police and firemen. Jenckes also focused on consumers' issues. She drafted legislation to overhaul the Food and Drugs Act, which would have extended protections to cosmetics, therapeutic devices, and other over-the-counter products.

Jenckes was an outspoken foe of Communism and a strong advocate of funding for the FBI. "If this House of Representatives refuses to appropriate the amount of money [FBI director] Mr. Hoover deems necessary, then this House of Representatives and the Congress must stand responsible for any increase in kidnapping, white slavery, extortion, and other crimes," she said.[128] She continued to fight Communism after leaving Congress, helping five Hungarian priests escape from a Budapest prison and enter the United States after the failed 1956 Hungarian uprisings.

Jenckes narrowly won her second term to Congress in 1934 by just 383 votes, but lost her bid for a third term to Republican Noble Johnson, who had previously served in the House from 1925 to 1931. Jenckes remained in Washington for a short time to work for the American Red Cross, but later returned to Terre Haute, Ind., where she died in 1975.

• EDDIE BERNICE JOHNSON (D-Texas)
(Dec. 3, 1935–)
House: Jan. 5, 1993, to present

Throughout her legislative career, Eddie Bernice Johnson has established herself as a political trailblazer. She first entered public service in 1972 when she won a seat in the Texas House of Representatives and became the first black woman ever elected to public office in Dallas. During her five years in the state legislature, Johnson reached another milestone. She became the chair of the Labor Committee—the first woman in state history to chair a major committee.

In 1977, Johnson resigned from office to accept an appointment by President Carter as the regional director of the Department of Health, Education, and Welfare. She worked under the Carter administration until 1981, when she opened her own consulting company to promote minority businesses. In 1986, Johnson returned to politics and won a seat in the Texas Senate, becoming the first black to serve in the Senate since Reconstruction. During the next six years, Johnson focused much of her legislative attention on combatting racism in the state's hiring practices and held hearings investigating racial discrimination in state contracts. Johnson also chaired the Committee on Reapportionment—a position that helped pave her way to the U.S. Congress. As chair of the panel, Johnson personally mapped out the majority black congressional district she would run for in 1992.

Despite the criticism, Johnson went on to win the newly drawn House district with a whopping 72 percent of the vote. Johnson was assigned to the Science Committee and the Committee on Transportation and Infrastructure. She was also elected as the whip for the Congressional Black Caucus. A former nurse, Johnson is a strong advocate of health care for women and children. In 1998, she and other Black Caucus members called on the White House to declare a state of emergency in the black community because of the spread of AIDS. She also pushed legislation to study why more women do not enter into the field of science and investigate pay gaps between men and women in science-based professions.

Johnson has also focused on increasing jobs and job training. She split with many liberals in the Democratic party and supported the North American Free Trade Agreement in 1993, saying it would bring more job opportunities to her constituents. She voted to continue funding for the superconducting supercollider and backed the production of additional B-2 bombers in 1995, again arguing that both projects would create jobs.

In 1996, the U.S. Supreme Court ruled that Johnson's majority black district, along with similar districts in other states, was unconstitutional. Johnson's district was redrawn to include more white voters, but Johnson easily won re-election that year with 61 percent of the vote.

NANCY JOHNSON (R-Conn.)
(Jan. 5, 1935–   )
House: Jan. 3, 1983, to present

Nancy Johnson is one of only a handful of women to have chaired a full congressional committee. But her service at the helm of the House Committee on Standards of Official Conduct, ironically, caused her great political damage. Johnson chaired the panel—better known as the Ethics

Committee—during its consideration of misconduct charges filed against House Speaker Newt Gingrich (R-Ga.) Although the committee eventually found Gingrich guilty of breaking House rules and issued a $300,000 penalty against him, Johnson was criticized by her own hometown paper as "the willing tool of Republican leaders trying to protect Mr. Gingrich."[129]

Along with her chairmanship of the Ethics Committee—which she left following the Gingrich ruling in 1997—Johnson also holds an exclusive post at the helm of the Ways and Means subcommittee on oversight. She is the first Republican woman to serve on Ways and Means and the only woman to chair one of its subcommittees. The panel gives Johnson the opportunity to work on two of her favorite issues: health and trade. She has worked to lower tariffs to help domestic manufacturers trade their goods overseas and in 1993 she voted for the North American Free Trade Agreement. On the committee, Johnson also worked to craft a comprehensive package on child care. She proposed giving families vouchers to pay for fees at licensed day-care centers and financing them by restricting child-care tax credits for higher-income families. In 1997, her child health bill was signed into law, providing health care for millions of uninsured children.

Johnson is a moderate on social issues and is often voting against her fellow Republicans. She voted with liberals on such issues as mandated family leave and a waiting period for handgun purchases. When President Bush vetoed a bill that would have funded abortions for poor women who were the victims of rape or incest, Johnson blasted the move as "deeply, profoundly inhumane and unjust."[130] In 1997, Johnson became co-chair of the Congressional Caucus on Women's Issues. She has worked to allow homemakers to contribute to IRAs at the same level as their wage-earning spouses and she fought—unsuccessfully—to allow federal workers the opportunity to buy health insurance that covers abortions. She sought to soften the GOP welfare reform bill and won an amendment that guaranteed Medicaid benefits for welfare recipients. However, she lost an effort to exempt mothers with children under 10 years of age from the five-year welfare cut-off limit.

Johnson's moderate stance has helped her win re-election over and over in a district that often votes Democratic in other political contests. Johnson, in fact, has relied on crossover voters throughout her political career. She won her very first campaign for political office in 1976 to became the first Republican in 30 years to represent the city of New Britain in the state Senate. Before entering the political arena, Johnson was a longtime activist in New Britain community affairs. She worked as a volunteer in local school programs, community children's services, and fund-raising campaigns for libraries and charities.

STEPHANIE TUBBS JONES (D-Ohio)
(Sept. 10, 1949–   )
House: Jan. 6, 1999, to present

Stephanie Tubbs Jones made history when she won election to Congress, becoming the first black woman to represent Ohio in the U.S. House of Representatives. She succeeded longtime Rep. Louis Stokes (D), the only other black to serve in the Ohio delegation.

Before coming to Congress, Tubbs had never previously served in a legislative position, but had an extensive career as a lawyer. She was a trial attorney for the Equal Employment Opportunity Commission in Cleveland, Ohio, and assistant prosecutor for Cuyahoga County. In 1983, Jones was appointed to the Court of Common Pleas in Cuyahoga County—the first black woman to serve on that court. She held that judgeship until 1991, when she was appointed as Cuyahoga County Prosecutor, the first black and first woman to hold that position.

Jones decided to run for Congress following Stokes's announcement that he was retiring after 30 years in office. She easily won the five-way Democratic primary, which virtually guaranteed her election in the overwhelmingly Democratic district. Just three weeks before her election, she was inducted into the Ohio Women's Hall of Fame. In the House, Jones was assigned to the Banking Committee and the Small Business Committee.

BARBARA JORDAN (D-Texas)
(Feb. 21, 1936–Jan. 17, 1996)
House: Jan. 3, 1973, to Jan. 3, 1979

In her very first term in Congress, Barbara Jordan gained national attention for her eloquent but hard-hitting speeches during the Watergate impeachment hearings of President Nixon. Although she was a little-known freshman, she helped set the serious tone of the hearings by using constitutional arguments to defend her votes for all five articles of impeachment. "My faith in the Constitution is whole, it is complete, it is

total. I am not going to sit here and be an idle spectator to the diminu-
tion, the subversion, the destruction of the Constitution," Jordan said in
her opening salvo at the Judiciary Committee hearings.[131] The committee
ultimately passed three of the impeachment articles.

Jordan began developing her powerful oratory skills at an early age.
She was a member of her high school debate team and won first prize
in a national oratorical contest. When Jordan enrolled at the historically
black Texas Southern University, she became the first female to travel
across the country with the school's debate team and helped lead the
school to numerous championships. After graduation, Jordan went on to
earn her law degree from Boston University in 1959. Jordan initially had
difficulty finding a job, so she set up her own law practice in her parents'
kitchen. During the summer, she taught at Tuskegee Institute to earn
enough money to move from the kitchen to her own office. She also
worked as an administrative assistant to a county judge, where she first
became interested in politics and began working with the local Democratic party. She helped mobilize black voters across Houston during the
1960 presidential race of John Kennedy.

In 1962—at the age of 26—Jordan launched her first political campaign
for the state House. She lost, but managed to garner a respectable 46,000
votes. "I figured anybody who could get 46,000 people to vote for them
for any office should keep on trying," she said.[132] Two years later, she
ran and lost again. After her second defeat, Jordan turned her sights on
the state Senate and in 1966 became the first black woman elected to that
body. "I didn't play up the fact of being a Negro or a woman," Jordan
said of her campaign. "It feels good to know that people recognize a
qualified candidate when they see one."[133] Although the 1960s were a
time of racial upheaval and protest, Jordan's noncombative style won
her many friends among her all-white male colleagues. She proved herself an effective legislator, seeing about half of all the bills she introduced
become law. She helped create the Texas Fair Employment Practices
Commission and the first state minimum wage law designed specifically
to include low wage earners such as farm and domestic workers. She
also forced the state government to include anti-discrimination language
in business contracts. During her time in the state Senate, Jordan became
the first black to preside over the proceedings and the first black woman
given the honor of "Governor for a Day." Although the honor was
largely ceremonial, it made her the first black chief executive in the country.

In 1971, Jordan decided to run for the newly drawn U.S. congressional
district centered around Houston. The race turned ugly when her black
primary challenger accused her of "selling out." He charged that she
had cooperated with white lawmakers to create the new congressional

district at the expense of her "safe black" Senate seat that was drawn out of existence. In the end, however, Jordan won with 80 percent of the votes in the primary and 81 percent in the general election. She became the first black woman from the South ever elected to the U.S. Congress.

Soon after she was sworn in, Jordan contacted fellow Texan former President Lyndon Johnson—with whom she had become friends during her time in the state Senate—and asked him to help her secure a seat on the prestigious Judiciary Committee. She got the seat, and also later served on the Government Operations Committee.

Although Jordan was a liberal legislator, she was not an active member of the Congressional Black Caucus. She instead preferred to work closely with fellow Texans, including many conservative Democrats. Jordan, however, did work hard on behalf of civil rights. She was one of 35 Democrats who tried to block the confirmation of Gerald Ford as vice president because of his poor civil rights record. In 1975, she also fought to create bilingual ballots for Hispanics, Native Americans, and Asian Americans under the Voting Rights Act. She co-sponsored with Rep. Martha Griffiths (D-Mich.) a bill to extend Social Security coverage to housewives and pushed to include domestic workers in the minimum wage bill. She also fought to give free legal services to the poor.

In 1976, Jordan became the first black to serve as the keynote speaker at a Democratic National Convention. She was again asked to serve as keynote speaker in 1991—12 years after leaving office—at the presidential convention that nominated Bill Clinton.

In 1978, Jordan—suffering from multiple sclerosis that would eventually confine her to a wheelchair—declined to run for a fourth term in the House. She returned to Texas and taught at the University of Texas's Lyndon B. Johnson School of Public Affairs. In 1990, she was voted by the National Women's Hall of Fame as one of the most influential women of the twentieth century, and in 1994 Jordan received the Presidential Medal of Freedom. She was also named by President Clinton to chair the U.S. Immigration Reform Commission, charged with reviewing immigration policy. The commission issued its final report in 1995, recommending significant reductions in legal immigration, an unpopular proposal among ethnic groups and lawmakers. Six months later, Jordan died of pneumonia as a complication of leukemia.

BOOK BY JORDAN

Barbara Jordan: A Self-Portrait (1979)

FLORENCE KAHN (R-Calif.)
(Nov. 9, 1866–Nov. 16, 1948)
House: May 4, 1925, to Jan. 3, 1937

Florence Kahn came to Congress after she won the special election to succeed her husband, broadway actor-turned-congressman Julius Kahn, who died while in office. Mrs. Kahn served as an unpaid aide to her husband during his 25 years representing the San Francisco area and worked particularly closely with him in the final years of his life when illness kept him from devoting full time to his duties.

After winning office, Mrs. Kahn quickly became known for her sharp wit and constant mimickry of her congressional colleagues. She was anything but timid. Once, at a hearing on a proposed national movie censorship measure, a colleague on the Education Committee charged that anyone opposed to censorship was unclean. Kahn shot back, "Don't you dare call me unclean." And later at the hearing, when she was accused of having been influenced by one of the witnesses, a young and handsome motion picture man, Kahn yelled, "Of course I have been. Look at him and tell me if I am to blame!"[134]

When she first came to Congress, Kahn was assigned to the Indian Affairs Committee, a minor panel usually reserved for women and Independents. The outspoken Kahn refused the seat, declaring, "The only Indians in my district are in front of cigar stores and I can't do anything for them."[135] She later accepted a post on the Education Committee but continued to fight her leadership until she finally won a seat on the Military Affairs panel, a major committee that had once been chaired by her husband. In her third term in office, she became the first woman to be named to the powerful Appropriations Committee. As a member of that committee, she helped secure the $75 million needed to construct the San Francisco Bay Bridge and another $4 million to build a dirigible base in her district.

Kahn was a strong advocate of national defense and federal crime fighting. She fought for and won passage of controversial legislation expanding the budget and authority of the Federal Bureau of Investigation. FBI Director J. Edgar Hoover praised her as the "Mother of the FBI" and even served as an honorary pallbearer at her funeral in 1948.[136] A strong believer in women's rights, Kahn once told a group of Republican women planning to run for public office that they had the responsibility "to obliterate sex in politics." After she won her third race for office—

getting twice as many voters as her late husband ever did—she was asked how she did it. Her response: "Sex appeal!" But when she was asked if she had aspirations to move up to the Senate, she replied, "No use kidding myself. I couldn't make it."[137]

Kahn finally lost her bid for a seventh term in office during the Democratic landslide of 1936, but remained active in civic affairs for years to come. She was women's division chairman of the 1939 Golden Gate Exposition and co-chair for northern California of the American Women's Voluntary Service (a World War II citizens organization).

MARCY KAPTUR (D-Ohio)
(June 17, 1946–   )
House: Jan. 3, 1983, to present

Marcy Kaptur's unyielding concern for jobs in her local Toledo area has made her one of the most outspoken opponents of the two biggest international trade agreements to pass the Congress in recent years. In 1993, she fought strenuously against NAFTA, arguing that millions of U.S. jobs would be lost as companies moved to Mexico for cheap labor. A year later, she turned her sights on the GATT trade agreement and the World Trade Organization, which she said would harm the U.S. economy and undo international environmental, consumer protection, and labor laws. She worked with labor unions in an attempt to kill the deals, but lost both fights. Kaptur's strong stance on trade caught the eye of independent presidential candidate Ross Perot, who asked her to be his running mate in 1996. She declined.

Kaptur's staunch support for organized labor and U.S. jobs stems from her working-class background. Her mother was an original organizer of an auto trade union in Ohio. Kaptur was the first member of her family to go to college and even went on to pursue a doctorate at the Massachusetts Institute of Technology. She worked as an urban planner and in 1977 became an assistant for urban affairs with the Carter White House, where she helped steer 17 housing and neighborhood revitalization bills through Congress.

Kaptur had worked with the Ohio Democratic party as a volunteer since the age of 13, but when she won her House seat in 1982, it was a surprise to everyone. She took the Democratic nomination essentially by default after the local party gave up on finding a proven vote-getter to challenge the popular Republican incumbent. Nobody thought she had a chance, but she won the race by focusing on the declining local economy and attacking the incumbent for his support of President Reagan's free trade policies.

Once in the House, Kaptur tried to win a spot on the powerful Appropriations Committee, but was told the "woman's slot" was already filled. She was instead assigned to the Banking, Finance, and Urban Affairs Committee and the Committee on Veterans' Affairs. She forged a close relationship with the Speaker Jim Wright (D-Texas), who later named her vice chair of a task force on trade and appointed her to the Steering and Policy Committee that oversees committee assignments. In her fourth term in office, Kaptur was given a seat on the prestigious Budget Committee, and soon thereafter finally won a spot on the Appropriations Committee, where today she serves as the top Democrat on the subcommittee on agriculture—a spot from which she can look out for the wheat, corn, and soybean farmers in her district.

Along with her opposition to the NAFTA and GATT trade agreements, Kaptur spent years pushing for Japan to open its markets to U.S.-made auto parts. She also fought against President Clinton's policy to grant China Most-Favored-Nation (MFN) trade status, under which Chinese goods are allowed into the United States at low tariff rates. Kaptur attacked China for its poor human rights record and called MFN for China "a triumph of commercialism over balanced foreign policy and a triumph of fascism over liberty."[138] As with her fights against NAFTA and GATT, Kaptur also lost her attempt to kill China's MFN.

Kaptur generally votes along party lines in the House, although she often splits with her Democratic colleagues on abortion issues. Kaptur describes herself as neither pro-choice nor pro-life, but opposes federal funds for abortions. In 1996, she voted against an amendment that would have allowed privately financed abortions at overseas military hospitals and she also supports a ban on the so-called partial birth abortion. She has, however, backed a requirement that states fund Medicaid abortions for poor women in the cases of rape, incest and threat to the life of the mother.

BOOK BY KAPTUR

Women of Congress: A Twentieth-Century Odyssey (1996)

NANCY KASSEBAUM (R-Kan.)
(July 29, 1932–   )
Senate: Jan. 3, 1979, to Jan. 3, 1997

Nancy Kassebaum grew up in a political family, but had little personal experience in public life before coming to the Senate. Her father, Alfred Landon, served as the governor of Kansas and was the Republican presidential nominee in 1936. Although she was surrounded by major political figures during her youth, her father never encouraged her to enter the political arena. Instead, Kassebaum married soon after graduating from the University of Kansas in 1954. She went on to earn a master's in history from the University of Michigan and soon found herself raising a family.

It wasn't until her four children were older that Kassebaum began her public service career. In 1973, she was elected to the local school board and served a single term, as president. It was her only elective office before coming to the Senate. Kassebaum also served on the Kansas Governmental Ethics Commission and the Kansas Committee on the Humanities. After divorcing her husband in 1975, Kassebaum dealt with the prospect of single motherhood by calling Sen. James Pearson of Kansas— whose campaign her ex-husband had chaired. Pearson offered her a job in his Washington office and she served as a caseworker for one year before returning back to Wichita, Kan., to help manage the family radio station business.

In 1978, Sen. Pearson announced his retirement and Kassebaum decided to make a bid for the seat. Although she had little political experience, her family name helped her win an easy victory over eight other Republicans and she went on to become the first woman elected to the Senate who was not the widow of a congressman.

In the Senate, Kassebaum served on a variety of committees: Banking, Housing and Urban Affairs; Budget; Commerce, Science and Transportation; Foreign Relations; and Labor and Human Resources. In 1994, Kassebaum became chair of the Labor Committee, the first woman to lead a major panel (Sen. Margaret Chase Smith had chaired the minor Committee on Rates and Compensation in 1955). At the helm of the Labor Committee, Kassebaum dealt with issues of job training, welfare, and the minimum wage. She opposed efforts to hike the minimum wage, arguing that it would hurt small businesses and reduce job opportunities. She also worked to streamline the government's job training programs and held hearings exposing wasteful spending and faulty management of the Job Corps program.

On the Foreign Relations committee, Kassebaum chaired the African affairs subcommittee. She helped push for sanctions against the apartheid government in South Africa despite opposition from GOP President Reagan.

Kassebaum was generally conservative on fiscal issues, but moderate on many social matters. Although she was petite and soft-spoken, she was not afraid to stand apart from her fellow Republicans—and often did. In 1989, she was the only Republican to vote against confirming John Tower, President Bush's nominee for defense secretary. She was pro-choice on abortion issues and a strong advocate of arms control. In 1986, she backed a Democratic amendment cutting Reagan's request for the strategic defense initiative. In 1992, Kassebaum helped found the Republican Majority Coalition, a group aimed at fighting the rise of the religious right. In her final years in office, she worked closely with Democratic Sen. Ted Kennedy (Mass.) to overhaul the nation's health insurance system to allow greater portability of benefits from job to job and provide coverage for people with preexisting conditions. In 1994, she faced sharp anger from her fellow Republicans when she voted for President Clinton's crime bill. The vote prompted some Republicans to try to strip her of her seniority, but she survived the storm.

Despite her support of the Equal Rights Amendment and abortion rights, Kassebaum was careful not to brand herself a "feminist," and she considered herself a "U.S. Senator, not a woman Senator." "It diminishes women to say that we have one voice and everything in the Senate would change if we were there," she said. She added that she wasn't so much concerned about bringing more women to Congress as she was about electing more moderate Republicans.[139]

In her final year in office, Kassebaum married former Tennessee senator and majority leader Howard Baker. After retiring from the Senate in 1997, Kassebaum was named by Defense Secretary William Cohen to head a special panel to study mixed-gender training in the military.

MAUDE KEE (D-W.Va.)
(June 7, 1895–Feb. 15, 1975)
House: July 26, 1951, to Jan. 3, 1963

The only woman ever elected to represent West Virginia in Congress, Maude Kee succeeded her husband in office following his death, and was later succeeded by her son after she retired from office. Kee's husband, Rep. John Kee, was known as a progressive Democrat and his wife followed closely in his footsteps once she took his seat. She voted against cuts in economic aid for Europe and backed increased foreign assistance. In 1952, Kee took a self-financed 16,000-mile trip through seven South American countries, fulfilling what had been her husband's lifelong dream. Kee was strongly pro-labor—opposing the use of the Taft-Hartley Act to end a steelworkers strike in 1952—and supported the continuation of consumer price and rent controls.

Kee also dedicated herself to helping the physically disabled, a cause sparked by her only daughter's lifelong bout with cerebral palsey and polio. She was able to work on behalf of the disabled as chair of the Veterans' Affairs subcommittee on hospitals. She investigated veterans' facilities during the Korean War and worked to improve the medical care at military hospitals. She helped establish a library for the disabled at the Woodrow Wilson Rehabilitation Center in Virginia and launched a book drive that brought in more than 10,000 texts for the project. Along with her assignment on the Veterans' Affairs Committee, Kee served on the Government Operations Committee and the Interior and Insular Affairs Committee.

Kee also worked hard for her constituents, helping to bring federally funded highways, flood control projects, and courthouses back home to her district. She fought to attract new industry and jobs to West Virginia and established centers to retrain idle miners.

Before winning election to the House, Kee served as the administrative assistant in her husband's congressional office and wrote a weekly column from Washington for a chain of West Virginia newspapers. She stopped writing the column when her husband became chair of the Foreign Affairs Committee so that she could spend more time helping him with his office work.

In 1964, ill health forced Kee to retire from office. Her son, James— who had worked as Kee's administrative assistant—successfully ran to replace his mother.

EDNA FLANNERY KELLY (D-N.Y.)
(Aug. 20, 1906–Dec. 14, 1997)
House: Nov. 8, 1949, to Jan. 3, 1969

During her nearly 20 years in office—through the Korean and Vietnam War eras—Edna Flannery Kelly established an impressive record on some of the most controversial issues of her time. On the domestic front, she was a consistent fighter for civil rights and equal pay for women. She also worked tirelessly on foreign affairs and was a staunch anti-Communist.

Unlike many of her predecessors, Kelly did not come to Congress to replace a deceased husband. Instead, she was elected in her own right, but credited her husband's death for her early interest in politics. Edward Leo Kelly had been active in New York politics, serving as the head of the Madison Democratic Club and later as a city court justice. After he was killed in a car accident in 1942, Mrs. Kelly decided to enter politics "to carry on in the Kelly family tradition."[140] The local Democratic boss—New York state Assemblyman Irwin Steingut—took Edna Kelly under his wing and helped get her elected to the King's County Democratic executive committee. He also secured her appointment as research director of the Democratic party in the state legislature in 1943. In that job, she was responsible for analyzing bills and comparing them to similar legislation introduced in other states. It was the perfect training ground for the U.S. Congress.

In 1949, when Brooklyn's U.S. representative died in office, the local Democratic machine decided that Kelly should run for the seat. Campaigning on a platform that included support for the United Nations, the Marshall Plan, aid to Israel, civil rights, federal aid for education, slum clearing, and low-cost housing, Kelly polled twice as many voters as her nearest rival. She also became the first Democratic woman elected by New York City.

In Congress, Kelly won a seat on the prestigious Foreign Affairs Committee and would eventually chair its subcommittee on Europe. As a member of that committee, she led five overseas investigations in Europe to study U.S. foreign policy. During her 19 years in office—which spanned the height of the Cold War—Kelly focused on the threat of Communism in Eastern Europe. In 1951, Kelly amended the Mutual Security Act to help 1.5 million refugees, mainly from Eastern Europe, resettle into new areas. A year later, Kelly amended the foreign aid bill to suspend any further aid to Communist Yugoslavia. In 1954, when there were large U.S. farm surpluses available to needy nations, Kelly helped amend the Agricultural Trade Development and Assistance Act to exclude the Soviet Union and its satellites from the definition of "friendly nations." She also introduced a resolution—unanimously adopted by Congress—opposing Communist China's admission to the United Nations. Her work on international issues was recognized by President Kennedy when he appointed her a delegate to the 18th General Assembly of the UN.

On the domestic front, Kelly worked on behalf of women, blacks, and seniors. In 1951, Kelly introduced the first of her many bills calling for equal pay for equal work for women. Twelve years later, President Kennedy presented Kelly with one of the pens he used to sign the 1963 Equal Pay Act into law in recognition of her years of work. Kelly was also one of the first sponsors of a bill to allow working widows and widowers to deduct child care from their income taxes. That language was eventually incorporated into the 1954 tax law revision.

In 1967 alone, Kelly introduced 50 bills on subjects ranging from crime, drug abuse, conservation, to public health. During her lengthy career, she voted for the creation of the Civil Rights Commission and the Civil Rights Act of 1964. She fought for an increase in the minimum wage, a lowering of the retirement age, and for parents to be able to deduct the cost of their children's higher education from their taxes. Her hard work was rewarded by her party, which named her secretary of the House Democratic Caucus.

Kelly never had problems winning re-election until 1968, when her district lines were redrawn after a Supreme Court ruling. She was forced to run against her Democratic Colleague Rep. Emanuel Celler, chair of the House Judiciary Committee and the most senior member of the Brooklyn delegation. Although she was able to garner 32 percent in the three-way primary race, it was not enough to win and her congressional career came to an end.

SUE KELLY (R-N.Y.)
(Sept. 26, 1936–   )
House: Jan. 4 1995, to present

Although Sue Kelly's campaign for Congress in 1994 was her first run for political office, she had worked with the local Republican party and various civic groups for more than 30 years. She was the co-founder of the Bedford, N.Y., League of Women Voters, president of her local PTA, and founder of the Bedford Recreation Committee. Before coming to Congress, Kelly was also a rape crisis counselor, a high school teacher, and owner of a flower shop.

Her election to the House spelled the end of a political dynasty in New York's 19th district. The seat had been held by GOP Rep. Hamilton Fish for 26 years, and members of the Fish family had represented the area since 1843. But after Fish announced his retirement from office, Kelly defeated Fish's son, who was running for the seat as a Democrat.

On the campaign trail, Kelly balanced her strong pro-choice stance with her conservative positions on crime and fiscal policy. She supports capital punishment, a balanced budget constitutional amendment, and elimination of the capital gains tax. During her election campaign, the Westchester Coalition for Legal Abortion withdrew its earlier endorsement of Kelly, citing her support for the GOP Contract with America, which contained some positions objectionable to the abortion-rights coalition.

Kelly also came under attack from environmental groups soon after her arrival on Capitol Hill. Although she calls herself an environmentalist, many conservation groups criticized her for supporting a Republican-backed bill revising the 1972 clean water act—a revision they called a "polluter's bill of rights." She also supported a bill making it more difficult for federal agencies to issue health, safety, and environmental regulations.

But Kelly won back some environmental support when she fought efforts in 1995 to limit the regulatory authority of the Environmental Protection Agency and supported a bill in 1996 to provide $210 million to protect the Florida Everglades. She also helped push through legislation protecting Sterling Forest, a vast undeveloped parcel of land along the New York–New Jersey border. Kelly again irked environmentalists in 1998 when she introduced a bill to create the Congressional Office of Regulatory Analysis, which would examine the economic impact of all federal regulations on businesses. Environmental groups blasted the bill as an attempt to elevate industry profits over health and safety concerns.

Kelly has also come under attack from conservative members of her own party. She fought against many of her GOP colleagues when they tried to kill the National Endowment for the Arts, and is often on the opposite side of her colleagues on the abortion issue. She was one of just 17 Republicans in 1995 to vote against an appropriations bill that would have prohibited Medicaid funding for abortions for poor women in the cases of rape and incest. In 1996, she was one of only 15 Republicans to oppose a ban on so-called partial birth abortions. She, however, switched sides and voted for the ban in 1997. She is the only one of the seven GOP women elected to the House in 1994 to support abortion rights and to join the Congressional Woman's Caucus.

On the other women's issues, Kelly in 1998 called on Congress to adopt a resolution calling on federal agencies to increase the number of women-owned businesses receiving government contracts. That same year she also introduced a bill cracking down on stalkers.

Kelly sits on the Banking and Financial Services Committee, the Transportation and Infrastructure Committee, and the Committee on Small Business, where she chairs the subcommittee on regulatory reform and paperwork reduction.

Rep. Jeannette Rankin (R-Mont.), the first woman to serve in Congress. Courtesy of the Library of Congress.

Sen. Rebecca Latimer Felton (D-Ga.), appointed in 1922, was the first woman to serve in the Senate. Courtesy of the Senate Historian's office.

Rep. Alice Mary Robertson (R-Okla.), the second woman elected to Congress. Courtesy of the Library of Congress.

Left to right: Reps. Alice Mary Robertson (R-Okla.), Winnifred Huck (R-Ill.), and Mae Ella Nolan (R-Calif.), the second, third, and fourth women to serve in the House of Representatives. Courtesy of the Library of Congress.

Sen. Hattie Caraway (D-Ark.) was the first woman elected to the Senate and the first woman to chair a committee in that chamber. Courtesy of the Library of Congress.

Left to right: At the opening of the 71st Congress, Reps. Ruth Bryan Owen (D-Fla.), Mary Norton (D-N.J.), Florence Kahn (R-Calif.), Pearl Oldfield (D-Ark.), Edith Nourse Rogers (R-Mass.), Eliza Jane Pratt (D-N.C.), and Ruth Hanna McCormick (R-Ill.). Courtesy of the Library of Congress.

Left to right: Rep. Margaret Chase Smith (R-Maine), Rep. Edith Nourse Rogers (R-Mass.), Mrs. Ed Gann, and Rep. Frances Bolton (R-Ohio). Courtesy of the Senate Historian's office.

Rep. Clare Boothe Luce (R-Conn.) addresses the 1964 Republican National Convention. Courtesy of the Library of Congress.

Left to right: Sen. Margaret Chase Smith (R-Maine), President Lyndon B. Johnson, and Sen. Maurine Neuberger (D-Ore.). Courtesy of the Senate Historian's office.

Rep. Bella Abzug (D-N.Y.) addresses the 1972 Democratic National Convention. Courtesy of the Library of Congress.

In 1994, women legislators gathered to urge passage of the Violence Against Women Act. From right to left: Rep. Connie Morella (R-Md.), D.C. Delegate Eleanor Holmes Norton (D), Rep. Patricia Schroeder (D-Colo.), Rep. Elizabeth Furse (D-Ore.), Rep. Carolyn Maloney (D-N.Y.), and NOW President Patricia Ireland. Courtesy of the office of Rep. Connie Morella.

Women members of Congress hold a press conference in 1994 to show support for a ban against assault weapons. From left: Sen. Carol Moseley Brown (D-Ill.), Sen. Patty Murray (D-Wash.), Rep. Maxine Waters (D-Calif.), Rep. Nancy Pelosi (D-Calif.), Rep. Carolyn Maloney (D-N.Y.), Rep. Nita Lowey (D-N.Y.), Sen. Dianne Feinstein (D-Calif.), Rep. Elizabeth Furse (D-Ore.), Rep. Jane Harman (D-Calif.), Rep. Connie Morella (R-Md.), Rep. Marge Roukema (R-N.J.), Rep. Leslie Byrne (D-Va.), and Sen. Barbara Mikulski (D-Md.). Courtesy of the office of Rep. Nita Lowey.

BARBARA KENNELLY (D-Conn.)
(July 10, 1936–)
House: Jan. 12, 1982, to Jan. 6, 1999

Barbara Kennelly has spent her life surrounded by politicians. Her father was John Bailey, the legendary Connecticut Democratic boss and chairman of the Democratic National Committee under Presidents John Kennedy and Lyndon Johnson. She married James Kennelly, Speaker of the Connecticut House, but she didn't personally enter the political arena until relatively late in life. A graduate of Trinity College with a master's in government, Kennelly spent her early professional life as the director of two large social service agencies. She was almost 40 when she was appointed to fill a vacancy in the Hartford City Council in 1975. She went on to easily win a full term soon after, and in 1979 was elected as Connecticut secretary of state. Two years later she won a seat in Congress in a special election after the death of a longtime incumbent.

Accustomed as she was to politics, Kennelly began her climb up the House leadership ladder shortly after her election. She brushed up on her golf game—a sport she learned from her father—as a way to forge strong camaraderies with her mostly male colleagues. Kennelly was in the House less than a year when she won a seat on the powerful Ways and Means Committee—one of only a handful of women ever to serve on that panel. In her second year in office, Speaker Tip O'Neil named her to the Democratic Steering and Policy Committee, which makes committee assignments and helps develop legislative strategies. Later in her career, she became the first woman to serve on the Select Committee on Intelligence. She also served on the Committee on Government Operations and the Committee on Public Works and Transportation.

In 1989, Kennelly lost a longshot bid for chair of the House Democratic Caucus, but two years later she was appointed as one of three chief deputy whips, a top position in the leadership. In 1994, Kennelly ran against her friend and colleague Rep. Louise Slaughter (D-N.Y.) to win the vice chairmanship of the Democratic Caucus. She became the highest-ranking woman ever to serve in the Democratic leadership.

Kennelly has spent much of her career working on the issues of child support, housing, welfare reform, and tax reform. In 1983, Kennelly introduced the Child Support Enforcement Amendment requiring states to establish a system for mandatory wage withholdings if child support payments were 30 days overdue. The following year, the House and

Senate unanimously passed the bill. She and others also pushed for tougher laws to enforce child-care payments in the 1996 welfare reform bill.

Kennelly says she came late to feminist issues at the urging of her three daughters. In 1991, she joined other congressional women to protest the willingness of Congress to appoint Clarence Thomas to the Supreme Court without first hearing from Anita Hill about alleged sexual harassment. In 1993, Kennelly complained to the White House that no female lawmakers were invited to Bill Clinton's inauguration day luncheon on Capitol Hill. She was later asked to attend.

She supports abortion rights and opposed a ban on so-called partial birth abortions. Kennelly generally votes liberal—she supported a minimum wage hike and opposed denying public education to illegal immigrants—but she voted with Republicans to prohibit same-sex marriages and in 1995 backed a ban on flag desecration.

In 1997, Kennelly announced she would leave Congress to run for governor of Connecticut. She lost the race to incumbent Republican Gov. John Rowland.

MARTHA KEYS (D-Kan.)
(Aug. 10, 1930–   )
House: Jan. 3, 1975, to Jan. 3, 1979

Martha Keys may best be remembered for her marriage to former Rep. Andy Jacobs (D-Ind.), becoming the first congressional couple ever to marry while in office and serve side-by-side. The two began dating shortly after Keys was sworn into her seat, and they were married a year later in 1976. (It would be almost 20 years until a second congressional couple would fall in love and marry each other while serving on Capitol Hill—GOP Reps. Susan Molinari and Bill Paxon, both of New York.)

Before coming to Congress, Keys had worked in local Democratic politics and served as the Kansas state coordinator of George McGovern's 1972 presidential bid, which was managed by her brother-in-law and future senator, Gary Hart. Keys decided to run for the House two years later when Rep. William Roy (D-Kan.) resigned from his seat to challenge Sen. Bob Dole (R-Kan.). Keys was one of the few Democrats to win office in Kansas that year.

Keys was rewarded in her freshman year with a seat on the exclusive Ways and Means Committee, but spent much of her first term fighting for re-election to the Republican-leaning district. During her brief two terms in office, Keys concentrated on women's issues, tax reform, and health legislation, particularly the issue of national health insurance. She introduced a Social Security bill that required all covered earnings to be shared between a husband and wife, with each gaining credits on his or her separate Social Security account. The bill was aimed at ending a law that gave the second wife of a divorced man all of his Social Security benefits and left the first wife with nothing.

Keys lost re-election in 1978, but was named special adviser to the Secretary of Health, Education and Welfare a year later. In 1980 and 1981, she served as assistant secretary of education. She later worked as a consultant in Washington and served as director of the Center for a New Democracy in 1985 and 1986. In 1990, she joined several other former members of Congress to organize the Council for the National Interest, a nonprofit group aimed at representing Palestinian interests and counterweighing the influence of the American Israel Public Affairs Committee. That same year she was also named vice president of the National Multiple Sclerosis Society.

CAROLYN CHEEKS KILPATRICK
(D-Mich.)
(June 25, 1945–   )
House: Jan. 7, 1997, to present

Carolyn Kilpatrick was the only candidate in 1996 to defeat a sitting incumbent in a primary. She beat three-term Democratic Rep. Barbara-Rose Collins who was being investigated by the Justice Department and House Ethics Committee for misusing her congressional and campaign funds. After winning the Democratic nomination, Kilpatrick easily won the general election in the overwhelmingly Democratic district.

Kilpatrick is a divorced mother of two. She earned her master's degree in education from the University of Michigan and taught public school for eight years.

Kilpatrick also had a long career in public service before coming to Congress. She served for 17 years in the state House where she became the first African American in Michigan history to serve on the state House Appropriations Committee. She also served in the leadership as a Democratic whip.

In Congress, Kilpatrick serves on the Banking and Financial Services Committee, the House Oversight Committee, and the Joint Committee on the Library of Congress. Kilpatrick has worked to increase affordable health care to the poor and boost the wages of working families. She introduced legislation to give a $1,000 per month tax credit to doctors who locate in medically underserved areas. She also supported an increase in the minimum wage and fought Republican efforts to deny funds to colleges that used affirmative action in their admissions programs.

COYA KNUTSON (D-Minn.)
(Aug. 22, 1912–Oct. 10, 1996)
House: Jan. 3, 1955, to Jan. 3, 1959

Coya Knutson's promising congressional career was cut short when her husband conspired with her political opponents to oust her from office. During Knutson's campaign for a third term, her husband Andy wrote a public letter accusing her of infidelity and charging that her job on Capitol Hill had ruined their domestic bliss. In reality, Andy was an alcoholic who routinely abused his wife and their adopted son.

Knutson used politics as a means of escaping her ugly home life. She had earlier taught high school for 16 years, paying most of the family bills while her husband worked as a janitor. At one point, Knutson even bought a six-room lodge and named it Andy's Hotel, hoping it would spark her husband's interest. It didn't. Knutson later served as a field worker for the Agriculture Adjustment Administration and became involved in farming issues that would eventually dominate her legislative agenda.

Knutson first began working in civic affairs in 1948 when she joined the Red Lake County welfare board and helped establish a local clinic, Red Cross office, and community chest fund. That same year she was chosen to chair the Red Lake County Democratic-Farmer-Labor party. Two years later, she won a seat in the Minnesota state House where she served until 1954. During her time in the state House, Knutson authored a bill to increase the quality and sales of dairy products and sponsored educational programs for disabled children.

In 1954, Knutson ran for and won election to the U.S. House in an upset victory against a six-term Republican. Knutson campaigned on increased support for family farmers and criticized the farm policies of the Eisenhower administration. She also played the accordian and sang songs at all her campaign stops (Knutson in her youth had studied music at the Juilliard School in New York).

When she arrived on Capitol Hill, Knutson became the first woman assigned to the House Agriculture Committee. Over the next four years Knutson pushed for an extension of the food stamp program, for the distrubution of farm surpluses, and a federally supported school lunch program. Knutson also created the first federal appropriations for cystic fibrosis research. She introduced the first bill to include an income tax checkoff for presidential campaign financing. And she authored a bill that would eventually establish a federal student loan program.

Knutson seemed assured of a long and productive career in Congress, but her husband put an end to that. "Our home life has deteriorated to the extent that it is practically nonexistent," he wrote in a letter that made its way to the newspapers. "I want to have the happy home that we enjoyed for many years prior to her election."[141] Andy then issued a press release accusing his wife of having an affair with her young administrative assistant and threatened a $200,000 lawsuit. The letter became known as the "Coya Come Home" letter and it ruined her chances for re-election. She was defeated by 1,390 votes in 1958—the only Democratic incumbent to lose a seat that year.

Knutson filed a complaint with the House elections subcommittee charging that her defeat was the direct result of a "malicious conspiracy" on the part of her political foes. Andy Knutson admitted to the panel that he had been persuaded to write the letter by "friends" who included some of his wife's rivals within the Democratic party. It was also charged that the press release was drafted by the campaign manager for the GOP winner against Knutson, although the Republican denied the allegations. The subcommittee unanimously agreed that the "exploitation of the family life of Mrs. Knutson was a contributing case to her defeat," but it could not find any direct evidence of a plot.[142]

Knutson tried another run for office in 1960 but lost. "I ran in 1960 knowing that I couldn't possibly win, but as a candidate I had a platform from which to campaign for John Kennedy. And when all the ballots were counted, the ninth district was the one to put him over the top in Minnesota," she said.[143] A grateful Kennedy appointed her congressional liaison for the Office of Civilian Defense where she continued to serve until 1970. In 1977, Knutson made a final bid for the House, but was again defeated.

MARY LANDRIEU (D-La.)
(Nov. 23, 1955–   )
Senate: Jan. 7, 1997, to present

Most of Mary Landrieu's first year in office was spent defending her right to serve in the Senate. She had won election in 1996 by just 5,788 votes over her Republican opponent Woody Jenkins. Jenkins refused to concede and claimed voter fraud. The Senate Rules Committee opened a probe into the charges and, after spending eight months investigating the election, voted unanimously to drop the charges saying there was not enough evidence to overturn the election.

Despite the investigation, Landrieu continued to work on a number of high-profile issues. She voted for a balanced budget constitutional amendment and worked with Democrats and Republicans to draft legislation that would require the federal government to compensate Louisiana and other coastal states for the costs of supporting the offshore oil-drilling industry.

Landrieu calls herself a moderate or "new" Democrat. She supported an increase in the minimum wage, as well as tax cuts and the easing of government regulations on businesses. She is a supporter of a constitutional amendment banning desecration of the U.S. flag and, although she backs abortion rights, she voted for a ban on a certain type of abortion procedure called partial birth abortion by its opponents. Landrieu has also focused much of her attention on education and children's issues. She has pushed for full funding of the Head Start educational program, more federal dollars for computers in classrooms, and tax credits to help middle-class families pay for college tuition. Landrieu has also sponsored legislation to overhaul adoption and foster-care policies. Landrieu herself is the mother of two adopted children. Landrieu serves on the Agriculture Committee, the Committee on Energy and Natural Resources, and the Small Business Committee.

Landrieu comes from a well-known political family. Her father, Moon Landrieu, had been mayor of New Orleans and secretary of Housing and Urban Development under the administration of President Carter. Landrieu herself entered politics at a young age. She was just 23 when she was elected to the Louisiana House of Representatives, where she served on the powerful Appropriations Committee and championed issues important to women and children. After two terms in the House, she decided to make her first statewide run and was elected state treasurer in 1987 and re-elected without opposition four years later. In 1995, she ran for but lost her bid for governor.

KATHERINE LANGLEY (R-Ky.)
(Feb. 14, 1888–Aug. 15, 1948)
House: March 4, 1926, to March 3, 1931

Unlike most of her female predecessors in Congress, Katherine Langley did not come to Congress via the widow's path. Instead, Langley was elected to fill the House seat left vacant when her husband was sent to jail for trying to transport and sell whisky during Prohibition.

Langley had learned the ins and outs of politics long before she was elected to the House. She was the daughter of James Madison Gudger, a four-term congressman from North Carolina, and worked as secretary to her husband John Wesley Langley during his 18 years in office. She was an active member of the Kentucky Republican party, serving as the first woman member of the state central committee and founder of the Women's Republican State Committee. She was also a delegate to the Republican National Convention in 1924.

After Mr. Langley was caught trying to bribe a Prohibition officer and sent to the federal penitentiary in Atlanta, he made a plea to his constituents to elect his wife to "vindicate" his name. He also claimed that he was "practically penniless" and that the only hope of saving their home was to send his wife to serve a term in Congress while he sat in jail.[144]

The voters of Kentucky were undisturbed by Mr. Langley's conviction—many believing he was a victim of a conspiracy. While on the campaign trail in 1926, Mrs. Langley delivered more than 100 speeches, each time glorifying the name of her husband and promising to carry out his goals in office. Local papers praised Mrs. Langley as "better equipped intellectually than her husband for service in Congress" and claimed that "John Langley wears the breeches, but the lady has the brains."[145] Mrs. Langley won the seat by a sizeable margin, but was not wholly accepted by her new congressional colleagues. "She offends the squeamish by her unstinted display of gypsy colors on the floor and the conspicuousness with which she dresses her bushy blue-black hair," one newspaper wrote about her.[146] She was also criticized for her flowery oratory on the House floor, a result of her earlier career as a speech teacher. She remained popular with the voters however, and won a second term in 1928 by an even larger margin than her first election. During her second term in office, she was placed on the elite Committee on Committees—the first woman to serve on the powerful panel responsible for making all committee assignments for members.

During her time in office, Langley successfully pushed President Coolidge to grant clemency to her jailed husband—with the understanding that he would never again seek office. But in 1929, denying that he had agreed to the deal, Langley announced from the family home that he would try to regain his seat in Congress. Back in Washington, Mrs. Langley quickly announced that she had no intention to step aside "for John or anyone else."[147] Mrs. Langley's name eventually ended up on the ballot, but the family feud cost her enough votes to lose the election to her Democratic challenger. In 1932, a year after her loss, Langley was named by the governor to serve on the Kentucky Railroad Commission.

BARBARA LEE (D-Calif.)
(July 16, 1946–   )
House: April 21, 1998, to present

Barbara Lee came to Congress to fill the seat of the man she once worked for. And Lee was the perfect successor to liberal 14-term Rep. Ron Dellums (D). Like Dellums, Lee supports spending less money on the military and more to help the poor, the environment, and public education. During the special election to replace Dellums—who resigned halfway through his 14th term—Lee campaigned on the slogan "Carrying the baton."

Lee's liberal views were shaped at a young age when she and her family were the victims of racial discrimination. Her mother, when she was in labor with Lee, was initially refused treatment at an El Paso, Texas, hospital because she was black. Years later, Lee became the first black cheerleader at her high school, which touched off rioting.

Lee is an accomplished pianist who received music scholarships to college. She first became involved in politics while attending Mills College in Oakland, Calif., where she was faced with a course requirement to work for a political campaign during the presidential year of 1972.

Lee signed on with Rep. Shirley Chisholm (D-N.Y.), the country's first black candidate for president. Lee rose quickly through the ranks and eventually ran Chisholm's Northern California campaign. For another class project, Lee started a community mental health center that thrived for 12 years until Gov. Ronald Reagan ended the program.

In 1975, Lee joined Dellums's congressional staff, working in both his Washington and California offices. Lee served as his senior adviser and chief of staff for 12 years.

In 1991, Lee was elected to the California assembly, where she passed bills to convert closed military facilities, provide health insurance to poor children, and improve day care and mental health programs under the state's welfare system. After serving six years in the assembly, Lee won election to the state Senate, where she served until her election to Congress.

On Capitol Hill, Lee has pledged to continue working for the under-privileged. On her first day in Congress, Lee called for universal health care coverage, better wages and benefits for working men and women, and more public transportation to help clean up the environment. She serves on the Committee on Banking and Financial Services and the Science Committee.

BLANCHE LAMBERT LINCOLN (D-Ark.)
(Sept. 30, 1960–)
House: Jan. 5, 1993, to Jan. 3, 1997
Senate: Jan. 6, 1999, to present

Blanche Lambert Lincoln first came to Congress by defeating the very lawmaker she once worked for. From 1987 to 1989, Lincoln served as a receptionist to Rep. Bill Alexander (D-Ark.). After leaving Alexander's office and working for several years as a researcher for lobbying firms, Lincoln decided she wanted to return to Capitol Hill—this time as an elected official.

Alexander had been politically hurt by several financial and ethical controversies, and Lincoln easily defeated him in the Democratic primary. In the heavily Democratic district, the nomination was tantamount to election to Congress. Lincoln was assigned to the prestigious Energy and Commerce Committee as well as the Agriculture and Merchant Marine Committees.

Although Lincoln's district was overwhelmingly Democratic in voter registration, the constituency was largely urban and conservative-leaning. A farmer's daughter and avid duck-hunter, Lincoln's southern twang and straight-talking style proved popular with voters. She also generally voted along moderate lines. She opposed the 1993 Brady bill, which imposed a waiting period for handgun purchases, but she supported a ban on certain assault weapons a year later. She also joined the "Blue Dog" caucus, a group of conservative House Democrats. She backed a constitutional amendment requiring a balanced budget and voted against lifting the ban on homosexuals in the military.

After winning election to a second term in 1994, Lincoln—who had run under her maiden name of Lambert during her first two campaigns—began using her husband's last name of Lincoln. The two had married in 1993. During her second term, Lincoln also announced she was pregnant with twins and declined to run for a third term. She returned home to Arkansas to raise her family, but in 1998 ran for the open seat of retiring Sen. Dale Bumpers (D-Ark.). She won the Democratic nomination and went on to easily win the general election. In the Senate, Lincoln was assigned to the Energy and Natural Resources Committee, the Agriculture Committee, and the Special Committee on Aging.

MARILYN LLOYD (D-Md.)
(Jan. 3, 1929–   )
House: Jan. 3, 1975, to Jan. 3, 1995

Marilyn Lloyd was first elected to Congress in a surprise victory and as a relative unknown. Her husband, a local TV personality with little political background, had won the Democratic nomination for the seat, but was subsequently killed in a plane crash. The county Democratic chairman immediately looked to his widow as a replacement in the race, although she appeared to have little chance of winning. Lloyd was a political neophyte—she had previously owned and operated a local radio station with her husband. But Lloyd turned out to be an aggressive campaigner, taking popular stands for women's rights, against busing, and against President Ford's pardon of Richard Nixon following the Watergate scandal.

During her first term in the House, Lloyd won a seat on the Science, Space, and Technology Committee—the perfect position to work on behalf of her district's Oak Ridge National Laboratory, a nuclear facility that provided many jobs for her constituents. She eventually rose to become chair of the panel's subcommittee on energy research and development, and throughout her time in office she worked to advance the nation's science and technology policies. She also fought unabashedly to win science and military contracts for her district.

Lloyd was one of the most conservative Democrats in the House and, as a member of the Armed Services Committee, was a solid supporter of a strong military.

Throughout her 20 years in office, Lloyd served on the Select Committee on Aging and eventually chaired its subcommittee on housing and consumer interests. As chairwoman, she held hearings on women's health concerns and compiled a handbook on women's health entitled, "Staying Healthy, Being Aware: Health Care After Forty." In 1992, during the controversy over whether or not to ban silicone-gel breast implants, Lloyd went public with the story of her own mastectomy and asked the National Institutes of Health, on behalf of herself and other breast cancer survivors, to allow women to continue having breast replacement surgery.

In 1994, after 20 years in office, Lloyd retired from Congress.

ZOE LOFGREN (D-Calif.)
(Dec. 21, 1947–)
House: Jan. 4, 1995, to present

The issue of motherhood played a major role in Zoe Lofgren's first election to Congress. One of only four Democratic women elected to the House during the Republican landslide in the 1994 elections, Lofgren launched her campaign while standing on a kitchen breadbox in the living room of her house, stressing her middle-class roots and motherly concerns about violence in schools and the streets. She had originally been considered the underdog in the Democratic primary against a male opponent, but Lofgren benefited from an uproar that ensued when state election officials barred her from describing herself as a "mother" on the primary ballot. The officials said California law prohibited such descriptions under the heading of occupation.

"They're telling me motherhood is not a job," fumed Lofgren, who also happened to be a Santa Clara County supervisor. "As any mother will tell you, it is a job, 24 hours a day. It seems to me that being a parent is probably the most important job to the future of our country. If the law says that doesn't count, the law is wrong."[148]

The controversy drew national attention and helped Lofgren narrowly win the Democratic nomination by just 1,107 votes. She then went on to easily win the general election. Although motherhood was a winning issue for Lofgren, she was no political novice before coming to Congress. She traces her political roots to walking precincts for presidential candidate Adlai Stevenson in 1952 at the age of five. Her first job after graduating from Stanford University was as an aide to Rep. Don Edwards (D-Calif.)—the man Lofgren would succeed in Congress following his retirement. She later opened a private law practice, focusing on immigration law, and headed a nonprofit group aimed at creating low-income housing. In 1995, she was elected to the Santa Clara County Board of Supervisors, where she worked to maintain health care for the poor.

After winning election to the House, Lofgren continued to speak out on behalf of women, families, and the poor. During debate in her first term on a Republican bill aimed at curbing immigration, she won approval of four amendments that restored protections for battered women and children. She also voted against Republican legislation to overhaul the welfare system and opposed efforts to deny public education to illegal immigrants. In 1998, she introduced legislation that would provide federal grants to allow schools to start and end classes later in the day. She cited scientific studies showing that teenagers are better able to concentrate in the afternoon and evening, rather than in the morning.

A solid liberal vote, Lofgren has voted to increase the minimum wage, freeze defense spending, and ban certain assault weapons. She is also a strong supporter of abortion rights and opposed the ban on a particular type of abortion, labeled partial birth abortion by its opponents.

She serves on the Judiciary Committee and the Science Committee.

CATHERINE LONG (D-La.)
(Feb. 7, 1924–   )
House: April 4, 1985, to Jan. 3, 1987

Catherine Long came to Congress to fill the seat of her husband, Rep. Gillis Long, who died while serving his eighth term in office. Louisiana constituents proved their affection for Gillis Long when they gave his widow more than 50 percent of the vote against four other challengers.

Catherine Long's early career ranged from the military to politics. She worked as a pharmacist's mate in the U.S. Navy and later served as an aide to Sen. Wayne Morse (D-Ore.) and Rep. James Polk (D-Ohio). She also served as a delegate to Democratic National Conventions and was a member of the Louisiana Democratic Finance Council and the state party's central committee.

After winning the special election to Congress, Long paid special attention to Louisiana's economic needs. She sought to preserve price supports for sugar and opposed efforts to require local governments to share the cost of federal flood control programs. She co-sponsored the Economic Equity Act of 1985, which secured pension and health benefits for women, and sought to restrict racial and sex discrimination in insurance practices. She also supported economic sanctions against South Africa and aid for Nicaraguan refugees.

Long declined to run for re-election in 1986, citing overwhelming debts left over from her first campaign.

JILL LONG (D-Ind.)
(July 12, 1952–   )
House: March 28, 1989, to Jan. 3, 1995

Jill Long's election to the House was not only a shock to Republicans, but a huge embarrassment. The seat had been in solid GOP hands for 12 years and was once held by former GOP Vice President Dan Quayle. Long won the special election to fill the open seat created when Rep. Dan Coats (R) was appointed to fill Quayle's Senate seat after he won election as vice president. It was Long's third try for Congress. She was soundly defeated by Quayle in a 1986 Senate bid and by Coats in a bid for the House in 1988. But the two elections helped her win wide name recognition and taught her the political lessons she needed to win in 1989. During her first two bids, Long campaigned on liberal issues that included support for abortion rights and a ban on school prayer. In her third try, she shifted her focus to conservative economic issues and hammered away on an anti-tax platform.

In her successful 1990 re-election campaign, Long continued her strong anti-tax position, stating, "I'm cautious and moderate by nature. I was raised not to like taxes, to save money, to darn socks and refinish furniture—all the 4-H Club stuff."[149]

Long was not joking about being a member of the 4-H Club. She grew up on a grain and dairy farm, where she milked cows, fed hogs, and cut hay. Long went on to earn a master's degree and later a doctorate in business. Up until her election, she taught business at Indiana University. Even on election day in 1989, Long had to break away from greeting voters at the polls to teach a noontime class. Her only prior political experience before coming to Congress was a three-year stint on the Valparaiso City (Ind.) Council.

Long maintained her interest in farm issues after coming to Congress. She was assigned to the Agriculture Committee, where she persuaded her colleagues to hold a field hearing in her district—the first in the area in nearly 30 years. She wanted her committee colleagues to hear firsthand from concerned farmers about the proposed program changes in the 1990 Farm Bill. Long pushed through several amendments to the bill, including incentives to farmers who practice effective conservation-oriented techniques and ensuring fair planting flexibility for farmers.

Long—the daughter of a World War II veteran—served on the Veterans' Affairs Committee and fought for better treatment of posttraumatic stress disorder and expanded hospice care for terminally ill veterans. She pushed for comprehensive health care services for women vets, including counseling for women who were sexually harassed while in the military. Long was also a member of the Select Committee on Hunger.

On social issues, Long was generally liberal. She voted to allow federal funds for abortion in cases of rape and incest, and supported raising the minimum wage. In 1991, she voted against authorizing President Bush to use force in the Persian Gulf. But Long was strictly conservative on fiscal issues. She was a member of the Task Force on Government Waste, which investigated federal agencies to identify wasteful uses of taxpayer money. She voted against the congressional pay raise and supported a strict gift ban for members of Congress. She opposed any bill that increased taxes, including President Clinton's 1994 budget package. Despite her conservative fiscal votes, she was defeated by a Republican in her 1994 bid for re-election.

ROSE LONG (D-La.)
(April 8, 1892–May 27, 1970)
Senate: Feb. 10, 1936, to Jan. 3, 1937

When Rose Long was sworn in to the Senate in 1936, it was the first time in history that two women had ever served together in that chamber. Sen. Hattie Caraway (D-Ark.) had held Senate office since 1931. (The record of two women serving simultaneously would not be broken until 1992, when the number of women in the Senate tripled to six.) Long also has the distinction of being part of the only father–mother–son combination to serve in the institution. Long's husband, Huey—whom she succeeded after his death—was a senator for three years, and her son Russell served in the Senate from 1948 to 1987.

Long was appointed by Gov. James Noe after her husband's brutal assassination in the Louisiana state capitol building. But Long was not the top choice of the state's Democratic machine. When the front-runner for the open seat, Gov. O. K. Allen, died before he could be sworn into office, his successor Noe named Long to avoid a divisive intraparty struggle. On Long's appointment to the open seat, Caraway mused, "It will be nice to have a woman's company in the Senate."[150]

Unlike like her husband, who was known for his boisterous and flamboyant style, Rose Long was reserved and soft-spoken. She rarely rose to speak on the Senate floor, but instead focused on her five committee assignments. She served on the Claims Committee, the Immigration Committee, the Interoceanic Canals Committee, the Post Offices and Post Roads Committee, and the Public Lands and Surveys Committee. Long was most proud of her work on the latter panel, where she successfully pushed through a measure to enlarge the Chalmette National Park on the site of the battle of New Orleans.

Long had learned politics from watching her husband's career. She helped manage his early campaigns and served as his secretary and stenographer. She is also said to have helped her husband complete his three-year law course at Tulane University in just seven months. He once proclaimed that she had the best political judgment of anyone he knew and that he would rather trust her advice than that of anyone else.

Although Long remained low key during her brief one year in office, she drew much attention from her male colleagues for her quiet charm and youthful looks—she was just 43 when sworn into office. She is said to have suffered constant rumors of a remarriage as well as frequent flirtation from other senators.

Long accepted her role as little more than the legatee of her husband's estate and quietly left Washington for her home in Shreveport, La., when the remainder of her husband's term expired in 1937.

NITA LOWEY (D-N.Y.)
(July 5, 1937–   )
House: Jan. 3, 1989, to present

Nita Lowey is one of Congress's most outspoken supporters of women's rights and abortion rights. A former co-chair of the Congressional Caucus for Women's Issues, Lowey now serves as the chair of the Pro-Choice Task Force. She opposes a ban on so-called partial birth abortions, saying doctors, not Congress, should make medical decisions. She has also focused much of her legislative attention on women's health issues and uses her seat on the Appropriations Committee to push for greater funding for breast cancer research.

Lowey started her political career in 1974 as a campaign aide to her neighbor, Mario Cuomo, who was running for lieutenant governor of New York. Lowey, a homemaker at the time, opened her house up as a meeting spot for Cuomo supporters. Cuomo lost his bid, but was later appointed secretary of state and paid Lowey back by hiring her to work in his department's anti-poverty division. After Cuomo became governor in 1982, Lowey remained in the secretary of state's office and eventually rose to become a top aide there.

Her successful bid for Congress in 1988 was her first run for elective office. In her freshman term, Lowey was named to the Education and Labor Committee, the Merchant Marine and Fisheries Committee, and the Select Committee on Narcotics Abuse and Control. But at the start of her second term, Lowey aggressively lobbied her Democratic leadership and won a seat on the exclusive Appropriations Committee. Years later, following the Republican takeover of Congress in 1994, Lowey successfully fought to keep her seat on the panel. Republicans had planned to cut back on committee rosters, but Lowey went directly to top GOP leaders and argued that by sparing a few Democratic seats, they could maintain important diversity on the powerful spending panel. They agreed and let her keep her seat.

As a member of the Appropriations subcommittee on health services, Lowey fought unsuccessfully to allow federal research on human embryos in medical studies. She has been more successful in winning funding hikes for the National Institutes of Health and the National Cancer Institute. She has also pushed to maintain breast cancer research programs within the Department of Defense.

Lowey has established herself as a leader in the women's rights movement. She fought to require federal health insurance plans to cover abortion services and to end restrictions on federal funding for abortions under the Medicaid program. She lost on both fronts. She has pushed to create federal programs addressing violence against women and supported the 1994 ban on assault weapons, calling violence and crime women's issues.

On other issues, she has tried to trim the budget by cutting federal subsidy programs for farmers and peanut growers. She is however, a strong proponent of U.S. aid to Israel.

In 1998, she fought aggressively to add a provision to a national highway bill that encouraged states to lower their drunk driving limits, but was blocked from offering her amendment on the House floor. It would have withheld federal transportation funds from states that didn't drop their blood alcohol limits from .10 to .08. She said the move would save 500 lives a year.

CLARE BOOTHE LUCE (R-Conn.)
(April 10, 1903–Oct. 9, 1987)
House: Jan. 3, 1943, to Jan. 3, 1947

The life of Clare Booth Luce reads like a novel, with her four years in Congress just one short chapter. Luce was the illegitimate daughter of a failed concert violinist and a chorus girl, but she would eventually go on to be a journalist, playwright, legislator and ambassador to Italy. In 1953, a Gallup poll ranked her the fourth "most admired woman" in the world, just after Eleanor Roosevelt, Queen Elizabeth II, and Mrs. Dwight D. Eisenhower.

Luce's humble beginnings in Manhattan were a far cry from the sophisticated lifestyle she would lead as an adult. Luce's father deserted the family when she was just eight years old. Her mother struggled to give her daughter a good education, but Luce's schooling was at best intermittent. She studied acting as a child and worked as an understudy to actress Mary Pickford. Her mother later remarried a wealthy doctor, Albert Austin, who went on to serve in Congress from the same district Luce would eventually represent.

Luce first became involved in politics as a teenager when she joined the National Women's Party and campaigned for suffrage. Luce later married multimillionaire George Tuttle Brokaw, 23 years her senior. He was the heir to a clothing fortune, but also a drunkard and a brute. The marriage lasted six years and produced Luce's only child. Thanks in part to Brokaw's generous alimony, Luce became one of Manhattan's gayest divorcées. Following her divorce, Luce joined the staff of *Vogue* as an editorial assistant. A year later, she became associate editor of *Vanity Fair* and within two years was named managing editor.

In 1934, Luce left journalism and began devoting her energy to writing plays. *The Women* opened on Broadway in 1936 to huge audiences. The satire about idle, rich women toured the country and was eventually made into a Hollywood film. In 1935, Luce married Henry Luce, the co-founder of *Time* magazine, and the couple quickly began collaborating on a new publication called *Life*. Soon after the outbreak of World War

II, Luce toured the world as a war correspondent for *Time, Life,* and *Fortune* magazines. She traveled 75,000 miles through Europe, North Africa, and China. On her return to the United States, she published her reports in a book entitled *Europe in the Spring,* which was eventually translated into five languages.

In 1942, Luce agreed to run for Congress in hopes of recapturing the seat her stepfather had lost two years earlier. She easily won the GOP nomination over six opponents and narrowly ousted the Democratic incumbent in the general election. During that campaign, Luce made President Franklin Roosevelt her main target, accusing him of inefficiency at home and of "talking a tough war but waging a soft one."[151] Once in office, Luce requested a seat on the Foreign Affairs Committee. Despite being well qualified for the post due to her extensive travels as a reporter, she was considered "insufferably arrogant" for having asked for such a prestigious seat and quickly turned down.[152] Instead, Luce was placed on the Military Affairs Committee.

In her maiden speech on the House floor, Luce attacked Vice President Henry Wallace's foreign policy as "globaloney." Her speech made front-page headlines and Luce was thereafter branded an isolationist—a charge she strongly denied. Throughout the war, Luce used her seat in Congress as a platform to attack the Roosevelt administration. Her nonstop opposition to the Democratic president prompted Republicans to select her as the keynote speaker at their national convention in 1944—the first woman ever given such an honor. During her emotional speech Luce referred to all the "GI Joes and GI Jims" who had lost their lives during the war and suggested that the massive casualties were due to Democratic bungling. During her race for a second term in Congress, Roosevelt himself campaigned for Luce's opponent, but Luce narrowly managed to win reelection by just 2,000 votes.

Luce's notoriety for a sharp tongue tended to obscure much of her legislative efforts. During her two terms in Congress, Luce proposed a nonaggression pact with England, France, and other European countries. She called for racial equality in the armed services and condemned the Daughters of the American Revolution for refusing to let Marian Anderson—a black singer—perform at Constitution Hall. She also fought for India's independence from Britain and voted against the Smith-Connally Anti-Strike Bill. Her very first bill in Congress was to create a special branch of the military for 4-Fs to work in nonessential activities. She offered legislation to establish a Department of Children's Welfare and to create a bureau in the Labor Department to ensure equal pay for equal work regardless of race or sex. Neither of these bills ever made it out of committee. As World War II came to a close, Luce increased her warnings about the threat of the Soviet Union and introduced a resolution urging Congress to acknowledge American responsibility for Soviet domination of Poland following the Yalta conference.

In 1946, Luce announced she would not run for a third term in office. She, however, remained active in Republican politics as a writer and lecturer and in 1948 went on to describe Democratic presidential nominee Harry Truman as a "man of phlegm, not fire."[153] In 1952, Luce campaigned for Dwight D. Eisenhower, but after the election declined his offer to join the cabinet as secretary of labor. Instead, she agreed to become the ambassador to Italy, a post she held for five years. In 1959, Eisenhower nominated her as ambassador to Brazil, but Luce withdrew her name following a bitter Senate confirmation process in which Sen. Wayne Morse (D-Ore.)—who still held a grudge over her wartime attacks against Roosevelt—blocked her nomination.

In 1964, Luce co-chaired Barry Goldwater's bid for the White House and later served on the President's Foreign Intelligence Advisory Board under Nixon, Ford, and Reagan. Following the death of her husband in 1967, Luce moved to Hawaii, but in the 1980s returned to Washington, where she remained until her death in 1987.

GEORGIA LUSK (D-N.M.)
(May 12, 1893–Jan. 5, 1971)
House: Jan. 3, 1947, to Jan. 3, 1949

Before coming to Congress, Georgia Lusk dedicated herself to improving the educational system of her home state of New Mexico. A school teacher by profession, Lusk was elected superintendent of Lea County in 1924 and served in that post for six years before winning a bid for state superintendent of public instruction. During her time overseeing the state's schools, she discovered severe problems within the system—most notably a lack of textbooks. In classes held in one-room adobes she would see as many as 25 students sharing a single book. Lusk successfully lobbied the state legislature to use a $28,000 slush fund to buy books for the schools. She also pushed the legislature to fund a school construction plan, raise teachers' salaries, and institute a teachers' retirement program. "It's just as important for the government to look over the business of education as it is too look over farming or railroading or anything else," Lusk once said.[154] The *National Education Association Journal* reported in 1932 that Lusk had raised the standards of New Mexico's school system while at the same time eliminated teacher testing as a requirement of certification.

Lusk attended the Democratic National Convention in 1928 and 1948 and served as a delegate in 1944 to the first White House Conference on Rural Education. Two years later, she decided to run for one of New Mexico's two at-large seats to the House. After winning election to the House, Lusk was assigned to the Committee on Veteran Affairs—a seat not quite suited to her background, but she continued to call for educational improvements. She pushed for federal support of educational programs and backed the establishment of a cabinet-level Department of Education. On other issues, she was considered an independent voter. She was a staunch backer of the Truman administration's foreign policies, voting for assistance to Greece and Turkey and endorsing universal military training. But she voted to overturn Truman's veto of the Taft-Hartley Act—a bill that limited the ability of unions to strike and weakened national labor standards.

Lusk lost her bid for a second term in 1948. Some charged she had been the victim of illegal campaign maneuvers, but she declined to demand a recount, saying, "I didn't have the money and, anyway, I thought they'd only say a woman can't take a licking."[155] In 1949, Truman appointed Lusk to the War Claims Commission, where she served with other Democratic appointees until the election of President Eisenhower in 1953. Lusk then returned to New Mexico and was again elected to two terms as state superintendent of schools.

CAROLYN MALONEY (D-N.Y.)
(Feb. 19, 1948–   )
House: Jan. 5, 1993, to present

Carolyn Maloney won election to Congress in the 1992 "Year of the Woman" by defeating seven-term Republican Rep. Bill Green. Although Green was a liberal Republican who had defeated past big names such as former Rep. Bella Abzug, Maloney ran a tough campaign and used the slogan "there are too many millionaires and not enough women" in Congress to narrowly oust Green by just 4,000 votes. Maloney was also helped by her strong name recognition from 10 years in the New York City Council.

Maloney, a former teacher and administrator for the New York City Board of Education, began her work in the political arena in 1977 when she served as a legislative aide for the New York state assembly. She also worked as the director of special projects for the state Senate minority leader. Maloney made her first run for public office in 1982 and won a seat on the New York City Council. During her time on the Council, Maloney authored the landmark New York City Campaign Finance Act, which helped level the playing field for political challengers and incumbents.

Maloney, the first city legislator to give birth to a child while serving on the council, also focused much of her legislative attention on women's issues. She proposed a comprehensive legislative package to make day care more available and affordable. She also led efforts to create the Joint Mayoral-Council Commission on Early Childhood Development programs.

After winning election to Congress, Maloney continued to focus on women's issues and campaign finance reform. During debate in 1998 on overhauling the way federal campaigns are funded, Maloney offered a bill creating a commission to study the problem. She later withdrew the legislation in an effort to pass a more comprehensive bill that cracked down on large, unregulated donations.

During her time in Congress, Maloney has served on the Banking and Financial Services Committee, the Government Reform and Oversight Committee, and the Joint Economic Committee. On the Government Reform and Oversight Committee, Maloney was an outspoken opponent of the Republican investigation into fund-raising by Democrats and the Clinton White House.

A strong supporter of abortion rights, Maloney backed legislation to increase access to abortion clinics and require states to provide federally funded abortions to poor women in cases of rape and incest.

During a string of sexual harassment controversies involving the armed services, Maloney in 1997 introduced a bill to set up a commission to investigate the military justice system. That same year she reintroduced the Equal Rights Amendment to the Constitution, 25 years after Congress first passed it only to have it die in 1982 lacking ratification. In 1997, Maloney also offered legislation encouraging women to breast feed their children and offering tax breaks to businesses that set up "lactation locations" for new mothers.

HELEN DOUGLAS MANKIN (D-Ga.)
(Sept. 11, 1894–July 25, 1956)
House: Feb. 12, 1946, to Jan. 3, 1947

Helen Douglas Mankin's congressional record and political background were much more substantial than her brief House service would suggest. Before and after coming to Congress, Mankin fought to reform Georgia politics and give blacks a greater voice in public affairs. It was the black vote, in fact, that pushed her to victory in the 1946 special election to fill the seat of Rep. Robert Ramspeck, who resigned to take a seat with the Air Transport Association. She was the only woman in a field of 18 candidates. On election night, Mankin was running behind until the ballot box from Atlanta's Ward 3, Precinct B, was opened. All but 10 of the registered voters in that precinct were black. In the ballot box were 956 votes for Mankin, 35 for her opponents. Mankin won the election by 770 votes.

Mankin had won the favor of black voters largely due to her earlier reputation as a lawyer who gave fair treatment to her black clients. Mankin had also fought to end the Georgia state poll tax while she served in the state legislature. Her bid for the U.S. House was the first election in the state following the repeal of that voting restriction.

Mankin first became involved in politics in 1935 when she led an unsuccessful campaign to pass a child labor law. She decided she might be more successful if she were on the inside of the political arena. She took $150 that she had been saving to paint the house, posted it, and declared herself a candidate for the Georgia General Assembly. "Nobody thought I had a chance," she said. "But I got an 800-vote plurality."[156] During her next 10 years in the state legislature, Mankin worked for higher salaries for teachers, segregation for teen prisoners, and a state department of labor.

In her youth, Mankin interrupted her law studies to join a women's hospital unit attached to the French Army and spent a year driving an ambulance in France. On her return to the United States, Mankin earned her law degree at the Atlanta Law School. She later traveled extensively across America and Europe—all by car—and did some freelance newspaper writing about her adventures. After winning election to the House, Mankin was appointed to the Civil Service Committee, Claims Committee, Elections Committee, and the Committee on Revision of the Laws.

In contrast to many of her Georgia colleagues, she opposed funding for the House Committee on Un-American Activities and pushed for a federal ban on the poll tax. She supported federal housing programs, price controls, and international cooperation to maintain peace. "I'm a liberal but not a radical," Mankin once said.[157]

In the Democratic primary for the following full term, Mankin garnered nearly 11,000 more votes than her opponent. But under the state's "county unit system," which heavily favored rural districts, Mankin was awarded just six unit votes for carrying Fulton County while her opponent received eight units for carrying two less populous counties. Attempts by the Georgia Democratic Executive Committee to place Mankin's name on the ballot failed, but she refused to give up and continued to campaign as a write-in candidate. She received an impressive 16,000 write-in votes, but it was not enough to defeat her opponent who garnered 22,000 ballot votes. After losing the race, Mankin launched a legal battle against the unit system, charging that it was unconstitutional. The U.S. District Court in Atlanta ruled against her in 1950 and that decision was upheld later that year by the U.S. Supreme Court. It was not until 1962—six years after Mankin was killed in a car accident—that the high court would rule the unit voting system unconstitutional.

MARJORIE MARGOLIES-MEZVINSKY
(D-Pa.)
(June 21, 1942–   )
House: Jan. 5, 1993, to Jan. 3, 1995

Marjorie Margolies-Mezvinsky was elected to Congress by a narrow 1,400 votes in a district that was 2-to-1 registered Republican. On the night of her election, she actually composed a concession speech in which she simply changed the word "defeat" to "victory" throughout the text. She was the first Democrat to represent the Montgomery County, Pa., area in 77 years.

A graduate of the University of Pennsylvania and a CBS News Foundation fellow at Columbia University, Margolies-Mezvinsky began her career as a television journalist in 1967. One of her first assignments covered the plight of Southeast Asian war orphans. She was so moved by the story that in 1970, at the age of 28, she adopted an orphan from Korea and became the first unmarried American to adopt a foreign child. Four years later, she adopted another orphan from Vietnam.

In 1975, while working with NBC on assignment in Washington, she met and married Iowa Congressman Edward Mezvinsky, who served on the House Judiciary Committee during the Watergate investigation. The couple eventually had two children, and together with his four sons, her two adopted children, and three other children the couple adopted together, they raised a total of 11 children.

Five of those children were still living at home when Margolies-Mezvinsky decided to leave journalism and run for Congress in 1992. It was the "Year of the Woman," and Margolies-Mezvinsky won an open seat to join 24 other new women in the House. She was one of five freshman Democrats named to the powerful Energy and Commerce Committee. She also served on the Government Operations and the Small Business Committees. She focused on many women's issues, working unsuccessfully to defeat the "Hyde amendment" that prohibited government-funded abortions and to pass a bill which banned intimidation of women seeking access to abortion clinics. She also supported the Family and Medical Leave Act, giving workers unpaid time off to deal with family emergencies. Along with women's concerns, Margolies-Mezvinsky worked on a variety of budget issues. She introduced bills to link cost-of-living increases for Social Security to a person's means and to raise the retirement age to 70 by the year 2012.

But it was Margolies-Mezvinsky's vote for President Clinton's budget package that caused her political downfall. During her campaign, Margolies-Mezvinsky had pledged to oppose the budget deal. Once in office, she actually cast three preliminary votes against the package, saying that it should have contained more spending cuts and less tax increases. Just hours before the final vote on the bill, Margolies-Mezvinsky appeared on local television telling constituents she remained opposed to the budget plan. But just minutes before the vote, she received a call from President Clinton asking for her support. She agreed, but only if hers was the deciding vote. In the end, her support was needed and she voted yes to give Clinton a razor-thin victory of 218 to 216.

"I knew at the time that changing my vote at the 11th hour may have been tantamount to political suicide," she said later. "But the vote would resolve itself into one simple question: Was my political future more important than the agenda that the President had laid out for America?" She added, "I have another life. I've never had problems figuring out what I was going to do. Win or lose, I've won."[158] Sure enough, her flip-flop was used against her in her bid for a second term and she was defeated by about 10,000 votes.

After leaving Congress, Margolies-Mezvinsky served as executive director of the Women's Campaign Fund, a group that assists pro-choice women candidates. In 1998, Margolies-Mezvinsky resigned from the group to run for lieutenant governor of Pennsylvania. She and her gubernatorial running mate were overwhelmingly defeated by the incumbent Republican team. Shortly after the defeat, Margolies-Mezvinsky launched a campaign for the Senate in the year 2000.

BOOKS BY MARGOLIES-MEZVINSKY

Finding Someone to Love (1980)
They Came to Stay (1976)
A Woman's Place: The Freshman Women Who Changed the Face of Congress (1994)

LYNN MARTIN (R-Ill.)
(Dec. 26, 1939–   )
House: Jan. 3, 1981, to Jan. 3, 1991

Once called the "political version of Joan Rivers" by the *Chicago Tribune*, Lynn Martin used her quick tongue and sarcastic wit to rise her way up through state and national elected office and eventually into the presidential cabinet. A moderate Republican, she often crossed her own party leaders—particularly when it came to women's issues and abortion rights. She, however, established many strong ties to top GOP leaders, and was chosen in 1984 by Vice President George Bush to coach him in his debate against vice presidential hopeful Geraldine Ferraro. Eight years later, she seconded his nomination at the 1992 Republican Convention for his re-election as president. Bush later rewarded her by naming her secretary of labor.

Martin started in politics in 1972 when she was elected to the Winnebago County, Ill., Board. Four years later she won a seat in the Illinois state House and later moved to the state Senate. In 1980, when Rep. John Anderson (R-Ill.) left Congress to run for president, Martin defeated four other Republicans to take Anderson's seat.

Once in the House, Martin rose quickly within her party hierarchy. During her first term in the House, she was appointed to the powerful Budget Committee. On that committee, Martin led the effort to push through the 1986 reconciliation package, a bill of deficit-cutting measures that was batted back and forth between the House and Senate an unprecedented nine times. Martin held firm against Democratic leadership attempts to increase federal spending and eventually brokered a deal with moderate Democrats, convincing enough of them to join Republicans in passing the bill.

Martin often used her wit to bring the inflated egos of her male colleagues back down to earth. Once, during a late-night session of the House when tempers began to flare, Martin—a former school teacher—quipped, "It's never wise to keep the House in after 11. It's like managing a nursery school without a nap." Another time, when Democrats on the Budget Committee tried to approve a costly spending measure, Martin blurted out, "Maybe girls learn to say 'no' easier than boys."[159]

In her third term in the House, Martin was elected vice chair of the Republican Conference, the first woman ever to serve in the Republican House leadership. She was re-elected to that post in 1986, but was defeated in her bid for full chair of the conference two years later. Her defeat was due, in part, to her liberal social stances. She supported the Equal Rights Amendment and backed abortion rights for women. After visiting South Africa, Martin defied the Reagan administration by voting to support economic sanctions against the country's apartheid government. She also opposed the Bush administration by voting to override the president's veto of family and medical leave legislation.

In her position on the House Administration Committee, Martin challenged Democratic chairmen of other committees to tell her how many women they employed and how much they were being paid. She conducted a survey that showed women congressional workers were concentrated at the low end of the salary spectrum while men held the majority of high-paying jobs. She also pushed Congress to comply with job safety and worker protection laws imposed on private sector businesses.

Martin also served on the Committee on Public Works and Transportation, the Committee on Armed Services, and the powerful Rules Committee.

In 1990, Martin left the House to run an unsuccessful bid against Sen. Paul Simon (D). After her loss, President Bush quickly appointed her his secretary of labor, even though she differed with him on a number of social issues, especially abortion. "I can't imagine that the only people who should work for a president are those who sycophantically agree on everything," she said after her appointment. "It would be the most boring Cabinet in the world and it would be of no use to the president."[160]

After Bush left office, Martin remained active as a political analyst and television commentator. She taught government at Northwestern University and worked with the international accounting firm Deloitte & Touche on their program to help women break into top management positions. In 1995, Martin briefly threw her hat into the presidential race, but later withdrew.

CATHERINE MAY (R-Wash.)
(May 18, 1914–   )
House: Jan. 3, 1959, to Jan. 3, 1971

Catherine May, the first woman to represent Washington state in the U.S. House of Representatives, devoted most of her congressional career to protecting the farmers of her largely agricultural district. She served on the House Agriculture Committee throughout her 12 years in office and repeatedly pushed to increase domestic production of beet sugar— a major crop in her district. She backed placing special fees on imported sugar and in 1964 proposed a higher permanent quota for domestic sugar beets. In 1964, she was one of 15 presidential appointees named to the National Commission on Food Marketing, which studied and made recommendations on the marketing structure of the food industry.

May was also concerned with children's issues. In her first year in office, May introduced a bill to strengthen and improve state and local programs to fight juvenile delinquency. She also amended in 1966 the Child Nutrition Act to extend the school milk program to children attending overseas schools administered by the Defense Department. In 1970, she sponsored a proposal by President Nixon to provide extremely poor families with free food stamps.

Along with her Agriculture seat, May also served briefly on the District of Columbia Committee and the Joint Committee on Atomic Energy. May generally voted along party lines and supported the Eisenhower administration. In 1965, she was honored by being placed on the House GOP Policy and Research Committee and the GOP Committee on Committees—two powerful panels charged with shaping Republican legislation and handing out committee assignments. May, however, did split with her party leadership during her second term in office when she was one of just 23 Republicans who voted for federal funding of power transmission lines for electric plants in the Upper Colorado Basin. May also broke with her party when she pushed to keep alive a nuclear reactor in her state, arguing it would create jobs and help private industry.

May was also a strong supporter of women's rights. She fought for passage of the Equal Pay Act of 1963 and was also part of a small group of congressional women who tried to have the House gym opened up to women lawmakers.

May lost her bid for a seventh term in 1970. In 1971, she was appointed to the U.S. International Trade Commission and became the first woman to chair that panel.

Ironically, May says it was her husband who first encouraged her to enter politics and that she would never have done so without his approval. "I feel strongly that any woman who pursues a career outside the home without her husband's blessing is in for trouble. I would not have gone into politics if my husband had not wanted me to," she said.[161]

May was elected to the Washington state legislature in 1952—only the second woman ever to achieve that honor—and served there for six years. While in the state House, May served on the Education Committee and took a special interest in the special needs of retarded children and juvenile delinquency. She also served as vice chair of the Governor's statewide Committee on Educational Television.

Before entering politics, May worked as a writer, editor, and broadcaster for several radio stations in Washington and New York.

CAROLYN MCCARTHY (D-N.Y.)
(Jan. 5, 1944–   )
House: Jan. 7, 1997, to present

Carolyn McCarthy was first thrust into the political spotlight when a gunman opened fire on a Long Island Rail Road commuter train in 1993, killing her husband and seriously wounding her son. Following the tragedy, McCarthy, a nurse who had never before been a political activist, began to lobby Congress to pass tougher gun laws. When her local congressman, Rep. Dan Frisa (R), rebuffed her pleas to oppose a repeal of an assault weapons ban, McCarthy decided to run against him.

A lifelong Republican, McCarthy at first tried to challenge him in the primary election. But local Republican officials discouraged her. Democrats then quickly jumped into the fray and asked her to run on their ticket. The national Democratic party even gave her a high-profile speaking role at the party's 1996 national convention.

McCarthy's tragic tale made her a top media story and she went on to easily defeat Frisa by a 16-point margin. In Congress, McCarthy has maintained her focus on passing tougher restrictions on gun ownership. She called on gun manufacturers to produce childproof guns, and introduced legislation to penalize adults who do not keep firearms out of the reach of children.

McCarthy has also focused on education issues and worked to pass legislation creating a program to help train more teachers across the country. Although she was a lifelong Republican, she backs many stances usually thought to be Democratic, including abortion rights, increased funding for educational programs, and environmental protection. She also opposes the death penalty. She serves on the Education and Work-force Committee and the Small Business Committee.

McCarthy's story even prompted Barbra Streisand and the NBC tele-vision network to produce a movie together about McCarthy's life and her rise to political power. The 1998 movie sparked a political uproar when actor Charleton Heston, the national spokesman for the National Rifle Association, attacked the movie as being slanted against the gun community.

KAREN MCCARTHY (D-Mo.)
(March, 18, 1947–   )
House: Jan. 4, 1995, to present

Karen McCarthy had extensive experience as a legislator before winning election to Congress. She served for 18 years in the Missouri legislature, devoting much of her attention to energy and environmental issues. She also focused on financial matters as chair of the Ways and Means Com-mittee for 12 years. McCarthy made a name for herself by successfully sponsoring legislation that provides job training and day-care services to Missouri women on welfare to help them get off public assistance and into the job market. The state program won national attention and praise from President Clinton. In 1994, her last year in the state legislature, she became president of the National Conference of State Legislatures, the first woman to serve as the group's leader.

McCarthy started her professional career as an English teacher. She holds two masters' degrees, in business and English. During her time in the state legislature, McCarthy also worked as a financial analyst for several private corporations.

McCarthy won her seat in Congress by defeating 10 other Democrats who had lined up to replace retiring Democratic Rep. Alan Wheat in 1994. After coming to Capitol Hill, she was assigned to the Science Com-mittee and the Small Business Committee. In 1995, she joined the Trans-portation and Infrastructure Committee, but, at the start of 1997, House leaders awarded McCarthy an exclusive spot on the Commerce Committee where she focuses on energy issues.

McCarthy considers herself a moderate or "new" Democrat, although she generally toes the party line. She has criticized Republicans for cutting public assistance to the poor while increasing spending on the military. She, however, ultimately supported the Republican-backed welfare reform bill that was signed by President Clinton in 1996. McCarthy has also sided with Republicans in backing states' rights and opposing "unfunded mandates"—federal regulations that states must enforce without economic assistance from the federal government. She said that her time in the Missouri state House had made her sensitive to the burdens on state governments.

But on social issues, McCarthy is a solid Democratic vote. She supports abortion rights and gun control, and voted to increase the minimum wage in 1996. She also backed Democratic efforts in 1998 to create a "patients' bill of rights" that would allow patients to sue their HMOs. In 1997, she pushed for the "brown fields" initiative that offered tax credits to businesses to clean up polluted areas.

KATHRYN O'LAUGHLIN MCCARTHY
(D-Kan.)
(April 24, 1894–Jan. 16, 1952)
House: March 4, 1933, to Jan. 3, 1935

Kathryn O'Laughlin came to Congress after defeating eight male challengers in the Democratic primary and going on to oust the incumbent Republican who held the western Kansas seat. She successfully addressed her campaign to the poor farmers and ranchers of the state. She supported tariff cuts and a dollar based on commodity prices rather than the gold standard. Just one month before she was sworn into office, O'Laughlin married Daniel McCarthy, a state senator who had worked on her campaign.

Kathryn McCarthy started down the path to politics long before winning election in 1932. As a young woman, she defied her father and enrolled in the University of Chicago to study law. After graduation, she worked as a lawyer in Chicago and later set up a practice back in her home state of Kansas. She soon began looking for the right opportunity to enter the political arena. She was a delegate to three state Democratic conventions and in 1931 won a seat in the state House.

After taking office in the U.S. House, McCarthy was assigned to the Insular Affairs Committee, a post that afforded her little chance to work on behalf of her farming constituents. Unlike most freshmen members who quietly accepted their assignments, McCarthy protested and asked to be switched to the Agriculture Committee. Her request was denied, but she was able to land a seat on the Education panel and fought for increased federal funding for vocational schools.

McCarthy also continued her work on behalf of farmers and supported most New Deal legislation. She backed the Agricultural Adjustment Act in hopes of saving farmers through greater government control of agricultural programs. But Kansas's agricultural workers quickly tired of government regulations and refused to back McCarthy in her bid for a second term. After a hard-fought race, McCarthy lost re-election by just over 7,500 votes. After leaving office in 1935, McCarthy returned to her law practice and later owned a car dealership. She also remained active in politics, serving as a delegate to state and national Democratic conventions until 1944.

RUTH HANNA MCCORMICK (R-Ill.)
(March 27, 1880–Dec. 31, 1944)
House: March 4, 1929, to March 3, 1931

Ruth Hanna McCormick was born into politics. Her father was Mark Hanna, the wealthy industrialist and Republican leader who went on to serve in the U.S. Senate and as campaign manager for William McKinley's presidential bid. McCormick rang doorbells for her father during political campaigns and made her first political speech on behalf of McKinley from the rear platform of a private railroad car—she was just 16 at the time. She also worked as a secretary for her father during his tenure in the Senate, spending time on Capitol Hill to "absorb the language and the routine of the legislative branch."[162]

McCormick entered into another political family when she married Medill McCormick, the heir to the *Chicago Tribune*, who would eventually serve as a state legislator, U.S. congressman, and senator. She campaigned for her husband during his bid for the House in 1916, and after he came to office the two worked together for the Suffrage Amendment. She became chair of the Congressional Committee of the National American Woman Suffrage Association, lobbying for the woman's vote in the halls of the Capitol while he argued for it on the House floor. When he decided to run for the Senate in 1924, McCormick organized a network of Republican women's clubs across Illinois—a network that would later back her in her own political campaigns.

Throughout the 1920s, McCormick became increasingly influential in the Republican party. She was the first woman on the executive committee of the Republican National Committee and was an associate member of the National Committee from 1919 to 1924, when she became the first elected national committeewoman from Illinois.

Her husband, who had suffered from manic depression and later became an alcoholic, killed himself in 1925 at the age of 47. For the first few years following his death, McCormick worked as a farmer and newspaper publisher. In 1928, however, she decided to return to the political arena and entered the race for one of two open House seats. Later that year she became the first woman in politics to grace the cover of *Time* magazine.

"Usually, when a candidate announces his candidacy, we read in the papers that owing to the demand of his constituency and the pressure of his friends he has reluctantly agreed to make this great sacrifice and run for office," she said when announcing her candidacy. "In all candor and honesty I must say that nobody asked me to run. I have no demand upon me from constituents, friends, enemies, neighbors or family, and as far as I know, nobody wants me to run. But I hope at the end of the campaign that I am going to find a sufficient number of people who think I ought to run."[163]

She defeated seven men in the Republican primary and led the entire state ticket during the November general elections. Within a month after taking office, McCormick announced her intention to run for the Senate against the man who had defeated her husband for reelection in 1924— fellow Republican Sen. Charles Deneen.

With a campaign slogan of "No promises and no bunk," McCormick defeated the incumbent by 170,000 votes in the primary—with strong backing from women voters—and became the first woman to beat a sitting male senator. Although winning the Republican nomination should have been tantamount to winning the seat, several issues hurt her general election campaign. First, she was a "dry" candidate and supported Prohibition. She was also hurt by the public's growing dislike for President Hoover, whom she had supported. But the greatest blow to McCormick's campaign was the accusation that she had "bought" her victory in the Republican primary. It was revealed that she spent $252,572 on her campaign compared to Deneen's $24,495. There was nothing illegal about her expenditures, but the press attacked her strategy as "may the best dollar win."[164]

The 1930 elections swept Democrats into office across the country. The party gained eight seats in the Senate and 51 in the House. McCormick was buried in the landslide.

Two years after her defeat, McCormick married Albert Simms, a former House colleague from New Mexico. She devoted her time to her dairy, two newspapers, a radio station, a cattle and sheep ranch, and her school for girls in Albuquerque, N.M. In 1940, she returned to politics to manage Thomas Dewey's unsuccessful presidential campaign, and again worked with Dewey in 1944 during his second bid for the White House. She died in Chicago later that year.

CYNTHIA MCKINNEY (D-Ga.)
(March 17, 1955–   )
House: Jan. 3, 1993, to present

Cynthia McKinney, the first black woman ever elected to Congress from Georgia, was forced to fight for her political life in 1996 after the Supreme Court invalidated her majority black congressional district and ordered it to be redrawn to include a majority of white voters. Although most pundits predicted the liberal McKinney would be unable to win in a majority white district, she won a surprisingly comfortable 58 to 42 percent victory over her GOP opponent.

McKinney, a former state legislator, helped create her original majority black district when she served on the state Reapportionment Committee in the early 1990s. She was first elected to the state House in 1988 and served alongside her father, veteran state lawmaker Bill McKinney. She quickly established herself as an outspoken liberal. In 1991, she received national attention when she took to the state House floor and denounced the Persian Gulf War. Two-thirds of the members walked out on the speech in protest, and many began calling her "Hanoi Cynthia," after the actress Jane Fonda who was called "Hanoi Jane" for her opposition to the Vietnam War.

A single mother known for her braided hair and youthful attire, which often includes gold tennis shoes, McKinney is one of the more controversial members of Congress. She made headlines in 1993 when the House debated an amendment prohibiting Medicaid funding for abortions. McKinney attacked the amendment, introduced by Rep. Henry Hyde (R-Ill.), as racist.

"The Hyde amendment is nothing but a discriminatory policy against poor women who happen to be disproportionately black," McKinney said on the floor. "This is about equity and fairness for all women, and, quite frankly, I have just about had it with my colleagues who vote against people of color, vote against the poor, and vote against women."[165]

McKinney also drew attention in 1994 when she refused to support a House resolution condemning an anti-Semitic speech made by an aide to Nation of Islam leader Louis Farrakhan. McKinney, one of just 33 members to vote against the resolution, said she believed Congress should not attack anyone's right to free speech. She said she refused to support similar resolutions denouncing ex-Nixon aide and talk show host G. Gordon Liddy on the same grounds.

McKinney serves on the Banking and Financial Services Committee and the Committee on International Relations, where she has worked—largely unsuccessfully—to curb U.S. arms sales to foreign dictators and countries with poor human rights records. Her efforts were often opposed by the Clinton White House.

McKinney also bumped heads with Clinton in 1998 when she tried to bring two Pakistani-American constituents to a White House ceremony. The two constituents were stopped by White House guards, even though McKinney had previously cleared them with security officials. When McKinney tried to enter the White House, she said a guard refused to talk to her and instead addressed all questions to her 23-year-old white aide. Once in the White House, another guard stopped her until a white male congressman explained who McKinney was.

"I am absolutely sick and tired of having to have my appearance at the White House validated by white people," McKinney wrote to Clinton, demanding an apology. "I am a member of Congress and I don't need to be stopped and questioned because I happen to look like the hired help."[166]

CLARA MCMILLAN (D-S.C.)
(Aug. 17, 1894–Nov. 8, 1976)
House: Jan. 3, 1940, to Jan. 3, 1941

Clara McMillan came to Congress by way of the widow's path. State Democratic leaders picked her to carry on the name of her husband, eight-term Rep. Thomas McMillan, who died in office, and she easily defeated two minor opponents in the Nov. 7, 1939, special election to fill out his unexpired term. She was sworn in at the start of the following session and assigned to the Committee on Patents, the Committee on Public Buildings and Grounds, and the Committee on the Election of the President, Vice President and Representatives in Congress.

When McMillan entered office, Congress was in the midst of debating what role the United States should play in the war raging in Europe. Although McMillen hoped the country could stay out of the fight, she backed military preparedness and supported the Burke-Wadsworth Selective Service Bill, which created the country's first peacetime draft. "I have five sons. The oldest will come immediately under the operation of the bill and be subject to its provisions, as he is past 21 years. My second son is almost 19 years old and is now taking military training in a school organized for that purpose. If and when my sons are needed for the defense of their country, I do not want them to go up against experienced soldiers, untrained and unskilled," she said in explaining her support for the bill.[167] During her one year in office, McMillan also introduced legislation to allow police officers to mail firearms for repairs.

As the 1940 elections approached, popular lawyer L. Mendel Rivers announced his candidacy and McMillan declined to make a second bid for office. Rivers went on to represent the district for nearly 30 years.

After leaving Congress, McMillan served with the National Youth Administration and the Office of War Information. From 1946 to 1957, she served as the information liaison officer with the Department of State.

CARRIE MEEK (D-Fla.)
(April 29, 1926–   )
House: Jan. 5, 1993, to present

The daughter of a sharecropper and granddaughter of slaves, Carrie Meek fought prejudice and poverty most of her life to ultimately win election to the House in 1992 and—along with two other black lawmakers elected that year—became one of the first African Americans in 129 years to represent Florida in Congress.

Meek was raised in a family of 12 children. At the age of 11 she worked as a domestic servant and supported her way through college. A track and field star as an undergraduate at Florida A&M, she graduated in 1946 with a bachelor's degree in biology and physical education.

Because of Florida's segregated education system, Meek was not allowed to go to graduate school in state. But under the separate but equal ruling, the state provided funds for her to seek an education somewhere else and she headed to the University of Michigan, where she received a master's degree in physical education and public health. She went on to coach women's basketball at Bethune-Cookman College and taught biology at Florida A&M. She also later served as special assistant to the vice president of Miami-Dade Community College in Miami, Fla.

In 1979, Meek ran for and won an open seat in the Florida state House, where she served for three years. In 1982, she ran for the state Senate and became the first black state legislator in Florida since Reconstruction. In the state Senate, Meek chaired the Education Appropriations Committee. She developed much of Florida's current housing finance policy and sponsored legislation that promoted minority businesses.

After winning election to the U.S. Congress in 1992, Meek won a prestigious seat on the Appropriations Committee by painstakingly introducing herself to all the members of the Democratic leadership and the Steering and Policy Committee, which decides committee assignments. After the 1994 GOP takeover of Congress, Meek lost the committee seat when Republicans reduced the number of Democrats on the panel. She moved over to the Budget Committee and the Committee on Government Reform and Oversight, but in 1996, when a number of Democrats retired from office, Meek returned to Appropriations to fill a vacancy.

Despite her grandmotherly appearance and soft voice, Meek is an outspoken legislator who's not afraid of a fight. In January 1995, Meek caused a stir on the House floor when she rose to make a speech denouncing House Speaker Newt Gingrich's (R-Ga.) lucrative book deal.

"News accounts tell us that while the Speaker may have given up a $4.5 million advance, he stands to gain that amount and much more in royalties. Where I come from that's a lot of dust," Meek said. "If anything, now, how much the Speaker earns has grown much more dependent upon how hard his publishing house hawks his book. Which leads me to the question of exactly who does this Speaker really work for. . . . Is it the America people or his New York publishing house?"[168]

During her speech, Republicans began to shout her down and demanded that her words be stricken from the permanent record. They were.

Meek generally votes along liberal lines, supporting a ban on assault weapons, access to abortion clinics, and President Clinton's initiative lifting the ban on gays in the military. She, however, opposed the Clinton White House on its policy of returning Haitian refugees to their homeland.

Meek also drew on her experience as a domestic worker during congressional debate on raising the income threshold for paying Social Security taxes for domestic workers. Although some wanted to increase the limit from $50 a quarter to $1,800 a year, Meek argued that if it was raised too high, employers may never have to pay Social Security taxes and the workers would be left without financial security in their old age. The House eventually agreed to a new $1,000-a-year threshold.

JAN MEYERS (R-Kan.)
(July 20, 1928–   )
House: Jan. 3, 1985, to Jan. 3, 1997

In 1994, when the Republicans took control of Congress, Jan Meyers became chair of the Small Business Committee—the first Republican woman to head a legislative panel in the House in 40 years and the first woman of either party since 1977. The top assignment was perfect for Meyers who, although soft-spoken and prone to compromise, had spent years tirelessly fighting to ease the tax burden and federal regulation of small businesses.

Before coming to Congress, Meyers spent more than 15 years in city and state government. From 1967 to 1972, Meyers was a member of the Overland Park City Council in Kansas—serving as its president for two years. She then moved on to the Kansas state Senate and focused on care for the elderly and prevention of child abuse. During her 12 years there, she held top leadership posts, including chair of the Public Health and Welfare Committee and chair of the Local Government Committee.

In 1978, Meyers ran for the U.S. Senate, but lost the GOP nomination to Nancy Kassebaum who would go on to hold the seat for 18 years. Meyers turned her sights on the U.S. House in 1984 and this time she won. She was elected by her fellow House freshmen as class president and won seats on the Committee on Science, Space, and Technology; the Committee on Small Business; and the Select Committee on Aging. She later moved from the science panel to the Committee on Foreign Affairs, where she focused on fighting international drug trafficking. She also served on the Economic and Educational Opportunities Committee.

On the Small Business Committee, Meyers introduced legislation to elevate the Small Business Administration to Cabinet-level rank, give permanent tax credits to small businesses, restore the small-business exemption to minimum wage laws, and increase the health care deduction for the self-employed from 25 to 100 percent. Meyers also opposed the Family and Medical Leave Act that required businesses to give employees unpaid leave for family emergencies. Her efforts won her awards from numerous business groups, including the Chamber of Commerce and the National Federation of Independent Businesses.

While on the Small Business Committee, Meyers also took on President Clinton when it was revealed that the SBA may have given an improper loan to one of Clinton's business partners in the controversial Whitewater land deal. Meyers fought the SBA to hand over its Whitewater documents and called on Clinton to answer questions about the shady arrangement.

A fiscal conservative, Meyers voted against congressional pay raises and worked to stop tax increases and wasteful government spending. Meyers, however, was a moderate on social issues such as abortion and gun control. She was among the few Republicans to support Clinton's anti-crime bill in 1994, and she backed a five-day waiting period for handgun purchases as well as a ban on certain assault weapons. A consistent supporter of abortion rights, she opposed requiring parental notification for minors' abortions and voted to guarantee access to abortion clinics.

Meyers retired in 1997 after 12 years in office.

HELEN MEYNER (D-N.J.)
(March 5, 1929–Nov. 2, 1997)
House: Jan. 3, 1975, to Jan. 3, 1979

Other than being the wife of former New Jersey Gov. Robert Meyner, Helen Meyner had relatively little political experience when she ran for the House. She launched her first campaign belatedly in 1972 when the Democratic nominee withdrew because he failed to meet a seven-year citizenship requirement for public office. Meyner entered the race at the request of the Democratic state committee, but lost in the general election. She tried again two years later, and this time won.

Before entering politics, Meyner served from 1950 to 1952 in Korea as an American Red Cross field worker and later as a guide to the United Nations. She also worked as a consumer affairs officer with Trans World Airlines. After her husband left the governor's mansion in 1962, Meyner began to write a twice-weekly column for the *Newark Star-Ledger*. She also conducted a New Jersey and New York City television interview program from 1965 to 1968 and later served on the New Jersey State Rehabilitation Commission.

After coming to Congress, Meyner was assigned to the Foreign Affairs Committee, the District of Columbia Committee, and the Select Committee on Aging. A self-proclaimed liberal, Meyner declared shortly after coming to the House, "People have been waiting for the President to do something, and he just doesn't seem to be doing it. I hope the Congress will—and that we can quicken the flow of liberal legislation this session."[169]

During her two terms in office, Meyner opposed efforts to expel Israel from the United Nations and condemned the 1975 resolution equating Zionism with racism. She did not think, however, that the United States should withdraw from the UN. Meyner also introduced an amendment to a Philippines assistance bill, reducing aid by $5 million in hopes of curtailing human rights abuses there.

Along with her interest in foreign affairs, Meyner worked on issues important to her constituents. She joined other members of the New Jersey delegation in a successful fight to save the Picatinny Arsenal in her district from closure. She also fought to protect her state's textile industry from less expensive foreign imports. In late 1976, she lobbied Democratic members of the state Senate not to rescind New Jersey's endorsement of the Equal Rights Amendment.

Meyner was defeated for re-election in 1978 and returned to work with the State Rehabilitation Commission. She later served on the board of several major companies, including Prudential Insurance, where she was known for her efforts to create opportunities for women. She also served as honorary co-chair of the Campaign for United Nations Reform, a bipartisan organization that promoted peace around the world.

BARBARA MIKULSKI (D-Md.)
(July 20, 1936–   )
House: Jan. 3, 1977, to Jan. 2, 1987
Senate: Jan. 3, 1987, to present

Barbara Mikulski is proof that size can be deceiving. At just 4 feet, 11 inches, she is one of Congress's toughest legislators and has been called the most powerful woman in the Senate. As the top Democrat on the Appropriations subcommittee on VA, HUD, and Independent Agencies, she helps oversee a discretionary fund of almost $100 billion. (Before the Republicans took control of Congress in 1994, Mikulski served as chair of the subcommittee—the first woman ever to head a spending panel in the Senate.)

Mikulski fought her way to the top from the working-class neighborhoods of Baltimore. She first became involved in politics during the 1960s, registering blacks to vote and organizing tenant strikes. Mikulski earned her degree in social service and worked for Catholic Charities and the Baltimore Welfare Department. Known as a hell-raiser, Mikulski in the late 1960s led the fight to save the east Baltimore ethnic neighborhoods that were slated for destruction to make way for a 16-lane highway. After years of fighting on the grass-roots level, she decided she could do even more in elected office and in 1971 she ran for the Baltimore City Council. In 1974, Mikulski turned her sights to the federal level, but lost a race for the Senate. Two years later, she launched another bid, this time for the House, and won with 75 percent of the vote.

In the House, Mikulski served on the Merchant Marine and Fisheries Committee, the Committee on Interstate and Foreign Commerce, and the powerful Committee on Energy and Commerce. Mikulski quickly earned the reputation as a hard-as-nails fighter for women, minorities, and the underdog. She helped draft legislation to provide federal assistance to abused spouses, and crafted the Child Abuse Act, which passed Congress in 1984. She advocated "unisex" insurance legislation that would end the practice of giving women lower life insurance annuity payments than men because they tend to live longer.

In 1986, Mikulski risked her safe seat in the House to run for the Senate. Despite an ugly race where her GOP opponent raised questions about Mikulski's sexuality, Mikulski easily won the race. In the Senate, Mikulski has continued her fight for social justice. She has fought against bans on taxpayer-financed abortions, pushed for universal health care coverage for women—including mammography, contraceptive drugs, and pap smears—and even pressured Congress's own Architect of the Capitol to improve job opportunities for minorities and women.

In her post on the Appropriations Committee, Mikulski has helped secure millions of dollars worth of projects for her home state of Maryland. She strongly backs the space program—NASA is stationed in Maryland and employs many of her constituents.

Along with her Appropriations assignment, Mikulski has served on the Labor and Human Resources Committee, the Small Business Committee, and the Ethics Committee. She was the only woman on the Ethics Committee at the time of her appointment and its only member to vocally support public hearings on sexual harassment charges against her colleague, Sen. Bob Packwood (R-Ore.). Public hearings were never held. Mikulski was also a leader in the unsuccessful fight to stop the promotion of Navy Adm. Frank Kelso in 1994 in the wake of the Tailhook sex scandal. "The Tailhook matter is a sordid, sleazy stain on the U.S. Navy,"

Mikulski said on the Senate floor. "I believe that if we do not take action to change the culture, as well as the law and the rules, this type of activity that went on at Tailhook and other forms of sexual harassment will happen again and again and again."[170]

In 1992, Mikulski was named assistant Democratic floor leader—the first woman to hold a Senate leadership post—and in 1996 she was elected Secretary of the Democratic Conference, a position she still holds today.

BOOKS BY MIKULSKI

Capitol Offense (1996)
Capitol Venture: A Novel (1997)

JUANITA MILLENDER-MCDONALD
(D-Calif.)
(Sept. 7, 1938–   )
House: March 26, 1996, to present

Juanita Millender-McDonald was elected to Congress to fill the seat of Rep. Walter Tucker (D) after he was convicted of felony charges of extortion and tax evasion. The charges against Tucker stemmed from his service as mayor of Compton, Calif., prior to his election to Congress.

Millender-McDonald, a former Carson City Council member and California state assemblywoman, narrowly won the Democratic nomination for the open seat, defeating eight other candidates, including Tucker's wife. She then went on to easily win the general election in the majority-minority district. African Americans and Hispanics make up about three-fourths of the district, which is one of the poorest in California.

On Capitol Hill, Millender-McDonald was assigned to the Small Business Committee and the Transportation and Infrastructure Committee. Just months after being sworn into office, Millender-McDonald convened a congressional inquiry back in her district to look into charges that the CIA led a conspiracy to flood Los Angeles with crack cocaine in order to bankroll Nicaraguan rebels. She also introduced legislation to create a select congressional committee to look into the highly publicized allegations.

A regional whip with the House Democratic Caucus, Millender-McDonald is a reliable liberal vote. She voted to raise the minimum wage and increase funding for bilingual education, while opposing GOP efforts to ban same-sex marriages and keep illegal immigrants out of the public school system. Millender-McDonald, a former teacher, is also a vocal supporter of the Goals 2000 national educational standards initiative. As the daughter of a minister in Alabama, Millender-McDonald spoke out strongly in favor of federalizing the crime of church burnings after a rash of black churches in the South were torched.

Millender-McDonald is an active member of the Women's Congressional Caucus. She co-chaired the group's task force on women-owned businesses and introduced legislation to encourage the federal government to grant more contracts to firms owned by women. She also introduced a bill to grant the Small Business Administration more money to train and counsel women business owners.

PATSY MINK (D-Hawaii)
(Dec. 6, 1927–   )
House: Jan. 3, 1965, to Jan. 3, 1977;
Sept. 22, 1990, to present

Throughout Patsy Mink's long and varied political career, she has established herself as one of the country's most liberal lawmakers, focusing on women's rights and educational issues. Of Japanese descent, Mink was the first woman of color ever to be elected to Congress. She has held elective office on the city, state, and national levels, and even made a bid for U.S. president.

Mink's educational background was as varied as her political career. She first entered the University of Hawaii as a pre-med student, but graduated in 1948 with a degree in zoology and chemistry. After graduation, she decided to enter law school and became the second woman of Oriental ancestry ever to be admitted to the Hawaii bar. After she was turned down for jobs at various law firms because she was a woman, she decided to open her own practice. She also lectured on business law at the University of Hawaii and served as attorney of the Hawaii House of Representatives.

In 1954, Mink established the Oahu Young Democrats and in 1960 served as a delegate to the Democratic National Convention where, as a member of the platform committee, she helped negotiate adoption of the civil rights plank. She had already won election to the Hawaii House of Representatives in 1956 and to the state Senate in 1958. In the Senate, she chaired the Education Committee and sponsored an equal-pay-for-equal-work bill while also pushing for Hawaiian statehood.

In 1959—the year Hawaii was admitted to the Union—Mink lost a bid for the U.S. House, but made a second try in 1964 and became the first woman from Hawaii to enter Congress. She was assigned to the Education and Labor Committee and introduced the first child-care bill as well as bills to set up bilingual education, student loans, and special education. In her first year in office, she gained passage of a bill calling for the construction of schools in all U.S. Pacific territories. One of Mink's greatest legislative successes was her Women's Education Equity Act, first introduced in 1971 and eventually passed as part of a broader educational bill in 1974. It was aimed at removing sexual stereotypes from schoolbooks and curricula and provided educational funds to develop programs that promoted equity among boys and girls.

When Mink first came to the House, she was a strong supporter of President Johnson's domestic programs, but quickly bumped heads with him over the escalation of the Vietnam War. She refused to support his request for a tax increase in 1967 fearing the money would be used for military action and continued her anti-war efforts during the Nixon administration. She introduced a censure motion against him and compared his military policy to Hitler's. She advocated amnesty for men who evaded the draft and executive clemency for soldiers discharged for protesting the war.

Throughout her House career, Mink has fought for women's rights. When Nixon nominated George Harold Carswell for the Supreme Court, she was the first member of Congress to oppose the nomination on the grounds that he refused, while serving as an appeals court judge, to consider a woman's complaint that she was denied a job because she had young children. Her objection eventually led to the rejection of Carswell's nomination.

Mink frequently found herself confronted by sexual discrimination within her own party. When she urged the Democratic Party's Committee on National Priorities in 1970 to consider more women for leadership and policy-making positions, she was confronted by fellow committee member Dr. Edgar Berman, Hubert Humphrey's personal physician. Berman claimed that women were limited in their leadership ability because of physiological and psychological factors caused by menopause and their menstrual cycles. "Suppose," he asked, "that we had a menopausal woman president who had to make the decision on the Bay of Pigs or the Russian contretemps with Cuba at the time? [She would be] subject to the curious mental aberrations of that age group." Mink shot back an angry letter calling Berman a "bigot" and demanded his ouster from the panel. Berman consequently resigned from the committee, but left with a parting remark saying that Mink's anger was "a typical example of an ordinarily controlled woman under the raging hormonal imbalance of the periodical lunar cycle."[171]

A year after the incident, Mink accepted an invitation from Oregon Democrats to enter their 1972 state presidential primary. She accepted saying, "Without a woman contending for the presidency, the concept of absolute equality will continue to be placed on the backburner as warmed-over lip service."[172] Mink flew at her own expense to Oregon every weekend to campaign, but she ended up winning just 2 percent of the vote.

In 1976, Mink decided to seek the Democratic nomination for the Senate rather than run for a seventh term in the House. She lost that contest, but was subsequently appointed by President Carter as Assistant Secretary of State for Oceans, International Environment, and Scientific Affairs. She held that post until 1978, when she took over as president of the liberal Americans for Democratic Action. In 1983, she returned to Hawaii, where she served on the Honolulu City Council until 1987.

Mink ran again for the U.S. House in 1990, winning a special election to fill the seat left vacant when Rep. Daniel Akaka (D) was appointed to the Senate. She was assigned again to the Education and Labor Committee and also the Budget Committee, where she says she can fight to "redirect our budget priorities" to education, health, and job creation.[173] During the 103rd Congress she headed a task force aimed at promoting equity for women and girls in job training and educational programs. In 1995, she created the Democratic Womens' Caucus and served as its first chair.

SUSAN MOLINARI (R-N.Y.)
(March 27, 1958–   )
House: March 27, 1990 to Aug. 1, 1997

Susan Molinari was not your typical GOP lawmaker. A liberal on such issues as abortion and gun control, she often found herself voting against her Republican leadership. But that same leadership helped her rise to the top ranks, where they hoped she would became a beacon for more women and moderates to join the party. Following the 1994 Republican takeover of Congress, Molinari won election as the vice chair of the House Republican Conference—the fifth highest-ranking post in the House. Molinari was again pushed into the spotlight in 1996 when presidential candidate Bob Dole named her as the keynote speaker at the Republican convention.

Molinari's personal life was as much in the news as her political career. Shortly after coming to Congress, Molinari caused waves when she became the first woman to wear pants on the House floor. In 1994, Molinari married fellow New York Republican Rep. Bill Paxon. Paxon served as chair of the National Republican Campaign Committee and the two became the first married couple in the congressional leadership. Two years later, Molinari gave birth to a baby girl—only the third woman to have a baby while serving in Congress.

Molinari was used to being in the spotlight. Her grandfather was a fixture in Staten Island politics, and her father, Guy Molinari, served in the House for nine years. When he resigned to become Staten Island Borough president in 1990, Molinari easily won the special election to fill his seat. Before coming to Congress, Molinari was the youngest member of the New York City Council, elected at the age of 26. She was the only Republican on the council, which automatically gave her the honor of minority leader, a post that entitled her to sit on every committee. During her five years on the council she was known for wearing black high-top sneakers and driving a Jeep.

After winning her father's seat in the House, Molinari was assigned to the Small Business Committee and the Public Works and Transportation Committee, where she eventually rose to chair the railroad subcommittee. In her third term she gave up her seat on Small Business to take a spot on the prestigious Budget Committee.

Molinari generally cast liberal votes on social issues. She supported legislation to guarantee access to abortion clinics and opposed Republican efforts to ban federal funding for abortions. She, however, supported a ban on so-called partial birth abortions. On gun control, Molinari backed a five-day waiting period for handgun purchases and a ban on certain assault weapons. In 1994, she and other moderate Republicans worked with the White House to modify President Clinton's anti-crime bill. She was one of the few Republicans to later vote for its passage.

But Molinari was more conservative on economic issues. She supported a balanced budget amendment to the Constitution and voted for a Republican budget plan to eliminate the deficit by 2002 by curbing spending growth on Medicare and Medicaid. Molinari was also a strong supporter of Speaker Newt Gingrich and stood by him while he was under investigation by the House Ethics Committee. After the panel found Gingrich guilty of wrongdoing, Molinari called his transgression an innocent mistake and helped garner votes for his re-election as Speaker.

On international affairs, Molinari was an outspoken critic of Clinton's decision to send troops to Bosnia during the civil war there. She led a congressional delegation to the war-torn area in 1995 and called on the House to end U.S. compliance with the UN-imposed embargo on arms to Bosnian Muslims.

In 1997, Molinari resigned from the House to become a co-anchor of a CBS Saturday morning news program. She left the show after nine months, and in January 1999 gave birth to her second child. She appears frequently as a television political analyst.

CONNIE MORELLA (R-Md.)
(Feb. 12, 1931–)
House: Jan. 3, 1987, to present

During her years in Congress, Connie Morella has established herself as the most liberal Republican in the House. She votes for President Clinton's policies more than any other House Republican and backs such liberal causes as abortion rights and gun control. During the Persian Gulf War she was one of only three Republicans to oppose a resolution authorizing President Bush to use force in Iraq. In 1997, she was one of just nine Republicans who refused to support Newt Gingrich's re-election as House Speaker. It wasn't until 1992—after 30 years of being a Republican—that she attended her first GOP convention. And then it was only to oppose the platform plank that described abortion as murder.

But Morella is a fiscal conservative who supports a constitutional balanced budget amendment. She toes the party line more often than not and signed the GOP Contract with America in 1994—even though she voted against many of the bills included in it. Her liberalism is a perfect fit for her district, where Democratic voters far outnumber Republicans but consistently return Morella to office with comfortable margins.

Her district also is home to 60,000 current and retired federal workers—a constituency to which she devotes much of her legislative attention. As a member of the Government Reform and Oversight Committee (formerly called the Post Office and Civil Service Committee), she has worked to retrain and relocate federal workers displaced by government downsizing and fought to keep health care insurance costs down for federal employees. She introduced legislation that would raise the pay of federal workers in her district, and has worked to prevent future federal government shutdowns. She also sits on the Science Committee, where she chairs the subcommittee on technology. That post also helps her look after her constituents, giving her jurisdiction over several federal agencies, including the National Institute of Standards and Technology and the National Institutes of Health.

Along with her attention to federal workers, Morella has focused much of her time on women's and children's issues. She co-chaired the Congressional Women's Caucus in 1995 and 1996 and currently co-chairs two of its task forces on AIDS and preventive health care for women. She was a sponsor of the Violence Against Women Act and pushed for federal funding for battered women's shelters and child abuse prevention programs. She backed tax breaks to help low-income families get quality child care and introduced the Comprehensive Fetal Alcohol Syndrome Prevention Act to improve federal efforts to fight alcohol consumption by pregnant women. Perhaps much of Morella's concern for children's issues is sparked by her own busy family life. Morella and her husband are parents to nine children—three of their own, the rest her late sister's children.

Before entering politics, Morella taught for 15 years at Montgomery College in Maryland. After working with a variety of community organizations, Morella formally entered politics in 1979 as a member of the Maryland General Assembly. In 1980, Morella ran for the U.S. House, but lost in the primary. She waited six years before launching a second bid for the House—and winning.

CAROL MOSELEY-BRAUN (D-Ill.)
(Aug. 16, 1947–)
Senate: Jan. 5, 1993, to Jan. 6, 1999

After winning election in 1992 as the country's first African-American female senator, Carol Moseley-Braun wasted little time leaving her mark in the white male-dominated institution. Just seven months into her term, Moseley-Braun took on one of the most senior and conservative members of the chamber, Sen. Jesse Helms (R-N.C.). Moseley-Braun launched a filibuster against a Helms amendment that would have granted a patent renewal to the Daughters of the Confederacy for the group's insignia featuring the Confederate flag.

"The issue is whether or not Americans such as myself who believe in the promise of this country, who feel strongly and who are patriots in this country, will have to suffer the indignity of being reminded time and time again, that at one point in this country's history we were hu-

man chattel. We were property. We could be traded, bought, and sold,"
Moseley-Braun said on the Senate floor.[174] In the end, she won over a
majority of her colleagues who agreed to kill the amendment.

Although her stance won her the respect of many, Helms never forgot.
Shortly after the floor battle, Moseley-Braun was on a Senate elevator
when Helms got on. "He saw me standing there, and he started to sing,
'I wish I was in the land of cotton. . . . ' And he looked at Senator [Orin]
Hatch and said, 'I'm going to sing Dixie until she cries.' And I looked
at him and said, 'Senator Helms, your singing would make me cry if
you sang Rock of Ages.' "[175]

Moseley-Braun won election to the Senate in the wake of national female anger over the treatment of Anita Hill by the Senate Judiciary Committee during the confirmation hearings of Supreme Court Justice
Clarence Thomas. She defeated two-term incumbent Sen. Alan Dixon in
the Democratic primary and went on to easily win the general election.
Once on Capitol Hill, Moseley-Braun won a seat on the same Judiciary
Committee she had criticized during her campaign. She also served on
the Banking, Housing and Urban Affairs Committee and the Committee
on Small Business. She later gave up her post on Judiciary for a slot on
the powerful Finance Committee.

Moseley-Braun had a long and distinguished political career before
coming to Congress. A graduate of the University of Chicago law school,
Moseley-Braun worked as a prosecutor in the U.S. Attorney's Office from
1972 until she entered the political arena in 1978. She ran for and won
a seat in the Illinois House of Representatives, where she served for the
next 10 years. During her time in the state House, she introduced legislation to bar the state of Illinois from investing in South Africa and
sponsored bills to ban discrimination in housing and private clubs. Her
political ally while in the state House was Chicago's first black mayor,
Harold Washington, who made her the city's floor leader in the legislature in 1983. She later rose to become the first woman assistant majority
leader. In 1987, she won election as the Cook County recorder of deeds,
the first black in the state to serve in a countywide elected position.

When Moseley-Braun launched her bid for U.S. Senate, she began with
great promise. Her campaign, however, soon became bogged down with
financial and ethics problems. A month before the elections, Moseley-
Braun came under scrutiny for her handling of her mother's finances.
She, along with her siblings, had accepted an inheritance from her
mother even though the older woman was being supported by Medicaid.
She was criticized for keeping the money rather than paying back the
state for the taxpayer-financed assistance given to her mother. A state
investigation was completed just days before the election, and Moseley-
Braun paid the state roughly $15,000 in back medical expenses for her
mother.

Moseley-Braun also came under scrutiny for mishandling campaign funds, and a court eventually ordered the campaign committee to pay $56,000 in back rent and interest to a landlord who had leased office space for her political headquarters. Her staff was plagued by an unusually high turnover rate and her campaign manager and former fiancé faced accusations of sexual harassment.

Controversy continued to haunt Moseley-Braun following her election. In 1996, she took an unofficial trip to Nigeria to visit with dictator Sani Abache. The State Department and several human rights groups rebuked her, but Moseley-Braun defended the trip and said it was part of her duty as a lawmaker to keep contact with world leaders.

Despite the controversies, Moseley-Braun continued to work on a liberal legislative agenda to help minorities and the poor. She introduced the Women's Pension Equity Act of 1996 and fought to stop Republican cuts in social programs. She backed an increase in the minimum wage, voted against a constitutional amendment barring flag desecration, and supported a bill to outlaw job discrimination based on sexual orientation.

When Sen. Bob Packwood (R-Ore.) came under investigation for sexual misconduct, she called for public hearings by the Ethics Committee. She also was a leader in the fight to deny Navy Adm. Frank Kelso an increase in rank and pension in the wake of the Tailhook sexual harassment scandal. But Moseley-Braun sometimes took stands contrary to her liberal backers. She supported a constitutional balanced-budget amendment and sponsored language to allow children as young as 13 to be tried as adults for violent crimes.

Moseley-Braun's personal controversies and her generally liberal voting record led Republicans to make her their top target in the 1998 elections. She lost her bid for re-election to conservative state Sen. Peter Fitzgerald (R) and vowed never again to run for public office.

PATTY MURRAY (D-Wash.)
(Oct. 11, 1950–   )
Senate: Jan. 5, 1993, to present

Patty Murray became Washington state's first female senator after being heralded in the press as the "mom in tennis shoes." The label was first applied disparagingly to Murray in 1979 when she petitioned the state legislature not to cut funding for a co-op preschool program in which she was involved. A state legislator gave Murray the nickname to imply that she would have little influence, but Murray went on to organize 12,000 families statewide and preserved the preschool program. Years later, when she campaigned for the U.S. Senate in 1992, she successfully used the nickname to portray herself as someone who could relate to the average voter.

Murray first entered public office in 1983 when she joined the Shoreline school board just outside of Seattle. Five years later, she won a seat on the state Senate and was soon named to serve as minority whip.

Murray says she was motivated to run for the U.S. Senate after watching the hearings on Supreme Court nominee Clarence Thomas and the sexual harassment charges launched against him by Anita Hill. Murray got the opportunity to run when incumbent Sen. Brock Adams (D-Wash.) was tainted by charges of sexual harassment from eight different women. Murray was the first Democrat to announce a challenge to Adams, but when he withdrew from the race, other candidates quickly jumped in. Murray easily defeated three Democrats in the primary and went on to win the general election with 54 percent of the vote.

Joining the Senate at the age of 42, Murray was at least 10 years younger than any other female senator and the only one whose children still lived at home. She was assigned to the Appropriations Committee, the Banking Committee, and the Budget Committee. Later in her first term, she left the Banking Committee and took spots on the Labor and Human Resources Committee, the Select Committee on Ethics, and the Veterans' Affairs Committee.

Murray is a strong proponent of abortion rights and women's rights. She won Senate passage of an amendment in 1996 to allow women to have abortions at U.S. military bases overseas. She was also one of the most ardent backers of surgeon general nominee Dr. Henry Foster, who was rejected for confirmation after he came under intense scrutiny for his abortion stance.

Murray fought hard for passage of the Family and Medical Leave Act in 1993. She spoke out on the Senate floor, telling how the measure would have helped her when she was a 26-year-old pregnant secretary. Murray was also an outspoken critic of Sen. Bob Packwood (D-Ore.) when he came under charges for sexual harassment in 1995. Murray was one of five women senators to pressure the Ethics Committee to hold public hearings on the charges. Following Packwood's resignation, she called for the establishment of a clear sexual harassment policy for the U.S. Senate, similar to one she had written while in the Washington state Senate.

In 1994, Murray tried to block the Senate from allowing Navy Adam. Henry Mauz, Jr., to retire with honors. Murray wanted an investigation into complaints that the admiral did not act promptly to deal with sexual harassment charges brought by a woman sailor. Murray withdrew her motion after she received assurances from Pentagon officials that they would work to change procedures for reviewing future retirement nominations.

Along with her work on behalf of women's rights, Murray is a strong supporter of Most Favored Nation trade status for China, an issue that can be very popular with the large technology industry in her state that provides computer and other assistance to China. Murray also supported the North American Free Trade Agreement.

In 1998, Murray was challenged by GOP Rep. Linda Smith, but easily won re-election. It was only the third time in history that two women ran against each other for a Senate seat. In 1960, Sen. Margaret Chase Smith (R-Maine) defeated Democratic challenger Lucia Cormier and, in 1986, Sen. Barbara Mikulski defeated Republican challenger Linda Chavez.

SUE MYRICK (R-N.C.)
(Aug. 1, 1941–)
House: Jan. 4, 1995, to present

Sue Myrick had plenty of campaign experience before winning election to Congress in 1994. An advertising executive, Myrick made her first run for political office in 1981 but lost her bid for the Charlotte, N.C., City Council. She ran again for that office two years later and finally won. In 1985, she ran for Charlotte mayor and lost, but ran again and won in 1987 and was re-elected in 1989. Three years later, Myrick ran for the GOP nomination to the U.S. Senate, but lost.

Her lengthy campaign experience gave her the name recognition she needed in 1994 going into a five-way primary for the U.S. House. On the campaign trail, Myrick focused on tougher sentences for criminals and reining in the budget deficit. She has maintained those focuses during her time in Congress.

After winning her first term in office, Myrick was assigned to the Budget Committee, the Science Committee, and the Small Business Committee. She was also selected by her fellow freshmen to serve as a liaison between her class and the House leadership. Her negotiating and organization skills soon caught the eye of the leadership, which awarded her a seat on the exclusive Rules Committee in her second term.

A staunch conservative, Myrick is a member of the House Conservative Action Team (CATs) and the Congressional Family Caucus—two groups that push for conservative legislation. She strongly opposes abortion and voted to override President Clinton's veto of the ban on so-called partial birth abortions. She supports the death penalty and voted to repeal the ban on certain assault weapons. She also backed a constitutional "Religious Freedom Amendment" that would allow prayer and other religious ceremonies in public places, including schools. "The amendment protects the right of every American to acknowledge their God without state interference," Myrick said of the legislation, which was defeated by the House in 1998.[176]

Myrick has fought continuously to cut government spending. During her first year in Washington, she co-chaired a task force of freshman Republicans that scrutinized the Department of Housing and Urban Development (HUD) and recommended its termination. In 1996, she was one of just 19 Republicans who voted against their party leadership on the fiscal 1997 budget resolution, complaining the plan did not zero out the deficit fast enough.

Myrick has even fought for budget cuts at the risk of alienating her constituents. During 1998 debate on the huge $217-billion highway funding bill, Myrick turned down an offer from her leadership to bring home $15 million in federal funds for the building of a Charlotte beltway. Myrick said the offer came with a string attached: Vote for the bill.

"I ran on a campaign of, 'If you want pork, don't send me,' because I am not going to bring home the bacon," Myrick said. "I'm going to take a lot of heat, but . . . it is a fact that government is not there to take care of all of us."[177]

GRACE NAPOLITANO (D-Calif.)
(Dec. 4, 1936–   )
House: Jan. 6, 1999, to present

Grace Napolitano was the grandmother of 12 when she was first elected to Congress. She, however, was a tough campaigner and won a hard-fought Democratic primary against the top aide of the previous congressman, who was retiring after 16 years in office. After securing the nomination, she easily won the general election in the overwhelmingly Democratic district. She was assigned to the Small Business Committee and the Energy and Natural Resources Committee.

Before coming to Congress, Napolitano served for six years in the Cal-

ifornia state assembly where she chaired the International Trade and
Development Committee. In that position, she traveled to places like
China, Thailand, and Mexico to promote California economic interests.
During her time in the state legislature, Napolitano helped secure more
than 1,400 acres of open land in her district for one of the largest new
parks and wilderness areas in Southern California. Napolitano also made
a name for herself by regularly bringing homemade green chili enchi-
ladas and tacos to her fellow state legislators.

Before her time in the state legislature, Napolitino served from 1986
to 1992 on the Norwalk City Council—two of those years holding the
title of mayor.

Napolitano's election to the U.S. Congress came in the midst of impeachment hearings against President Clinton, who lied under oath
about an extramarital affair. Napolitano was blunt in her opposition to
the impeachment proceedings.

"He is a person who just didn't know how to keep it in his pants,"
she said. "The fact that they are trying to impeach him for it is wrong."[178]

MAURINE NEUBERGER (D-Ore.)
(Jan. 9, 1907–   )
Senate: Nov. 8, 1960, to Jan. 3, 1967

When first-term Sen. Richard Neuberger died of a cerebral hemorrhage
on March, 9, 1960, his widow Maurine wasn't given much time to grieve.
With just two days left before the filing deadline for the upcoming primary election, local and national Democrats descended on Maurine to
ask her to run in her husband's place. Several thousand Oregonians
signed petitions urging her to enter the race and she even received a
personal plea from Sen. Margaret Chase Smith (R-Maine), the only
woman in the Senate at the time.

"I couldn't think of anything except going back to Washington and
getting Muffet, our cat, closing the office and moving out of our apart-
ment," Neuberger recalled of the hours after her husband's death. "But
as I thought more about it, I began to realize I was probably as qualified
as any other potential candidate. And, above all, I knew in my heart that
Dick would have wanted me to run."[179]

Neuberger went on to defeat four men in the primary and a former
governor in the general election by almost 70,000 votes. Her victory came

in large part because of the Neuberger name, but she had also established herself as a skilled campaigner and politician over the years. Neuberger first met her husband when she was a high school teacher and he was a freelance writer. After their marriage, they worked together on magazine articles as well as publishing pieces individually. In 1948, Neuberger headed her husband's successful campaign to the state Senate. Two years later, she would go on to win election herself to the state House. During her time in the state legislature, she focused on women's issues. She fought for passage of a bill that allowed working mothers to deduct child-care costs from their taxes. She also gained notoriety when she arrived at a committee hearing with an apron and mixing bowl to show how much trouble it was for women to color margarine. The display helped lift a ban on colored margarine.

In 1954, Neuberger headed her husband's campaign for the U.S. Senate, helping him to become the first Democrat in 40 years to go to the Senate from Oregon. After his election, Mr. Neuberger wrote a magazine article titled "My Wife Put Me in the Senate." In it he wrote, "Wherever I went campaigning with Maurine, I did much better at the polls than where I stumped the countryside alone."[180] In 1955, Neuberger gave up her seat in the state legislature to join her husband in Washington as his unpaid assistant. She sat in on committees on which he was not a member so he could learn about pending bills and spent hours at the Library of Congress researching legislation for him.

Her experience as a Senate aide helped her become an effective legislator when she succeeded her husband in office. On the Commerce Committee, she co-sponsored a truth-in-packaging bill that required commercial products, such as cosmetics, to list ingredients on their labels. She initiated a nationwide anti-smoking campaign, outraging the tobacco industry and anticipating the subsequent surgeon general's report linking smoking to lung cancer. As a result, Congress gave the Federal Trade Commission the authority to regulate cigarette advertising and labeling.

Along with the Commerce Committee, Neuberger also sat on the Agriculture and Forestry Committee, the Banking and Currency Committee, and the Special Committee on Aging—on which she pushed for improvements in the nation's health care system. During her one term in the Senate, Neuberger sponsored a bill to create a U.S. travel service to encourage tourism and also backed an amendment to make it easier to deduct child-care expenses from income taxes. She worked on legislation requiring lawmakers and federal officials to disclose their finances and helped secure funds for the creation of a Presidential Commission on the Status of Women. In 1964, Neuberger came under attack for lending the Oregon flag to participants in the Selma civil rights march.

Neuberger declined to run for a second term in 1966. She instead went on to serve as chair of the Commission on the Status of Women and taught American government at Boston University, Radcliffe Institute, and Reed College. She also remained active in the American Cancer Society's campaign against smoking.

MAE ELLA NOLAN (R-Calif.)
(Sept. 20, 1886–July 9, 1973)
House: Jan. 23, 1923, to March 3, 1925

Mae Ella Nolan is known for two distinctions: She was the first woman to chair a House committee, and, during her two years in office, she managed never to give a single speech on the House floor. Nolan came to Congress after winning a special election to succeed her husband, Rep. John Nolan, who had died one week after being re-elected to a sixth term. With the strong backing of the Labor party, women, and government employees, she defeated six men running for the same seat and garnered over 4,000 more votes than the man who ran second. Following her victory, the *New York Times* quoted friends who described Mrs. Nolan as "warm-hearted, home-loving, plain-spoken and amply supplied with horse sense." She brought her only sister, Teresa Glenn, to Congress with her to manage her office. Glenn had earlier worked as Mr. Nolan's private secretary.

Nolan followed closely in the footsteps of her pro-labor husband and helped pushed through the House a bill he authored that called for a minimum wage of $3 a day for federal workers. The bill, however, was later killed in the Senate. She was appointed to the Labor Committee— which her husband had chaired—and the Committee on Woman Suffrage, a seat she later gave up to chair the Committee on Expenditures in the Post Office Department.

At the end of her first term, Nolan announced she would not seek a second, declaring, "Politics is entirely too masculine to have any attraction for feminine responsibilities."[181] She also cited the happiness of her ten-year-old daughter who disliked living in a boarding school. The two returned to San Francisco and Nolan later moved to Sacramento, where she died at the age of 86.

CATHERINE NORRELL (D-Ark.)
(March 30, 1901–Aug. 26, 1981)
House: April 18, 1961, to Jan. 3, 1963

Catherine Norrell was elected to Congress to fill the seat of her husband, 11-term Rep. Bill Norrell, who died in office. She already knew much about the legislative process, having served as her husband's unpaid assistant during his time in the state Senate and the U.S. House. She also served as the president of the Congressional Wives Club, working side-by-side with such prominent women as Lady Bird Johnson.

Norrell campaigned on the promise of continuing her husband's policies and spent much of her time in office working to improve the Arkansas economy. She looked out for the interests of the clay, textile, and lumber industry that dominated her district. She served on the Post Office and Civil Service Committee.

When Norrell was first elected, she knew her district was targeted for elimination because of the most recent census numbers, which showed a decline in the local population. She had to choose between retiring after her first term or challenging the veteran congressman who represented a neighboring district. She chose to leave office.

After her retirement, President Kennedy appointed Norrell to serve as Deputy Assistant Secretary of State for Education and Cultural Affairs. She later served from 1965 to 1969 as the director of the State Department's reception center in Honolulu, Hawaii.

ANNE NORTHUP (R-Ky.)
(Jan. 22, 1948–   )
House: Jan. 7, 1997, to present

Anne Northup made headlines in 1996 when she was one of just three Republicans to defeat a House incumbent. She was also the only Republican that year to win in a district Bill Clinton carried during his re-election campaign for president. As a reward, House Republican leaders gave Northup a coveted seat on the Appropriations Committee.

Northup is a conservative who generally votes along party lines. She opposes abortion, supports tax cuts, and wants to scale back government programs to return more power to the states. She also opposes government regulations placed on small businesses.

Much of Northup's time in the House has been focused on education issues. She sits on the Appropriations subcommittee on education and backs sending federal block grants to states to allow localities to shape their school programs rather than forcing states to follow federal guidelines.

She also co-founded the House Reading Caucus with Democratic Rep. Carrie Meek (Fla.). The Caucus is aimed at informing lawmakers about the national costs of illiteracy and the best research on how children learn to read.

Much of Northup's concern about literacy comes from her personal experience as a mother of a dyslexic child. Northup, in fact, is the mother of six children, two of them adopted. Before entering politics, Northup worked as a school teacher. She later served in the Kentucky state House from 1987 until her election to Congress in 1996.

ELEANOR HOLMES NORTON
(D-District of Columbia)
(June 13, 1937–   )
House: Jan 3, 1991, to present

Since coming to Congress, Eleanor Holmes Norton has established herself as a crusader for granting statehood to Washington, D.C. But before she came to Capitol Hill, Norton was nationally known as a fighter for civil rights for women and minorities. A graduate of Yale Law School, Norton was active with the Student Nonviolent Coordinating Committee and worked as a staff member of the 1963 civil rights march on Washington. After passing the bar, she took her first law job with the American Civil Liberties Union in New York, focusing on First Amendment cases. Her work on behalf of free speech led her to represent two unlikely clients. In 1968, Norton argued and won her first case before the Supreme Court on behalf of the National States Rights party, a white supremacist group that had been denied permission for a rally in Maryland. Norton also worked with the lawsuit of segregationist Alabama Gov. George Wallace who sued New York City after he was denied a permit to hold a rally at Shea Stadium. "If people like George Wallace are denied free expression, then the same thing can happen to black people," Norton said. "To implement my belief in free speech, I represent anyone whose free speech has been infringed."[182]

Norton's work on behalf of Wallace caught the eye of New York Mayor John Lindsay, who appointed Norton chair of the city's Commission on Human Rights in 1970. During the next seven years, Norton worked to obtain liberal maternity benefits for women, expanded abortion laws, and updated state laws on workmen's compensation and minimum wages. She convened public hearings on the Board of Education's employment practices and conducted a census of city employees to check for racial and sexual discrimination. In 1973, Norton helped found the National Black Feminist Organization. In 1977, Norton was named by President Carter to become the first woman to head the Equal Employment Opportunity Commission. As chair of the EEOC, Norton is credited with reducing the commission's backlog of cases and overhauling its administration practices.

Norton left the EEOC when Carter left the White House in 1981 and she went to work for the Urban Institute, a liberal think tank and later joined the faculty of Georgetown University Law School. In 1990, Norton ran for Congress as the nonvoting delegate for Washington, D.C. She was considered a shoe-in for the seat, until shortly before the election when it was revealed that she and her husband owed more than $80,000 in back taxes. Norton denied knowing anything about it and said her husband had been responsible for taking care of the family finances. Despite a barrage of negative press, Norton went on to narrowly win the seat. She later divorced her husband.

In Congress, Norton has focused her attention on winning statehood for Washington. In her first term in office, Norton managed to bring to the floor a vote on District statehood. Although the bill was overwhelmingly defeated, it was the first time in 200 years that such a debate had been held. Norton has also fought to keep jobs in the District and won extra money for District schools and public safety. Norton also worked with the Republican-led Congress to establish a presidentially appointed Financial Control Board to oversee the District's economy. Norton has also been active on women's issues and in 1997 became the Democratic co-chair of the Congressional Caucus for Women's Issues. She serves on the Government Reform and Oversight Committee and the Committee on Transportation and Infrastructure.

MARY TERESA NORTON (D-N.J.)
(March 7, 1875–Aug. 2, 1959)
House: March 25, 1925, to Jan. 3, 1951

During her 26 years of congressional service, Mary Teresa Norton earned an impressive collection of honors: She was the first Democratic woman ever elected to Congress, she was the first woman to serve as a state party chair, the first to chair a national party Platform Committee, and the first member of Congress—male or female—to chair three committees. As chair of the powerful Labor Committee, she single-handedly shepherded the Fair Labor Standards Act of 1938 through the House and, as head of the District of Columbia Committee, she helped enact laws to allow women police officers in the District and to grant women the right to serve on juries. She also served as chair of the House Administration Committee, and in 1932 she would have been nominated for vice president of the United States had she not declined the honor.

Norton entered the world of politics in 1910 shortly after the death of her only child, a son who died when he was just one week old. To help overcome her grief, Norton volunteered in a day-care center for young children of working mothers and later worked to expand and establish new centers, including the Queen's Daughters Day Nursery in New Jersey City. She became president of the Day Nursery Association of New Jersey, and it was during this time, as she sought financial support from local business and political leaders, that she met her political mentor—Jersey City's all-powerful mayor Frank Hague.

Hague, eager to win support from the newly enfranchised women voters for the Democratic party, convinced Norton to join the Democratic State Committee in 1920 and later helped her win election as the first woman to serve on the Hudson County Board of Freeholders in 1923. Her first act as freeholder was to draft a resolution creating a maternity hospital with county funds. A year later, Norton won election to the U.S. House of Representatives. Soon after taking office, she introduced the first constitutional amendment to repeal Prohibition. A strong Catholic, she later opposed the Gillette bill, which would have allowed the use of federal funds to disseminate information about birth control. Declaring, "It's up to women to stand for each other," Norton spent much of her energy working to better the status of poor and working-class women. She introduced a bill to allow American women who married foreigners to keep their U.S. citizenship—just as men could. She helped secure $6 million to support federal nursery schools for the children of working mothers in war industries and co-authored a bill that would have prohibited sexual discrimination. Eleanor Roosevelt once wrote of Norton, "She fought for the underdog."[183]

When Norton took over the chair of the D.C. Committee—a position she held from 1931 to 1937—she became known as the "Mayor of Washington." At the opening of her first committee meeting, Rep. Frank Bowman (R-W.Va) remarked, "This is the first time in my life I have been controlled by a woman." Norton shot back, "It's the first time I've had the privilege of presiding over a body of men, and I rather like the prospect."[184]

She referred to the more than 400,000 voteless citizens of the District as her "adopted people" and vowed "to seek home rule for democracy's stepchildren."[185] She failed in her effort to get the vote for Washingtonians and could not convince her colleagues to legalize gambling in the city, but she was able to improve public transportation and clean up the capital's slums. She also won passage of the first old-age pension bill for the District's residents and secured $1.5 million to build the Glenn Dale Hospital for children with tuberculosis.

A turning point in Norton's career came in 1937 when the chairmanship of the Labor Committee opened up. The male members of the panel were shocked to discover Norton was next in line for the top spot. Despite the pleas of House Speaker William Bankhead, Norton refused to stay on the District panel and took over the Labor chairmanship. She worked hard to pass the New Deal programs of President Franklin Roosevelt, including the National Recovery Act, the Home Owner's Loan Corporation, the Works Progress Administration, the Glass-Steagall Banking Act, and the creation of the Securities and Exchange Commission.

But Norton's greatest and most difficult achievement was passage of the Fair Labor Standards Act, which provided a 25-cent per hour minimum wage, a 40-hour work week, time-and-a-half for overtime work, and a prohibition of child labor. In order to release the bill trapped in the unsympathetic Rules Committee, Norton used a rare parliamentary procedure called the discharge petition, which required her to gain the signatures of 218 of her colleagues. She even went on national radio to urge voters to support the bill. Once it came to the House floor, a bitter debate ensued and the bill was defeated. Undaunted, Norton again used the discharge petition to bring a revised bill to the floor, which passed the second time around.

"I'm prouder of getting that bill through the House than anything else I've done in my life," Norton declared.[186]

In 1947, Norton resigned from the Labor Committee when the Republicans gained control of Congress and Rep. Fred Hartley (R-N.J.) became chairman. Norton declared she had "no respect" for Hartley, whom she charged had only attended 10 meetings of the committee in the past 10 years. "I refuse to serve under him. It would be too hard on my blood pressure."[187]

Norton later became chair of the House Administration Committee and introduced a bill eliminating the poll tax—a fee that was imposed at polling stations and aimed at preventing blacks from voting. The bill passed the House but died in the Senate.

In 1950, Norton declined to run for re-election but remained in Washington to work as a consultant for the Department of Labor. She died at the age of 84 at her sister's house in Greenwich, Conn.

MARY ROSE OAKAR (D-Ohio)
(March 5, 1940–   )
House: Jan. 3, 1977, to Jan. 3, 1993

Mary Rose Oakar made her name in Congress by concentrating on internal House rules and procedures. She served in the Democratic leadership and chaired a subcommittee on the House Administration Committee, which oversaw House operations. Ironically, it was the same rules and procedures she helped control that plagued her throughout her career and brought her eventual downfall from office.

Before entering politics, Oakar worked as a high school and community college teacher in Cleveland for 12 years. She earned her master's degree in 1966 from John Carroll University and also studied acting at the Royal Academy of Dramatic Arts in London.

From 1973 to 1976, Oakar served on the Cleveland City Council, where she won considerable media attention for her plan to make "creative use" of vacant lots and for working to outlaw the sale of airplane glue to minors. In 1976, Oakar joined 11 other Democrats in a bid for an open House seat. Her campaign focused on the fact that she was the only woman in the race and the only one without a law degree. She won the primary with 24 percent and went on to easily win the general election.

Early in her House career, Oakar joined the Democratic whip organization and proved herself a hard worker on routine leadership tasks. She joined the House Administration Committee in 1984 to protect leadership interests and eventually took over the subcommittee on police and personnel. As part of the leadership, she traveled across the country campaigning for her colleagues. When Rep. Geraldine Ferraro (D-N.Y.)

left the House in 1984 to run for vice president, Oakar took her place as secretary of the Democratic Caucus—and quickly renamed the post vice chairman. Four years later, Oakar ran for chair of the Caucus, but was soundly defeated.

Oakar also served on the Post Office and Civil Service Committee and the Banking, Finance and Urban Affairs Committee, where she chaired the subcommittee on economic stabilization. That chairmanship gave her the opportunity to look out for the financial redevelopment of older industrial areas such as her own district. On the Post Office Committee, Oakar fought for pay equity for women. She pushed for a study of federal pay scales to determine whether women were paid less than men, not only in the same jobs, but for work of equivalent responsibility that tended to attract women rather than men. Although she worked for women's rights, Oakar—a staunch Catholic—opposed abortion. Throughout her career, Oakar also pushed to give congressional employees many of the same benefits enjoyed by other federal and private sector workers.

Despite her work on internal House procedure, Oakar was investigated by the Ethics Committee in 1987 and found to have broken House rules on two occasions. In one case, Oakar kept a former aide and housemate on salary for two years after the woman moved to New York. In another case, Oakar gave a $10,000 salary increase to an aide the same month she and Oakar bought a house together. She did not face any punishment, but was forced to repay the money.

In 1992, during her bid for a ninth term, Oakar was one of dozens of lawmakers caught in the House bank scandal and was found to have 213 overdrafts on her House bank account. The scandal led to her defeat for re-election. Oakar got into even more trouble when Justice Department investigators looking into the scandal discovered that she had faked the names of campaign contributors to cover up $16,000 in improper donations. Oakar was indicted on seven felony counts, but ended up pleading guilty to two misdemeanors. In 1998, a judge sentenced Oakar to two year's probation, $32,000 in fines, and 200 hours of community service.

CAROLINE O'DAY (D-N.Y.)
(June 22, 1875–Jan. 4, 1943)
House: Jan. 3, 1935, to Jan. 3, 1943

Caroline O'Day had extensive political experience before coming to Congress. A fighter for suffrage, O'Day in 1917 lobbied beside Jeannette Rankin to give women the vote in New York. O'Day was later rewarded for her efforts and named to the post of vice chair of the New York Democratic committee and directed its women's division and served as a delegate to every Democratic National Convention between 1924 and 1936. During her work in state politics, O'Day became good friends with Eleanor Roosevelt and together they worked to organize women Democrats into a powerful political force. Roosevelt would later campaign for O'Day, helping her win her first election to the House.

Along with her work for women's suffrage, O'Day was also an activist for fair labor and social welfare. In 1921, Gov. Alfred E. Smith named her to the State Board of Social Welfare—the agency that oversaw public institutions caring for displaced children. She was a member of the Consumer League and helped expose the exploitation of workers in the candy industry, she also helped win the first minimum wage scale for laundry workers. She even occasionally turned her New York estate over to trade unions for their conferences and meetings.

But the cause of peace may have been O'Day's biggest concern. She was vice chair of the Women's International League for Peace and Freedom, an offshoot of the National Women's Party. A pacifist throughout World War I, O'Day turned her estate after the Armistice into a home for convalescent soldiers.

O'Day brought her pacifist beliefs with her to Congress, and during her first year in office she flew to Buenos Aires to present to the Inter-American Conference for the Maintenance of Peace an anti-war petition containing more than one million signatures. "Women will no longer consent to war," she told the conference's delegates. As World War II approached, O'Day unsuccessfully fought to keep America out of the battle. She assailed the U.S. Army and Navy as the "most powerful lobby in the nation" and offered to endorse any Republican who backed peace legislation. Her pacifist beliefs also forced her to break on several occasions with President Roosevelt. She voted against the repeal of the arms embargo in 1939 and opposed the 1940 selective service bill. With those exceptions, O'Day otherwise consistently supported Roosevelt's New Deal legislation. She helped attach a child labor amendment to the 1936 Walsh-Healey Act and the 1938 Fair Labor Standards Act.

O'Day's first election to Congress came largely through the efforts of Eleanor Roosevelt, who campaigned for her—it was the first time a First Lady had ever stumped for a candidate. O'Day ultimately won the election by defeating the woman candidate nominated by the Republicans. The Republicans continued to pit female challengers against O'Day in each of her three bids for re-election and she defeated them all.

After coming to the House, O'Day served on the Immigration and Naturalization Committee and the Insular Affairs Committee. She also chaired the Committee on the Election of the President, Vice President, and Representatives in Congress from 1937 to 1943. When the Dies Bill to Deport Alien Fascists and Communists was reported from the Immigration Committee, O'Day attacked it as repressive and charged that if it passed, it would put America on a par with Communist and Fascist countries that limited civil liberties.

In 1939, O'Day joined in the public protest against the Daughters of the American Revolution, which refused to permit the African-American singer Marian Anderson to perform at Constitution Hall. She followed up her protest by sending invitations to prominent people, asking them to support the concert after it was rescheduled in front of the Lincoln Memorial.

O'Day, who had been in failing health for several years, declined to run for re-election in 1942. She was succeeded by a Republican woman— Winnifred Stanley. O'Day died on Jan. 4, 1943, one day after her fourth term in office expired.

Before O'Day became involved in politics, she was a successful painter, magazine illustrator, and costume designer. She studied art in Paris, Munich, and Holland for eight years. Her works were exhibited at the Paris Salon in 1899 and 1900.

PEARL OLDFIELD (D-Ark.)
(Dec. 2, 1876–April 12, 1962)
House: Jan. 11, 1929, to March 3, 1931

Pearl Oldfield—or Miss Pearl as she was popularly known—came to Congress to fill the seat left vacant by the death of her husband, 10-term Rep. William Oldfield. She ran unopposed to fill out the remaining three months of her husband's term and defeated an Independent candidate for the next full term.

During her service, she sponsored legislation to provide federal disaster aid for farmlands damaged by flooding of the Mississippi River in 1927. She also pushed for a $15-million appropriation to buy food in drought-stricken areas, including her own district, and sponsored legislation to authorize the Arkansas Highway Commission to construct free bridges across her local Black and White Rivers.

Just weeks after coming to office, Oldfield announced she would not seek re-election, but would simply serve out the remainder of her term in the spirit of "taking care of things" for her husband. She said she would then gladly retire to where women belong—in the home.[188] She later said that no woman should be elected to public office simply because of her gender. "I think that women in the public service should consider all public questions broadly, keeping in mind constantly the entire citizenship, rather than endeavor to serve their own sex separately by injecting essentially feminine views," she said. "No one should seek or expect public office simply because of her sex, but she has an equal right to appeal to the voters for support on the basis of her comparative ability to render public service."[189]

RUTH BRYAN OWEN (D-Fla.)
(Oct. 2, 1885–July 26, 1954)
House: March 4, 1929, to March 3, 1933

Ruth Bryan Owen, the first woman to be elected to the House from the Deep South, was indoctrinated into the world of politics by her father, three-time presidential nominee Rep. William Jennings Bryan (D). Owen was just 11 when her father made his first bid for the White House and by the time of his third run in 1908 she had joined the campaign as his secretary.

Owen married at a young age, and when she divorced her husband after less than two years, she became the single mother of two small children. To support her new family, she lectured for the Nebraska Extension Service and wrote for a newspaper syndicate. She remarried a year later to Reginald Owen, a British officer in the Royal Engineers, whom she met during a trip overseas with her parents. She accompanied her new husband to his posts in Jamaica, the West Indies, and London. At the age of 30, she took a nursing course and joined the British Volunteer Aid Detachment in Cairo, where she served for three years caring for the injured. She later formed the "Optimists"—a company of entertainers who performed at military hospitals and rest camps in Palestine.

Major Owen eventually fell ill, and the couple moved to Florida with Ruth's parents. Because of her husband's illness, Mrs. Owen was again forced to support her family and she returned to the lecture circuit, where she spoke to more than one million people.

In 1926, Mrs. Owen decided to run for the House of Representatives, but lost the Democratic primary for the Florida seat by just 776 votes— not bad in a state that never ratified the Women's Suffrage Amendment. A year later, Major Owen died, and shortly thereafter Mrs. Owen decided to make a second try for the House. She bought a brand-new 1928 green Ford coupe, christened it "the Spirit of Florida," and traveled across the district talking to voters. This time she soundly defeated the seven-term incumbent by 14,000 votes in the primary and sailed to victory in the general election.

Shortly after Owen was sworn into office, the man she defeated in the general election contested her victory, charging that she had lost her American citizenship when she married Major Owen and therefore could not hold office. Owen argued before the House Committee on Elections that her citizenship had not been taken away because she had married a foreigner, but because she was a woman. Never had a man lost his citizenship because of marriage. "You cannot deny my claim without saying to millions of American women that they are not entitled to the same treatment as men," she argued.[190] In the end, Owen was allowed to keep her seat.

Once in office, Owen requested a position on the Foreign Affairs Committee, and the House voted to expand the panel's membership to make room for her. Owen also concentrated on issues important to her state. She helped secure $8 million to develop the state's rivers and harbors, and just three weeks after the Mediterranean fruit fly appeared in Florida, Owen won $4.25 million to eradicate the pest. In her second term, Owen introduced legislation to set aside 2,000 square miles of the Everglades as a national park. Landowners opposed it, arguing the land was full of snakes, and even brought one of the reptiles to a committee hearing to demonstrate their point. Owen, who had never touched a snake in her life, grabbed it, wrapped it around her neck, and declared, "That's how afraid of snakes we are in the Everglades."[191] Her bill lost, but it ultimately led to the creation of the Everglades National Park decades later.

Owen also pushed for women's issues. She spoke out for mothers' pensions and for the creation of a Department of Home and Child. She also created an educational program that brought a boy and girl from each of the 18 counties in her district to Washington each year. She would personally lead the kids on tours through the Library of Congress and the White House, teaching them about government and politics.

In 1932, Owen lost her bid for a third term after her challenger attacked her for supporting Prohibition. A year later, President Franklin Roosevelt appointed her as minister to Denmark—the first American woman named to such a high post. She resigned from her post in 1936 after she married a captain in the Danish Royal Guard, and spent the following months campaigning for Roosevelt's re-election. In 1945, President Truman made her a special assistant with the State Department to aid in the creation of the United Nations and in 1949 made her an alternate delegate to the UN General Assembly. She spent the final years of her life writing, lecturing, and actively promoting the

UN. She died in 1954 while in Copenhagen to accept a decoration awarded by King Frederick IX.

ELIZABETH PATTERSON (D-S.C.)
(Nov. 18, 1939–)
House: Jan. 3, 1987, to Jan. 3, 1993

Elizabeth Patterson grew up surrounded by politics. As a young girl she worked on the campaigns of her father, Olin Johnston, who served as South Carolina's governor and U.S. Senator for more than 25 years. Patterson continued on the path of government service following college when she worked as a recruiting officer for the Peace Corps and VISTA. She later served as the Head Start coordinator for the South Carolina Office of Economic Opportunity and as a staff assistant for U.S. Rep. James Mann (D-S.C.). Patterson first won political office in 1975 as a member of the Spartanburg County Council. From 1979 to 1987, she served in the South Carolina state Senate.

When Patterson decided to run for Congress, she wasn't given much of a chance. Her district had been in Republican hands for eight years. But Patterson just narrowly defeated the well-financed GOP candidate and gave Democrats a major victory in the South. Patterson was able to hold on to the seat—just narrowly—through two more elections largely due to her down-home style and fiscal conservatism.

In the House, Patterson served on the Banking, Finance, and Urban Affairs Committee, the Veterans' Affairs Committee, and the Select Committee on Hunger. Shortly after first coming to the House, Patterson joined a group of moderate Democrats and Republicans dedicated to reducing the federal deficit with across-the-board spending cuts. In 1989, she introduced her own budget plan that gave the president more power to kill spending programs and removed the Social Security trust fund from calculations of the size of the deficit.

Patterson generally voted conservatively, and frequently broke with her fellow Democrats. In her second term, she voted against a Democratic bill to increase the minimum wage to $4.55 an hour and instead backed a Republican plan that hiked it by 20 cents less. She opposed a bill that required employers to give their workers family and medical leave and sponsored a constitutional amendment banning physical desecration of the U.S. flag.

NANCY PELOSI (D-Calif.)
(March 26, 1940–   )
House: June 2, 1987, to present

Nancy Pelosi came to the House after winning the special election to replace another woman, Rep. Sala Burton (D-Calif.), who died while in office. Just days before her death from cancer, Burton let it be known that she backed Pelosi as her successor—an endorsement that virtually assured Pelosi's victory. Although Pelosi had never before held national office, she had a long history of political involvement. Her father, Thomas D'Alesandro, served in the House from 1939 to 1947 representing Baltimore, and he later became mayor of that city. Pelosi's brother also served as Baltimore's mayor. After growing up on the East Coast, Pelosi moved across country to San Francisco and quickly became involved in the Democratic party and helped secure San Francisco as the site of the national convention in 1984. She lost a bid for national party chair in 1985, but went on to take over as the finance chair of the Democratic Senatorial Campaign Committee a year later.

After coming to the House in 1987, Pelosi was assigned to the Banking, Finance, and Urban Affairs Committee and the Committee on Government Operations. She quickly established herself as a solid liberal, opposing aid to Nicaraguan contras, supporting gun control, and introducing legislation to fight the AIDS virus—a serious problem in her district where the voting population is about one-fifth homosexual. She has continuously pushed for increased funding for AIDS research and for federally funded needle exchange programs aimed at preventing the spread of the deadly disease among intravenous drug users. In 1998, Pelosi led the unsuccessful opposition to a GOP bill banning all federal funding for such programs. "Science, not politics, should lead on public health policy," Pelosi said during floor debate on the bill. "The science is irrefutable. Needle exchange works and works well."[192]

Throughout her House career, Pelosi has fought strenuously to deny special trade status to China. Pelosi—whose district includes thousands of Chinese Americans—currently serves as chair of the Congressional Working Group on China. She has fought both President George Bush and Bill Clinton—unsuccessfully—to deny "Most Favored Nation" trade status to China until it improves its human rights record. In 1989, following the Tiananmen Square massacre, Pelosi introduced legislation to allow Chinese students in America to seek permanent U.S. residence without having to return home first. Congress cleared the measure, but it was vetoed by Bush.

In 1991, during her third term in office, Pelosi gave up her other two panel assignments for a seat on the powerful Appropriations Committee—where her father once served. She is currently the top Democrat on its subcommittee on foreign operations and regularly fights GOP efforts to reduce foreign aid, particularly for international family planning programs. In 1991, House leaders also drafted Pelosi to serve on the Ethics Committee. She remained on that panel for six years and in 1995 became one of two Democrats on the ethics subcommittee that looked into the political fund-raising practices of Speaker Newt Gingrich (R-Ga.). Following the panel's in-depth probe, Pelosi felt Gingrich should have been censured by the House and forced out of the Speaker's chair. She, however, agreed to back the lighter punishment of a reprimand and $300,000 penalty, saying she was concerned that an extended battle would have torn apart the House. Pelosi also currently serves on the Select Committee on Intelligence.

SHIRLEY PETTIS (R-Calif.)
(July 12, 1924–   )
House: April 29, 1975, to Jan. 3, 1979

Shirley Pettis came to the House in a special election to fill the seat of her husband, Rep. Jerry Pettis, who was killed in a plane crash. She won more than 60 percent of the vote against a field of 12 other candidates.

Before joining Congress, Pettis worked as a journalist and helped her husband run the family ranch. She was the founder and manager of the Audio-Digest Foundation and after her husband was elected to the House in 1966, she wrote a newspaper column for the *San Bernardino Sun-Telegram*. During her husband's time in office, Pettis also served as vice president of the Republican Congressional Wives Club.

After winning her husband's seat, Pettis was assigned to the Interior and Insular Affairs Committee. When she won election to a second term, she took posts on the Education and Labor Committee and the International Relations Committee. In her first term, she used her position on the Interior Committee to gain legislation protecting desert lands in her district. She secured wilderness status for almost a half million acres in the Joshua Tree National Monument and established the California Desert Conservation area.

During her time in office, Pettis generally voted along party lines. She supported banning federal funds for abortions, opposed the creation of a Consumer Protection Agency, and opposed cutting President's Ford request for military aid to South Korea.

Pettis declined a bid for a third term in office.

GRACIE PFOST (D-Idaho)
(March 12, 1906–Aug. 11, 1965)
House: Jan. 3, 1953, to Jan. 3, 1963

Throughout her 10 years in Congress, Gracie Pfost was a strong advocate of liberal causes, including a higher minimum wage, federal work programs, and women's rights. But she was best known for her unyielding fight to bring a federally funded dam project to the Hell's Canyon branch of the Snake River in her district—a fight that earned her the nickname of "Hell's Belle." In her maiden speech on the House floor, Pfost introduced a bill to authorize the construction of the dam and power plant. She opposed the private construction of the plant, saying the federal project would be more efficient and cost effective. She repeatedly bumped heads with the administration and private power companies, but vowed she would not be "bluffed, bullied or frightened by the private monopolies."[193] She finally lost her battle in 1957 when the House Interior and Insular Affairs Committee killed her bill for the dam and power plant.

Pfost first ran for Congress in 1950, but lost to the Republican incumbent by just 783 votes. In a rematch two years later, she used a slogan that let the voters know how to pronounce her name: "Tie Your Vote to a Solid Post—Gracie Pfost." This time, she narrowly defeated Rep. John Wood by 591 votes. Wood's request to have the House conduct a recount was turned down.

Pfost was assigned to the Public Works Committee, the Post Office and Civil Service Committee, and the Interior and Insular Affairs Committee, where she went on to chair the public lands subcommittee. She was also appointed by House Speaker Joseph Martin to a special five-member panel charged with investigating tax-exempt charities to determine if they had used funds for "un-American activities." In the midst of McCarthyism and anti-Communist hysteria, Pfost made a brave stand. After serving nine months on the panel, Pfost and the only other Democrat on the committee, Rep. Wayne Hays (Ohio), walked out of the hearings condemning them for publicizing unsubstantiated charges against foundation employees. "[The] foundations have been indicted and convicted under procedures which can only be characterized as barbaric," Pfost said.[194] The panel was forced to disband.

Later in her career, Pfost served on a 15-member commission to survey the nation's outdoor recreational resources, the first time such an inventory was ever taken. During her long congressional career she opposed the anti-labor Taft-Hartley Act, introduced a bill to expand the school milk program for children, and worked to create a Youth Conservation Program to find jobs for young men. In her 1954 re-election bid, she campaigned in favor of the Equal Rights Amendment and in 1955 she voted against a $10,000 pay raise for members of Congress.

In 1962, Pfost turned her sights on the Senate. She was nominated as the Democratic candidate for the Senate seat, but narrowly lost the general election. After leaving Congress, Pfost was named special assistant of housing for the elderly in the Federal Housing Administration. She held that post for two years until her death from Hodgkin's disease in 1965.

Before entering politics, Pfost worked as a chemist for a milk products company for two years until 1929, when she took on the jobs of deputy county clerk, auditor, and recorder of Canyon County, Idaho. She held those posts for 10 years and in 1940 was elected county treasurer, where she remained for another 10 years. She was a delegate to every Democratic National Convention between 1944 and 1960 and served on the convention's Platform and Resolutions Committee.

ELIZA JANE PRATT (D-N.C.)
(March 5, 1902–May 13, 1981)
House: June 3, 1946, to Jan. 3, 1947

Eliza Jane Pratt held her House seat for just seven months, but her career in Congress spanned more than two decades. Between 1924 and 1946, Pratt served as the top assistant to a parade of representatives from North Carolina's eighth district. When her last boss, Rep. William Burgin, died in office with less than a year left in his term, his successor was obvious. The state Democratic Executive Committee deliberated just 30 minutes before nominating Pratt to fill the vacancy. She campaigned for five weeks—paying all her own expenses—and won a lopsided victory over the Republican candidate.

Pratt first came to Capitol Hill when Rep. William Hammer asked her to give up her editor's post at a North Carolina weekly paper and move to Washington to serve as his assistant. During the next 22 years as congressional aide, Pratt became as well known to the voters as any of her bosses. She had mastered the legislative system and knew the background, purpose, and prospect of nearly every bill that was pending in Congress. During her time on Capitol Hill she witnessed such historic events as Charles Lindbergh's appearance before a joint session of Congress and President Roosevelt's request before Congress for a declaration of war against Japan.

Once sworn into office, Pratt was assigned to the Committee on Pensions, the Committee on Territories, and the Committee on Flood Control. Although she was encouraged by the local press to run for the following full term, she reluctantly declined, citing the high cost of campaigning. After leaving Congress, Pratt remained active in Washington politics. She worked for the Office of Alien Property from 1947 to 1951, the Department of Agriculture from 1951 to 1954, and the Library of Congress from 1954 to 1956. She returned to Capitol Hill in 1957 to work again for a North Carolina lawmaker, Rep. Alvin Kitchin. She later moved back to North Carolina, where she was active in the state Democratic Executive Committee. Pratt once lamented the fact that while women had become more active in politics, they too often stood behind the scenes rather then in the starring role. "I can remember the time when only a handful of women would turn out for a rally. Now they sometimes outnumber the men. And they work as regular members of a campaign organization. Unfortunately, when a campaign ends, they are all too often relegated to their former roles as second-class politicians."[195]

RUTH BAKER PRATT (R-N.Y.)
(Aug. 24, 1877–Aug. 23, 1965)
House: March 4, 1929, to March 3, 1933

Unlike many of her predecessors, Ruth Baker Pratt did not suceed a father or husband in Congress, but was elected in her own right. She ran for the House on her record as the only female alderman New York City ever had. During her two terms on the alderman board, she often found herself at odds with her 64 male colleagues, but Pratt had learned the art of political warfare years earlier from her extensive work in civic affairs. During World War I Pratt chaired the Second Federal Reserve District's Woman's Liberty Loan Committee. In 1918, she was appoined vice chair of the Republican National Ways and Means Committee and worked for Herbert Hoover's presidential nomination in 1920. She was a delegate at the Republican state conventions between 1920 and 1938 and served as a delegate to the national conventions from 1924 to 1944. She seconded President Hoover's renomination in 1932, the same year she was voted out of her House seat.

One year before winning election to the House in 1928, Pratt's husband John Teele Pratt—the heir of Standard Oil—died. His family wealth made Pratt one of the richest members of Congress at the time. She is noted to have leased "Evermay"—an eighteenth-century Georgian manor in Georgetown, Washington—shortly after her arrival in Washington. She also kept a manor home in New York that boasted greenhouses, stables, and 35 servants.

During her four years in Congress, Pratt served on the Committee on Education, the Committee on Banking and Currency, and the Committee on the Library. Her maiden speech on the floor was in opposition to a provision in the Hawley tariff bill that would increase the duty on sugar. During her speech, Pratt read a letter of protest from the president of the American Federation of Labor addressed to a Republican male colleague. Pratt was allowed to read the letter because "it had so much more weight coming from her."[196]

Pratt later introduced a bill for a $75,000 appropriation to publish books for the blind. She supported the repeal of Prohibition and concentrated on constituent service, often cutting through red tape to help immigrant constituents bring their families overseas to the United States. Pratt narrowly won a second term in 1930 by just 651 votes, but was unable to survive a challenge two years later. Her bid for a third term was hurt by charges she abused the franking privilege by mailing 70,000 pamphlets to her district detailing her achievements in office. She also fell victim to the 1932 Democratic tide that replaced Republicans across the country with followers of Franklin Roosevelt's New Deal.

After her defeat, Pratt remained active in civic affairs. She sat on the board of directors of the New York Philharmonic Symphony Society and served as chair of the Fine Arts Foundation—a forerunner of the National Endowment for the Humanities. She was also appointed to the advisory committee of the Republican Builders—a group aimed at rejuvenating the party after its defeats in 1932 and 1934—and was president of the Women's National Republican Club from 1943 to 1946.

Throughout her career, Pratt insisted that "sex has no place whatever in politics." She once wrote: "A man enters public life and not the slightest attention is paid to the fact that he is a man. A woman runs for office and there is more interest in the fact that she is a woman than in her qualifications for the job she seeks. She is completely shackled by her sex. At every turn she is confronted with the fact that the activities of the world have been cut from a he pattern."[197]

DEBORAH PRYCE (R-Ohio)
(July 29, 1951–   )
House: Jan, 5, 1993, to present

Deborah Pryce has made a steady rise up the Republican leadership since coming to Congress. She first caught the attention of national Republicans when she was one of just three GOP women elected to Congress during the 1992 "Year of the Woman." She quickly established herself as a leader when her fellow freshman colleagues elected her as their first class president.

Pryce was assigned to the Banking and Financial Services Committee and the Government Reform and Oversight Committee. During her first term in office, she distinguished herself as one of the more outspoken critics of President Clinton's economic policies.

Following the 1994 GOP takeover of Congress, House Speaker Newt Gingrich (R-Ga) named Pryce to the 10-member task force assembled to ensure a smooth transition of power to the new Republican majority. Pryce chaired the team's Legal Committee. Republicans also awarded Pryce with a prestigious spot on the House Rules Committee, which oversees all legislation that comes to the floor. Pryce accepted the exclusive assignment and gave up her other two committee seats. In 1997, Pryce won another leadership post. She defeated three Republicans to be elected the Secretary of the House Republican Conference. The spot is the sixth-ranking leadership position in the House. In 1998, Gingrich named Pryce the chief coordinator and spokeswoman for the GOP policy on the landmark tobacco settlement between 40 states and tobacco companies.

Legislatively, Pryce is conservative on most fiscal issues but more moderate on social matters. She supports abortion rights and voted to lift the "gag rule" barring staff at federally funded clinics from discussing abortion with patients. She also voted to allow federal employees' health care plans to cover abortions. She, however, supports a ban on a certain type of procedure called partial birth abortions by its opponents. Pryce was one of several GOP women lawmakers in 1995 to ask the House leadership to limit the number of times members would be forced to vote on the issue of abortion. "If Republicans are going to attract women voters, this is not the way to do it," Pryce said. "Every time we have to make an issue of it, the party loses."[198]

Pryce found herself at odds with the majority of her GOP colleagues when she supported a ban on certain assault weapons. Pryce also helped win Democratic support for a Republican overhaul of the welfare system in 1996 when she offered an amendment to the GOP bill that increased federal money for child-care programs by $160 million a year over five years.

Pryce has also worked to promote adoption. The mother of an adopted daughter, Pryce unsuccessfully fought to reform the Indian Child Welfare Act, which makes it difficult for non-American Indians to adopt Indian children.

On fiscal matters, Pryce is a straight conservative. She supports a balanced budget constitutional amendment and a presidential line-item veto. She also has fought federal mandates on businesses. In 1993, she was one of only a few women lawmakers to oppose legislation requiring businesses to offer family and medical leave to workers. She said the bill would be too costly for businesses.

Before coming to Congress, Pryce was a lawyer and judge. From 1985 to 1992 she was the presiding judge on the Franklin County, Ohio, Municipal Court. She previously worked for six years as the senior assistant Columbus City prosecutor.

GLADYS PYLE (R-S.D.)
(Oct. 4, 1890–March 14, 1989)
Senate: Nov. 9, 1938, to Jan. 3, 1939
(never sworn into office)

Gladys Pyle was the first Republican woman elected to the Senate, although she was never actually sworn into office. Pyle won the Nov. 9, 1938, special election to fill out the last few weeks of the term of Sen. Peter Norbeck, who had died in office, but the Senate had already adjourned for the year five months earlier. Although she never had the chance to take the oath of office, Pyle made the most of her two months on Capitol Hill. After her election, she drove all the way from South Dakota to Washington with her mother, a stenographer and clerk, because, she said, "I wouldn't feel like a Senator unless I did.[199] As soon as she arrived on Capitol Hill, she personally screwed her nameplate on the door of her temporary office, spoke at a luncheon of the Republican National Committee about the 1940 presidential campaign, and organized meetings with officials at the Interior Department to discuss South Dakota issues. "This life is a hectic whirl," she exclaimed.[200]

Pyle's service in the Senate may have been uneventful, but she had developed an impressive record in public service years before coming to Washington. Pyle grew up in a political family. Her mother led the Universal Franchise League, which won suffrage for South Dakota women in 1918, and Pyle's father was the state's attorney general. After doing graduate work at the American Conservatory of Music and the University of Chicago, she returned to South Dakota to work as a high school teacher and principal.

In 1923, Pyle became the first woman elected to the South Dakota state legislature, and four years later she became the first woman to serve as South Dakota secretary of state. In 1930, she made an unsuccessful bid for governor. She also served on the state Securities Commission where she helped write a budget law credited with giving South Dakota a "greatly improved fiscal policy."[201] Before winning election to the U.S. Senate, Pyle ran a life insurance business.

After her brief service in the Senate, Pyle continued her work in politics. In 1940, she gave the nominating speech at the GOP National Convention in Philadelphia for South Dakota's favorite-son presidential candidate, Gov. Harlan Bushfield. She later served for 14 years on the South Dakota State Board of Charities and Corrections. From 1950 to 1986, Pyle returned to her insurance business. She died in 1989 at the age of 98.

JEANNETTE RANKIN (R-Mont.)
(June 11, 1880–May 18, 1973)
House: March 4, 1917, to Jan. 3, 1919;
Jan. 3, 1941, to Jan. 3, 1943

Jeannette Rankin was not only the first woman ever elected to Congress, but also the only person in congressional history to vote against the United States' entry into both World Wars. She cast those votes—24 years apart—based on her lifetime commitment to peace and despite the knowledge they would bring her certain defeat for re-election.

Rankin's political strength and courage were likely products of her rugged upbringing on a ranch just outside Missoula, Mont. As a young woman, she led cows home by lantern in the pitch dark of night and accompanied her father on trips to his lumber camp, where she cooked for crews of 50 or 60. Rankin eventually attended the University of Montana and graduated with a degree in biology—an unusual feat for any woman at the turn of the century. The entire Rankin family was intellectually minded and pursued lofty goals. Her father had served as the local county commissioner. Her sister Harriet became dean of women at the University of Montana, and her sister Mary worked as an English professor at the same school. Her sister Edna was a lawyer and pioneer in the field of planned parenthood, and her only brother, Wellington, served as state attorney general.

Shortly after graduating college, Rankin decided she wanted to travel and left to visit her brother in Boston. During this trip she first became aware of the social injustices that plagued the country. She toured the Boston slums, where she was shocked to see women and children living in abject poverty. She later went to San Francisco's Latin Quarter and worked in a shelter for homeless women. In 1908, she spent a year at the New York School of Philanthropy, an institution whose progressive philosophy claimed that American women suffered because they had no voice in creating the power that ruled over them. Rankin soon became a leader in the national suffrage movement, traveling across the country and to New Zealand, where women had received the vote in 1893. She was chairman of the Montana Suffrage Association and served as field secretary for the National Suffrage Association.

When Montana gave women the right to vote in 1914—thanks in large part to Rankin's work—the door was open for her to run for public office. She decided to run for the U.S. House, and her brother Wellington signed on as campaign manager. During her exhaustive campaign, Rankin toured every village and town in Montana by train, buggy, car, and horseback. She promised to work for a women's suffrage amendment, an eight-hour workday for women, improved health care for mothers and children, and prohibition. When asked why a woman should be elected to Congress, she answered: "There are hundreds of men to care for the nation's tariff and foreign policy and irrigation projects. But there isn't a single woman to look after the nation's greatest asset: its children."[202] When she won election to the House in 1916, Rankin, 36, became the only Republican to win major elective office in Montana that year. Her victory came four years before women across the country had the right to vote.

Just four days after being sworn into office, Rankin faced one of the most important votes of her career—a resolution declaring the United States' entry into World War I. Rankin had campaigned against sending any Montanan to fight in the war, but she was under heavy pressure to support the resolution. Her brother urged her to "vote a man's vote" and warned that she could never win re-election if she did not. Rival women's groups put pressure on her from both sides, declaring that her vote would speak for all women. Carrie Chapman Catt of the National American Woman Suffrage Assocation feared that a vote against the war would brand suffragists as unpatriotic, while Alice Paul of the Woman's Party thought women in politics should speak for peace.

When her name was called to cast her ballot, Rankin rose and softly said, "I want to stand by my country, but I cannot vote for war."[203] Although Rankin was joined by 55 of her male colleagues in voting "nay," she was singled out for criticism in the press and was erroneously described as weeping on the floor during the vote.

Rankin spent the rest of her first term devoting herself to winning passage of the Suffrage Amendment. She co-sponsored a constitutional amendment giving women the right to vote. When the House Judiciary Committee tried to bottle up the measure, Rankin successfully introduced legislation creating a 13-member Woman Suffrage Committee, on which she served as ranking minority member. She was then chosen to lead the floor debate on suffrage.

"Can we afford to allow these men and women [of the United States] to doubt for a single instant the sincerity of our protestations of democracy?" she asked. "How shall we answer their challenge, gentlemen; how shall we explain to them the meaning of democracy if the same Congress that voted for war to make the world safe for democracy refuses to give this small measure of democracy to the women of our country."[204]

The House approved the amendment with exactly the two-thirds vote needed in 1918, but the Senate failed to pass it until a year later. Ironically, Rankin was no longer in Congress during that vote. In 1918, redistricting had vastly changed Rankin's base of support, and she chose to run for the Senate instead of the House. She lost the GOP primary, but decided to run in the general election as a candidate of the National Party, a coalition of socialists, prohibitionists, progressives, and farmers.

Her vote against the war, however, was used against her, and she came in a distant third. For the next 20 years, she worked as a field secretary of the National Consumer's League, lobbying for federal wage-and-hour laws, for a child-labor amendment, and for the maternity and infancy bill she had introduced while in office. She also worked with the Women's International League for Peace and Freedom and the Women's Peace Union, lobbying for a constitutional amendment "forbidding the United States from preparing for, or engaging in war." She later became legislative secretary for the National Council for the Prevention of War.

In 1940, as she approached 60 years of age, Rankin again ran for the House. She won by more than 9,000 votes and was the only Republican to win national office in Montana. On Dec. 8, 1941, the day after the Japanese attacked Pearl Harbor, the Senate unanimously approved President Roosevelt's request to declare war. As the House took up the vote, Rankin tried futilely to voice her opposition on the floor, but was ignored by Speaker Sam Rayburn. When her name was called during the roll call, Rankin cast the sole "no" vote to a chorus of jeers and hisses.

She did not run for re-election the following year, but continued to work for peace outside of elected office. She made several trips to India to study the pacifism of Gandhi. In the late 1960s, when she was in her 80s, Rankin helped organize the Jeannette Rankin Brigade and marched on Washington to protest the Vietnam War. She died in 1973, one month shy of her 93rd birthday.

Even after her death, 50 year after she left Congress, Rankin's absolute opposition to war still provoked praise and controversy. During the Persian Gulf War in 1991, Rankin's name was invoked at anti-war rallies as a role model for women peacemakers.

In 1996, Rankin's pacifism once again sparked debate on Capitol Hill. As Republican leaders discussed placing a statue of a woman in the Capitol's rotunda—none had ever stood there before—Republican women members of the House blocked efforts to move Rankin's bronze likeness to that most prominent area of the building. The GOP women said they did not want a pacifist to symbolize them or their party in the rotunda.

LOUISE REECE (R-Tenn.)
(Nov. 6, 1898–May 14, 1970)
House: May 16, 1961, to Jan. 3, 1963

When Louise Reece won election to Congress, she was following in a long family tradition. Her father, Guy Goff, was a U.S. senator from West Virginia and her grandfather, Nathan Goff, represented West Virginia in both the House and Senate. Reece herself came to the House to fill the seat of her husband, Rep. B. Carroll Reece, who died in his 12th term.

During her husband's lengthy House service, Reece regularly campaigned side-by-side with him. Because he could not drive, she served as his chauffeur on the campaign trail and Tennessee voters grew to know her as well they knew him. Reece also worked as an assistant to her husband when he chaired the Republican National Committee. Reece herself served as a delegate to the Republican National Convention in 1956.

In the special election to fill out her husband's unfinished term, Reece defeated her Democratic opponent with an almost two-to-one margin. After the election, Reece was assigned to the Public Works Committee. She focused on legislation dealing with the education, health, and welfare of children. She paid particular attention to school construction and juvenile delinquency. Reece also worked to protect her district's glass industry and pressed President Kennedy to restore tariff rates on certain glass products. In honor of the 45th anniversary of the Suffrage Amendment granting women the right to vote, Reece gave a speech on the House floor, giving special recognition to her state of Tennessee for providing the final vote for ratification.

At the end of her first term in office, Reece—suffering from severe arthritis—opted not to run for re-election.

CHARLOTTE REID (R-Ill.)
(Sept. 27, 1913–   )
House: Jan. 3, 1963, to Oct. 7, 1971

Before coming to Congress, Charlotte Reid was a well-known radio singer in the 1930s, entertaining millions as the featured vocalist on NBC and Don McNeill's popular show, *Breakfast Club*. Reid was elected to the House after her husband, who had won the GOP nomination for the seat, died during the campaign. The local Republican party chairman convinced Reid to run in his place and she went on to defeat the Democratic opponent with more than 60 percent of the vote.

Reid was not totally new to politics. She had spent years working in civic and charitable groups including the March of Dimes, the Child Welfare Society, the Girl Scouts, and the PTA. After her election to the House, Reid's prominence from her show business past was quickly recognized by her colleagues. During her first term in office, she received 19 invitations to campaign for GOP candidates and was one of just two freshmen selected to speak at the 1964 Republican National Convention.

A solid conservative, Reid fought for fiscal restraint and reduced federal power. She supported the military action in Vietnam and in 1965 traveled at her own expense to that country to meet with U.S. soldiers. As the first member of Congress to be cleared by the Defense Department to visit the war zone, Reid spent four days flying over the jungle in open helicopters, talking to the wounded and touring military outposts.

Legislatively, Reid backed an amendment to a 1968 higher education bill that denied federal loans to students who participated in anti-war protests. Reid later introduced a constitutional amendment to overturn the Supreme Court ruling against prayer in public schools. She also backed proposals to outlaw mail-order and out-of-state sales of rifles and supported a truth-in-lending law that required the disclosure of interest on loans. Although Reid never considered herself a feminist, she spoke out in favor of the Equal Rights Amendment and, along with Reps. Patsy Mink (D-Hawaii) and Catherine May Bedell (R-Wash.), pushed to open up the House gym to women lawmakers.

During her first two terms in the House, Reid served on the Interior and Insular Affairs Committee and the Public Works Committee. She later gave up those assignments to accept a seat on the powerful Appropriations Committee. She also served on the House Ethics Committee.

In 1971, President Nixon nominated Reid to serve on the Federal Communications Commission. She was unanimously confirmed by the Senate and resigned her seat in the House on Oct. 7. She later served as a member of the President's task force on International Private Enterprise from 1983 to 1985.

CORRINE RILEY (D-S.C.)
(July 4, 1893–April 12, 1979)
House: April 10, 1962, to Jan. 3, 1963

Corrine Riley won a special election to the House—to fill the seat of her husband Rep. Jacob Riley who died in office—without making one campaign appearance. Riley had no political experience and at first resisted the efforts of local Democrats to get her to run. But with the party behind her, she went on to win the primary against Martha Fitzgerald, an 11-term state legislator, by almost a three-to-one margin. She had no challengers in the special general election.

Riley was given a seat on the Science and Astronautics Committee after she turned down assignments on what she considered two lesser panels—the Post Office and Civil Service Committee and the Education and Labor Committee. During her eight months in the House, Riley introduced a bill authorizing the General Services Administration to transfer surplus property to the Aiken, S.C., Historical Society. She also supported a bill that required television sets to be equipped with high-frequency channels—something she hoped would benefit an educational television station back in her district. At the end of her brief term, Riley decided not to run for re-election.

Before coming to Congress, Riley worked as a high school teacher from 1915 to 1937 and served as a field representative for the South Carolina textbook commission from 1938 to 1942. During World War II, Riley also worked for the Civilian Personnel Office at Shaw Air Force Base in South Carolina.

LYNN RIVERS (D-Mich.)
(Dec. 19, 1956–)
House: Jan. 4, 1995, to present

Lynn Rivers says she entered politics as a "mom who got mad at the system."[205] A central theme of Rivers's campaign for Congress was her life story, which she said voters could identify with. Rivers got married the day after her high school graduation and had her first child when she was 18. She entered politics at the age of 28, joining the Ann Arbor Board of Education while she was still pursuing an undergraduate degree at the University of Michigan. She stayed on the board from 1984 to 1992, serving as its president for three years. In 1992, Rivers was elected to the Michigan state legislature—the same year she earned her law degree from Wayne State University.

In 1994, Rivers won the seat of retiring U.S. Democratic Rep. William Ford. On the campaign trail, she highlighted the differences between herself and her conservative Republican opponent, speaking out in favor of abortion rights, gay rights, and gun control. Once arriving on Capitol Hill, she was assigned to the Science and the Budget Committees. She was also elected by her fellow Democratic freshmen to serve as class president. In 1996, Rivers was asked by the Democratic party to speak at the 1996 National Convention during the "families first" segment that preceded First Lady Hillary Rodham Clinton's speech.

Rivers has focused much of her legislative attention on education. She believes the federal government should help set standards for public education and that by spending more money on public education—and less on the military—the government can better prepare students for a global job market and ultimately reduce the costs of public assistance. She has been an outspoken opponent of Republican efforts to create school vouchers that parents can use to pay tuition at private schools.

Rivers is generally a solid Democratic vote, opposing Republican efforts to reduce the cost of Medicare spending, deny public education to illegal immigrants, and ban a certain abortion technique labeled partial birth abortion by its opponents. She, however, joined most Republicans in voting to overhaul the welfare system in 1996. She said she did not agree with many of the plan's provisions, but feared it would be the only chance Congress got to make changes in the welfare system. She also joined with many freshmen Republicans in 1995 in pushing to reform the internal operations of Congress. She supported GOP legislation prohibiting House members from receiving gifts from lobbyists.

ALICE MARY ROBERTSON (R-Okla.)
(Jan. 2, 1854–July 1, 1931)
House: March 4, 1921, to March 3, 1923

The second woman ever to serve in Congress and the first to serve after women received the right to vote, Alice Mary Robertson bore little resemblance to her predecessor Jeannette Rankin (R-Mont.)—the first woman to serve in Congress. Unlike Rankin, Robertson was a staunch anti-suffragist who believed that exchanging women's "privileges" for men's "rights" was a poor swap. Even the press painted her as the exact opposite of Rankin.

"She is no tender Miss Rankin," wrote the *New York Times*. "She wouldn't have wept and she wouldn't have voted No on the declaration of war with Germany. An ardent Rooseveltian, she says that 'we ought to have gotten in a long time before we did.' " The paper also described her as a "total abstainer, never wore a pair of silk stockings and won't wear high-heeled shoes."[206]

Robertson was born at the Tullahassee Mission of the Creek Nation in Indian Territory (what is now Oklahoma) to missionary parents. She attended Elmira College in New York and went on to be the first woman clerk in the Office of Indian Affairs in Washington. Robertson later taught at schools in Pennsylvania and at a mission she founded among the Creek nation. From 1905 to 1913, she served as postmaster of Muskogee, Okla., and later ran a dairy farm and cafeteria in Muskogee.

Indeed, it was from that cafeteria that Robertson, at the age of 67, ran her successful campaign for the House. She advertised her run for office and her business in the same modest newspaper ads. She made no speeches and solicited no votes outside the restaurant, but would sit down with voters who came in for a bite and over "a bowl of soup talk politics." She reportedly had a record of 17 bowls of soup in one dinner hour.[207]

Robertson made her opposition to women's rights well known soon after she was elected to Congress. She incurred the wrath of such groups as the League of Women Voters, the National Women's Party, and the Daughters of the American Revolution when she refused to support the Sheppard-Towner Bill, a measure originally authored by Jeannette Rankin, which was aimed at reducing the number of deaths of mothers and newborn infants. She charged that "the 'sob stuff' claim that 680 babies die every day from the failure in enacting this bill . . . is absurd."[208]

She later voted against the creation of a federal Department of Education, explaining that, unlike the North, southern states would never accept the seating of "colored" school children next to whites. She also opposed U.S. entry into the League of Nations. On June 20, 1921, during a vote on funding for a U.S. delegation to the centennial celebrations of Peru's independence, Robertson became the first woman to preside over a session of the House.

During World War I, Robertson had run a canteen for servicemen in Muskogee, but after she came to Congress she voted against a measure that would have given bonuses to veterans of the war. That opposition contributed to her loss for re-election in 1922 against William Hastings, the man she had ousted from office two years earlier. On her defeat, Robertson returned to Oklahoma and worked in the Veterans' Hospital in Muskogee and for the Oklahoma Historical Society.

EDITH NOURSE ROGERS (R-Mass.)
(March 19, 1881–Sept. 10, 1960)
House: June 30, 1925, to Sept. 10, 1960

Like many of the women who came to Congress before her, Edith Nourse Rogers was first elected to fill out the unexpired term of her deceased husband, Rep. John Jacob Rogers. Mrs. Rogers, however, went on to win re-election 17 times to become the longest serving congresswoman in history. Rogers reluctantly decided to run for Congress only after being pushed by friends and local political leaders, but she won her first election with more votes than her husband garnered a year earlier, and she defeated her opponent with a more than two-to-one margin.

Her work with her husband during his time in the House helped her learn the ropes of congressional service and paved the way for what would later be her top priority in office—veterans. During World War I, her husband took a leave of absence from Congress to enlist as a private in the army. Mrs. Rogers went with her husband to war-torn Europe and volunteered in hospitals with the YMCA and the Red Cross. After returning to the United States, Mrs. Rogers continued her work with the Red Cross and volunteered at the Walter Reed Hospital from 1918 to 1922, often working 18 hours a day. Her work with disabled veterans earned her the title "Angel of Walter Reed." By now, her volunteerism had captured the attention of President Harding, who appointed her as his personal representative in charge of assistance for disabled veterans. The next year she was reappointed by President Coolidge, and President Hoover named her to the same post in 1929.

Rogers continued her dedication to veterans issues after coming to Congress. She was assigned to the World War Veterans Committee (later named the Veterans Affairs Committee) and later served as its chair. One of her first pieces of legislation after coming to Congress was a $15-million appropriation to build a nationwide network of veterans hospitals, which she steered to passage despite the opposition of the committee chairman.

Rogers quickly became known for her love of a good floor fight and her aggressive pursuit of legislation. One congressional reporter wrote that she "conducts herself like a man. She doesn't get on her mark, get set, and then recite her speech in schoolgirl fashion. Bouncing out of her seat, she shoots a question in a high-pitched Boston accent and leaps in where other gentlewomen fear to tread."[209]

In 1941, Rogers introduced a bill to establish the Woman's Army Auxiliary Corps (WAACs). It was the forerunner of all women's military units and gave women the right to wear a uniform, live in barracks, and earn the same pay as members of the regular army. Three years later, Rogers helped draft the 1944 GI Bill of Rights, which gave returning veterans such benefits as college scholarships and low-interest home loans. Rogers was so instrumental in getting the bill passed that after President Franklin Roosevelt signed it into law, he gave her the pen he used to sign his name. Rogers was also one of the first members to protest the persecution of Jews by Nazi Germany. She opposed U.S. neutrality at the beginning of World War II, voted for the Selective Service Act, sponsored a bill establishing a Nurses Corps in the Veterans' Administration, and backed all defense appropriations through 1945.

Along with her dedication to veterans and a strong national defense, Rogers also fought hard to protect the interests of cotton millworkers and other industrial workers in her district. Herself a daughter of a cotton mill official, Rogers pushed for tariff laws helpful to mill owners and legislation to benefit mill hands and their families. She made it a habit to wear cotton dresses and hose, and urged her male colleagues to wear cotton suits. Other legislative successes included the establishment of the National Cancer Institute and a $50,000 bill for an accident prevention study, the first step by Congress in national highway safety.

In 1960—at the age of 79 and just three weeks before her primary race for election to a 19th terms—Rogers fell ill and quietly checked herself into a hospital under an assumed name. She died two days before the election, in which she was unopposed. She probably would have approved of the man who succeeded her in Congress—deputy director of the Veterans Administration, F. Bradford Morse.

ILEANA ROS-LEHTINEN (R-Fla.)
(July 15, 1952–)
House: Aug. 29, 1989, to present

Ileana Ros-Lehtinen, the first Cuban American elected to Congress, has spent most of her political career working to oust Cuban leader Fidel Castro from office. Born in Havana, Cuba, Ros-Lehtinen immigrated to the United States when she was seven years old. She went on to earn a master's degree from Florida International University and became a school teacher and founder of a private elementary school. In 1982, Ros-Lehtinen won a seat in the Florida state House, becoming the first Hispanic ever elected to the state legislature. Four years later she won a seat in the state Senate.

In 1989, when 13-term Democratic Rep. Claude Pepper died, Republicans looked to Ros-Lehtinen as their best chance to capture the seat. The district's Hispanic population was growing quickly, and Ros-Lehtinen had established herself as a leader in the Cuban community. She defeated 10 opponents in the special election. After coming to Congress, she was assigned to the Government Reform and Oversight Committee and the Committee on International Relations, where she now chairs the economic policy and trade subcommittee. As a member of the committee, she has backed bills aimed at reducing foreign spending and eliminating certain international agencies such as the U.S. Information Agency and the Arms Control and Disarmament Agency.

But Ros-Lehtinen's primary legislative focus has been aimed against Castro. She supported the ban against subsidiaries of U.S. corporations from conducting business in Cuba and a bill to punish foreign companies that invest in Cuba. In 1997, Ros-Lehtinen resigned from the Congressional Hispanic Caucus after its chair, Rep. Xavier Becerra (D-Calif.), took a trip to Cuba.

Although Ros-Lehtinen has worked closely with conservatives to punish Castro, her Hispanic background has often led her to oppose her party on immigration issues. She was one of only a handful of Republicans who refused to sign the GOP Contract with America in 1994.

She opposed the welfare provision in the Contract that denied benefits to legal immigrants. When the welfare bill passed the House in 1996, she was one of only two Republicans to vote against it. (The other was fellow Cuban immigrant Rep. Lincoln Diaz-Balart.) Ros-Lehtinen voted against GOP bills to make English the official U.S. language and end federal funding for bilingual education programs. She also fought a plan to prohibit children of illegal immigrants from attending public schools, calling it "a mean-spirited attempt that will hold children responsible for their parents' actions."[210]

Ros-Lehtinen has also opposed her Republican leadership on several non-immigration issues. She broke ranks with her party in 1996 and voted to raise the minimum wage by 90 cents and was one of just 42 Republicans to vote against the repeal of a ban on assault weapons.

MARGE ROUKEMA (R-N.J.)
(Sept. 19, 1929–   )
House: Jan. 3, 1981, to present

Marge Roukema, the most senior woman in the House today, is also one of the most moderate Republicans in Congress. She has voted with Democrats on many social issues—including abortion rights and gun control—but she is a strong fiscal conservative and favors a balanced budget amendment to the Constitution.

A former school teacher, Roukema first entered public life as a member of the Ridgewood, N.J., Board of Education from 1970 to 1973. Roukema also worked in local GOP politics, serving as president of the Ridgewood Republican Club for two years. She made her first run for the House in 1978, but lost to the Democratic nominee. Two years later she tried again and this time won by nearly 10,000 votes.

After coming to the House, Roukema was assigned to the Education and Labor Committee and the Committee on Banking, Finance, and Urban Affairs where, following the GOP takeover of Congress in 1994, she became chair of its subcommittee on financial institutions and consumer credit. In 1984, Roukema was named the ranking Republican of the newly formed Select Committee on Hunger, a post she held until the committee's elimination in 1995.

One of Roukema's biggest achievements during her long career was the enactment of the Family and Medical Leave Act in 1993. Roukema had worked on the legislation for years, despite opposition from most members of her party and GOP President Bush who vetoed the bill twice. Roukema was the lead Republican sponsor of the act, which she calls "a bedrock family issue," and requires large firms to provide unpaid leave to new parents, disabled workers, and those caring for seriously ill relatives. Roukema negotiated a crucial compromise in the bill to exempt small businesses—a compromise that helped win enough GOP support to pass the bill out of Congress. Roukema's undying support for the act came from her own personal experience with her 17-year-old son who died after battling leukemia. "When my son Todd was stricken with leukemia and needed home care, I was free to remain at home and give him the loving care he needed. But what of the millions of mothers who work for the thousands of companies that do not have family leave policies?" Roukema said during House floor debate on the bill.[211]

Roukema has often found herself bumping heads with her more conservative Republican colleagues. She fought efforts by President Reagan to cut funding for student loans. In 1994, she was one of only 11 Republicans to vote to bring a Democratic anti-crime bill to the House floor. She also voted for a Democratic bill to ban 19 different types of assault weapons.

In 1997, Roukema called on her party to appoint an interim Speaker until the House ethics committee finished its investigation of Speaker Newt Gingrich (R-Ga.). Later, after Gingrich was slapped with a $300,000 fine for breaking House rules, Roukema called on Gingrich to pay out of his own pocket, rather than from campaign funds.

On women's issues, Roukema has voted to allow abortions at overseas military hospitals, provide federal workers with health care plans that cover abortions, and require states to fund Medicaid abortions for poor women in the cases of rape and incest and to protect the life of the woman. She did, however, vote to ban so-called partial birth abortions. Roukema has also fought to help parents collect child support payments.

A fiscal conservative, she voted to freeze defense spending and opposed funding for two big-ticket projects favored by many Republicans—the superconducting supercollider and NASA's space station.

LUCILLE ROYBALL-ALLARD (D-Calif.)
(June 12, 1941–   )
House: Jan. 5, 1993, to present

Lucille Royball-Allard, the first Mexican-American woman elected to Congress, succeeded her father, 15-term Rep. Ed Royball (D-Calif.), after his retirement from the House. But Royball-Allard has established herself as a savvy legislator in her own right. From 1995 to 1996, she served as second vice chair of the Hispanic Caucus, and in 1997 she was elected chair of the California Democratic Congressional Delegation. The delegation bucked its tradition of giving the top post to its most senior member and made her the first woman and first Hispanic to chair the group.

Royball-Allard honed her legislative skills during her three terms in the California state assembly. During her time at the state level, Royball-Allard received national acclaim for her work on behalf of battered women, prompting the California chapter of the National Organization for Women to name her Legislator of the Year in 1991. She pushed through the assembly a bill requiring state courts to consider a batterer's history of domestic violence during child custody hearings and fought for enactment of the nation's first state statute establishing penalties for sexual misconduct by attorneys against their clients.

In Congress, Royball-Allard has continued to focus on women's issues. She chairs the Women's Caucus Task Force on Violence Against Women. She introduced the Battered Women's Economic Protection Act to ensure that battered women can take leave from their jobs to seek counseling and obtain unemployment insurance if they are forced to quit their jobs as a direct result of domestic violence. As a member of the Budget Committee, she successfully amended the budget resolution in 1996 to ensure that no changes in the welfare system will exacerbate domestic violence problems faced by low income women. Her proposal was the only Democratic amendment adopted by the committee.

Royball-Allard also sits on the Banking and Financial Services Committee, where she works to stimulate the economy of her financially strapped district. She has worked to bring special mortgage programs to poor constituents looking to buy homes and strongly supports small business development. She pushed through an amendment in 1994 authorizing the Small Business Administration to create mobile resource centers to provide on-site assistance to small businesses. Royball-Allard sat on the Small Business Committee when she first came to Congress, but later gave up the seat to serve on the Budget Committee.

Representing a majority Hispanic district, Royball-Allard strongly opposes Republican efforts to end bilingual education in public schools and make English the official language of the United States. Although she is staunchly liberal, she is not considered a partisan zealot. She has used her chairmanship of the California Democratic delegation to try to build a bridge to Republicans. "As I tell my colleagues from other states, I want their worst nightmare to come true: the California delegation coming together on key issues."[212] Her ability to work on a bipartisan level prompted House leaders to name her in 1998 to a special committee to investigate whether President Clinton illegally traded sensitive technology to China in exchange for campaign contributions.

Following the 1998 elections, Roybal-Allard was elected to serve as chair of the Congressional Hispanic Caucus for the 106th Congress. She was the first woman ever elected to head that organization.

KATHARINE ST. GEORGE (R-N.Y.)
(July 12, 1894–May 2, 1983)
House: Jan. 3, 1947, to Jan. 3, 1965

During her 18 years in the House, Katharine St. George established herself as a solid conservative, but, ironically, she is best known for championing what is generally considered a liberal cause—equal rights and pay for women. When the chair of the House Judiciary Committee refused to act on the Equal Rights Amendment in 1950, St. George led the fight to bring the bill to the floor for a vote. She tried but failed to collect the signatures of 218 of her colleagues, the number needed to "discharge" the amendment from committee. Although she was unable to push the ERA through Congress, she proposed in 1959 a bill to require equal pay for equal work among the sexes. That proposal was eventually signed into law as the Equal Pay Act of 1963.

During her first term in office, St. George also proposed a bill to strengthen the mandate for the Women's Army Corps by expanding Veteran's Administration law to WAC personnel. And in 1964, during House consideration of the Civil Rights Act prohibiting racial discrimination, St. George joined other women lawmakers to include sexual discrimination under the ban. "I can think of nothing more logical than this amendment at this point," St. George told her male colleagues.

"[Women] do not need any special privileges. We outlast you. We out-live you. We nag you to death . . . [and] we are entitled to this little crumb of equality. The addition of the little, terrifying word 's-e-x' will not hurt this legislation in any way."[213]

Despite her efforts to put women and men on an equal playing field, St. George did not consider herself a feminist and sometimes even ex-pressed frustration with her own sex. "It's lucky that men don't under-stand women, because women do, and they don't like them," she said.[214] She also sometimes suggested that women should not enter federal office because it puts too much of a strain on the family.

St. George was born in England to a wealthy family. Her father was the European editor for *Forum* magazine, and St. George received much of her early education in France, Switzerland, and Germany. She was also a first cousin to Franklin Roosevelt—a relationship that sometimes left St. George in a political quandry. After the Democratic Roosevelt was elected President in 1932, St. George stopped campaigning for her fellow Republicans during his first two terms in the White House. She, did, however, re-enter the political arena when Roosevelt ran for a third term, which she opposed.

St. George first entered public service in 1926 when she was elected to the Tuxedo, N.Y., board of education and the town board—positions she held until her bid for Congress 20 years later. She also served as treasurer and chair of the Orange County Republicans—the first woman in New York to head a GOP committee. In 1942, she suffered her first political defeat when she lost the nomination for state assembly.

St. George decided to run for federal office after her friend Rep. Ham-ilton Fish (R-N.Y.) was defeated in 1944 by a Republican-turned-Democrat. When the party-switcher ran for re-election two years later—this time as a Republican—St. George trounced him in the primary. She then sailed on to victory in the general election. On her arrival on Capitol Hill, St. George was turned down for seats on the Foreign Affairs and Agriculture Committees and was instead assigned to the Post Office and Civil Service Committee. She was later given a spot on the Government Operations Committee, the Armed Services Committee, and the power-ful Rules Committee—the first time a woman had ever won a seat on that panel. As a member on Armed Services, St. George was the first woman passenger on the F-104 B (Starfighter) plane when it broke the sound barrier.

As a member of the Post Office and Civil Service Committee, St. George introduced bills to establish a federal employee's code of ethics and increase federal salaries according to the cost of living index. She was, however, one of only two members on the panel to oppose a bill in 1963 granting broader raises to federal career employees—including members of Congress. She also proposed the creation of a federal safety division in the Labor Department and called for a ban on veterans' benefits to anyone belonging to organizations advocating the overthrow of the U.S. government. In her very first speech on the House floor, she called for secrecy on the atomic bomb until the country could find a defense against it.

In 1961, St. George voted to kill a Kennedy administration proposal to give states federal funds for school construction and teacher salaries. The following year, just four days after the Supreme Court ruled to ban prayer in New York state schools, St. George introduced a joint resolution authorizing Congress to override high court decisions by a two-thirds vote of both houses.

As a reward for her loyalty to the GOP, St. George was given a seat on the Republican Policy Committee and the Committee on Committee, which was in charge of handing out assignments to Republicans. St. George was also made a regional whip, responsible for gathering votes on leadership proposals.

In her bid for a 10th term in Congress, St. George was narrowly defeated by a liberal Democrat. She returned to New York and chaired the Tuxedo Park Republican town committee until her retirement in 1979.

PATRICIA SAIKI (R-Hawaii)
(May 28, 1930–   )
House: Jan. 3, 1987, to Jan. 3, 1991

Pat Saiki holds a distinct honor in Hawaiian politics—she is the only Republican ever elected to the House from Hawaii since it became a state in 1959. Saiki's moderate stance on issues and her extensive political background helped her win that distinction in the solidly Democratic state. A former high school teacher, Saiki first entered politics in the 1960s as the secretary, and later vice chairman, of the state Republican party. In 1968 she won election to the Hawaii House of Representatives and served as a delegate to the state Constitutional Convention, where she sponsored an Equal Rights Amendment to the state constitution. In 1974, Saiki won election to the state Senate, where she served until 1982 when she ran for lieutenant governor. After losing that bid, Saiki served as state GOP chairman until 1985. During her time at the helm of the party, she tripled membership and helped raised $800,000.

Saiki decided to run for Congress in 1986 to fill the seat of Rep. Cecil Heftel (D), who had resigned to run for governor. In an odd twist of political fate, Saiki lost the September special election to fill out the remaining months in Heftel's term, but won the GOP nomination for the general election two months later. She went on to win the November election for the full two-year term.

Once in office, Saiki was assigned to the Banking, Finance, and Urban Affairs Committee; the Merchant Marine and Fisheries Committee; and the Select Committee on Aging. In her first term, Saiki—a Japanese American—co-sponsored a bill to offer compensation and an official apology from the U.S. government to the thousands of Japanese Americans interned during World War II. Saiki's uncle was one of the Japanese Americans held in U.S. camps during the war. The bill became law in 1987.

Saiki was a moderate Republican, frequently opposing her party on social issues. She supported a seven-day waiting period for handguns and voted to overturn President Ronald Reagan's veto of the Civil Rights Restoration Act. She, however, backed Reagan's request for military aid to the Nicaraguan Contras and supported the death penalty for drug-related murders. Saiki also concentrated on constituent services during her two terms in office and helped secure a $2.6-million authorization to add land to Hawaii's Kilauea Point National Wildlife Refuge.

In 1990, following the death of Sen. Spark Matsunaga (D), Saiki ran in the special election to fill out the remainder of the Senate term but lost the bid to her Democratic House colleague Daniel Akaka. Four years later, Saiki ran for governor. She won the Republican nomination—the first woman in the state to win nomination for governor—but lost the general election to the Democratic candidate.

LORETTA SANCHEZ (D-Calif.)
(Jan. 7, 1960–   )
House: Jan. 7, 1997, to present

Much of Loretta Sanchez's first term in office was consumed by a House investigation into whether she legally won her seat. Sanchez had defeated nine-term Rep. Bob Dornan (R) by less than 1,000 votes. Dornan, a firebrand conservative, challenged the election and charged that illegal immigrants and noncitizens had voted for Sanchez to give her the narrow margin of victory. After 14 months of investigation, a bipartisan House task force ruled that although it had found some instances of illegal voting, it was not widespread enough to warrant Sanchez's removal from office. Dornan launched a rematch against Sanchez in 1998, but was defeated.

Sanchez was a political newcomer when she ran for Congress. A financial adviser, she had only run for public office once before, losing a bid in 1994 for the Anaheim city council. After coming to Capitol Hill, Sanchez was assigned to the Education and Workforce Committee and the National Security Committee.

Although Sanchez is generally liberal on social issues, she is more conservative on money matters. A former Republican—she switched registration in 1992— Sanchez believes in a smaller government and lower taxes and has called for an overhaul of the IRS. She is a member of the House Blue Dog Caucus, a group of moderate to conservative Democrats. During her campaign for Congress, she took a tough stance against crime and supports the death penalty.

But on most social issues, Sanchez is a reliable Democratic vote. She supports abortion rights and opposed a ban on a controversial procedure labled partial birth abortion by its opponents. She also opposed federal efforts to overturn a California state-passed initiative that legalized the medical use of marijuana.

The daughter of Mexican immigrants, Sanchez supports most affirmative action programs and has fought various English-only initiatives. From her seat on the Education and Workforce Committee, Sanchez has also fought to expand the Head Start preschool program. Sanchez was one of the first children to graduate from the program in 1965 and said that it helped her overcome emotional and learning difficulties.

JAN SCHAKOWSKY (D-Ill.)
(May 26, 1944–   )
House: Jan. 6, 1999, to present

Long before coming to Congress, Jan Schakowsky had established a reputation as a ceaseless fighter for liberal causes. She first became involved in politics during the 1970s when, as a housewife, she helped launch a successful nationwide campaign to require freshness dates on food products. She later became the program director of Illinois Public Action, the state's largest public interest organization, where she fought for energy reform and stronger protection from toxic chemicals. As Director of the Illinois State Council of Senior Citizens from 1985 to 1990, she organized across the state for lower cost prescription drugs and tax relief for seniors.

In 1991, Schakowsky was elected to the Illinois general assembly, where she fought for union rights, expanded family leave benefits, and nursing home protections. She also helped pass the first bill in the nation guaranteeing homeless people the right to vote. During her eight years on the state assembly, Schakowsky served as a Democratic Floor Leader and Secretary of the Conference of Women Legislators.

In the U.S. House of Representatives, Schakowsky has vowed to support gun control, abortion rights, and alternative sentencing for nonviolent criminals to alleviate prison crowding. She was assigned to the Banking Committee and Small Business Committee.

LYNN SCHENK (D-Calif.)
(Jan. 5, 1945–   )
House: Jan. 5, 1993, to Jan. 3, 1995

Long before coming to Congress, Lynn Schenk had established herself as an effective and liberal politician. A graduate of the University of San Diego law school, she forced the university to build a woman's restroom in the male-dominated institution. In 1972, she co-founded the San Diego Lawyers Club to help female attorneys, and a year later co-founded the Women's Bank in San Diego. She formally entered the world of politics in 1976 as a White House fellow under the Carter administration. In 1980, she served with California Gov. Jerry Brown (D) as the state's first female secretary of business, transportation, and housing. She unsuccessfully ran for the San Diego Board of Supervisors in 1984 and in 1990 became a commissioner of the San Diego Unified Port District, a post she held until her election to the U.S. House during the historic 1992 "Year of the Woman."

Once in Congress, Schenk served on the Energy and Commerce Committee and the Committee on Merchant Marine and Fisheries. Schenk maintained a liberal voting record on social issues such as abortion and the environment, and a more conservative one on fiscal matters. She boasted that she "stood up to the president" by voting for a balanced budget amendment and was one of only 33 House Democrats to support a Republican line-item veto bill. She was a pro-business Democrat, supporting tax incentives for business investment and cuts on capital gains taxes. She also focused on health care issues and looked out for the interests of biomedical research companies in her district.

But Schenk was hurt politically when she voted in favor of President Clinton's tax-raising budget in 1993. During her re-election bid in 1994, her GOP opponent ran ads accompanied by the sound of a cash register, claiming that Schenk's budget vote cost local taxpayers more than $500 million. The ads proved effective, and Schenk lost her bid for a second term.

In 1998, Schenk made another try for office, this time running for California's attorney general. She was defeated for the Democratic nomination.

CLAUDINE SCHNEIDER (R-R.I.)
(March 25, 1947–   )
House: Jan. 3, 1981, to Jan. 3, 1991

When Claudine Schneider won election to Congress in 1980, she became the first Republican from Rhode Island to serve in the House in more than 40 years. Schneider's liberal voting record—she voted against GOP President Reagan three-quarters of the time, more than the average Democrat—helped her win solid re-elections to the traditionally Democratic seat for the next eight years.

Schneider first became involved in politics during the 1970s when she led the fight against the construction of a nuclear power plant near her home. She worked closely with a number of environmental issues and in 1973 founded the Rhode Island Committee on Energy. She later worked as executive director of the Conservation Law Foundation and became the federal coordinator of the Rhode Island Coastal Management Program in 1978. That same year, Schneider decided to run for Congress. Although she was little known and underfinanced, Schneider came within 9,000 votes of defeating the Democratic incumbent.

Following her defeat for the House, Schneider remained in the public eye by hosting a Sunday morning talk show in Providence. When she ran again in 1980, she was much better known and financed, and this time defeated the Democrat by more than 22,000 votes.

Once in Congress, Schneider was assigned to the Merchant Marine and Fisheries Committee and the Committee on Science, Space, and Technology, where she eventually became the top Republican on the subcommittee on natural resources, agriculture research, and the environment.

She quickly established herself as one of the most liberal Republicans in Congress, focusing on environmental, energy, and women's issues. In her first year in office, Schneider introduced a bill aimed at preventing the repeal of Title IX, an act that prevents sexual discrimination in federally funded schools. She later sponsored legislation that would help older women go to college by expanding financial aid to part-time and other "nontraditional" students. Parts of her bill were included in a broader education bill approved in 1986.

On environmental issues, Schneider played a central role in halting construction of the Clinch River nuclear reactor—a project backed by Reagan and other top Republicans. She led the effort to ban ocean dumping of sewage sludge and medical waste and tried unsuccessfully to place a tax on hazardous waste disposal.

In 1990, Schneider made a bid for the Senate against 30-year incumbent Claiborne Pell (D). Schneider was reluctant to attack the 71-year-old Pell personally, and there was little difference between the two liberals' voting records. Rhode Island voters decided to stick with the incumbent Pell, and Schneider lost with only 38 percent of the vote.

PATRICIA SCHROEDER (D-Colo.)
(July 30, 1940–   )
House: Jan. 3, 1973, to Jan. 3, 1997

When Pat Schroeder won her seat in 1972, she was the first woman ever elected to Congress from Colorado and the first female member with young children—a son, six, and a daughter, two. By the time she retired from office 24 years later, she had become the dean of House women— the longest-serving woman at the time—and had established herself as a liberal outsider who refused to play by the rules of the male-dominated Congress.

"I have a brain and a uterus, and I use them both," Schroeder once declared after a male colleague asked how she could hold office and raise children.[215]

Schroeder's fight for women's rights began long before she ran for Congress. A graduate of Harvard Law School, Schroeder was one of only 19 women in a class of 554 and she often faced blatant hostility from her male colleagues. On graduation in 1964, she was told no law firm would ever hire her out of fear she would eventually quit to raise children. After being turned down for several jobs, she accepted a government position as a field attorney for Colorado with the National Labor Relations Board. Two years later she started her own private practice and did volunteer work for Rocky Mountain Planned Parenthood. She also worked for a year as a precinct committeewoman and taught law at Denver-area colleges.

Schroeder decided to run for Congress at the urging of her husband. The Denver district was considered a Republican stronghold, and few Democrats were willing to run. "I was the only person he could talk into it," she said. Because she was so sure she would lose, Schroeder continued to work in her law practice throughout the campaign so that she would have "something to go back to."[216] She ran on an anti-Vietnam platform and called for a reordering of national priorities to emphasize education, child care, health services, and environmental protection. Despite being frequently criticized for running for office while also raising two children, she won the general election in an upset victory, beating the Republican incumbent with 51.6 percent of the vote.

Once in office, Schroeder pushed her way onto the all-male Armed Services Committee, where she fought what she considered was an excessive military budget. She immediately bumped heads with the committee's conservative southern chair, Edward Herbert. Herbert did not want Schroeder on his panel and punished her by forcing her to share a seat with another new member he didn't like, black liberal Ron Dellums. Despite her early confrontations with Herbert, Schroeder eventually rose to chair the panel's subcommittee on military installations in 1990. Schroeder also served on the Judiciary Committee and the Post Office and Civil Service Committee and chaired the Select Committee on Children, Youth, and Families. Schroeder also co-chaired the Congressional Women's Caucus, which she helped found in 1977.

During her congressional career, Schroeder fought for a ban on nuclear testing, better housing and day-care facilities on military bases, increased medical research on women's health, and abortion availability on overseas military bases. She passed legislation that allowed divorced armed service wives to receive a portion of their husband's military pensions, and successfully pushed to lift the ban on gays in the military and on women in combat. Schroeder co-sponsored the Pregnancy Discrimination Act that became law in 1978 and required employers to treat pregnancy like any other temporary disability and include it as part of their insurance coverage.

One of Schroeder's most hard-fought battles was for passage of the Family and Medical Leave Act. Schroeder spent almost a decade pushing for its passage, which required employers to give workers 12 weeks unpaid leave to take care of sick relatives or newborn children. When Congress finally passed the bill and President Clinton signed it in 1993, many male lawmakers were invited to participate in the White House signing ceremony, but no women were asked to join in. "I had worked on it for nine years, but when it finally passes, it's the guys who take the credit."[217]

Along with her extensive legislative successes, Schroeder also became famous for her quick wit and memorable one-liners. She labeled President Reagan "the Teflon president" and said Vice President Dan Quayle thought the Supreme Court decision "Roe versus Wade are two ways to cross the Potomac." She chastised Pentagon allies on the Armed Services Committee, telling them "If you guys were women, you'd always be pregnant. You just can't say no." She is also well remembered for her brief entrance into—and withdrawal from—the presidential race in 1987. After three months of campaigning, she dropped out of the race in an emotional press conference. Choking back tears, she finished her speech and threw herself into the arms of her husband. "What began . . . as an exciting quest for the presidency of the United States ended three months later . . . as a search for Kleenex," she would later quip.[218]

After leaving Congress in 1997, Schroeder became president of the Association of American Publishers, a trade association that works on behalf of First Amendment rights.

BOOKS BY SCHROEDER

Champion of the Great American Family (1989)
24 Years of House Work . . . and the Place Is Still a Mess (1998)

ANDREA SEASTRAND (R-Calif.)
(Aug. 5, 1941–)
House: Jan. 4, 1995, to Jan. 7, 1997

Andrea Seastrand narrowly won her House seat in 1994 by just 1,500 votes—a less than 1 percent margin of victory over her Democratic opponent. She became one of seven new GOP women elected to the House that year—the largest number of Republican women ever elected to Congress.

Seastrand entered politics late in life. A former teacher, she first ran for office in 1990, winning the state assembly seat her late husband had held for eight years. During her 1994 campaign for Congress, Seastrand emphasized the Republican Contract with America and drew much of her support from the Christian Coalition and the conservative Eagle Forum. A strong opponent of abortion, gun control, and gay rights, Seastrand also supported California's anti-immigrant Proposition 187 that was on the state ballot that year.

Religion also played a role in her race. During one campaign speech, she suggested that God was sending warnings to sinful Californians: "Floods, drought, fires, earthquakes, lifting mountains two feet high in Northridge."[219]

Once on Capitol Hill, Seastrand was assigned to the Science Committee and the Committee on Transportation and Infrastructure. During her one term in office she backed GOP efforts to overhaul the welfare system, cut taxes, and balance the budget. She and her fellow freshmen also killed a longtime congressional perk—free ice delivered every day to members' offices. Seastrand said the elimination of the perk symbolized Republicans' goals to reduce the size of government.

In 1996, Democrat Walter Capps—the man Seastrand narrowly defeated two years earlier—launched a rematch and defeated her by more than 10,000 votes.

KAREN SHEPHERD (D-Utah)
(July 5, 1940–   )
House: Jan. 5, 1993, to Jan. 3, 1995

Karen Shepherd came to Congress on shaky political ground. She represented a district that gave President Clinton only 32 percent of the vote; she herself won election with a bare 51 percent. She was only the second woman sent to Congress from Utah and the only non-Mormon in the state's delegation.

A former English teacher, Shepherd said she went into politics after reading one too many term papers. She worked in the Democratic party on a grass-roots level, and in 1978 launched *Network*, a magazine for working women. After selling the magazine in 1988, Shepherd became the community relations director for the University of Utah business school. In 1990, she was elected to the Utah state senate, where she served until her election to Congress in the historic 1992 "Year of the Woman."

Shepherd ran on a liberal platform, stressing children's issues. She even opened a children's play area at her campaign headquarters. After winning the race, Shepherd was assigned to the Natural Resources Committee and the Public Works and Transportation Committee, where she worked to convert the nation's defense industry to post-Cold War businesses.

Shepherd also co-chaired a freshman class task force on Congressional reform. The task force developed a package recommending such changes as prohibiting members from chairing more than one committee or subcommittee and banning gifts from lobbyists to lawmakers. Many of the recommendations, however, were never adopted by the House. On her own, Shepherd refused to accept a cost-of-living pay raise and instead returned the money to the U.S. Treasury. Shepherd also bucked her leadership by being the first House Democrat to call for an independent prosecutor to investigate Clinton's controversial Whitewater land deal.

Although Shepherd tried to establish herself as an independent thinker, she was hurt politically when she voted for Clinton's crime bill and his 1993 deficit-cutting tax package. During her campaign, she had pledged to support deficit reduction, but also to oppose any tax increases. "I was wrong when I said it, and I wish I hadn't," she said.[220] She later added, "Look, I'm old and I've had a good life. What's the worst thing that can happen to me? That I lose."[221]

That's exactly what happened. Her votes for Clinton's bills were used against her and she was defeated by Republican Enid Green Waldholtz—the same woman Shepherd beat two years earlier in her first election to the House. After leaving Congress, Shepherd in 1996 was appointed to be the U.S. executive director of the European Bank for Reconstruction and Development—an organization that makes loans to emerging democracies in Eastern Europe.

EDNA SIMPSON (R-Ill.)
(Oct. 26, 1891–May 15, 1984)
House: Jan. 3, 1959, to Jan. 3, 1961

Edna Simpson won election to the House just nine days after the death of her husband, eight-term Rep. Sidney Simpson (R). The local GOP persuaded Simpson to allow her name to be placed on the ballot for the seat to which her husband had already been nominated. Simpson did not make a single campaign speech, yet she easily defeated her Democratic opponent.

After the election, Simpson brought her daughter Janet to Washington with her to work as a legislative aide. Once in office, Simpson remained in the shadows. During her two years of service, she never once spoke on the House floor. She did, however, introduce an amendment to the Railroad Retirement Act allowing retirees who received veterans' benefits to also receive their full retirement pay. Simpson was assigned to the House Administration Committee and the Committee on Interior and Insular Affairs. She declined to run for re-election to a second term.

LOUISE SLAUGHTER (D-N.Y.)
(Aug. 14, 1929–   )
House: Jan. 3, 1987, to present

Louise Slaughter has been called "a combination of Southern charm and back-room politics, a Southern belle with a cigar in her mouth."[222] Born and raised in Kentucky, Slaughter still carries a heavy southern accent, despite decades of living in and representing upstate New York. She did not enter the world of politics until late in life, after getting married and raising a family. But her early life taught her many of the traits needed in the political arena. A graduate of the University of Kentucky, Slaughter holds a master's in public health—a subject she has focused on in Congress, particularly women's health issues. After college, Slaughter worked as a marketing research assistant for Procter & Gamble. The job required her to go across the country, knocking on doors and asking women for their opinions on different brands of cake mix and laundry detergent. The experience helped train her for the door-to-door campaigning she would need later in her political career.

Slaughter first became involved in politics in 1971 when she and her husband led a citizens' campaign against the commercial development of a forest area across the street from their home. The effort failed, but a year later Slaughter ran for the Monroe County (NY) legislature as the "ecology-minded housewife."[223] She lost, but tried again in 1975, and this time won. From 1979 to 1982, Slaughter ran the Rochester regional office of New York Lieutenant Governor Mario Cuomo and in 1983 she was elected to the New York state assembly. In 1986, when she won her House seat, she was the only woman to defeat a sitting member of Congress that year. Slaughter quickly endeared herself to the House leadership. Early in her second term, Speaker Tom Foley (D-Wash.) named Slaughter to the powerful Rules Committee. Slaughter happily gave up her other assignments on the Government Operations Committee and the Public Works and Transportation Committee to accept the post. Her position on the Rules Committee prompted the *Washington Post* to call her "one of the most powerful women in Congress." Slaughter's position as the only woman on Rules was magnified when she was assigned to the powerful Budget Committee in 1991. That year she also was named to chair the Committee on Organization, Study and Review, a panel responsible for developing the rules for the Democratic Caucus and full House.

Although Slaughter won high-profile assignments early in her congressional career, she faced several high-profile disappointments later on. In 1994, Slaughter ran for vice chair of the Caucus against her friend Rep. Barbara Kennelly (Conn.), losing the race by a 93 to 90 margin. In 1997, Slaughter sought the top Democratic slot on the Budget Committee. Slaughter campaigned in part on the fact that no other women held the ranking Democratic slot on any committee, but was defeated by the more conservative Rep. Jack Spratt (S.C.). She left the committee altogether following her defeat.

Throughout her congressional career, Slaughter has been an outspoken proponent of feminist issues. She sponsored a law to ban blockades of abortion clinics and in 1995 spoke out loudly for surgeon general nominee Henry Foster who was attacked for having performed abortions. In 1991, she was one of seven House women to march over to the Senate to protest the treatment of Anita Hill, and three years later she again marched with House women to the upper chamber to protest the Tailhook Navy sex scandal.

As the chair of the Task Force on Women's Health, Slaughter has advocated increased funding for research on women's health. She introduced legislation—later signed into law—to increase education about the dangers of the drug DES, a synthetic hormone given to 5 million pregnant women between 1941 and 1971 that has been found to cause severe health problems in their offspring. Slaughter has pushed to crack down on sexual predators and create federal studies on environmental health risks to women.

Slaughter has also fought to ensure that homeless children can attend public schools and sponsored a provision in the 1994 crime bill that requires sexual offenders released from prison to alert law enforcement officials about their new addresses. She supports gun control and has called for tougher restrictions on anyone buying explosives.

LINDA SMITH (R-Wash.)
(July 16, 1950–   )
House: Jan. 4, 1995, to Jan. 6, 1999

Linda Smith was elected to the House during the historic 1994 elections that brought Republicans into control after 40 years of Democratic rule. Although she was one of the more conservative members of her class, she was also one of the more rebellious who frequently bumped heads with her own GOP leadership.

Long before coming to Congress, Smith had established a reputation as someone who often challenged the political mainstream. She first ran for office in 1983 and won a seat in the Washington state House. She said she had entered the political arena because of anger over a state tax increase. Four years later, she ran for and won a seat in the state Senate where she pushed for campaign ethics and tax reform. After the Senate blocked her campaign finance reform bills, she decided to go directly to the voters in the form of a ballot initiative to limit campaign spending and donations from special interests, which passed in 1992.

Smith turned her sights on Congress in 1994 after the Republican front-runner for the 3rd congressional district dropped out of the race just a month before the primary. Smith launched a write-in campaign with an all-volunteer organization and large support from Christian activists. She easily won the nomination—the only candidate in Washington state ever to win the GOP nomination as a write-in candidate—and went on to defeat three-term incumbent Rep. Jolene Unsoeld (D) in the general election.

Smith continued her fight for reform after coming to Capitol Hill—much to the chagrin of the veteran Republican leadership. One of her first acts in Congress was to introduce the "Clean Government Resolution of 1995" that sought to ban gifts, trips, meals, and entertainment to lawmakers except from family and close friends. It also sought to restrict special interests from contributing to political campaigns and require candidates to raise all their money from within their states. The House would eventually pass its own gift ban legislation, but Smith's calls for campaign finance reform were never enacted by Congress. She also fought unsuccessfully to deny members of Congress a yearly cost-of-living salary increase.

On other legislative issues, Smith was a staunch opponent of abortion, offering legislation early in her first term to deny federal funds for abortions for poor women in cases of rape or incest. She voted conservatively on most social issues—she supported prayer in public schools and voted to repeal the ban on certain assault weapons—but she did support an increase in the minimum wage.

Smith opposed her leadership on a number of high-profile issues. In 1996, she was one of just a handful of Republicans who voted against a spending bill that reopened the government after a record-length shutdown. Her vote against the bill came despite pleas and threats from GOP House Speaker Newt Gingrich. In 1997, after Gingrich was reprimanded by the House Ethics Committee for breaking House rules, Smith again bucked her leadership when she was one of just nine Republicans to vote against Gingrich's re-election as Speaker.

Smith served on the Resources and Small Business Committees. During her first term, she chaired the Small Business subcommittee on tax and finance—the first GOP woman to chair a subcommittee in her first term. Smith, however, lost that chairmanship in her second term.

In 1997, Smith announced that she was leaving the House to challenge Democratic Sen. Patty Murray. She won the Republican nomination after a hard-fought primary, but lost to Murray in the general election. It was only the third time in history that two women ran against each other for the Senate. The previous times occured in 1960 when Sen. Margaret Chase Smith (R-Maine) defeated Democratic challenger Lucia Cormier and in 1986 when Sen. Barbara Mikulski (D-Md.) defeated Republican challenger Linda Chavez.

MARGARET CHASE SMITH (R-Maine)
(Dec. 14, 1897–May 29, 1995)
House: June 3, 1940, to Jan. 3, 1949
Senate: Jan. 3, 1949, to Jan. 3, 1973

Margaret Chase Smith's 32-year congressional career is filled with firsts: She was the first woman to be elected to both the House and Senate, the first woman to be elected to the Senate leadership, the first woman to enter the Senate without first being appointed, and the first woman to have her name placed in nomination for the presidency of the United States. She also holds the record as the longest serving female in Senate history. But despite these milestones, Smith is probably best known for her "Declaration of Conscience" speech, given on June 1, 1950, criticizing Wisconsin Sen. Joseph McCarthy for his tactics of accusing people—

without any proof—of being Communists. Smith was barely in the Senate for more than a year when she made the historic speech.

"I do not like the way the Senate has been made a rendezvous for vilification, for selfish political gain at the sacrifice of individual reputations and national unity. . . . I do not want to see the party ride to political victory on the Four Horsemen of Calumny—fear, ignorance, bigotry and smear."[224]

Her words made Smith an overnight celebrity. *Newsweek* ran a picture of her on its cover and floated her as possible vice presidential candidate. The speech cemented her role as an independent voice in the Senate, but it also won her a lifelong enemy in McCarthy. He bitterly called Smith and the six other Republicans who joined her cause "Snow White and the six dwarfs." McCarthy, who chaired the Senate panel that made subcommittee assignments, removed her from the Permanent Investigations subcommittee and replaced her with Sen. Richard Nixon.

McCarthy demonstrated his grudge against Smith years later when he entered a candidate against her in the 1954 primary race. Smith managed to trounce McCarthy's candidate—a staffer for his Investigations Committee—with 82 percent of the vote. That same year, McCarthy was censured by the Senate for his reckless charges of Communism.

Smith first came to Congress in 1940 to fill out the unexpired House term of her husband, Rep. Clyde Smith. Shortly before his death, he appealed to the voters to elect his "partner in public life" to succeed him. Smith had served as her husband's secretary, often putting in 15 hours a day handling his mail, writing his speeches, and researching his bills. She also served as treasurer of the Congressional Wives Club, and years earlier had been elected to the state Republican party. In the special election for her husband's seat, Smith won nearly three times the vote her husband had garnered in his last election. Smith quickly asked for a seat on the Labor Committee, where her husband had served. She was denied her request and instead was assigned to three lesser committees— Education, Invalid Pensions, and Post Offices and Post Roads. Later in her career she would win a seat on the Naval Affairs Committee—later called the Armed Services Committee.

During her House service, Smith generally voted with the Republicans against the Roosevelt administration. She, however, broke with her party on several contentious issues. A defense hawk, Smith supported Roosevelt's Lend-Lease Act that gave food and weapons to European nations fighting the Nazis in World War II. She also broke with the Republican party when she supported the Selective Service Act, and she voted to arm U.S. merchant vessels to enable them to sail into combat areas. Smith distinguished herself as a strong supporter of military preparedness, and was the first woman to sail on a U.S. destroyer in wartime. One of Smith's greatest legislative achievements was passage of her bill creating a permanant female branch of the Navy—Women Accepted for Volunteer Emergency Service (WAVES).

Although Smith worked to advance women's rights—she supported the Equal Rights Amendment—she insisted that she never considered herself a "woman in Congress." "I was a member. . . . I was elected as a person. I served as a member. It was never a question of serving as a woman."[225]

In 1948, Smith decided to run for an open seat in the Senate. She easily defeated three primary challengers—including the state's governor and a former governor—winning more votes than all three other candidates combined. While in the Senate she served on the Rules and Administration Committee, the Appropriations Committee, the Government Operations Committee, the Aeronautical and Space Sciences Committee, and the Armed Services Committee, where she eventually rose to become the panel's top Republican.

While in the Senate, Smith didn't miss a single roll-call vote between 1955 and 1968. Her record of 2,941 consecutive ballots ended only after she suffered a broken hip. Smith refused to campaign while the Senate was in session—believing that voting was one of the most important duties of a legislator—and even introduced a constitutional amendment to expel any senator who missed more than 60 percent of roll calls. Smith also scuttled tradition by never accepting campaign donations—saying she didn't want to be indebted to any special interest.

Among the highlights of Smith's Senate career were her efforts to enlarge the National Institutes of Health and expand assistance to medical schools and research facilities. Smith is also remembered for her attempt to have the rose declared the official flower of the United States. (Smith always wore a red rose on her lapel.) And in 1957, Smith led the fight against granting actor Jimmy Stewart the rank of brigadier general in the Air Force.

In 1961, Smith made a highly publicized speech attacking President Kennedy for not standing up to Soviet Premier Nikita Khrushchev. The speech prompted Khrushchev to call Smith "the devil in a disguise of a woman."[226] Three years later, Smith declared her candidacy for the White House. She received 27 delegate votes, more than anyone else except for the GOP nominee Sen. Barry Goldwater (Ariz.). She may have lost that race, but two years later she won the chairmanship of the powerful Senate Republican Conference—becoming the first woman to win a leadership post in the Senate.

In 1970—on the 20th anniversary of her "Declaration of Conscience" speech—Smith rose once again on the Senate floor, this time to criticize the militant student protests against the Vietnam War and President Nixon's repressive tactics to squelch their dissent.

Two years later, Smith was defeated in her bid for a fifth term in the Senate. Upon leaving office she declared, "I hate to leave the Senate when there is no indication another qualified woman is coming in. We've built a place here for quality service. If I leave and there's a long lapse, the next woman will have to rebuild entirely."[227] Smith returned to Maine where she established the Margaret Chase Smith Library, containing the extensive documentation of her congressional career. In 1989, she received the Presidential Medal of Freedom—the highest civilian award—from President Bush. When she died in 1995, nearly 900 people attended the funeral.

BOOK BY SMITH

Declaration of Conscience (1972)

VIRGINIA SMITH (R-Neb.)
(June 30, 1911–   )
House: Jan. 3, 1975, to Jan. 3, 1991

Virginia Smith came to Congress after four decades of involvement in farm organizations, and her House career was largely a continuation of her work back in Nebraska. The wife of a wheat farmer, Smith served for 20 years as the chair of the American Farm Bureau Federation's women's board. She worked with the U.S. Department of Agriculture's Home Economics Research Advisory Committee, the American Country Life Association, and she chaired the President's Task Force on Rural Development. She also was a county GOP chairwoman and a delegate to the Republican national conventions from 1956 to 1972.

So name recognition was not a problem for Smith when she decided to run for elected office in 1974 at the age of 63. But the race for the open House seat attracted seven other GOP candidates and Smith barely won the primary with a margin of 141 votes. The general election also proved tough in a year that favored Democrats. But Smith—a conservative who never considered herself a feminist and even ran under the name of "Mrs. Haven Smith"—got an unexpected boost when her Democratic challenger charged that women do not belong in politics. The remark energized female voters and gave Smith the edge she needed to win— by only 737 votes.

As a freshman in Congress, Smith served on the Committee on Education and Labor and the Committee on Interior and Insular Affairs. In her second term, she left those posts to take a seat on the powerful Appropriations Committee. For the next 15 years, Smith used that seat to secure funding for dozens of agriculture research and water projects for her Nebraska district. As the top Republican on the Appropriations subcommittee on agriculture, she also fought diligently to protect the interests of the many grain farmers and ranchers across her district. She spoke for meat whenever possible, defending the interests of the ranchers who produced it and urging consumers to eat it. She once denounced a federal agriculture appointee as an "avowed vegetarian."[228]

A strong conservative, Smith also pushed for legislation to ban abortion, legalize prayer in public schools, and establish English as the official language of the United States. In 1990, after 16 years in office, Smith decided to retire from Congress and declined to run for a ninth term.

OLYMPIA SNOWE (R-Maine)
(Feb. 21, 1947–)
House: Jan. 3, 1979, to Jan. 3, 1995
Senate: Jan. 3, 1995, to present

Olympia Snowe's life and rise to political power has a storybook quality. She was orphaned at the age of nine and raised in a blue-collar neighborhood by her aunt, a textile millworker, and her uncle, a barber. She was raised a Democrat, but after working as an intern for Democratic Gov. Kenneth Curtis, she met and fell in love with Peter Snowe, a Republican activist. After they married, she took on her husband's political allegiance and he went on to be elected to the Maine state legislature.

In 1973, just four months after Snowe began working in the district office of GOP Rep. William Cohen, Snowe's husband was killed in a car crash. Snowe decided to run for her husband's vacant seat and won. She would go on to win a second term to the legislature in her own right and was elected to the state Senate in 1976. Two years later, Snowe won a close House race to succeed Cohen, who had moved on to the Senate. Snowe would go on to serve for 16 years in the House before winning election to the Senate in the Republican takeover of Congress in 1994. She became only the fourth woman ever to serve in both the House and Senate.

Snowe has been one of Congress's most moderate Republicans. In the House she was the longtime co-chair with Rep. Pat Schroeder (D-Colo.) of the Congressional Caucus for Women's Issues. She pushed for abortion rights, federal research on women's health, and family and medical leave. "I think it's important for women in Congress to ensure equity for women," she said. "If we don't, who will?"[229]

While in the House she served on the Government Operations Committee, the Small Business Committee, the Select Committee on Aging, the Joint Economic Committee, and the Committee on Foreign Affairs, where she was ranking Republican on the international operations subcommittee. As the subcommittee's top Republican, Snowe traveled to Moscow in 1987 as part of a team to inspect the U.S. embassy there. She took the lead in calling for the demolition of the building that had been seeded with secret listening devices.

After moving to the Senate, Snowe continued to push for abortion rights. In 1996, she called on GOP presidential candidate Bob Dole to drop from the party platform support for an anti-abortion constitutional amendment. She also joined with Republican Governors Pete Wilson of California and William Weld of Massachusetts in trying to pressure the Republican platform committee to acknowledge pro-choice members of the party. She argued that the anti-abortion constitutional amendment "does not reflect the majority view of Republicans and certainly doesn't represent the views of a majority of Americans." She opposed the ban on so-called partial birth abortions and tried to block a ban on abortions being performed at overseas military hospitals. She called the ban "another frontal assault on the principle of reproductive freedom and the dignity of women's lives."[230]

Following the GOP takeover of Congress in 1995, Snowe joined with other moderate Republicans to block conservatives' efforts to cut welfare benefits to the poor. She opposed plans to deny welfare checks to unwed teenage mothers and pushed to add child-care funding for welfare recipients. She has regularly called for increased spending on social programs and was one of the leaders of an effort to restore funding for the student loan program. In 1998, Snowe was a key player in the failed effort to reform the campaign finance system. She worked with members from both parties to hammer out a compromise bill that would curb the high cost of running for office.

Although she is a moderate, she backs a strong military and has voted to increase defense spending. As a member of the Senate Armed Services Committee, Snowe works to protect Maine's military interests, including those of Bath Iron Works, a shipbuilding company that is the state's largest employer. Snowe also chairs the Commerce, Science, and Transportation subcommittee on oceans and fisheries, where she looks out for Maine's fishing industry. She also serves on the Budget and the Small Business Committees.

GLADYS SPELLMAN (D-Md.)
(March 1, 1918–June 19, 1988)
House: Jan. 3, 1975, to Feb. 24, 1981

Gladys Spellman's huge popularity with her constituents was proven in 1980 when she was overwhelmingly elected to a fourth term in the House with 80 percent of the vote, even though she had lapsed into a coma five days before the election. She had suffered a heart attack while judging a children's Halloween contest in her district and never regained consciousness. The election gave her back her seat, but after receiving a medical analysis stating that she was in a "trance-like state" and unable to take the oath of office, the House declared her seat vacant in February 1981. It was the first time the House ever vacated the seat of a member who had become mentally or physically disabled.

Spellman's popularity with the voters stemmed largely from her tireless support for federal employees. Almost 40 percent of the workers in her district were employed by the federal government—the highest percentage of any district in the nation—and Spellman was careful to respond to their needs. In Congress she played a key role in defeating efforts to merge the federal retirement system with Social Security. As chair of the Post Office and Civil Service subcommittee on compensation and employee benefits, she was influential in opposing measures that would have held down pay increases or required freezes on hiring. Periodically she would write a "Beautiful Bureaucrat" column in her newsletter commending a federal worker and insisting that most bureaucrats were people who "far from slowing down the wheels of government are really the people who keep them churning."[231]

As a member of the Banking Committee, Spellman backed legislation to establish a bank to make loans to cooperatives owned by consumers and legislation to extend the federal revenue-sharing program. She also voted for a 1975 proposal authorizing $7 billion in loan guarantees for financially troubled New York City.

Spellman first became involved in politics on the state level as a school teacher and a PTA activist who fought for higher teachers' wages. She was elected to the Prince George's County Board of Commissioners in 1962 and again in 1966 and served for two years as its chair. In 1967, she was appointed by President Johnson to the Advisory Commission on Intergovernmental Relations, and from 1971 to 1974 served as a county council-woman at large. During her service in county politics, Spellman was active on women's rights. She once recalled the hostility she faced as the first woman on the county's board of commissioners. "[The men would tell me] I thought just like a man. At first I was flattered, then I got angry and said, 'Well, I guess today was an off-day for me. Tomorrow I'll be myself and do better.'"[232] Spellman fought for equal home-purchasing opportunities for women, and introduced legislation calling for a study on the status of county women. She later drafted a bill creating the county's Commission for Women. Dismayed at the procedures of local police and hospitals in dealing with victims of sexual assault, she proposed a task force to study the treatment of rape victims. That task force later served as the model for a national center created by Congress for the study and prevention of rape. After coming to the Congress, Spellman continued to push for legislation granting women equal rights.

Following the House's move to vacate Spellman's seat in 1981, a crowded field of 32 candidates ran for the spot—including her husband Reuben. He, however, finished second in the Democratic primary to Steny Hoyer, who went on to win the general election. Spellman survived for eight more years in a coma before dying in a nursing home in 1988.

DEBBIE STABENOW (D-Mich.)
(April 29, 1950–   )
House: Jan. 7, 1997, to present

Debbie Stabenow made Democrats' dreams come true in 1996 when she defeated first-term Republican Rep. Dick Chrysler who had wrestled the House seat away from the party two years earlier. Stabenow was a well-known and popular local lawmaker who during her time in the state Senate helped push through the largest property tax cut in Michigan's history.

A social moderate and fiscal conservative, Stabenow began her career in elective politics in 1975 by serving a three-year stint on the Ingham County Commission. In 1978, she was elected to the state House where she made a name for herself by working on such issues as domestic violence, child abuse prevention, and mental health care. In 1990, she was elected to the state Senate and served for one term.

In 1994, Stabenow ran for the Democratic gubernatorial nomination. After losing the primary, she ran as the lieutenant governor candidate with the primary winner, but the ticket lost. Stabenow later co-founded the Michigan Leadership Institute that provided leadership training to private companies and local government.

Stabenow is a strong supporter of President Clinton's proposals to put computers in every classroom across the country. She also wants to expand students' access to college and financial aid. Stabenow serves on the Agriculture Committee and the Science Committee.

In the House, Stabenow has continued to fight against domestic violence. She introduced bills to reauthorize funding for a national toll-free hotline for domestic violence and continue funding for local law enforcement departments that create violence prevention programs. She also co-sponsored legislation adding $340 million over five years to help pay for more domestic violence treatment and prevention programs.

During the 1998 impeachment probe into whether Clinton lied under oath about having an affair with a White House intern, Stabenow was the only member of Congress to set up a special toll-free line to take constituent calls about their feelings on the investigation.

WINNIFRED STANLEY (R-N.Y.)
(Aug. 14, 1909–Feb. 29, 1996)
House: Jan. 3, 1943, to Jan. 3, 1945

Winnifred Stanley came to Congress knowing she would serve only one term. Redistricting was going to merge New York's two at-large seats into one, so Republicans wanted to recruit a candidate who would step down after two years. Stanley was willing to interrupt her distinguished legal career to answer the call of her party. In 1942, she set out across the state with gubernatorial candidate Thomas Dewey and campaigned on a win-the-war platform. She insisted on traveling by foot, bus, or train, refusing to take advantage of the special gas-rationing privileges allowed political candidates. In the general election she led a field of eight candidates for the two at-large seats and, at the age of 33, became the youngest woman ever elected to Congress.

New to national politics, Stanley had won the first political office she ever sought. Young and vivacious, she was heralded by *Newsweek* magazine as "pretty enough to 'twitterpate' some of her colleagues."[233] She was also voted by the Fashion Academy as one of the 10 best dressed women in the nation.

Stanley requested a seat on the Judiciary Committee, hoping to make full use of her legal prowess, but was instead assigned to the lesser Committee on Civil Service and the Committee on Patents. She was, however, honored in Congress by being chosen as one of the Republican tellers to count the votes on the election of House Speaker, and she was named as the only woman to the 41-member Republican Congressional Food Study Committee.

Stanley generally opposed President Roosevelt's New Deal programs for farm supports and soil conservation, but voted with the Democratic administration to eliminate the poll tax. She voted for the continuation of the Dies' Committee to Investigate Un-American Activities and for revocation of the President's order limiting salaries to $25,000 after taxes. Stanley was also a strong advocate of gender and racial equality. She spoke out for Army commissions for women physicians and crusaded for gainful employment for all people, regardless of race, religion, or sex. In 1943, she unsuccessfully pushed for an amendment to the National Labor Relations Act that would have made it illegal to pay women less than men for equal work.

"In the post war world, we will be in desperate need of the best brains available, regardless of whether those brains and talents happen to belong to men or women. Until there is equal opportunity for all, we shall be paying only lip service to those glorious and fundamental rules of our American heritage," she said.[234]

Stanley's concern for equality was rooted in her early days as a lawyer when she specialized in cases involving women and children. Stanley earned her law degree from the University of Buffalo—one of just four women in her class. She was honored as having the highest grade-point average in her law class, and she had earlier earned her undergraduate degree magna cum laude. During her four years in private practice, Stanley launched a campaign to allow women to serve on juries. In 1938, when Stanley was just 28, she was appointed assistant district attorney for Erie County—the first woman named to that position. Later that year, New York state granted women the right to serve on juries.

Along with her drive for sexual equality, Stanley also used her congressional seat to emphasize the need to prepare for peace and ensure jobs once the war was over. She endorsed a resolution that said "the only way to keep the United States out of future wars is not to have future wars. Our nation alone cannot police the world. Our nation alone cannot prevent wars. The world can progress toward permanent stability and peace only through the collaboration of its component peoples."[235]

After leaving Congress, Stanley was appointed by Gov. Dewey as chief counsel of the New York State Employees' Retirement System, a post she held for 10 years. From 1955 to 1979, Stanley served as assistant attorney general with the New York State Law Department. She later returned to private practice and established herself as an expert authority in administrative and constitutional law. She retired in 1986.

LEONOR SULLIVAN (D-Mo.)
(Aug. 21, 1902–Sept. 1, 1988)
House: Jan. 3, 1953, to Jan. 3, 1977

Years before men like Ralph Nader made a name for themselves, Leonor Sullivan was known as the nation's consumer watchdog. As chair of the Banking and Currency subcommittee on consumer affairs, Sullivan crusaded against harmful food additives, deceptive advertising, contaminated meat, and hidden finance charges. She kicked off her drive for consumer rights in her very first term in office when she joined 23 other members of the House to urge the creation of a permanent committee on consumer protection and authored an amendment to the Federal Food, Drug and Cosmetic Act to give FDA inspectors blanket authority to inspect factories where food, drugs, or cosmetics were made. In 1957, she shepherded through Congress the Poultry Inspection Act, establishing the first compulsory federal inspection of poultry sold in interstate commerce. A year later, she helped write and pass the Food Additives Act, which required pretesting of all chemical additives used in or on foodstuffs. And nearly every year after that she pushed for bills addressing the use of artificial colors, labeling of hazardous substances, and prescription drugs.

In 1961, she introduced a 41-page omnibus bill covering all food, drugs, and cosmetics. When warned that powerful commercial interests would be united against her, she said there were thousands of women who needed protection from products containing carcinogens. Her comprehensive bill was never passed, though she reintroduced it in every Congress. Nonetheless, a series of consumer protections laws eventually passed by Congress accomplished in a piecemeal fashion much of what she had advocated.

In 1959, Sullivan wrote the Food Stamp Act that replaced the "dumping" of surplus foods on the needy with a program of coupons that would allow the poor to shop at regular grocery stores. Congress passed the bill, but the secretary of agriculture refused to implement the program. Sullivan wrote President Kennedy asking his help in kicking off the plan. In 1961, Kennedy inaugurated a pilot program that was much smaller than what Sullivan had envisioned. In 1964, Sullivan introduced a new food stamp bill to expand the pilot project. President Johnson signed the bill establishing a permanent and nationwide program.

In 1968, Sullivan was the House floor manager for the Consumer Protection Act, which established "truth in lending" provisions requiring lenders to provide consumers with information about the cost of credit. She also authored and pushed through Congress the Fair Credit Reporting Act, which prevented credit companies from selling or distributing false or malicious information.

Sullivan was also active on women's issues. She co-sponsored the Equal Pay Act of 1963 and introduced bills to provide full Social Security benefits for women retiring at age 62. She backed efforts by her colleague Martha Griffiths (D-Mich.) to include a ban on sexual discrimination in the 1964 Civil Rights Act. She also held hearings on equal credit opportunities for women and worked to pass legislation providing such protections.

But despite her work on behalf of women's rights, Sullivan was the only woman in Congress to vote against the Equal Rights Amendment. Sullivan said she feared the ERA would kill the many labor and social laws that had been enacted in the name of protecting women. "For example, it will make it impossible for our courts to punish a deserting father for failure to provide support for his children," Sullivan argued.[236] She also feared the ERA would include women in the military draft. "ERA says you are my equal," Sullivan quipped. "I think I'm a whole lot better."[237]

In 1973, Sullivan was elected chair of the Merchant Marine and Fisheries Committee. In that position she passed the 1976 Fishery and Conservation Management Act, which established a 200-mile fisheries conservation zone off the U.S. coasts. She also was the first woman to serve on the House Democratic Steering Committee and was elected for five terms as the secretary of the House Democratic Caucus.

Sullivan grew up in a large and rather poor family of nine children. Her parents did not have the money to send her to college, so she got a job at the local telephone company and put herself through night school at Washington University in St. Louis. She later taught business accounting and became the director of the St. Louis Business School.

In 1941, she married Rep. John Sullivan and served as his campaign manager and congressional aide. When he died in 1951, Sullivan wanted to run for his seat, but the local Democratic party refused to nominate her. The man they did nominate ended up losing to the Republican candidate. Sullivan went to work as the administrative assistant to neighboring Rep. Theodore Irving and saved enough money to run for her husband's old seat the following year. She also enrolled in speech courses at the downtown Washington YWCA to overcome a fear of public speaking.

During the 1952 primary, she faced seven male challengers. The party-endorsed candidate promised voters "to give her a top position" in his office once he was elected. But Sullivan defeated them all and went on to beat the Republican incumbent by a nearly two-to-one margin.

Sullivan voluntarily retired from Congress in 1977 at the age of 75. She was succeeded by Rep. Richard Gephardt, who would later become the House Democratic leader.

JESSIE SUMNER (R-Ill.)
(July 17, 1898–Aug. 10, 1994)
House: Jan. 3, 1939, to Jan. 3, 1947

Jessie Sumner spent most of her congressional career fighting President Franklin Roosevelt's foreign policies and America's entry into World War II. She is said to have been a rough-and-tumble debater who was skilled in parliamentary maneuvering on the House floor. But her unyielding isolationism—even after the bombing of Pearl Harbor—often left her alone or among a very small minority in the House. She opposed amending the Neutrality Act to permit the arming of American merchant ships that were being attacked by the Nazis, she voted against the Burke-Waddsworth Selective Service Bill, which established the nation's first peacetime draft, and she was one of just 29 members who fought the 1943 Fulbright resolution that pledged the United States' participation in postwar international efforts to create and maintain peace. She called the resolution "the most dangerous bill ever presented to an American Congress" and a "Machiavellian" scheme to make permanent the policy of "handouts across the sea." She also introduced a resolution to appoint a special House committee to "investigate the cause and prevention of wars likely to involve the United States" and recommend peace offers.[238] In 1944, she unsuccessfully offered an amendment to postpone the D-Day invasion of Europe. "The invasions," she said, "will be costly and stupid."[239]

One of her few legislative victories came in 1942 during debate on a $20-billion naval appropriations bill. She secured an amendment that banned the use of funds for "extravagant christening services at battleship launchings." With escalating military costs, she urged the Navy to end its tradition of smashing a champagne bottle against the ships and presenting the typically female christener with an orchid and expensive piece of jewelry. "If Helen of Troy could launch a thousand ships without a diamond bracelet, our women can do the same," she told her House colleagues.[240]

Sumner's isolationist views continued after the war. In 1945, she was one of just 18 Republicans to oppose legislation authorizing the United States' entrance into the World Bank and International Monetary Fund, calling it the worst fraud in American history. She also spoke against funding the United Nations Relief and Rehabilitation Administration, warning that Soviet Leader Joseph Stalin could use the organization's relief efforts to become "a successor to Hitler." She was one of just 15 members opposed to the country's entrance into the United Nations, saying, "We have just joined the dance of death on the European and Asiatic battlefields."[241]

In an unusual move in 1943, Sumner joined with liberals and the House's other six female lawmakers to demand of the Appropriations Committee that women working in war factories be provided child care. A year later, however, she reversed her position and was the only woman to vote for a drastic cut in child-care funds.

Sumner won her first election to Congress running on an anti-New Deal platform. She was given a slot on the Committee on Banking and Currency, largely because of her earlier career as a lawyer and her service with the Chase National Bank of New York in 1928 and 1929. Sumner studied law at the University of Chicago, Columbia University, and at Oxford University where she was one of the first American women to take legal training at the British school. After being admitted to the bar in 1923, Sumner opened a law practice in Chicago. She was a member of the National Women Lawyers' Association, the Business and Professional Women's Club, the National Women's Republican Club, and the National Federation of Women's Clubs.

A family tragedy in 1932 first prompted Sumner to enter politics. Her brother was kidnapped by bank robbers, and after she helped secure the criminals' convictions she was inspired to run for State's attorney. She lost that first bid for office, but when her uncle—a county judge—died in 1937, she was elected to fill out his term. She was the first woman to sit on the judicial bench in Illinois.

After retiring from Congress in 1947, Sumner returned to Illinois where she served as president of the Sumner National Bank. She never married and once declared that "lots of women could succeed in politics if they didn't prefer the so-called A-1 career: marriage."[242]

ELLEN TAUSCHER (D-Calif.)
(Nov. 15, 1951–   )
House: Jan. 7, 1997, to present

When she was just 25, Ellen Tauscher became the first woman to have a seat on the New York Stock Exchange. Her time on Wall Street as an investment banker for Prudential-Bache Security and other top firms helped form Tauscher's sometimes conservative views on fiscal matters. It also helped her earn the finances she would use years later in her run for Congress. In 1996, Tauscher defeated two-term GOP Rep. Bill Baker after pouring more than $1.5 million of her own money into the campaign. Tauscher's finances were also helped by her husband, the CEO of Vanstar Corp, a $2-billion-a-year computer company.

Tauscher came from humble beginnings. She was the first person in her family ever to attend college. But Tauscher did grow up in a political family. Her father served as a local officeholder in New Jersey.

After 14 years on Wall Street, Tauscher in 1989 moved to California where she founded the Child Care Registry to help parents find safe child care. The registry was the country's first national screening service to conduct pre-employment background checks on child-care providers. She also published a child-care reference guide.

Tauscher became involved in politics working as a fund-raiser for Bay Area Democrats. In 1992 and 1994, Tauscher served as the co-chair of Sen. Dianne Feinstein's (D-Calif.) successful Senate campaigns. During her own campaign for office in 1996, Tauscher ran as a traditional pro-environment, pro-abortion rights Democrat, but she also promoted more moderate views on money matters, including support for a balanced budget constitutional amendment and opposition to new taxes. Despite the large amounts of money she spent on the race, she won by just 4,000 votes.

Once in office, Tauscher was assigned to the Transportation and Infrastructure Committee and the Science Committee. She is also an active member of the "Blue Dog" coalition—a group of fiscally conservative House Democrats. She supports targeted cuts in capital gains taxes and deficit reduction, although not at the expense of student loans, environmental protection, or programs that provide benefits to senior citizens.

Tauscher's background in child care has led her to push for child and educational programs in Congress. She helped author a successful amendment to the Higher Education Reauthorization Act in 1998 that creates a program to gradually forgive federal college loans for students who earn childhood education degrees and work in licensed child-care centers. She also co-authored a comprehensive child-care package in 1998 that calls for new tax credits to help working parents pay for child care and provides after-school programs for up to 1 million children a year.

BOOK BY TAUSCHER

The Childcare Sourcebook (1996)

LERA THOMAS (D-Texas)
(Aug. 3, 1900–July 23, 1993)
House: March 26, 1966, to Jan. 3, 1967

Lera Thomas came to Congress following the death of her husband, Rep. Albert Thomas, who had served for 29 years in the House and held the chairmanship of the Appropriations subcommittee on defense. The 64-year-old widow faced a GOP challenger in the special election for the open seat, but she still won the race with nearly 75 percent of the vote. Thomas was assigned to the Merchant Marine and Fisheries Committee, where she pushed for funding of the Houston Ship Channel—a project of her husband's. She also called on Congress to appropriate funds for a NASA lunar sample laboratory in Houston.

At the end of her brief nine-month term, Thomas traveled to South Korea and South Vietnam and personally delivered letters from Texas families to their relatives and friends on duty there.

Thomas decided not to run for re-election, and after leaving office she served briefly as a consultant on manpower information in the Vietnam Bureau of the Agency for International Development. Thomas then returned to Texas, where she ran the family farm and an antique shop.

RUTH THOMPSON (R-Mich.)
(Sept. 15, 1887–April 5, 1970)
House: Jan. 3, 1951, to Jan. 3, 1957

Ruth Thompson was not only the first woman sent to Congress from Michigan, but after she was sworn into the House, she also became the first woman to serve on the Judiciary Committee. Thompson's long and distinguished background in law helped her overcome the initial grumblings of her male colleagues. Thomspon first began her work in the legal profession as a registrar in the Probate Court of Muskegon County. At the age of 31, Thompson entered night school to study law while working days as a secretary in an attorney's office. Six years later she passed the bar and became Muskegon County's first woman lawyer.

Thompson's first elective position was as County Probate Judge, a post she held for 12 years until 1937. Two years later, Thompson won a seat in the Michigan state House and became the first woman to serve in that legislature. After one term, Thompson left Michigan and headed to Washington where she worked with the Civil Service Commission, the Social Security Board, and the Labor Department. During World War II, she spent three years with the War Department in Washington and was later transfered to Frankfurt, Germany, and Copenhagen, Denmark, before returning to Michigan to open her own law practice.

In 1950, when eight-term Rep. Albert Engel (R) decided to leave Congress to run for the governor's office, Thompson entered the race to fill the seat. She won the nomination after defeating a former lieutenant governor and a county Republican chairman. She went on to narrowly win the general election against the Democratic chairman of the state Labor Mediation Board.

In addition to her Judiciary seat, Thompson was also assigned to the Joint Committee on Immigration and Nationality Policy. Thompson quickly established herself as a strong opponent to the Truman Administration. In her first year in office she joined 13 conservative Republicans in signing a petition calling for "vigorous action" on domestic and foreign legislative programs, including reducing government nondefense spending. She later joined GOP colleagues in pushing for the ouster of Secretary of State Dean Acheson, who had come under attack for military setbacks in Korea. She also frequently voted against foreign military and economic aid.

On domestic issues, Thompson voted to limit further housing construction under the Public Housing Administration, supported a curtailment of price controls, and backed a cut in federal workers. In a protest against inflation, Thompson joined five other GOP women on the House floor, each carrying increasingly lighter baskets of groceries to show the falling purchasing power of the dollar over the years.

Thompson sponsored proposals to encourage development of public library service in rural areas and stimulate the growth of low-cost electric energy from a variety of power sources. She introduced bills to create a Department of Peace and to make it easier for World War I veterans with honorable discharges to claim benefits.

Thompson won re-election in 1952 and 1954 with pluralities of more than 20,000 votes, but her congressional career began to unravel in her third term when the Air Force announced its plans to build a new jet interceptor base outside of her district. Thompson claimed military officials had promised the base to her constituents and she fought to have its location changed. She succeeded in having the base moved to her district, but the resulting yearlong delay and additional $5 million in construction costs proved a political embarrassment and led to her primary defeat in 1956.

KAREN THURMAN (D-Fla.)
(Jan. 12, 1951–)
House: Jan. 5, 1993, to present

Karen Thurman had worked in public service for almost 20 years before she won election to a newly created House seat during the 1992 "Year of the Woman." Thurman, in fact, played a large role in creating that new district. Immediately before coming to Congress, Thurman served in the Florida state Senate where she chaired the Committee on Congressional Reapportionment. As chair of the committee, Thurman helped to carve out the new congressional district that included much of her state Senate district and preserved her strongest bases of support. She has easily won re-election ever since.

A 1973 graduate of the University of Florida, Thurman began her professional career as a mathematics teacher at a Florida middle school. In 1974, at the urging of her students, Thurman ran for a seat on the Dunnellon City Council, winning her first election by a margin of just five votes. During her eight years as a councilwoman, Thurman also served for two terms as the mayor of Dunnellon. In 1982, Thurman won election to the state Senate and six years later became the first woman in Florida history to chair the Senate Agriculture Committee.

After arriving on Capitol Hill, Thurman was assigned to the House Agriculture Committee and the Committee on Government Reform and Oversight. In 1997, she gave up those committees for a prestigious seat on the tax-writing Ways and Means Committee.

Legislatively, Thurman often straddles the line between her liberal Democratic colleagues and her more conservative southern constituents. She is a faithful backer of President Clinton's economic policies—voting in 1993 for his controversial deficit reduction plan that included tax increases. She also supports abortion rights, although she has voted for banning federal funding for abortions. But Thurman opposed two gun control bills pushed by the Clinton administration and has accepted campaign contributions from the National Rifle Association. In 1996, she supported a repeal of a ban on certain assault weapons.

Thurman's district includes a large number of senior citizens and Thurman has attacked Republicans for their attempts to scale back growth in the Medicare system. Thurman has also kept a close eye on efforts to overhaul the Social Security system. In 1998, Thurman, along with other women lawmakers, sent a letter to Clinton asking the administration to consider the special concerns of elderly women when looking at ways to reform Social Security.

Thurman has also looked out for the needs of the large agriculture industry in her district, fighting efforts to eliminate federal price supports for peanut growers. And she voted against the North American Free Trade Agreement in 1993, arguing it posed an economic threat to local farmers.

In 1996, Thurman was drawn into an ethics scandal involving Speaker Newt Gingrich (R-Ga.). Two of her constituents had secretly tapped into a cellular phone conversation between Gingrich and other GOP House leaders who were discussing an ethics investigation into wrongdoing by the Speaker. The constituents turned a tape of the conversation over to Thurman, who advised them to hand it over to the top Democrat on the House ethics committee, Rep. Jim McDermott (Wash.). McDermott then leaked the tape to several newspapers. The two constituents were charged with illegally intercepting a phone call, and Republicans filed a lawsuit against McDermott, but no action was ever taken against Thurman.

JOLENE UNSOELD (D-Wash.)
(Dec. 3, 1931–   )
House: Jan. 3, 1989, to Jan. 4, 1995

Jolene Unsoeld overcame great personal tragedy before entering the political arena. Unsoeld's husband, a legendary mountain climber and one of the first Americans to climb Mount Everest, was killed in an avalanche in 1979 during a hike up Mount Rainier in Washington state. Three years earlier, their daughter was killed during a hike in the Himalayas with her father. Unsoeld herself is an accomplished mountain climber and was the first woman to scale the North Face of Mount Teton in Wyoming.

Actor Robert Redford bought the rights to her life story for a possible film project.

Unsoeld entered the political arena by a less than traditional route. She and her husband spent five years with the Peace Corps and the Agency for International Development in Nepal during the 1960s. When they came home, Unsoeld embarked on a succession of environmental and consumer causes, including such projects as a 1974 report on the financing of state legislative races entitled, "Who Gave, Who Got, How Much."

In 1984, she was elected to the Washington state legislature and made a name for herself as an outspoken supporter of environmental protections. She led a successful ballot initiative to establish more stringent requirements for the clean up of toxic waste sites.

In 1988, Unsoeld ran for the U.S. House, winning an open seat by just 618 votes—the closest race in the country that year. Her narrow margin of victory and her strong liberal voting record made her an immediate target of the Republican party. She faced much criticism from the large logging industry in her district for her efforts to protect ancient forests and save the endangered spotted owl. She defended herself by citing her family's long involvement with the industry. "My father and grandfather were timbermen. My father started out as a kid working a donkey engine on Larch Mountain. My brother is the third generation in this proud industry and today owns a wood treatment plant. My family has long been supported by timber dollars," she said.[243]

Unsoeld was a solid liberal on most issues. She supported abortion rights, cuts in military spending, and in 1991 was one of seven female House members who marched to the Senate to urge a full hearing of Anita Hill's sexual harassment charges against Supreme Court nominee Clarence Thomas. She served on the Education and Labor Committee and the Merchant Marine and Fisheries Committee.

But Unsoeld stunned many of her liberal supporters when she set aside her past support for gun control to champion the National Rifle Association's views on semiautomatic assault weapons. She authored an amendment to the 1990 crime bill that essentially gutted a prohibition on semiautomatic weapons by banning only firearms assembled with foreign parts. She also voted against requiring a seven-day waiting period for handgun purchases.

Despite her gun stance, Unsoeld was branded as too liberal for her district and in 1994 was defeated for a fourth term by Republican Linda Smith.

After leaving Capitol Hill, Unsoeld was appointed by Washington Gov. Mike Lowry to serve on the state Fish and Wildlife Commission. But in 1998, the Republican-controlled state Senate voted to kick Unsoeld off the commission largely because of her stands against sport fishing.

NYDIA VELAZQUEZ (D-N.Y.)
(March 22, 1953–   )
House: Jan. 5, 1993, to present

Nydia Velazquez, the first Puerto Rican woman elected to Congress, has spent much of her political career working on behalf of immigrants. She has consistently opposed Republican efforts to deny public benefits to immigrants and has worked to expand job opportunities for her predominantly Hispanic constituents. In 1998, she made history when she was named ranking Democrat of the House Small Business Committee—the first Hispanic woman ever to serve as chair or ranking member of a full House or Senate committee.

Velazquez was born in the sugar cane region of Puerto Rico, one of nine children. She was the first person in her family to receive a college degree, graduating magna cum laude from the University of Puerto Rico. She moved to the U.S. mainland at the age of 19 to attend New York University, where she earned a master's degree in political science. She joined the faculty of Hunter College at the City University of New York in 1981 as an adjunct professor of Puerto Rican studies. In 1983, she served as a special assistant to U.S. Rep. Ed Towns (D-N.Y.) and the following year became the first Latina to serve on the New York City Council. She, however, was defeated for re-election to a second term. In 1986, she served as the Director of the Department of Puerto Rican Community Affairs.

Shortly before running for Congress in 1992, Velazquez launched a Hispanic voter registration drive financed by the Puerto Rican government. The drive registered 200,000 voters nationwide, but critics charged that she had targeted the Brooklyn sections that later became part of her congressional district. During Velazquez's congressional campaign, opponents also anonymously sent news outlets hospital records showing that she had attempted suicide in 1991 and that she had been battling depression with alcohol and pills. Velazquez said counseling had helped her overcome her depression and she later sued the hospital for violating her privacy by releasing the records. But Velazquez overcame the controversy and won the five-way primary for the newly drawn seat. One of her defeated primary opponents was nine-term Rep. Stephen Solarz (D-N.Y.), who ran for the seat after his district was dismantled in redistricting. Velazquez went on to easily win the general primary and become one of the 24 women elected to Congress during the historic "Year of the Woman."

In Congress, Velazquez has established herself as a solid liberal. She is a strong proponent of increasing the minimum wage and voted against efforts to overhaul the welfare system, to repeal the ban on certain assault weapons, and ban same-sex marriages. She has fought GOP measures allowing states to deny public education to illegal aliens and prohibiting illegal aliens from collecting certain benefits on behalf of their U.S.-born children. She also attacked legislation that would make English the official language of the U.S. government and require all official business to be in English. "It fuels the fire of anti-immigrant hatred, encouraging racism and discrimination," she said.[244]

Velazquez has generally supported the legislative agenda of President Clinton, although she did oppose him on the North American Free Trade Agreement and in 1994 was one of several Democratic lawmakers arrested outside the White House during a rally against Clinton's policy of returning Haitian refugees to their homeland.

BARBARA VUCANOVICH (R-Nev.)
(June 22, 1921–   )
House: Jan. 3, 1983, to Jan. 3, 1997

Although Barbara Vucanovich had never held elected office before coming to Congress, she steadily rose through the party hierarchy to become one of the highest-ranking women in the House and to chair one of its most powerful subcommittees. Vucanovich was 62 years old when she first won election, having spent 30 years working in local Republican politics. She had worked in presidential campaigns since the Eisenhower era, headed a number of local women's political groups, and served as a delegate to state GOP conventions. A widow, Vucanovich supported her five children by operating a successful speed reading school and a travel agency. For 20 years she also worked as a state aide to U.S. Sen. Paul Laxalt (R-Nev.). Vucanovich's grandmotherly image—along with the backing of Laxalt—helped her win the support of voters who elected Vucanovich as the first woman from Nevada to hold federal office.

Once in the House, Vucanovich served on the House Administration Committee, the Select Committee on Children, Youth, and Families, and the Committee on Interior and Insular Affairs, where she fought efforts to create a nuclear waste dump in her state and opposed a plan to designate large areas of Nevada as federal wilderness land. She also fought attempts to overhaul the 1872 Mining Law, which Vucanovich said would hurt the state's mining industry and cost jobs.

In 1992, Vucanovich was given a seat on the powerful Appropriations Committee. With the Republican takeover of Congress in 1994, Vucanovich became the chair of the Appropriations subcommittee on military construction—only the second woman in history to chair an appropriations subcommittee. [The first was Rep. Julia Butler Hansen (D-Wash.) from 1967 to 1974]. Vucanovich had come from a military family—her grandfather, father, and two brothers were in the military and her son served two tours in Vietnam—and she promised to use the chairmanship to improve the quality of life for military personnel and their families.

Vucanovich was the lead sponsor of the Family Reinforcement Act, a prominent part of the Republicans' Contract with America. The bill called for tougher sentences for crimes against kids, beefed up child support enforcement, and provided tax credits for adoption and elder care.

Vucanovich was a solid conservative on both fiscal and social issues, opposing abortion and family and medical leave. Her personal battle with breast cancer led her to make preventive care and affordable mammograms a legislative priority. She introduced legislation to provide annual coverage under the Social Security Act of mammography screening for women over 65.

During her final term in office, Vucanovich was elected by her fellow Republicans as the secretary of the GOP Conference—the seventh-ranking spot in the House. Vucanovich said she wanted to use her post as a beacon for women and minorities to join the Republican party. "I hope this says Republicans are trying to bring some balance to the party," she said. "I think women bring a lot more compassion. Rather than just looking at things from the point of view of the white male, we need to offer alternative views. We need to find ways that Republicans can offer an agenda for women and minorities. They have allowed the Democrats to set the agenda for women."[245]

Vucanovich declined to seek election to an eighth term and retired in 1997.

MAXINE WATERS (D-Calif.)
(Aug. 15, 1938–   )
House: Jan. 3, 1991, to present

Maxine Waters, who describes herself as a lawmaker who "does not have time to be polite," has established herself as one of the more outspoken and combative liberals in the House.[246] As the representative of the very poor south-central Los Angeles district, Waters is a crusader for the underprivileged and a relentless opponent of Republican efforts to cut federal aid programs for the needy. Waters' concern for the poor stems from her own humble beginnings. She was raised in public housing projects in St. Louis, one of 13 children. As a teenager she bused tables in a segregated restaurant and married just after high school. By the age of 21 she was the mother of two children and working in a garment factory.

Waters' public career began in 1966 when she volunteered as an assistant teacher in the new Head Start program while pursuing a college degree. From Head Start she became involved in community and political affairs. In 1976, Waters won a seat in the California assembly and quickly made a name for herself as a combative politician. On her first day in the assembly, Waters pushed to have the gender-neutral term "assembly member" replace the official title of "assemblyman." She initially won that battle but it was later overturned. During the next 14 years, Waters helped create the first public school in a public housing project and successfully fought to get the state of California to divest its pension funds from South African investments. A protégé of the legendary state House Speaker Willi Brown, Waters eventually rose to become majority whip, chair of the Democratic Caucus, and chair of the Rules Committee.

In 1990, after 28-year U.S. Rep. Augustus Hawkins (D-Calif.) announced his retirement, Waters ran for and easily won the open House seat. She once again quickly established herself as an agitator of the status quo. Assigned to the Veterans' Affairs Committee, Waters challenged the chairman to hire more blacks for the staff. She also served on the Banking Committee and later gave up her Veterans' Affairs seat for a spot on the Judiciary Committee.

On Judiciary Waters participated in the historic impeachment hearings against President Clinton in 1998 and was one of his most outspoken supporters. She had served as national co-chair of Clinton's 1992 presidential bid.

Despite her liberal positions and general support for Clinton, Waters was not afraid to challenge Clinton or her own party on a variety of legislative issues. In 1995, when Clinton considered cutting affirmative action programs, Waters threatened to leave the Democratic party. "No president is so important that we will belong to him if he undermines us on this issue," said.[247] Waters also criticized Clinton for his policy on detaining Haitian refugees. In 1994, she was arrested after she chained herself to the White House gates in protest of the policy.

But Waters generally reserves her wrath for Republicans. In 1992, after the Los Angeles riots that were sparked by the Rodney King verdict, GOP President Bush invited a group of congressional members to the

White House to discuss the disturbance. When Waters found out she was not invited, she showed up at the White House and insisted she be allowed into the meeting.

Waters has successfully fought for federally funded job training programs for the poor and is a strong opponent of the death penalty, which she says is disproportionately applied to minorities and the poor. She also pushed for hearings and investigations into allegations that the CIA had been complicit in inner-city crack cocaine dealing, with the cash proceeds going to the Nicaraguan contras. In 1996, Waters was named chair of the Congressional Black Caucus, the first woman to head that organization since 1979.

JESSICA WEIS (R-N.Y.)
(July 8, 1901–May 1, 1963)
House: Jan. 3, 1959, to Jan. 3, 1963

Jessica Weis was a stranger to politics until 1935 when she was approached by the local county Republican leader who was looking for party workers. He named Weis—the wife of a businessman and mother of three—as the vice chairman of the Citizens' Republican Finance Committee and Weis quickly immersed herself in party activities. She led a successful campaign to raise money for the party and a year later organized motorcades for Kansas Gov. Alfred Landon's presidential bid against Franklin Roosevelt. In 1937, Weis became vice chair of the Monroe County Republican Committee, a post she held until 1952. In 1941 and 1942, Weis was president of the National Federation of Republican Women, a post that carried her across the nation meeting with the group's 380,000 members. She was a delegate-at-large at six national Republican conventions, and in 1948 she was among the speakers who seconded Thomas E. Dewey's presidential nomination. In 1953, President Eisenhower appointed Weis as a member of the National Civil Defense Advisory Council, and a year later she was named by the State Department as an adviser to the U.S. delegate to the Inter-American Commission of Women.

"I really went into politics because I got tired sitting around the sitting room and objecting to the way things were being run. I decided I ought to do something about it or stop objecting," Weis said.[248]

In 1958, Weis finally decided she was ready to run for national office. She bested three men for the GOP nomination and went on to defeat the

Democratic nominee for the open seat. In her first term she was assigned to the Committee on Government Operations and the Committee on the District of Columbia. In her second term Weis left Government Operations for a seat on the brand new Committee on Science and Astronautics.

While in office, Weis introduced an equal-pay bill for women and supported an Equal Rights Amendment to the Constitution. She also proposed a bill that would allow tax deductions for educational expenses. She generally supported the Eisenhower administration and fought for cuts in government spending. She opposed domestic spending plans for veterans' housing, airport, and power plant construction, and water pollution controls. While in the House, Weis also conducted a personal poll to help select a national flower. She reported that the rose won by a count of six-to-one.

In 1962, Weis learned she was dying of cancer and opted not to run for election to a third term. She died in May 1963, just four months after retiring from the House.

HEATHER WILSON (R-N.M.)
(Dec. 30, 1960–   )
House: June 25, 1998, to present

Heather Wilson's victory in the special election to replace five-term Republican Rep. Steve Schiff, who died of skin cancer, made her the first woman in 50 years and the first Republican woman to represent New Mexico in Congress. The race for the vacant seat proved the most expensive in New Mexico history, with Wilson spending about $1 million on her campaign and her Democratic opponent, millionaire businessman Phil Maloof, spending more than $1.5 million from his own pocket.

Just months after her June victory in the special election, Wilson faced Maloof again in the race for the following full two-year term. She again won.

Wilson serves on the Commerce Committee. She supports limited abortion rights but opposes public funding of the procedure and a particular technique critics call partial birth abortion. She opposes an increase in the minimum wage and backs school vouchers. She has also called for a simpler tax code.

Before coming to Congress, Wilson was the secretary of the state Children, Youth and Families Department. She is an Air Force Academy graduate and Rhodes Scholar, and once served on President George Bush's National Security Council staff.

EFFIEGENE WINGO (D-Ark.)
(April 13, 1883–Sept. 19, 1962)
House: Nov. 4, 1930, to March 3, 1933

Just weeks after Rep. Otis Wingo died while serving his ninth term in office, the Arkansas state Democratic and Republican parties threw aside partisan differences to assure his dying wish—that his widow Effiegene succeed him in Congress. The state Democratic Cental Committee unanimously nominated Wingo to fill out the five months remaining in her husband's unexpired term and also for the following two-year term that began in 1931. The Republican committee met a few minutes later and also endorsed Wingo.

Wingo had learned the ins and outs of Congress during the final four years of her husband's service in the House, during which she worked in his office while he recuperated from an automobile accident. Wingo also had politics in her blood—she was the great-great-great-granddaughter of Rep. Matthew Locke of North Carolina.

Wingo took office in the midst of the Depression and in the wake of severe droughts that devastated Arkansas's agricultural economy. Wingo worked in Congress for various relief measures for her district, but when federal help and Red Cross aid ran dry, Wingo herself went "begging"—asking affluent citizens groups to donate food, clothing, and medicine.

Wingo sponsored legislation to establish a game refuge in Ouachita National Forest and an Ouachita National Park. With the aid of the staff hired previously by her husband, Wingo also helped win the construction of a veterans' hospital, highways, and railroad bridges for her district.

Wingo retired from office after just one term and subsequently cofounded the National Institute of Public Affairs, which provided students with internships in Washington.

Before coming to Congress, Wingo studied music at the Union Female College in Oxford, Miss., and graduated from Maddox Seminary in Little Rock, Ark. She died in 1962.

CHASE GOING WOODHOUSE (D-Conn.)
(March 3, 1890–Dec. 12, 1984)
House: Jan. 3, 1945, to Jan. 3, 1947;
Jan. 3, 1949, to Jan. 3, 1951

Chase Going Woodhouse, who before coming to Congress worked for years as an economist and college professor, used her academic background once in office to push for jobs, a revamped tax system, and increased educational opportunities for the poor. Her economic experience won her a seat on the House Committee on Banking and Currency, where she ardently worked for implementation of the Bretton Woods agreement to establish an international monetary fund and a world bank for redevelopment in the postwar era. "Only the fighting is over. We still must win the war, and that means working out a system of economic cooperation between nations," she said.[249] Domestically, Woodhouse fought for full employment in the United States, insisting that such a goal could be reached if there was a rapid conversion from a wartime to a peacetime economy.

Woodhouse was described as "one of the most liberal minded women in Connecticut" by the American Federation of Labor.[250] She voted to end the poll tax and against funding for the Dies Committee on Un-American Activities. She supported an increase in the minimum wage, an expansion of Social Security benefits, and introduced a bill calling for equal pay for equal work for women. Her son once commented, "Dad talks about Thomas Jefferson and mother talks about better jobs for women."[251] Woodhouse also pushed for liberalized immigration laws, proposing that the unfilled quotas of England, Iceland, and other northern European countries be reassigned to Poland, Austria, and the Balkans.

Woodhouse narrowly won her first election to Congress in 1944 by upsetting the GOP incumbent in the traditionally Republican district. Voters, however, chose not to send her back in 1946. For the next two years, Woodhouse served as the executive director of the women's bureau of the Democratic National Committee. She also worked in 1948 as an economic adviser to General Lucius Clay, the Allied military governor of Germany. Later that year she returned to Connecticut and recaptured her House seat. She was re-assigned to the Committee on Banking and Currency and also the Committee on House Administration. In 1950, she was again ousted from office by the same Republican who had previously defeated her.

Woodhouse remained active in public affairs after leaving Congress. She was appointed by the President as assistant to the director of Price Stabilization from 1951 to 1953, and from 1952 to 1980 she was director of the Service Bureau for Women's Organizations in Hartford, Conn. In 1965, she was a delegate to the Connecticut Constitutional Convention.

Before coming to Congress, Woodhouse taught economics at a variety of colleges including Connecticut College, the University of Texas, the University of Iowa, and Smith College, where one of her students—Jessie Sumner—would go on to serve in Congress and sit with Woodhouse on the Banking and Currency Committee. In 1925, Woodhouse worked as a senior economist for the home economics bureau of the Department of Agriculture and, as part of her duties, lectured in every state in the country. She later founded the Institute of Women's Professional Relations to study the status of working women and served as president of the Connecticut Federation of Democratic Women's Clubs. She also organized the first Business Women's Club in Mexico while serving with the Federation of Business and Professional Women's Clubs.

In 1941, Woodhouse was elected as secretary of state for Connecticut with the highest majority of any state official that year. While in that position, Woodhouse created "election law schools" to better educate the public about voting.

Born in British Columbia, Canada, Woodhouse earned her bachelor's and master's degree in economics from McGill University in Montreal. She graduated with honors and was the first woman to earn an economics degree from the school. She later went to Germany for advanced work at the University of Berlin, but was forced to cut her studies short with the outbreak of World War I.

LYNN WOOLSEY (D-Calif.)
(Nov. 3, 1937–   )
House: Jan. 5, 1993, to present

During her time in Congress, Lynn Woolsey has focused on issues affecting women, children, and the needy. Her concern for these groups stems directly from her own life experience. When Woolsey was 29 years old, she divorced her successful stockbroker husband and found herself with three small children, no house, and little job experience. She was forced to go on welfare and food stamps to support her family. After three years of depending on federal assistance while working at a low-paying job, Woolsey remarried and left the welfare system. She eventually went back to college and completed her bachelor's degree at age 42. That same year she started her own temporary employment business. She was later elected to the Petaluma city council in California where she served for eight years before winning election to Congress. But Woolsey never forgot her time on the welfare rolls and has used that experience to fight for the poor. While on the city council, Woolsey was instrumental in expanding low- and moderate-income housing and she led the fight to build Sonoma County's first emergency family shelter for the homeless. She was elected to Congress to fill the seat left open when Rep. Barbara Boxer (D-Calif.) ran for the Senate.

In Congress, Woolsey has fought for family and medical leave, expanding early education programs, and creating jobs that pay a living wage. When the Republican-led Congress in 1995 began to look at overhauling the nation's welfare system, Woolsey helped lead efforts to protect the poor from harsh reforms. She tried to amend GOP proposals to provide welfare parents with child-care services, arguing that such assistance is essential to moving people from welfare to work. She charged that Republican efforts to place time limits on welfare assistance would hurt the poor, especially children.

"Without the guarantee of a safety net, mothers in the situation I was in would have felt very vulnerable. I knew I had time to get my life together. The welfare investment gave me that space. It took me three years. Now in some states, [the cutoff] will be two years or less. With that kind of pressure, you don't always do your best," Woolsey said after President Clinton signed the GOP welfare reform bill in 1996.[252]

Woolsey has also made education a top legislative priority. She introduced a bill to create partnerships between universities and public schools to improve classroom instruction and teacher training. She successfully fought for tax relief for parents of college students and graduates paying off student loans. She also introduced legislation to make college more accessible to families by making prepaid tuition programs for state colleges and universities more easily available.

Woolsey backs most liberal issues. She supports increasing the minimum wage, cutting military spending, protecting the environment, and abortion rights. She also broke a Capitol Hill gender barrier when in 1993 she became the first woman to play in the annual congressional basketball game. Her concern for the environment led her to oppose the North American Free Trade Agreement because of Mexico's lax environmental regulations. She, however, joined with conservative Rep. Henry Hyde (R-Ill.) in 1995 to try to enlist the Internal Revenue Service to help track down parents who fail to make child support payments. Woolsey and Hyde tried to attach the proposal to the welfare overhaul bill, but failed. Woolsey serves on the Budget Committee and the Committee on Education and the Workforce.

NOTES

1. "The Senate: Lady from Nebraska," *Newsweek*, Dec. 20, 1954, p. 20.

2. Hope Chamberlin, *A Minority of Members: Women in the U.S. Congress* (New York: Praeger, 1973), p. 246.

3. Clara Bingham, *Women on the Hill: Challenging the Culture of Congress* (New York: Random House, 1997), p. 23.

4. William Miller, *Fishbait: The Memoirs of the Congressional Doorkeeper* (Englewood Cliffs, N.J.: Prentice-Hall, Inc., 1977), p. 82.

5. Rudolf Engelbarts, *Women in the United States Congress, 1917–1972* (Littleton, Colo.: Libraries Unlimited, 1974), p. 118.

6. "The New House Members," *CQ Daily Monitor*, Nov. 5, 1998, p. 3.

7. Philip Duncan, *Politics in America 1990* (Washington, D.C.: CQ Press, 1989), p. 658.

8. Philip Duncan and Christine C. Lawrence, *Politics in America 1992* (Washington, D.C.: CQ Press, 1991), p. 653.

9. "The New House Members," *CQ Daily Monitor*, Nov. 5, 1998, p. 26.

10. Anna Rothe, ed., *Current Biography 1948* (New York: H. W. Wilson Company, 1948), p. 57.

11. Engelbarts, *Women in the United States Congress, 1917–1972*, p. 76.

12. Marcy Kaptur, *Women of Congress: A Twentieth-Century Odyssey* (Washington, D.C.: Congressional Quarterly, 1996), p. 161.

13. Sarah Booth Conroy, "Plucky Lindy: In New Book, Boggs Recalls Life in the Limelight," *Washington Post*, Oct. 24, 1994, p. B1.

14. Duncan, *Politics in America 1990*, p. 613.

15. Conroy, "Plucky Lindy: In New Book, Boggs Recalls Life in the Limelight," p. B1.

16. Kaptur, *Women of Congress: A Twentieth-Century Odyssey*, p. 165.

17. Ibid., p. 77.

18. Chamberlin, *A Minority of Members: Women in the U.S. Congress*, p. 133.

19. Kaptur, *Women of Congress: A Twentieth-Century Odyssey*, p. 80.

20. Chamberlin, *A Minority of Members: Women in the U.S. Congress*, p. 136.

21. *New York Times* Oral History Program, Former Members of Congress Oral History Collection, No. 11, Reva Bosone (Sanford, N.C.: Microfilming Corporation of America, 1981).

22. "The Lady from Bar 99," *Time,* April 26, 1954, p. 28.

23. Chamberlin, *A Minority of Members: Women in the U.S. Congress,* p. 227.

24. Charles Moritz, ed., *Current Biography 1975* (New York: H. W. Wilson Company, 1975), p. 60.

25. Robert Byrd, *The United States Senate, 1789–1989: Addresses on the History of the United States Senate,* Vol. 2 (Washington, D.C.: Government Printing Office, 1986), p. 522.

26. Chamberlin, *A Minority of Members: Women in the U.S. Congress,* p. 197.

27. Duncan, *Politics in America 1990,* p. 669.

28. Chamberlin, *A Minority of Members: Women in the U.S. Congress,* p. 157.

29. Karen Foerstel and Herbert Foerstel, *Climbing the Hill: Gender Conflict in Congress* (Westport, Conn.: Praeger, 1996), p. 56.

30. Ibid.

31. Byrd, *The United States Senate, 1789–1989: Addresses on the History of the United States Senate,* Vol. 2, p. 518.

32. Hattie Wyatt Caraway, *Silent Hattie Speaks: The Personal Journal of Senator Hattie Caraway,* edited by Diane D. Kincaid (Westport, Conn.: Greenwood Press, 1979), p. 9.

33. Byrd, *The United States Senate 1789–1989: Addresses on the History of the United States Senate,* Vol. 2, p. 519.

34. Chamberlin, *A Minority of Members: Women in the U.S. Congress,* p. 93.

35. Bingham, *Women on the Hill: Challenging the Culture of Congress,* p. 12.

36. Kaptur, *Women of Congress: A Twentieth-Century Odyssey,* p. 20.

37. Lloyd Grove, Al Kamen, and Bill McAllister, "One-Upmanship," *Washington Post,* Sept. 11, 1994, p. A21.

38. Thomas Galvin, "Disinvite Minorities—Idaho Pol," *New York Daily News,* May 14, 1997, p. 18.

39. Linda Killian, *The Freshmen: What Happened to the Republican Revolution?* (Boulder, Colo.: Westview Press, 1998), p. 18.

40. Columbus Salley, *The Black 100: A Ranking of the Most Influential African-Americans, Past and Present* (New York: Citadel Press, 1993), p. 248.

41. Ibid., p. 250.

42. Charles Moritz, ed., *Current Biography 1969* (New York: H. W. Wilson Company, 1969), p. 94.

43. Foerstel and Foerstel, *Climbing the Hill: Gender Conflict in Congress,* p. 97.

44. Moritz, *Current Biography 1969,* p. 94.

45. Foerstel and Foerstel, *Climbing the Hill: Gender Conflict in Congress,* p. 30.

46. Chamberlin, *A Minority of Members: Women in the U.S. Congress,* p. 222.

47. LaVerne McCain Gill, *African-American Women in Congress: Forming and Transforming History* (New Brunswick, N.J.: Rutgers University Press, 1997), p. 142.

48. Duncan, *Politics in America 1996,* p. 685.

49. Gill, *African-American Women in Congress: Forming and Transforming History,* p. 80.

50. Kaptur, *Women in Congress: A Twentieth-Century Odyssey,* p. 186.

51. Foerstel and Foerstel, *Climbing the Hill: Gender Conflict in Congress*, p. 130.

52. Kevin Merida, "Rush Limbaugh Saluted As a 'Majority Maker,' " *Washington Post*, Dec. 11, 1994, p. A30.

53. Marcia Gelbart, "GOP Women Tell Leaders to Soft-Pedal Abortion," *The Hill*, July 26, 1995, p. 1.

54. Linda Witt, Karen M. Paget, and Glenna Matthews, *Running as a Woman: Gender and Power in American Politics* (New York, The Free Press, 1994), p. 99.

55. *New York Times* Oral History Program, Former Members of Congress Oral History Collection, No. 23, Emily Taft Douglas (Sanford, N.C.: Microfilming Corporation of America, 1981), p. 13.

56. Anna Rothe, ed., *Current Biography 1945* (New York: H. W. Wilson Company, 1945), p. 20.

57. Chamberlin, *A Minority of Members: Women in the U.S. Congress*, p. 179.

58. Ibid., p. 179.

59. Ibid., p. 18.

60. Allida Black, *Casting Her Own Shadow: Eleanor Roosevelt and the Shaping of Postwar Liberalism* (New York: Columbia University Press, 1996), p. 163.

61. Maxine Block, ed., *Current Biography 1944* (New York: H. W. Wilson Company, 1944), p. 17.

62. Chamberlin, *A Minority of Members: Women in the U.S. Congress*, p. 183.

63. Ibid., p. 184.

64. Ibid., p. 188.

65. Philip Duncan, *Politics in America 1998* (Washington, D.C.: Congressional Quarterly, 1997), p. 1542.

66. *NBC Today Show*, U.S. Representative Jennifer Dunn (R-Wash.) interview, Nov. 10, 1998.

67. Chamberlin, *A Minority of Members: Women in the U.S. Congress*, p. 270.

68. Marybeth Weston, "Ladies' Day on the Hustings," *New York Times Magazine*, Oct. 19, 1958, p. 93.

69. Chamberlin, *A Minority of Members: Women in the U.S. Congress*, p. 349.

70. Mary McGrory, "Democrats Gallant in Defeat," *Washington Post*, Dec. 1, 1994, p. A2.

71. Charles Moritz, ed., *Current Biography 1955* (New York: H. W. Wilson Company, 1955), p. 196.

72. Duncan, *Politics in America 1998*, p. 85.

73. Chamberlin, *A Minority of Members: Women in the U.S. Congress*, p. 28.

74. Foerstel and Foerstel, *Climbing the Hill: Gender Conflict in Congress*, p. 6.

75. Ibid., p. 7.

76. Ibid., p. 8.

77. Chamberlin, *A Minority of Members: Women in the U.S. Congress*, p. 37.

78. LeeAnn Whites, "Rebecca Latimer Felton and the Wife's Farm: The Class and Racial Politics of Gender Reform," *Georgia Historical Quarterly* 76, no. 2 (Summer 1992), p. 363.

79. Millicent Fenwick, *Speaking Up* (New York: Harper & Row, 1982), p. 150.

80. Ibid., p. 33.

81. Jean Stafford, "In Congress, New Jersey's Perfect Lady Makes a Tough Campaigner, an Adroit Politician,"*Vogue*, June 1975, p. 140.

82. Devon Spurgeon, "Ferraro Enters Race to Take on Sen. D'Amato," *Washington Post,* Jan. 6, 1998, p. A5.

83. Duncan, *Politics in America 1996,* p. 1094.

84. Bob Baum, "Lawmaker Reveals Her Painful Choice," Associated Press, Jan. 22, 1997.

85. Chamberlin, *A Minority of Members: Women in the U.S. Congress,* p. 156.

86. Marjorie Dent, ed., *Current Biography 1959* (New York: H. W. Wilson Company, 1959), p. 156.

87. Byrd, *The United States Senate 1789–1989: Addresses on the History of the United States Senate,* Vol. 2, p. 521.

88. Chamberlin, *A Minority of Members: Women in the U.S. Congress,* p. 123.

89. Byrd, *The United States Senate 1789–1989: Addresses on the History of the United States Senate,* Vol. 2, p. 521.

90. Chamberlin, *A Minority of Members: Women in the U.S. Congress,* p. 124.

91. Byrd, *The United States Senate 1789–1989: Addresses on the History of the United States Senate,* Vol. 2, p. 521.

92. Barbara Boxer, *Strangers in the Senate: Politics and the New Revolution of Women in America* (Washington, D.C.: National Press Books, 1994), p. 98.

93. "Mrs. Graves Ends Service in Senate," *New York Times,* Jan. 11, 1938, p. 19.

94. Chamberlin, *A Minority of Members: Women in the U.S. Congress,* p. 251.

95. Irene Tinker, *Women in Washington: Advocates for Public Policy* (Beverly Hills: Sage Publications, 1983), p. 205.

96. Ibid., p. 202.

97. Kaptur, *Women of Congress: A Twentieth-Century Odyssey,* p. 114.

98. Emily Newell Blair, "If You Were Gadding About Washington," *Good Housekeeping,* March 1934, p. 26.

99. Emily George, *Martha Griffiths* (Washington, D.C.: University Press of America, 1982), pp. 110, 113.

100. Ibid., pp. 149–150.

101. Tinker, *Women in Washington: Advocates of Public Policy,* p. 197.

102. Ibid., p. 198.

103. Chamberlin, *A Minority of Members: Women in the U.S. Congress,* p. 260.

104. Gill, *African-American Women in Congress: Forming and Transforming History,* p. 94.

105. Mary Russell, "Rep. Julia Butler Hansen to Retire," *Washington Post,* Feb. 7, 1974, p. A3.

106. *New York Times* Oral History Program, Former Members of Congress Oral History Collection, No. 37, Julia Butler Hansen (Sanford, N.C.: Microfilming Corporation of America, 1981), p. 9.

107. Engelbarts, *Women in the United States Congress, 1917–1972,* p. 62.

108. Boxer, *Strangers in the Senate: Politics and the New Revolution of Women in America,* p. 104.

109. Charles Moritz, ed., *Current Biography 1985* (New York: H. W. Wilson Company, 1985), p. 176.

110. Chamberlin, *A Minority of Members: Women in the U.S. Congress,* p. 320.

111. Kaptur, *Women of Congress: A Twentieth-Century Odyssey,* p. 134.

112. Charles Moritz, ed., *Current Biography 1974* (New York: H. W. Wilson Company, 1974), p. 175.

113. Sue McCauley Patterson, "From Maryland with Promise (and Reservations)," *Ms.*, April 1975, p. 78.

114. Ibid.

115. Ibid.

116. Ibid.

117. Chamberlin, *A Minority of Members: Women in the U.S. Congress*, p. 353.

118. "The Women's Caucus, 20 and Roaring," *Washington Post*, Oct. 20, 1997, p. C3.

119. Chamberlin, *A Minority of Members: Women in the U.S. Congress*, p. 114.

120. Ibid., p. 113.

121. Charlotte Grimes, "Horn Shows She's Learned Art of Rough-and-Tumble, Congresswoman Finds Footing Among Washington Politicians," *St. Louis Post-Dispatch*, Oct. 3, 1992, p. 1B.

122. Chamberlin, *A Minority of Members: Women in the U.S. Congress*, p. 44.

123. Ibid., p. 45.

124. "Mrs. Huck Says If Equal Rights Bill Fails, Women Will Pass It in the Next Congress," *New York Times*, Dec. 10, 1923, p. 5.

125. Irvin Molotsky, "Muriel Humphrey Brown, 86; Finished Husband's Senate Term," *New York Times*, Sept. 22, 1998.

126. *Congressional Record*, April 19, 1994, p. S4435.

127. Annabel Paxton, *Women in Congress* (Richmond: Dietz Press, 1945), p. 11.

128. Chamberlin, *A Minority of Members: Women in the U.S. Congress*, p. 99.

129. Kevin Merida, "After Bruising Ethics Ordeal, Time to Mend Fences at Home," *Washington Post*, Jan. 25, 1997, p. A1.

130. Witt, Paget, and Matthews, *Running as a Woman: Gender and Power in American Politics*, p. 220.

131. Gill, *African-American Women in Congress: Forming and Transforming History*, p. 40.

132. Moritz, *Current Biography 1974*, p. 190.

133. Ibid., p. 190.

134. Duff Gilfond, "Gentlewomen of the House," *American Mercury*, Oct. 1929, p. 151.

135. Ibid.

136. Chamberlin, *A Minority of Members: Women in the U.S. Congress*, p. 51.

137. Gilfond, "Gentlewomen of the House," p. 151.

138. Duncan, *Politics in America 1998*, p. 1136.

139. Foerstel and Foerstel, *Climbing the Hill: Gender Conflict in Congress*, p. 185.

140. Kaptur, *Women of Congress: A Twentieth-Century Odyssey*, p. 103.

141. Elizabeth Kastor, "A Woman's Place," *Washington Post*, Nov. 17, 1996, p. F1.

142. "Conspiracy Denied," *Newsweek*, Dec. 29, 1958, p. 16.

143. Chamberlin, *A Minority of Members: Women in the U.S. Congress*, p. 267.

144. "Will It Be Congresswoman Langley," *The Literary Digest*, Jan. 30, 1926, p. 9.

145. "Kentucky's First Congresswoman," *The Literary Digest*, Aug. 21, 1926, p. 14.

146. Gilfond, "Gentlewomen of the House," p. 151.

147. Chamberlin, *A Minority of Members: Women in the U.S. Congress*, p. 65.

148. Foerstel and Foerstel, *Climbing the Hill: Gender Conflict in Congress*, p. 83.

149. B. W. Apple, "Indiana House Race Shows Incumbency Is Still of Value," *New York Times*, Nov. 3, 1990, p. 32.

150. "Lady from Louisiana," *Time*, Feb. 10, 1936, p. 12.

151. Chamberlin, *A Minority of Members: Women in the U.S. Congress*, p. 169.

152. Bingham, *Women on the Hill: Challenging the Culture of Congress*, p. 13.

153. Chamberlin, *A Minority of Members: Women in the U.S. Congress*, p. 173.

154. Emily Geer, "A Study of the Activities of Women in Congress with Special Reference to the Congressional Careers of Margaret Chase Smith, Mary T. Norton, and Edith Nourse Rogers" (Ph.D. diss. Bowling Green State University, 1952), p. 70.

155. Chamberlin, *A Minority of Members: Women in the U.S. Congress*, p. 202.

156. Maxine Block, ed., *Current Biography 1946* (New York: H. W. Wilson Company, 1946), p. 38.

157. Chamberlin, *A Minority of Members: Women in the U.S. Congress*, p. 192.

158. Barbara Slavin, "This Woman's Place," *Los Angeles Times*, May 30, 1994, p. E1.

159. Duncan, *Politics in America 1990*, p. 464.

160. Charles Trueheart, "Lynn Martin, No Yes Woman," *Washington Post*, Aug. 19, 1992, p. B1.

161. Charles Moritz, ed., *Current Biography 1960* (New York: H. W. Wilson Company, 1960), p. 270.

162. Chamberlin, *A Minority of Members: Women in the U.S. Congress*, p. 67.

163. Gilfond, "Gentlewomen of the House," p. 151.

164. Chamberlin, *A Minority of Members: Women in the U.S. Congress*, p. 72.

165. Foerstel and Foerstel, *Climbing the Hill: Gender Conflict in Congress*, p. 130.

166. Francesca Contiguglia, "McKinney Demands Apology for Racist Incident," *Roll Call*, May 11, 1998.

167. Chamberlin, *A Minority of Members: Women in the U.S. Congress*, p. 155.

168. Gill, *African-American Women in Congress: Forming and Transforming History*, p. 189.

169. Patterson, "From Maryland with Promise (and Reservations)," p. 80.

170. *Congressional Record*, April 19, 1994, p. S4422.

171. "The Sexes: Hormones in the White House," *Time*, Aug. 10, 1970, p. 13.

172. Chamberlin, *A Minority of Members: Women in the U.S. Congress*, p. 313.

173. Duncan, *Politics in America 1996*, p. 376.

174. Gill, *African-American Women in Congress: Forming and Transforming History*, p. 157.

175. Foerstel and Foerstel, *Climbing the Hill: Gender Conflict in Congress*, p. 68.

176. Kelly Wolfe, "Prayer Amendment Fails," *Hartford Courant*, June 5, 1998, p. A15.

177. Duncan, *Politics in America 1998*, p. 1083.

178. "The New House Members," *CQ Daily Monitor*, Nov. 5, 1998, p. 22.

179. Robert Cahn, "Madam Senator from Oregon," *Saturday Evening Post*, Jan. 7, 1961, p. 80.

180. Richard L. Neuberger, "My Wife Put Me in the Senate," *Harpers*, June 1955, p. 44.

181. Chamberlin, *A Minority of Members: Women in the U.S. Congress*, p. 350.

182. Moritz, *Current Biography 1976*, p. 295.

183. Chamberlin, *A Minority of Members: Women in the U.S. Congress*, p. 54.

184. Ibid.

185. Ibid.

186. Kaptur, *Women of Congress: A Twentieth-Century Odyssey*, p. 44.

187. Chamberlin, *A Minority of Members: Women in the U.S. Congress*, p. 57.

188. Associated Press, "Mrs. Oldfield To Quit Congress at Term End," *New York Times*, May 30, 1929, p. 8.

189. "Mrs. Oldfied Decries Feminist in Politics," *New York Times*, Feb. 19, 1931, p. 3.

190. Marjory Stoneman Douglas, *Voice of the River* (Englewood, Fla.: Pineapple Press, 1987), p. 150.

191. Ibid., pp. 176–177.

192. House floor debate, April 28, 1998.

193. Chamberlin, *A Minority of Members: Women in the U.S. Congress*, p. 230.

194. Anna Rothe, ed., *Current Biography 1955* (New York: H. W. Wilson Company, 1955), p. 487.

195. Chamberlin, *A Minority of Members: Women in the U.S. Congress*, p. 195.

196. Gilfond, "Gentlewomen of the House," p. 151.

197. Chamberlin, *A Minority of Members: Women in the U.S. Congress*, p. 79.

198. Marcia Gelbart, "GOP Women Tell Leaders to Soft-pedal Abortion," *The Hill*, July 26, 1995, p. 1.

199. "The Congress: In-Between Senators," *Time*, Dec. 19, 1938, p. 10.

200. Ibid.

201. Chamberlin, *A Minority of Members: Women in the U.S. Congress*, p. 126.

202. Kaptur, *Women of Congress: A Twentieth-Century Odyssey*, p. 25.

203. Ibid., p. 26.

204. Foerstel and Foerstel, *Climbing the Hill: Gender Conflict in Congress*, p. 119.

205. Ibid., p. 88.

206. "Mrs. Robertson of Oklahoma," *New York Times*, Nov. 13, 1920, p. 10.

207. Ibid.

208. Chamberlin, *A Minority of Members: Women in the U.S. Congress*, p. 41.

209. Ibid., p. 59.

210. Duncan, *Politics in America 1998*, p. 355.

211. Foerstel and Foerstel, *Climbing the Hill: Gender Conflict in Congress*, p. 129.

212. Francesca Contiguglia, "Leaders Pick Members of China Panel," *Roll Call*, June 22, 1998, p. 3.

213. *Congressional Record*—House, Feb. 8, 1964, pp. 2580–2581.

214. *New York Times* Oral History Program, Former Members of Congress Oral History Collection, No. 64, Katharine Price Collier St. George (Sanford, N.C.: Microfilming Corporation of America, 1981).

215. Charles Moritz, ed., *Current Biography 1978* (New York: H. W. Wilson Company, 1978), p. 369.

216. Ibid., p. 367.

217. Author's interview with Rep. Pat Schroeder (D-Colo.), Jan. 23, 1995.

218. Kaptur, *Women of Congress: A Twentieth-Century Odyssey*, p. 180.

219. Bob Sipchen, "California Elections: 22nd Congressional District; Race Becomes Test of GOP's '94 Ascension," *Los Angeles Times*, Sept. 25, 1996, p. 3.

220. Dennis Farney, "Utah's Shepherd Guards a Democratic Outpost As Party's Support Sags, GOP Challenge Grows," *Wall Street Journal,* Sept. 19, 1994.

221. E. J. Dionne Jr., "A Winner Either Way," *Washington Post,* Oct. 11, 1994, p. A7.

222. Foerstel and Foerstel, *Climbing the Hill: Gender Conflict in Congress,* p. 37.

223. Bingham, *Women on the Hill: Challenging the Culture of Congress,* p. 86.

224. Byrd, *The United States Senate 1789–1989: Addresses on the History of the United States Senate,* Vol. 2, p. 522.

225. Author's interview with Sen. Margaret Chase Smith, Nov. 9, 1994.

226. Kaptur, *Women of Congress: A Twentieth-Century Odyssey,* p. 93.

227. Boxer, *Strangers in the Senate: Politics and the New Revolution of Women in America,* p. 101.

228. Duncan, *Politics in America 1990,* p. 897.

229. Ibid., p. 643.

230. Duncan, *Politics in America 1998,* p. 628.

231. Bart Barnes, "Former Md. Representative Gladys N. Spellman, 70, Dies," *Washington Post,* June, 20, 1988, p. A1.

232. Patterson, "From Maryland with Promise," p. 80.

233. Chamberlin, *A Minority of Members: Women in the U.S. Congress,* p. 160.

234. Paxton, *Women in Congress,* p. 99.

235. Maxine Block, ed., *Current Biography 1943* (New York: H. W. Wilson Company, 1943), p. 75.

236. Chamberlin, *A Minority of Members: Women in the U.S. Congress,* p. 235.

237. Kaptur, *Women of Congress: A Twentieth-Century Odyssey,* p. 109.

238. Rothe, *Current Biography 1945,* p. 47.

239. Chamberlin, *A Minority of Members: Women in the U.S. Congress,* p. 154.

240. Ibid., p. 155.

241. Ibid., p. 154.

242. Ibid., p. 153.

243. Timothy Egan, "Debate Over Logging Means Trouble for Incumbent in Washington State," *New York Times,* Sept. 25, 1990, p. A18.

244. Duncan, *Politics in America 1988,* p. 995.

245. Foerstel and Foerstel, *Climbing the Hill: Gender Conflict in Congress,* p. 102.

246. La Verne McCain Gill, *African-American Women in Congress: Forming and Transforming History* (New Brunswick, N.J.: Rutgers University Press, 1997), p. 124.

247. Philip Duncan and Christine C. Lawrence, *Politics in America 1998* (Washington, D.C.: CQ Press, 1997), p. 186.

248. "Jessica McCullough Weis Dead," *New York Times,* May 2, 1963, p. 35.

249. Chamberlin, *A Minority of Members: Women in the U.S. Congress,* p. 190.

250. Rothe, *Current Biography 1945,* p. 61.

251. Paxton, *Women in Congress,* p. 120.

252. Colman McCarthy, "For One on Hill, Welfare Vote Was Personal," *Washington Post,* Aug. 13, 1996, p. C10.

SELECTED BIBLIOGRAPHY

Abzug, Bella, and Kelber, Mim. *Gender Gap, Bella Azbug's Guide to Political Power for American Women*. Boston: Houghton Mifflin, 1984.

Baxter, Sandra. *Women and Politics: The Invisible Majority*. Ann Arbor: University of Michigan Press, 1980.

Boxer, Barbara. *Strangers in the Senate: Politics and the New Revolution of Women in America*. Bethesda, Md.: National Press Books, 1993.

Burrell, Barbara C. *A Woman's Place Is in the House: Campaigning for Congress in the Feminist Era*. Ann Arbor: University of Michigan Press, 1994.

Carroll, Susan J. *Women as Candidates in American Politics*, 2d ed. Bloomington: Indiana University Press, 1994.

Chamberlin, Hope. *A Minority of Members: Women in the U.S. Congress*. New York: Praeger, 1973.

Chisholm, Shirley. *Unbought and Unbossed*. Boston: Houghton Mifflin and Co., 1970.

Conway, M. Margaret. *Women and Public Policy: A Revolution in Progress*. Washington, D.C.: CQ Press, 1995.

Cook, Elizabeth Adell, ed. *The Year of the Woman*. Boulder, Colo.: Westview Press, 1994.

Darcy, R. *Women, Elections, and Representation*. Lincoln: University of Nebraska Press, 1994.

Davidson, Sue. *A Heart in Politics: Jeannette Rankin and Patsy T. Mink*. Seattle: Seal Press, 1994.

Engelbarts, Rudolf. *Women in the United States Congress, 1917–1972: Their Accomplishments*. Littleton, Colo.: Libraries Unlimited, 1974.

Fenwick, Millicent. *Speaking Up*. New York: Harper & Row, 1982.

Ferraro, Geraldine. *Changing History: Women, Power and Politics*. Wakefield, R.I.: Moyer Bell, 1993.

Foerstel, Karen, and Foerstel, Herbert N. *Climbing the Hill: Gender Conflict in Congress*. Westport, Conn.: Praeger, 1996.

George, Emily. *Martha W. Griffiths*. Washington, D.C.: University Press of America, 1982.

Gertzog, Irwin N. *Congressional Women: Their Recruitment, Treatment, and Behavior.* New York: Praeger, 1984.

Gil, LaVerne McCain. *African-American Women in Congress: Forming and Transforming History.* New Brunswick, N.J.: Rutgers University Press. 1997.

Gould, Alberta. *First Lady of the Senate: A Life of Margaret Chase Smith.* Mt. Desert, Me.: Windswept House Publishers, 1990.

Holtzman, Elizabeth. *Who Said It Would Be Easy?: One Woman's Life in the Political Arena.* New York: Arcade, 1996.

Jordan, Barbara, and Hearon, Shelby. *Barbara Jordan: A Self-Portrait.* Garden City, N.Y.: Doubleday and Co., 1979.

Josephson, Hannah. *Jeannette Rankin, First Lady in Congress: A Biography.* Indianapolis: Bobbs-Merrill, 1974.

Kaptur, Marcy. *Women of Congress: A Twentieth-Century Odyssey.* Washington, D.C.: Congressional Quarterly, 1996.

Killian, Linda. *The Freshmen: What Happened to the Republican Revolution.* Boulder, Colo.: Westview Press, 1998.

Kinkaid, Diane, ed. *Silent Hattie Speaks: The Personal Journal of Senator Hattie Caraway.* Westport, Conn.: Greenwood Press, 1979.

Mandel, Ruth B. *In the Running: The New Woman Candidate.* Boston: Beacon Press, 1983.

Margolies-Mezvinsky, Marjorie. *A Woman's Place: The Freshman Women Who Changed the Face of Congress.* New York: Crown Publishers, 1994.

Miller, Kristie. *Ruth Hanna McCormick: A Life in Politics, 1880–1944.* Albuquerque: University of New Mexico Press, 1992.

Miller, William "Fishbait." *Fishbait: The Memoirs of the Congressional Doorkeeper.* Englewood Cliffs, N.J.: Prentice-Hall, 1977.

Paxton, Annabel. *Women in Congress.* Richmond, Va.: Dietz Press, 1945.

Roberts, Jerry. *Dianne Feinstein: Never Let Them See You Cry.* New York: HarperCollins West, 1994.

Schroeder, Patricia. *Champion of the Great American Family.* New York: Random House, 1989.

Scobie, Ingrid Winther. *Center Stage: Helen Gahagan Douglas, a Life.* New York: Oxford University Press, 1992.

Shadegg, Stephen. *Clare Boothe Luce: A Biography.* New York: Simon and Schuster, 1970.

Smith, Margaret Chase. *Declaration of Conscience,* edited by William C. Lewis, Jr. New York: Doubleday and Co., 1972.

Swerdlow, Amy. *Women Strike for Peace: Traditional Motherhood and Radical Politics in the 1960s.* Chicago: University of Chicago Press, 1993.

Tinker, Irene, ed. *Women in Washington: Advocates for Public Policy.* Beverly Hills: Sage Publications, 1983.

Witt, Linda. *Running as a Woman: Gender and Power in American Politics.* New York: Free Press, 1994.

Women in Congress, 1917–1990. Prepared under the direction of the Commission on the Bicentenary of the U.S. House of Representatives by the Office of the House Historian. Washington, D.C.: U.S. Government Printing Office, 1991.

INDEX

The page numbers set in **boldface** indicate the location of a main entry.

Abache, Sani, 197–198
Abel, Hazel, **17–18**
Abernathy, Thomas, 7
abortion, stance on: Jennifer Dunn, 76; Elizabeth Furse, 97; Sue Kelly, 148; Lynn Martin, 174; Cynthia McKinney, 181–182; Deborah Pryce, 222–223; Olympia Snowe, 258
Abrams, Robert, 92
Abzug, Bella, **18–20**
affirmative action, 42, 276
Agnew, Spiro, 122
AIDS, 216
Allen, Maryon, **20–21**
Anderson, Marian, 212
Andrews, Elizabeth, **21–22**
Anthony, Susan B., 40
apartheid, 32
Ashbrook, Jean, **22**

Baker, Howard, 144
Baker, Irene, **23**
Baldwin, Tammy, **23–24**
Barkley, Alben, 103–104
Becerra, Xavier, 235
Bentley, Helen Delich, **24–25**
Berkley, Shelley, **25–26**
Berman, Edgar, 191

Biggert, Judy, **26**
Blanchard, James, 111
Blitch, Iris, **26–27**
Boggs, Corrine "Lindy," **27–30**
Boggs, Hale, 27–28
Boggs, Thomas Hale, 29
Boland, Veronica, **30**
Bolton, Frances, **30–32**
Bono, Mary, **32–33**
Bono, Sonny, 33
Bosnia, 131, 193
Bosone, Reva, 7, **33–35**
Bowman, Frank, 208
Bowring, Eva, **35–36**
Boxer, Barbara, 12, **36–37**
Brown, Corrine, **38–39**
Bryan, William Jennings, 213
Buchanan, Vera, **39**
Burdick, Jocelyn, **39–40**
Burke, Yvonne Brathwaite, 8, **40–42**
Burrell, Barbara, 10
Burton, Sala, **42–43**, 216
Bush, George, 173
Bushfield, Vera, **43–44**
busing, 93, 105, 120
Byrne, Leslie, 8, **44–45**
Byron, Beverly, **45–46**
Byron, Katharine, 45, **46–47**

Cambodia, 123–124
Cantwell, Maria, **47–48**
Capps, Lois, **49**
Caraway, Hattie, 1, **50–52**, 103, 162–163
Carson, Julia, **52**
Carswell, George Harold, 191
Carter, Jimmy, 64
Castro, Fidel, 234
Celler, Emanuel, 6–7, 123
Chenoweth, Helen, **53–54**
children's issues, 116–117, 131, 136, 175
China, 142, 216
Chisholm, Shirley, 19, **54–57**, 156
Christian-Green, Donna, **57**
Church, Marguerite, **58–59**
CIA, 189, 277
cigarettes, 203
civil rights, 27, 29
Civil Rights Act, 5–6, 105, 109–110, 238
Clarke, Frank, 5
Clarke, Marian, **59–60**
Clayton, Eva, **60–61**
Clinton, Bill: affect of sex scandal, 12–13; Leslie Byrne and, 44; Maria Cantwell and, 48; Marjorie Margolies-Mezvinsky and, 172; Cynthia McKinney and, 182; Jan Meyers and, 186; Lucille Royball-Allard and, 238; Karen Shepherd and, 249; Maxine Waters and, 276
Cohen, Bill, 65
Collins, Barbara-Rose, **61–62**
Collins, Cardiss, **63–65**
Collins, Susan, **65–66**
communism, 22, 33, 73, 146
congressional baseball game, 48
Congressional Black Caucus: Yvonne Brathwaite Burke, 41; Cardiss Collins, 64; Eddie Bernice Johnson, 135; Maxine Waters, 277
Congressional Hispanic Caucus, 237, 238
Congressional Women's Caucus: Corrine "Lindy" Boggs, 28; Pat Danner, 67; Margaret Heckler, 119; Elizabeth Holtzman, 124; Nancy Johnson, 136; Nita Lowey, 164; Connie Morella, 195; Patricia Schroeder, 246
Consumer Protection Act, 264
consumer protections, 263
Contract with America, 106, 148, 194, 235
Cooper, Jere, 33
Cubin, Barbara, **66–67**
Cuomo, Mario, 164
Curtis, Charles, 3

D'Amato, Alfonse, 92
Danner, Pat, **67–68**
Davenport, Lacey, 91
DeGette, Diana, 2, **68–69**
DeLauro, Rosa, 2, **69–71**
Dellums, Ron, 246
Dole, Bob, 95
domestic violence, 28, 237
Dornan, Bob, 241
Douglas, Emily Taft, **71–73**
Douglas, Helen Gahagan, **73–75**
Dunn, Jennifer, 2, **75–77**
Dwyer, Florence, **77–79**

Edwards, Edwin, 79
Edwards, Elaine, **79**
Emerson, Jo Ann, **80**
EMILY's List, 10, 11, 70
English, Karan, **81–82**
Equal Employment Opportunity Commission, 110
Equal Pay Act, 105, 238
Equal Rights Amendment: Hattie Caraway, 51; Emanuel Celler, 123; floor debate, 6–7; Martha Griffiths, 109–111; Paula Hawkins, 117; Winnifred Mason Huck, 128; legislation introduced, 3; ratification extension, 124; Katharine St. George, 238; Leonor Sullivan, 264
Eshoo, Anna, **82–83**
Eslick, Willa, **83–84**

Fair Labor Standards Act, 208
Family and Medical Leave Act, 236, 246

Farmer, James, 55
Farrakhan, Louis, 181
Farrington, Mary, **84–85**
FBI, 134, 140
Feinstein, Dianne, 36, **85–86**
Felton, Rebecca, **87–89**
Fenwick, Millicent, **89–91**
Ferraro, Geraldine, **91–92**, 124, 209
Fiedler, Bobbi, **93**
Fong, Matt, 12
Ford, Gerald, 89,139
Fowler, Tillie, 13, **93–94**
Frahm, Sheila, **95**
Fulmer, Willa, **95–96**
fundraising, 10–11
Furse, Elizabeth, **96–97**

Gage, Matilda Joslyn, 40
Gasque, Elizabeth, **98**
gays in military, 38
General Agreement on Tariff and
    Trade (GATT), 141
Gephardt, Richard, 76
GI Bill of Rights, 233
Gibbs, Florence, **98**
Gingrich, Newt: Rosa DeLauro and,
    70; Jennifer Dunn and, 76; Nancy
    Johnson and, 136; Carrie Meek and,
    184; Susan Molinari and, 193; Con-
    nie Morella and, 194; Nancy Pelosi
    and, 217; Marge Roukema and, 236;
    Linda Smith and, 253; Karen Thur-
    man and, 271
Goldwater, Barry, 81
Granahan, Kathryn, **99–100**
Granger, Kay, **100–101**
Grasso, Ella, **101–102**
Graves, Dixie, **102–104**
Green, Edith, **104–106**
Greene, Enid, 8, 41, **106–107**
Greenway, Isabella, **107–108**
Griffiths, Martha, 6, **109–111**
gun control, stance on: Jean Ash-
    brook, 22; Barbara Boxer, 37; Julia
    Carson, 52; Diana DiGette, 68;
    Dianne Feinstein, 86; Carolyn Mc-
    Carthy, 176; Unsoeld, 272

Hague, Frank, 207
Haitian refugees, 38
Hall, Katie, **111–112**
Hansen, Julia Butler, **113–114**, 275
Harden, Cecil, **114–115**
Harding, Warren G., 87–88
Hardwick, Thomas, 87
Harman, Jane, 13, **115–116**
Hatche, Richard, 112
Hawkesworth, Mary, 10
Hawkins, Paula, **116–118**
Hayes, Wayne, 218
Heckler, Margaret, **118–120**
Helms, Jesse, 195
Herbert, Edward, 246
Hicks, Louise, **120–121**
Higher Education Facilities Act of
    1964, 104
Hill, Anita: Jill Long and, 8; Barbara
    Boxer and, 37; Barbara Kennelly
    and, 150; Carol Moseley-Braun and,
    196; Patty Murray and, 198; Louise
    Slaughter and, 251; Jolene Unsoeld
    and, 272
Holt, Marjorie, **121–122**
Holtzman, Elizabeth, 92, **123–124**
Honeyman, Nan, **124–125**
Hooley, Darlene, **125–126**
Hoover, J. Edgar, 20, 140
Horn, Joan Kelly, **126–127**
House Bank scandal, 210
Huck, Winnifred Mason, **128–129**
Huffington, Michael, 85
Humphrey, Muriel, **129–130**
Hutchison, Kay Bailey, **130–131**
Hyde, Henry, 64, 181–182

Ickes, Harold, 107

Jackson-Lee, Sheila, **132–133**
Jacobs, Andy, 150
Jenckes, Virginia, **133–134**
Johnson, Eddie Bernice, **134–135**
Johnson, Lyndon B., 139
Johnson, Nancy, 10, **135–136**
Jones, Stephanie Tubbs, **137**
Jordan, Barbara, **137–139**

Kahn, Florence, 11, **140–141**
Kaptur, Marcy, **141–142**
Kassebaum, Nancy, **143–144**, 185
Kee, Maude, **144–145**
Kefauver, Estes, 47
Kelly, Edna Flannery, **145–147**
Kelly, Sue, **147–148**
Kennedy, Edward, 109
Kennedy, John F., 105, 147, 153, 255
Kennelly, Barbara, **149–150**, 251
Keys, Martha, **150–151**
Khrushchev, Nikita, 255
Kilpatrick, Carolyn Cheeks, **151–152**
King, Martin Luther, Jr., 112
Knutson, Andy, 152–153
Knutson, Coya, **152–153**

Lake, Celinda, 11
Landrieu, Mary, **154–155**
Landrum, Phil, 105
Langley, Katherine, **155–156**
League of Nations, 71
Lee, Barbara, **156–157**
Lincoln, Blanche Lambert, **157–158**
Lloyd, Marilyn, **158–159**
Lofgren, Zoe, **159–160**
Long, Catherine, **160–161**
Long, Huey, 50, 163
Long, Jill, 8, **161–162**
Long, Rose, 79 **162–163**
Lowey, Nita, **163–165**
Luce, Clare Boothe, **165–167**
Lusk, Georgia, **167–168**

Malcolm, Ellen, 10
Maloney, Carolyn, **168–169**
Mankin, Helen Douglas, **170–171**
Marcantonio, Vito, 73
Margolies-Mezvinsky, Marjorie, **171–173**
Martin, Lynn, 11, **173–174**
May, Catherine, **175–176**
McCarthy, Carolyn, **176–177**
McCarthy, Joseph, 18, 73, 253–254
McCarthy, Karen, 13, **177–178**
McCarthy, Kathryn O'Laughlin, **178–179**
McCormack, John, 55

McCormick, Ruth Hanna, **179–181**
McKinney, Cynthia, **181–182**
McMillan, Clara, **182–183**
Meek, Carrie, **183–185**
Meyers, Jan, **185–186**
Meyner, Helen, **186–187**
Mikulski, Barbara, 2, **187–189**, 199
Millender-McDonald, Juanita, **189–190**
Mink, Patsy, **190–192**
Molinari, Susan, 8, 150, **192–194**
Mondale, Walter, 92
Morella, Connie, **194–195**
Morse, Wayne, 167
Moseley-Braun, Carol, 12, **195–197**
motherhood, 8, 41, 106, 159
Murray, Patty, 12, **197–199**
Myrick, Sue, 11, **199–200**

NAACP, 41, 43
Napolitano, Grace, **200–201**
NASA, 76
National Labor Relations Board, 262
National Women's Political Caucus, 11, 19, 55
Navy Tailhook scandal: Barbara Boxer and, 37; Kay Bailey Hutchison and, 131; Barbara Mikulski and, 188; political impact, 9; Louise Slaughter and, 251
Naziism, 72, 74
Neuberger, Maurine, **201–203**
Nixon, Richard: Bella Abzug and, 19; Helen Gahagan Douglas and, 73, 75; Margaret Heckler and, 119; Barbara Jordan and, 137; Patsy Mink and, 191
Nolan, Mae Ella, **203**
Norrell, Catherine, **204**
North American Free Trade Agreement (NAFTA), 25, 141
Northup, Anne, **204–205**
Norton, Eleanor Holmes, **205–206**
Norton, Mary Teresa, 3, **207–209**

Oakar, Mary Rose, **209–210**
O'Day, Caroline, **210–212**
Oldfield, Pearl, **212–213**
Owen, Ruth Bryan, **213–215**

Packwood, Bob: Barbara Boxer and, 37; critics of, 12; Elizabeth Furse and, 97; Barbara Mikulski and, 188
Parnell, Harvey, 50
Patterson, Elizabeth, 215
Paxon, Bill, 193
Pelosi, Nancy, 216–217
Perot, Ross, 9, 141
Persian Gulf War, 181, 227
Pettis, Shirley, 217–218
Pfost, Gracie, 218–219
pornography, 99
Pratt, Eliza Jane, 219–220
Pratt, Ruth Baker, 220–222
Pryce, Deborah, 222–223
Pyle, Gladys, 223–224

Raker, John, 4
Rankin, Jeannette, 1, 4, 210, 224–227, 231
Rayburn, Sam, 47
Reece, B. Carroll, 227
Reece, Louise, 227–228
Reid, Charlotte, 228–229
Riley, Corrine, 229–230
Rivers, Lynn, 230–231
Roberts, Cokie, 29
Robertson, Alice Mary, 231–232
Rogers, Edith Nourse, 3, 232–234
Roosevelt, Eleanor: Katharine Byron and, 47; Helen Gahagan Douglas and, 73; Isabella Greenway and, 108; Mary Teresa Norton and, 208; Caroline O'Day and, 211
Roosevelt, Franklin: Isabella Greenway and, 108; Nan Honeyman and, 124–125; Clare Booth Luce and, 166; Mary Teresa Norton and, 208; Katharine St. George and, 239
Ros-Lehtinen, Ileana, 234–235
Roukema, Marge, 235–236
Royball-Allard, Lucille, 237–238
Ryan, Bill Fitts, 20

St. George, Katharine, 238–240
Saiki, Patricia, 240–241
Sanchez, Loretta, 241–242
Schakowsky, Jan, 242–243

Schenk, Lynn, 243–244
Schneider, Claudine, 244–245
Schroeder, Patricia, 7, 8, 245–247
Seastrand, Andrea, 247–248
Shepherd, Karen, 106, 248–249
Sigmund, Barbara, 29
Simpson, Edna, 249–250
Slaughter, Louise, 2, 250–251
Smith, Howard, 5, 110
Smith, Linda, 12, 199, 252–253
Smith, Margaret Chase, 253–256; committee chairmanship, 143; on gender in politics, 12; member of Armed Services Committee, 19; missile destroyer named for, 66; Maurine Neuberger and, 201; race against female challenger, 199
Smith, Virginia, 256–257
Snowe, Olympia, 65, 257–258
Social Security, 109, 184, 271
Spellman, Gladys, 259–260
Stabenow, Debbie, 260–261
Stanley, Winnifred, 261–263
Stewart, Jimmy, 255
suffrage, 3–5, 179, 210, 225–226
Sullivan, Leonor, 3, 263–265
Sumner, Jessie, 265–266, 281

Tauscher, Ellen, 267–268
Thomas, Clarence: Barbara Boxer and, 37; critics of, 12; Barbara Kennelly and, 150; Jill Long and, 8; Carol Moseley-Braun and, 196; Patty Murray and, 198; political impact of scandal, 9; Jolene Unsoeld and, 272
Thomas, Lera, 268
Thompson, Ruth, 268–270
Thurman, Karen, 270–271
Title IX education act, 104–105
Tower, John, 144

United Nations, 32, 33, 71, 265
Unsoeld, Jolene, 271–272

Velazquez, Nydia, 273–274
Vietnam War, stance on: Bella Abzug, 18–19; Jean Ashbrook, 22; Shirley Chisholm, 56; Margaret Heckler,

119; Louise Hicks, 121; Patsy Mink, 191; Jeannette Rankin, 227; Charlotte Reid, 228

Vucanovich, Barbara, 113, **274–275**

Waldholtz, Enid Greene. *See* Greene, Enid

Wallace, George, 21, 206

Watergate, 137

Waters, Maxine, **275–277**

WAVES, 255

Weis, Jessica, **277–278**

welfare, 109, 133, 136, 282

Wilson, Heather, **278–279**

Wilson, Woodrow, 71

Wingo, Effiegene, **279**

women committee chairs, 1, 14

Women Strike for Peace, 19

Womens' Army Auxiliary Corps (WAACs), 233

women's health, 275

Woodhouse, Chase Going, **280–281**

Woods, Harriett, 11

Woolsey, Lynn, **281–283**

World War I, stance on: Caroline O'Day, 211; Jeannette Rankin, 224–226; Edith Nourse Rogers, 233

World War II, stance on: Frances Bolton, 31–33; Milicent Fenwick, 46–47; Caroline O'Day, 211; Jeannette Rankin, 224; Edith Nourse Rogers, 233; Pat Saiki, 241; Jessie Sumner, 265

About the Author

KAREN FOERSTEL is a reporter with *Congressional Quarterly Magazine*. She is the co-author, with Herbert Foerstel, of *Climbing the Hill* (Praeger, 1996).